DATE DUE

PROTEAN SHAPE

PROTEAN SHAPE

A STUDY IN EIGHTEENTH-CENTURY
VOCABULARY AND USAGE

SUSIE I. TUCKER

'the Proteus-nature. . . of ever-shifting language'
John Upton, *Critical Observations
on Shakespeare*, 1747, p. 237

UNIVERSITY OF LONDON
THE ATHLONE PRESS
1967

Published by
THE ATHLONE PRESS
UNIVERSITY OF LONDON
at 2 Gower Street, London WC1
Distributed by Constable & Co Ltd
12 Orange Street, London WC2

Canada
Oxford University Press
Toronto

U.S.A.
Oxford University Press Inc
New York

Printed in Great Britain by
WESTERN PRINTING SERVICES LTD
BRISTOL

PREFACE

THE pages that follow are no more than a trial shaft dug into the rich mine of eighteenth-century linguistic theory and practice. In Part One I have tried to find something of what the ordinary educated reader may have thought, or the man in the street, the lady in the drawing-room, the professional man, may have said, and how it struck contemporary critics. It has been interesting to look at the comments of one man of letters upon another, or of the verbal critic on the master-poet. In Part Two I have shifted the emphasis from the eighteenth century's views of itself to our views of the eighteenth century as we look back. It would have been impossible as well as unfruitful to keep our views out of Part One; but in Part Two I have been interested primarily in *our* difficulties, *our* discoveries, and *our* conclusions. The approach to the period is through double-doors.

In Part One I have used a few representative critical journals as the basis of evidence and discussion. They conceived it to be their duty not only to watch, but also to protect, the development of our language. This may well be to cry for the moon, but it does mean that they show us how people of education thought. Often English has developed in spite of them; the historian must chronicle the fact, and the educator take note. Sometimes they betray ignorance of the past course of English, and so serve to warn us against the pitfalls of uninformed judgment. Sometimes they issue warnings themselves that we should do well to heed, for they usually had the interests of clarity, decorum and reason very much at heart. If they all too often fail to kindle with poetic fire, they can be trusted to smother false lights. They were respected in their own day, as well they might be: we remember that Johnson and Goldsmith wrote for the *Gentleman's Magazine*, that the *Critical Review* was Smollett's periodical and had Johnson's support, and that Burke was concerned in the *Annual Register*. Perhaps they were also feared. The *Literary Magazine and British Review* in 1788 (p. 380) quotes the conclusion of one author who felt that a writer must set out as a 'Gladiator'. 'Should he escape the regular batteries of the "Monthly", "Critical" and "English" and "Analytical" Reviews, and the bombs and howitzers of the Gentleman's, the European, the Literary, etc. Magazines, it is still likely he may be mortally wounded by some irregular newspapers.'

At times the periodicals denigrated each other, as rivals in business and politics will: but they were not written by Grub Street hacks. Dr S. Nangle's book on the contributors to the *Monthly Review* shows that this Review was run by the scholars best qualified in their own fields to deal with the books on multifarious subjects that were submitted to them. The Memoir from Dr Aikin's preface to a publication by one of them, Dr Enfield, could have applied to many another. 'Dr. Enfield was especially fitted to take part in a literary journal, and to one of the most respectable of these works he was long a considerable contributor. The institution of a new magazine, under the name of the *Monthly* which in its plan embraced a larger circle of original literature than usual with these miscellanies, engaged him to exercise his powers as an essayist in a variety of topics, and the papers with which he enriched it, under the title of the Inquirer, obtained great applause from the manly freedom of their sentiment, and the correct elegance of their language.'

The *Monthly Review* began its career in 1749, and in 1791 an observant foreigner long resident in England, Dr F. A. Wendeborn, was saying that it was 'deservedly esteemed for communicating literary intelligence'. It did not stand alone.

Grammarians, philosophers, rhetoricians, translators, critics of the social scene, professional specialists, all afford comment on our vocabulary and how to use it—or how not to. If I have made little use of their discussions of syntax and spelling, it is not from any belief that the meaning and tone of words are all that matters, but because both have been discussed in detail. Dr S. A. Leonard's book on *The Standard of Correctness in English Usage 1700–1800*, for example, deals fully with disputed phrasing and structure, and I can only hope I have not trespassed on his ground. It would be impertinent in both senses of that word, to try to add any footnote to recent studies of eighteenth-century poetic diction in general or in relation to a particular poet: all I have tried to do here is to let the period express its own ideas on that subject.

My greatest obligations are first to Professor Geoffrey Tillotson of Birkbeck College for his initial suggestion of these studies and for constant advice and constructive comment: then to my colleague Professor C. H. Gifford of Bristol for the stimulus discussion with him always gives: to the staffs of the Bodleian Library and the University Libraries of Bristol and London for their unfailing help in providing basic material: and to the Bristol City Library for affording me unlooked-for facilities for my reading, as well as its run of the *Critical*

Review. I am greatly indebted to Miss D. M. Skews of Bexley Technical High School for saving me from many slips and for providing me with several modern instances: to Miss J. T. Wisely, and to Captain T. J. Jackson of the *Victory* Museum, H.M. Dockyard, Portsmouth, for information about the *Royal George* inscription; to Mr G. A. Forrest and the Clerk of the Peace of the County of Bedford for information about a misprision of felony case in 1961; to the three experts who turned my MS into legible typescript, Mrs L. K. Gay, Mrs E. D. Gilliard, and Mrs G. E. Roberts; to Dr A. Basil Cottle and Mr V. J. Scattergood for their eagle-eyed proof-reading, and particularly to the unfailing care and salutary advice of the officers of the Athlone Press.

The University   S.I.T.
Bristol

CONTENTS

ABBREVIATIONS   xi

PROLOGUE   1

PART ONE

THE EIGHTEENTH CENTURY LOOKS
AT ITS LANGUAGE

I. EXPOSITION AND DEFINITION   11
Foreigners, 12; Dialect, 19; Names of Diseases, 20; Technicalities,
20; Ambiguities, 23; Vogue Words, 25; Abstracts, 27

II. CENSURE AND PROTEST   33
New, Strange and Mainly French, 33; Latinate Diction, 39;
Americanisms, 46; Scotticisms, 46; Bombast, 48; Linguistic
Snobbery, 49; Literary Affectation, 51; Euphemism, 54; Inelegant
and Inappropriate Language, 56; Language and Literature, 57;
Low and Familiar, 61; Problems of Modernization, 62; Archaism,
67; Misuse, 69; Technical Terms, 72; Commercialese, 75; The
Professions, 76; Women's Usage, 78; Cant, 80; Political Language,
82; Advertisements, 83; Sailors' Language, 84; Levels of Language,
85; Short-cuts, 89

III. APOLOGY   91

IV. RECOMMENDATION   96
New Words, Wanted Words, 96; English for French, 104;
Foreigners, 106; Technicalities, Distinctions and Abstractions,
113; Confusions and Distinctions, 117; Taste and Colour, 122;
Art Terms, 124

PART TWO

THE TWENTIETH CENTURY LOOKS BACK

V. THE UNKNOWN   129

VI. THE ENLIGHTENING   137
Eighteenth-Century Attitudes,
(1) *Life*, 137; (2) *Letters*, 162

Light on our Vocabulary,
(1) *Reminders of the origins of terms now dulled,* 170; (2) *Special and General,* 171; (3) *Literal and Figurative,* 172; (4) *Variants,* 176; (5) *Enlivening our Words,* 178; (6) *Changed Reference,* 186

VII. THE UNDEVELOPED   189

VIII. THE MISLEADING   204

False Friends, 204; Mental Attitudes, 207; Changed Tone, 210; Approval and Disapproval, 212; Extension and Restriction, 217; Compliments?, 221; Weakening, 226; From Factual to Evaluative, 227; From Praise to Doubt, 228; New Words of Praise, 230; Loss of Etymological Sense, 238; Degeneracy, 240; Good Sense, Bad Sense, 245; Ambiguity, 249; Hesitation, 251; Words in Changed Contexts, 254; Specialisation, 257; Mistaken Identity, 263; Adjectives in Changed Contexts, 265; Misleading Verbs, 271; Changed Adverbial Usage, 275

EPILOGUE   279

APPENDIX: A Note on Eighteenth-Century
Periodicals   285

BIBLIOGRAPHY   287

INDEX OF WORDS AND TOPICS   302

INDEX OF PERSONS   317

ABBREVIATIONS AND
SHORT TITLES

Ann. Reg.	*The Annual Register*, 1758–
Brit. Crit.	*The British Critic*, 1793–1826
Brit. Syn.	Hester Lynch Piozzi, *British Synonymy*, 1794
Crit. Rev.	*The Critical Review*, 1756–1817
Dickins and Stanton	*An Eighteenth Century Correspondence*, ed. Dickins and Stanton, 1910
Dyche and Pardon	Thomas Dyche and William Pardon, *A New General English Dictionary*
Gent. Mag.	*Gentleman's Magazine*, 1731–1907
Gloss. Ang. Nova	*Glossographia Anglicana Nova*, 1722
Hertford-Pomfret Correspondence	*Correspondence between Frances Seymour, Countess of Hertford and Henrietta Louisa, Countess of Pomfret*
Melmoth, *Letters*	William Melmoth, *Letters of Sir Thomas Fitzosborne*, 1742
Month. Rev.	*The Monthly Review*, 1749–1845
M.P.	*Modern Philology*, 1903–
O.E.D.	*The Oxford English Dictionary*, 1933
Phil. of Rhet.	George Campbell, *The Philosophy of Rhetoric*, 1776
P.M.L.A.	*Publications of the Modern Language Association of America*, 1884–
Richardsons' Commentary	Jonathan Richardson Sr and Jr, *Explanatory Notes and Remarks on Milton's Paradise Lost*, 1734
Spect.	*The Spectator*, 1711–12; 1714

The busy and inquisitive nature of man is not content with knowing things are so, but will be prying into the causes and occasions of them: and this curiosity, which is certainly very laudable, when restrained within proper bounds, extends even to languages, in which there is hardly a word, a metaphor, or an allusion but what we want to know the bottom and original of: for tho' the meaning of the several expressions be well enough understood, that does not satisfy, but we are desirous of knowing, at the same time, *how* they came to import such and such things. Hence arises philology, etymology, annotations upon authors, books of rhetoric, and the like helps to literature.

The *Gentleman's Magazine*, XXIII (1753), 465

No inquiry can be more interesting to an inhabitant of Great Britain than that respecting the history of the English Language.

William Godwin: *Enquirer* (1797)
Essay XII, Of English Style

PROLOGUE

'A CRITIC whose labours are employed upon his native language,' the *Monthly Review* for 1778 points out, 'has, at hand, ample succours, which are not attainable by those who treat of either an ancient or foreign tongue. He can every moment consult men of letters, examine their decisions with respect to the real signification of words, and he may even appeal from their decisions to custom.'[1]

But what if the critic is employed upon his native language as it was spoken and written 200 or 250 years ago? In a sense the English of the eighteenth century is not the native language of any of us—we were not born in that period, and its English is partly a foreign tongue.[2] There are no recordings of the pronunciation and tune of English as they spoke it then, so we shall never hear it. Nevertheless, if we try to go back, we are provided with many helps and much enlightenment, for critics, theorists, and the mere observant man-in-the-street are all eagerly waiting to tell us how it struck contemporaries. They will tell us what they liked—perhaps more often, what they disliked—what was elegant and what was vulgar, what was correct and what was a solecism, what they felt to be new and what old-fashioned, what was impressive and what was funny. We must never assume that we shall agree with them when we eavesdrop on their comments: that is why their comments are so valuable. For if we read our reactions and prejudices back into their literature, we may prove bad critics for want of an elementary understanding of the language—there is nothing harder to grasp than the tone of a word or phrase. What was novel to them may be trite to us, what shocked them we take for granted. What was vivid or painful or embarrassing to them may have grown so dulled that it leaves us unmoved; and then we can be grateful to them for showing us the full original force of what we say so easily.

The eighteenth-century critics looked at their own language, at other people's, and at Language generally, with an all-embracing interest. It varied from the profundities of Philosophy to the superficialities of the

[1] *Month. Rev.* lix (1778), 499.
[2] Cp. John Symonds, *On revising the Epistles*, 'There is . . . a manifest difference between a person's *native language*, and the *language of his native country*.'

latest conversational catch-word: from attempts to analyse how language came into being, to a desire to know the origin of some bit of frothy slang or homely term or the name of a new invention. What is the reason for calling it *bubble-and-squeak*?[1] Is the Guillotine the same as the Scottish Maiden?[2]

Our twentieth-century worries were there—for instance, are we introducing too many foreign words, ought we to anglicise their pronunciation and spelling, or ought we to change back to their original correctness words already made thoroughly English? The argument usually concerns French and Latin, but there is the occasional refreshing excursion further afield. One writer is more impressed by the 'Stadthouse' at Amsterdam than by the use of 'the words High and Mighty repeated fifty times in a placaart'. The *Monthly Review* asks, 'Why not *placard*?', and points out that if 'our author had meant to follow the Dutch orthography, he should have written *plakaert*.[3] And here it is to be noted that no amount of laying down linguistic law at one period will bind its successors: for modern Dutch spells the word plakkaat, and modern English has to mention more informal placards than those of their High Mightinesses the States-General of the United Provinces.

On the other hand, Dr George Campbell thinks that *Zoroaster* is better in English than *Zerdusht*, *Alcoran* than *Koran*[4]—where we agree as to the Sage but not as to the Book. Opinions differed then: when Hume did use the form *the Alcoran*, the *Monthly Review* told him he should have said *The Koran*.[5] What we finally choose can be a hit-or-miss affair, as Campbell's example of *bashaw* makes plain. 'When some critics first thought of reforming it,' he tells us, one wanted *bassa*, another *pacha* and a third *pasha*—and with the last we seem now content.

How should we pronounce this, that, and the other? All too often the interesting thing is to see that what we insist on is what used to be thought low or careless, or what we accept without giving it a thought they make a centre of attack and defence. This is as true of structure as of sound. 'Litidzhus' for 'litigyus' is 'extremely improper', says the writer of *A Caution to Gentlemen who use Sheridan's Dictionary*, but we agree with Sheridan: *beerd* for *beard* is vulgar—the word is *bear* + *D*! *Leezhure* is 'ridiculous'—one hears strong dissent being registered on

---

[1] *Gent. Mag.* lx (1790), 801, 1075–6, lxi (1791), 216.
[2] *Gent. Mag.* lxiii (1793), 201.   [3] *Month. Rev.* xliv (1771), 281.
[4] *Phil. of Rhet.*, pp. 177, 178.   [5] *Month. Rev.* xvi (1757), 128.

the other side of the Atlantic. Edward Bysshe in the *Art of English Poetry* in 1702,[1] takes Dryden to task for giving *victorious* four syllables —and here we should hold that four is normal,[2] though a poet may reduce them to three if he wishes. In 1798[3] we find a critic declaring that he cannot believe such consummate authorities as Lord Mansfield and Mr Garrick would ever have said *inimĭcal* or *emĭgrant* instead of *inimīcal* and *emīgrant*. We find it surprising to suppose they ever said anything else. Discussions of sentence-structure often bring up the heavy guns of Latin grammar: we are bound to agree with Campbell, that Latin syntax is 'the genuine source of most of our grammatical scruples'.[4] In fact, eighteenth-century arguments about syntax and accidence suffer from far too much knowledge of Latin and far too little of Anglo-Saxon. This is why they make such heavy weather of 'I had rather'[5] or 'methinks'[6] or 'he *need* not' and suppose that rules proper to weak verbs may be applied to strong ones.[7]

There are iconoclasts, who care only for sense and want no truck with tradition. Dr James Beattie points out that we do not really need different persons in the verb 'to be'—either *am* or *is* would do for all the singular, as *are* does for all the plural. One wonders why he wanted to maintain a distinction of number. Dialect speakers, he notes, say 'I is', and 'says I' may be met with in good English authors as well as in common conversation. These barbarisms are as intelligible as the grammatical phrases, so inflections of the verb are not necessary. 'Custom . . . would soon render *we am, ye am, they am*, as expressive as *we are, ye are, they are*.'[8] He takes too a lenient view of *don't* and *shan't*, which we accept, and also of *ant* for 'are not' and *int* for 'is not'. His apostropheless spelling anticipates Bernard Shaw—but neither he nor Shaw was an Englishman: and the English on the whole disapproved. Beattie sees no need to regard inflections as proof of refinement,[9] and considers that many people now speak and write English without ever using a subjunctive or knowing that there is such a thing in the language.[10] But this is a view hardly more generally held—in scholastic circles—now than then, least of all in American English.

---

[1] p. 13.

[2] If we treat it as a word of three syllables, we improve the rhyme to *o'er us* in the National Anthem.

[3] *Gent. Mag.* lxviii (1798), 395: *Crit. Rev.* new arr. i, 295 disagrees.

[4] *Phil. of Rhet.*, p. 209.   [5] *Gent. Mag.* lxv (1795), 7.

[6] e.g. Sketch IX by Launcelot Temple (i.e. Dr J. Armstrong): *Two Grammatical Essays*.   [7] *Phil. of Rhet.*, pp. 148, 156.

[8] *Dissertations*, pp. 371–2.   [9] ibid., p. 376.   [10] ibid., p. 421.

We can watch new grammatical devices being tried out. Beattie defends 'the house is being built' construction as the answer to 'one of the greatest defects in the English tongue'. It was seriously opposed, but we should not like to be without it now. And we have found it useful to be able to say 'There was a Mr So and So there . . .',[1] though Beattie thinks this affected. After reading the many arguments about whether we should pray ' Our Father *who* art in Heaven' or '*which* art in Heaven', we may be tempted to sympathise with the critic—one Mr Vertue (did he really exist?)—who is reported to have written to the *Gentleman's Magazine* to say 'I am surprised that you admit dissertations which are merely philological disputes about the propriety of *who* and *which* when both equally convey the meaning of the writer.'[2] And yet, do we not also sympathise with his fellow-correspondent Mr Polyglot, who wants more philology—'What is there so worthy an object of our study as language; especially as truth itself dependeth upon the perspicuity of language.'

We are not much shocked (if at all) now by such expressions as to *leave in the lurch*, to *capture* a ship or to *crack* a joke. We *make up* our minds as a matter of course: all too many people *enjoy bad health*, though the eighteenth century was right to point out that this is a contradiction in terms, and to ask us to be explicit and not talk of being romantic *to a degree*. Withers[3] observes that no well-bred Londoners have ever *catched cold* or *taken cold*. To us, too, *catched* is vulgar—we forget that it is historically right—but *take cold* (the old phrase) sounds rather literary. Tennyson would more usually be accused of preciousness than inelegance, and it was he who made King Arthur say, echoing Malory,

My wound hath taken cold, and I shall die.

We do not look for a literal meaning when we *cast about* for an idea or an argument, and so we feel that Withers is hypercritical when he attacks Dr Blair for writing 'cast about for ornaments': 'the Imagination may be employed in *Quest* of Ornaments,—may contrive—investigate—invent etc, but what the Imagination is to cast about is inconceivable'.[4]

[1] ibid., p. 494.
[2] *Gent. Mag.* xxv (1755), Preface.
[3] *Aristarchus*, p. 149. So in 1787, the *Gent. Mag.* (lvii), 208, was calling it a barbarism frequently found in Scottish authors.
[4] Withers, op. cit., p. 206.

The purists fought and won their battle to preserve the proper distinction between *lie* and *lay*—('that intolerable vulgarism' sums up their verdict on the misuse of *lay*)—*teach* and *learn*. They routed *you was* even though they tell us that that 'expression sometimes occurs in books, is often heard in conversation, and frequently echoes through the caverns of Westminster Hall'.[1] But they did not rout *I have got*. Sir Alan Herbert in *What a Word* took up the same position in 1935 as Withers had taken in *Aristarchus* which came out in 1791.

The *Monthly Review* disliked the use of *got* in a Scottish medical treatise in 1759. But the nation in general has no more of a guilty conscience now than it had then. And we don't regard *don't* as suitable only to hairdressers and milliners' apprentices—we aren't as openly snobbish anyway. The critic is sure that Lord Mansfield, presiding at a trial involving the Duke of Cumberland and Lord Grosvenor[2], could not have used such a low turn of phrase—one suspects that his twentieth-century successors both could and would. Indeed, a broadcast by a minister of state or even Royalty would sound strangely stiff if it contained no abbreviations.

Most enlightening are the words. New ones are introduced as new things are invented—the development of *aerial* and *electric* offers exciting illustration; new moral or artistic insights are reflected as attitudes change—*enthusiasm* and *Gothic* are outstanding here, though there is plenty of food for thought in a consideration of what kind of action the eighteenth century thought *exemplary* or *benevolent*, or what they allowed to be covered by the term *accident*. Religious and political controversies are reflected in some of the uses of such words as *humanise*,[3] *Protestant*, and *mystery*, on the one hand, or *excise*, *influence* and *Whig* on the other. 'The meaning of words', as the *Monthly Review* so properly says, 'is not so permanent but that the lights and shades of the more delicate modes of expression are perpetually changing.'[4] The unwary reader can be completely deceived, or at best receive a bad jolt, if he thinks of the word in its modern sense or atmosphere: two extreme and comic examples are the name *Dolly Pinup*[5] for a sailor's sweetheart, and the *Red Flag* for a British red ensign.

---

[1] e.g. *Month. Rev.* lxvii (1797), 567. Cf. *Month. Rev.* l (1773–4), 11, on Hugh Kelly's *School for Wives*, produced at Drury Lane in 1773.

[2] *Month. Rev.* xliii (1771), 321.

[3] Not to 'turn bestial into human' but to 'reduce from divine to human'.

[4] *Month. Rev.* xxvii (1763), 218.

[5] *London Mag.* xxx (1764), 637. A lady's maid.

There are traps enough in such apparently normal words as *discover*, *supply*, *candour*, *enormous*—and *apparently* itself. On the other hand, eighteenth-century use at times throws a sudden light on terms that have grown dim. Examples are provided by such words and phrases as *alarm*, *stigma*, *flash in the pan*. There are too the words whose physical meaning we do not know from direct experience—such as *bosom-friend*, in two concrete meanings—or that we are unlikely to meet because manners and social conditions have changed, as in *bang-beggar*.[1] And finally, there are the missing words, some of which we have supplied since: we feel that if *Romanesque* had been applied to architecture in the eighteenth century, much of the confusion about Gothic might have been cleared up sooner.

The more thoughtful, the philosophers and aestheticians, put their energies into differentiation, into sharpening meanings of words. What exactly is *Taste?* Or the *Picturesque?* How does *Wonder* differ from *Surprise* or *Astonishment?* Here there are critics who contemplated the distinction between *Imagination* and *Fancy* before Coleridge. What distinguishes the Beautiful from the Sublime? Or, to come down to a more practical level, how does *swindling*[2] differ from any other sort of fraud, and what is its legal penalty? We don't seem any further on with that one.

The verbal critics at their best attack the muddled thinking that reveals itself in absurd mixtures of metaphor: at their worst, they would kill all imaginative life by their devastating earth-bound logic. Bentley on Milton is warning enough. Incidentally, the words that Bentley or the Richardsons think their readers would like explained when they come to *Paradise Lost*, or that John Upton places in the same category when he edits the *Faerie Queene*, are in themselves illuminating comments on the century's use of English. So are eighteenth-century explanations of Shakespeare's language. To us, it seems odd to be given expositions of *hideous*, *behest*, *curry favour*, *glee*, *sods*, *sway*: and the Richardsons' explanation of a *seal* as a *sea-calf* strikes us as an attempt to explain the normal by the rare. The changes of history are brought home to us when we find ourselves being told that Crete is now Candia, since to us Candia is now Crete again.

There is plenty of sound sense in eighteenth-century linguistic comment when it deals with propriety, the right language for translating the Bible or the ancient Classics, for moving an audience, for drawing

---

[1] 'A provincial term for a parish beadle.' (*Month. Rev.* xxxix (1768), 80.)
[2] *Gent. Mag.* lv (1788), 1154.

up a document, for writing precisely and avoiding bombast or affectation. The writers can discuss even English spelling sensibly and at times amusingly.[1]

There is too, in some quarters, a surprising amount of interest in the lower levels of English: from one of the most respectable of eighteenth-century journals[2] we can find the ninety-nine ways of saying a man is *drunk*, and a long list[3] of slang terms in use at Cambridge—not that they have remained restricted to that University or would need much explaining now to any undergraduates or their parents. E. Lloyd's poem *The Conversation*[4] is as near to a recording of different types of talk as can be found outside plays and novels—one feels it is truer to life than they usually are. To speak of 'the amazing *uncertainty* and diversity of colloquial jargon'[5] seems an understatement.

One by-product of investigating eighteenth-century vocabulary is the occasional finding of words not caught in the *O.E.D.*'s net from eighteenth-century sources and the more frequent instances of earlier occurrences.[6] There is a definition of *Tontine*[7] twenty-one years before *O.E.D.* The American *Blue Laws* are quoted by both *O.E.D.* and the *Dictionary of American English* from a *General History of Connecticut*, 1781, though *O.E.D*'s earliest British quotation comes from 1876. But readers of the *Monthly Review* were introduced to the expression in 1782, when the critic[8] of the book remarked that 'Considered as a specimen of the wisdom and spirit of the times, these Blue Laws (as they are called) give us no very favourable idea of either.'

Was the eighteenth century as good at anticipating what we tend to regard as more modern uses of words as it was in anticipating such diverse modernities as taxes on dogs and entertainments,[9] the reform of the monetary system,[10] and space-flight?[11] We see our own bad habits

---

[1] e.g. E. Thomas, *An Account of the Trial of the Letter Y* (1753): *The humble Petition of Z. Gent. Mag.* lii (1783), 19.

[2] *Gent. Mag.* xl (1770), 559–60.

[3] *Gent. Mag.* lxiv (1794), 1084, and lxv, 20 sq.

[4] 1768.   [5] *Month. Rev.* l (1780), 128.

[6] I have checked examples also with *The Stanford Dictionary of Anglicised Words and Phrases* (ed. C. A. M. Fennell), first published 1892 and reprinted 1965 by the Cambridge University Press.   [7] *Gent. Mag.* xiv (1744), 657.

[8] *Month. Rev.* lxvi (1782), 257.   [9] *Gent. Mag.* xxxii (1762), 31–2.

[10] Referred to in *Gent. Mag.* xv (1745), 378: 'An essay on the British computations of time, coin, weights and measures.' Our 'divisions of quantities are irregular, troublesome in practice and repugnant to the nature of things.'

[11] e.g. end of Gray's *Luna Habitabilis*, or, lightly, Repton's *Variety* (1788), xxx. Gray is noteworthy for not being satirical.

anticipated too. It may be a triviality like the rage for abbreviation on
the one hand and for pomposity on the other—or such a serious matter
as the notion that if we call a bad thing by a good name, we have cured
the situation. If *slave* sounds painful, say *Assistant-Planter*, and all is
well.[1]

The eighteenth century is a period so near to us that we can read
its writings without the apparatus needed for even the seventeenth, and
yet it is far enough away to make us perpetually on the alert lest we fall
into a sudden or routine pitfall. It is therefore an ideal training ground
for observant students. The chapters that follow are meant mainly for
them, to increase their capacity for observation, to sharpen their minds
for their reading of eighteenth-century poetry and prose, to enable
them to see how our language has developed, as a matter of history,
and to see it as a living and developing human activity.

[1] *Gent. Mag.* lix (1789), 334: see below, p. 56.

PART ONE

THE EIGHTEENTH CENTURY
LOOKS AT ITS LANGUAGE

The English Language ... without form, indigested, and irregularly combined; enriching itself daily by its piracies and depredations, seizes new terms from all quarters, which it assimilates without distinction into its vocabulary, without even deigning to disguise its thefts. In the disorder of its expressions, we see a people prepossessed with a rage of liberty, which they extend even to their diction, who would think themselves fettered, in submitting to any restraints in their language, and enslaved, in subjecting their periods to the rules either of logic or of grammar.

The Monthly Review, xliii (1771), 529.

I
EXPOSITION AND DEFINITION

DIRECT exposition of the meaning of a word occurs frequently enough to be both instructive and interesting. If the word needs no explanation for us, our historical sense is aroused; first we wonder what was odd about it, and then we realise that what is normal to us was strange 200 years ago: we try to put our minds back beyond the history familiar to us and see a different world. More important, it may be that we 'know' the word in a sense different from theirs: then it is our business to see how the change has come about.

What sort of words call for exposition? Foreigners obviously. They may be European; then they will give us the fruits of the Englishman's continental travels. They may be exotic; then they tell us of the eighteenth century's widening horizons. They may be simply new adaptations or applications of words from Greek and Latin. They stand for local colour, places, customs, people, things—or for scientific advances in need of a name.

But the words in need of explanation may be technical terms made of native stock, or old loans; they may stand for new fashions, new arts, new habits. They may also be the subjects of legal rulings that limit their application. They may be the jargon of one walk of life that needs explanation for the general public. Again, there are the ambiguous or unsettled words. Argument cannot be fruitful, unless the disputants are agreed on the sense they will stand to: literary critics may come to the defence of a poet's word that he meant in one sense, but that some perverse commentator has taken in another.

Vogue words may be known in London but not in the provinces, or in one social set and not elsewhere: kindly informants clear up the latest catch-words for their friends. It may interest us to see which of these expressions have ceased to be mere bits of fashionable jargon, and become lasting parts of the language—or to consider what are the modern equivalents of those that have not.

The expressions most in need of definition are those most difficult to define—the abstracts that the philosophers seek to settle, the all-embracing words that stand for a whole complex of shifting ideas. 'It

all depends on what you mean by . . .' and the serious exponents of
taste or *genius* or *pedantry* all try to sort out their beliefs and impressions in the spirit of Thomas Reid's remark,[1] 'that there is no greater
impediment to the advancement of knowledge than the ambiguity of
words'. They do not always remember the truth of another observation of his[2]—'When men attempt to define things which cannot be
defined, their definitions will always be either obscure or false.'

FOREIGNERS

Among the foreign words are a number of terms for geographical
phenomena, reflecting the increasing interest of the period in the wilder
aspects of natural scenery in remoter places. The *Critical Review*[3] defines *avalanche* as a 'gradually accumulating mass of snow rolling from
a mountain', adding pertinently 'there can be no English word for a
phenomenon of which there is no example in England'. Words suggested in the previous decade were *snow-ball* and *snow-fall*, which are
clearly inadequate since they have already English senses unrelated to
the idea of the avalanche. The word has since gained a metaphorical use
—we all know about avalanches of protests, complaints, invitations,
letters.

   Glacier had been introduced in 1744, but the word was being explained in travel-books much later. In 1779, the *Monthly Review*[4] was
explaining that the glaciers are 'mountains and vallies of ice', and in
1776 readers of the *Critical Review*[5] had been told that 'the Glaciers are
immense masses of ice, lodged upon the gentler declivities amidst the
Alps and exhibiting representations beyond conception fantastic and
picturesque'. If they were unfamiliar with *Glacier* it cannot be expected that they would know *Jökull*. They were introduced to it not in
1780 as *O.E.D.* says, but in 1758 when the *Monthly Review*[6] quoted
Horrebow's *Natural History of Iceland*, à propos of which the *Gentleman's Magazine*[7] explained that a 'Jokul is a mountain continually
covered with snow lying under another mountain that rises considerably higher, and is not covered with snow.' This is too detailed—Jökull
means simply *glacier*.

---

[1] *Intellectual Powers of Man*, I. i, 21.   [2] ibid., 24.
[3] *Crit. Rev.* 70 (1790), 311–12.   [4] *Month. Rev.* lx (1779), 344.
   [5] *Crit. Rev.* 41 (1776), 370, from Bourrit's *Journey to Glaciers in the Dutchy of
Savoy*, trans. C. F. Davy.
   [6] *Month. Rev.* xviii (1758), 195.   [7] *Gent. Mag.* xxviii (1758), 23.

The far North suggests ski-ing. The word and thing—*ski*—were introduced to English readers by the translation of Bishop Erich Pontoppidan's *Natural History of Norway*, which the *Monthly*[1] reviewed in 1755—'he says they have *skies* or long and thin pieces of wood, so smooth that the peasants wade through snow with them as lightly as ships under full sail. In war . . . a party of these skie-men are equal to light troops'. Ski-ing as a winter sport lay far in the future: *O.E.D.*'s first reference to *Ski* is circa 1885 (or 1854 in combination).

It surprises us to find the word *glen* in need of so much eighteenth-century comment, even if we recall that 'E.K.' was wider of the mark than anyone else has ever been when he said it was a 'country borough'. Upton's edition of Spenser says it is a valley. Dr Johnson refers it only to Spenser, and rightly enough considers it to be Erse—it is a Gaelic word occurring in Scotland, Wales and Ireland. The *O.E.D.* points out that in English at first it was a literary reminiscence of Spenser; but by the mid-century travel in Scotland was making it a real word. *An Account of Scotland* reviewed by the *Gentleman's Magazine*[2] in 1754 describes how among the mountains 'there are some flats called *glens*, which their situation renders totally barren, for the hollow in which they lie is sometimes so deep that the sun is not above this horizon more than three hours in the longest day'. A note on *glen* adds that it is also the name of a little spot of corn country by the sides of some small rivulet bounded by hills. In 1773 Dr Johnson[3] explained it to Mrs Thrale as the local name for a valley: she could have found as much from his *Dictionary* but in his letter he is speaking from personal experience. By 1779, the Edinburgh periodical the *Mirror*[4] was describing a journey through a glen that was romantic and picturesque.

Basaltes in its classical form is an old loan in English: *basaltine* was an eighteenth-century invention. But some people wanted a more English form, and introduced suggestions by way of a gloss on *basalt(es)*. The *Monthly Review*[5] remarks that Mr Pennant in his *Tour in Scotland* pronounces Staffa 'to be a genuine mass of *basaltes*; by which term he means "jointed columns".' This use of column for a natural formation dates from 1694 on the Stanford Dictionary's evidence. In 1775 the *Critical Review*[6] was reporting 'An Account of Two Giants' Causeways, or groups of prismatic basaltine columns, and other curious vulcanic concretions in the territories of Venice.' Its next

---

[1] *Month. Rev.* xii (1755), 451.   [2] *Gent. Mag.* xxiv (1754), 417.
[3] Letter of 21 September.   [4] No. 10.
[5] *Month. Rev.* li (1774), 458.   [6] *Crit. Rev.* 40 (1775), 91.

volume[1] was again describing a Royal Society *Philosophical Transactions* report which was an account of 'a curious Giants' Causeway or group of angular Columns, newly discovered ... near Padua'. Jointed, prismatic or angular, whatever the adjective, we are given a good picture of the formation: and the restriction of the general term Giants' Causeway to the one specifically so called in Ireland and so likely to be best known in England, is to be noticed.[2]

Among words for people we may notice *cicerone* which soon lost its suggestion of a 'rational and intelligent companion'[3] and *virtuoso* which likewise fell from grace. Joseph Spence[4] reminds us that *virtuoso* comes from *virtus*, and that word from *vir*—the Romans 'were of so military a turn that they called Fortitude *virtus* or "the Virtue", by way of excellence just as the same nation, now they are so debased and effeminated, call the love of the softer arts virtù'.

So Lord Lyttelton[5] in his *Persian Letters* makes his innocent oriental suppose that *virtuosi*, from the 'near relation their title bore to Virtue', must be 'a sett of rigid moralists', though he soon found they were a company of *fiddlers, eunuchs, painters, builders, gardeners,* and, above all, gentlemen that had *travelled into* Italy, who immediately came home perfect *virtuosi* though they went out the dullest fellows in the world. Twenty-five years earlier the *Tatler* (216) had ridiculed the Virtuosi in the absurd will of Nicholas Gimcrack,[6] and the *World* (98) nineteen years later was to say that the word referred only to Italian singers. It was still possible to use the word seriously, if it referred to a serious person. Sir Hans Sloane made a present of 'some Curiosities' to the Duke of Bourbon, 'his Highness being a Virtuoso'. This was reported by the *Gentleman's Magazine*[7] in the same year that saw the publication of the *Persian Letters*.

But Dr Johnson's Italian friend Giuseppe Baretti in his *Italian Library*[8] sums it all up sadly when he says: 'This word originally signified a *professor* or *follower* of *virtue*. At present it is synonymous with *musician*. I do not know how it came to signify in England a collector of shells and butterflies.'

Another foreign word disgraced because of the conduct of those

---

[1] *Crit. Rev.* 41 (1776), 182.   [2] *O.E.D.* 1779.   [3] *Month. Rev.* xxv (1762), 227.
[4] *Polymetis*, p. 139.   [5] Letter 32 (1735).
[6] Shebbeare in his *Letters* surely had this in mind when he mentioned how 'a gim-crack in shell-philosophy will lay out twenty guineas for a shell which is singular ... tho' ugly'. i, 131.
[7] *Gent. Mag.* v (1735), 331–2.   [8] Quoted, *Month. Rev.* xvi (1750), 182.

who bore it was *Nabob*. Dr Wendeborn[1] remarks that those 'who have acquired great riches in the East Indies' the English call Nabobs; but the *Critical Review*[2] tells us what many Englishmen thought of them— the word 'signifies in the modern acceptation . . . not a real nabob, but some worthy English gentleman who has amassed the fortune of one of those Indian monarchs, and who, in consequence of such exaltation, generally takes the liberty of acting in what manner he thinks proper, without a strict attention to the dictates of religion and morality'. It is a sufficient comment on the trial of Warren Hastings eight years later.

A word that quickly caught the fancy of the English was *Vampire*. In 1732 the *Gentleman's Magazine*[3] reported under Foreign Advices for March, that in Hungary 'certain dead Bodies called Vampires had kill'd Several Persons by sucking their Blood'. By May, the *Craftsman* was saying that this must be a political allegory, since the Hungarians, in subjection to Turks and Germans, must couch all their complaints under figures: the Vampire sounds like a leech or blood-sucker and ravenous ministers are Vampires when they bring in 'Taxes which must gradually drain the Body Politick of its Blood and Spirits'. By 1736 the Magazine[4] was looking nearer home, and declaring that gin would prove a Vampire to the nation, glossing *Vampire* as 'Dead Bodies in Hungary, said to suck the Blood of the Living.'

Divan in its social sense, as distinct from its legal, was an eighteenth- century importation. A good description is given in the *Monthly Review*,[5] where we are told that the '*Divan* is part of the room raised above the floor . . . this is spread with a carpet in winter, in summer with fine matts, along the sides are thick matrasses about 3 feet wide covered commonly with scarlet-cloth, and large bolsters of brocade, hard stuffed with cotton, are set against the walls . . . for the con- veniency of leaning. As they have no chairs, it is upon these they sit.' The word, beginning with the meaning of 'booklet', has had an extraordinary history at home as well as abroad. To the eighteenth century it suggested exotic furnishings; to the twentieth it has de- veloped its own specialist senses in the same department at home.

Though *hookah* was introduced in the 'sixties, twenty years later the author[6] of a travel-book felt that a note on it would be useful, and said—ambiguously—that it is the machine from which 'the smoke

[1] *View*, i, 46.   [2] *Crit. Rev.* 49 (1780), 319.
[3] *Gent. Mag.* ii (1732), 681.   [4] *Gent. Mag.* vi (1736), 311.
[5] From Russell's *Natural History of Aleppo*: *Month. Rev.* xv (1756), 137.
[6] *Crit. Rev.* 53 (1782), 430, Macintosh's *Travels in Europe, Asia and Africa*.

of tobacco and aromatics are inhaled'. And although *cummerbund* had been known since the early seventeenth century, he explains it as 'a long muslin belt wrapt round the waist'. That too had a future in the western world. *Kiosk* had been known from the early seventeenth century, but when Lady Craven[1] was describing her visit to Constantinople she added that 'kiosk means a summer house with blinds all round'. It is a far cry to the newspaper and tobacco kiosk of today.

More exotic still is *Tattoo*. In 1774[2] the *Gentleman's Magazine* reproduced a drawing of a New Zealand Chief 'curiously tataowed' with the comment that it 'exhibits at once the manner in which the New-Zealanders both paint and ornament themselves, and is different from anything of the like kind hitherto discovered as the reader will see by the plate'. This was *à propos* of an Epitome of 'Lieut. Cook's Voyage round the World'.

Casino needed explanation then, for it stood for a new idea: the eighteenth-century use of it needs explanation now, for it gives us the wrong idea—a socially wrong one, especially. In 1776 the *Critical Review*[3] was considering an Englishwoman's *Letters from Italy* in which she gave an account of the Casinos at Venice. The *Review* reports that they are 'small houses of one or two rooms on a floor, neatly fitted up, but never fine, intended for the reception of small coteries, where the company play at cards and generally sup together'. When it is considered, the *Review* continues, that, besides the regatta, a Venetian entertainment introduced to this metropolis last summer, a house also is lately opened under the title of a *casino*, there seems to be reason for apprehending that Venetian manners are making some progress among us. The *Review*'s choice of verb probably suggests some doubt whether Venetian manners were a desirable importation. Opinions differed. Nine years later, Lady Craven[4] was more detailed and enthusiastic. 'The Casini are very small houses hired by one person, or a set of people, to meet in of an evening, where cards, conversation, tea, coffee, lemonade, etc., and a well selected society conspire to give pleasure.' They were so elegant that she could have believed herself in 'a little fairy's palace'. No wonder Venetian ladies would often leave their own palaces to live

[1] *Journey*, p. 199.

[2] *Gent. Mag.* xliv (1774), 70.

[3] *Crit. Rev.* 41 (1776), 359. *O.E.D.* 1789. But in 1775 Sir William Chambers erected a small, elegant pleasure-house still known as the Casino on Lord Charlemont's estate, Marino, at Clontarf, Dublin. Horace Walpole used the word in 1744 (*Stanford Dictionary*).

[4] op. cit., pp. 94–5.

for months in a casino—of whose whereabouts, Lady Craven admits, their husbands might be totally ignorant. Perhaps it was not altogether surprising that these little apartments had the misfortune to labour under a very bad reputation—as temples of lawless love.[1] This was Dr Moore's report in his *View of Society and Manners in Italy*, though he considers that husbands would not let their wives go to them if it were true. Lady Craven's remark puts another complexion on that. At Bologna, the Casino was run by twelve men of the first quality, one of whom bore the expense for a month.[2] Obviously the society was more select then, the emphasis on gambling less strong, though the primary modern associations were there in germ.

'The word *Regatta* signifies *a struggle for the mastery*. When any foreign prince or nobleman of distinction visits Venice, it is customary to entertain them with a *regatta*; or rowing match on the Grand Canal.'[3] So said a booklet published in June 1775. It recommended a similar patriotic exhibition in this country—the first one was held the same month. The *Annual Register*[4] gave an account of 'the new Entertainment' and tells us that songs were sung in which Regatta was the rhyme for Ranelagh, as if to link an old form of amusement with a new. *Regatta* has become more democratic too.

In 1776–7 the magazines were explaining a new fashionable indoor amusement from France—the *Charade*. The word represented must be of two syllables and the game exercises the ingenuity of the ladies.[5] It has lasted well.

All these words suggest innocent pastimes. The eighteenth century however extended the use of *orgy*, a word that was two hundred years older in English in reference to classical religious rites. When Richardson[6] comments on Milton's use of it, he says 'generally by *orgies* is understood the Feasts of *Bacchus*, because they were Such, but Any other Mad Ceremonies may be So call'd.' As a result of the eighteenth-century wider application, they are.

The *Monthly Review*[7] offers a translation of *Lorgnette* (*O.E.D.* 1820)—'Achromatic Spying Glasses'—and explains that the French author means 'those tubes a few inches long, which have a convex

[1] *Ann. Reg.* xxiii (1780), Characters, 6.
[2] Hertford-Pomfret Correspondence, iii, 170.
[3] *Month Rev.* lii (1775), 554. Known in 1754.
[4] *Ann. Reg.* xviii, Appendix to Chronicle, 216.
[5] *Ann. Reg.* xix (1776), Miscellaneous Essays, 199. *Gent. Mag.* xlvii (1777), 24.
[6] The Richardsons' Commentary, p. 30.
[7] *Month. Rev.* liii (1775–6), 536.

object glass and a concave eye-glass, and are designed for the pocket'. Surely it was less clumsy to borrow the French word, even if we can't pronounce it properly by French standards.

Like us, the *Review*[1] could find no translation of *Raisonné* as it is now used in 'Catalogue Raisonné'. Confronted with a 'Dictionaire (*sic*) raisonné d'Anatomie, de Physiologie, etc.' the Reviewers asked their readers to observe that they had omitted the adjective when they translated the titles, for want of an English term of precisely the same sense. 'In its common acceptation it means rational, or, rather, argumentative or reasoning, none of which our idiom will permit, nor to apply in this instance, with propriety.' They added that the 'French are so fond of this term, that, as all science is congested into dictionaries, so all these dictionaries are raisonnés.' It has proved useful, especially to compilers of handbooks of Art Exhibitions. The Stanford Dictionary records its acceptance in 1803.

Coup d'œil for general use was disliked as a needless Gallicism, but as a military term there is something to be said for it. *O.E.D.* quotes it from 1839, but the author of an *Essay on War* reviewed by the *Monthly*[2] in 1762 was using it correctly to mean 'an ability to judge, at the very first glance, of the space necessary to contain any number of troops, and the far superior talent of knowing how to distinguish, in a moment, any advantage that can be taken of the ground'.

Another military term has become popular. Deane Swift[3] writes in humorous vein to Sanderson Miller in January 1755 to say he is 'prodigiously strict' and approaching very near what is called a Martinet, so he expects everything belonging to the 'Fortress' to be put in the best and most exact order that is possible. Their minds were running on Gothic battlements.

There was a tendency in the eighteenth century to confuse *character* and *caricature*, on the mistaken assumption that they are related words. Hogarth had said that good drawing is no part of 'Caracatura', and was taken to task by an anonymous critic[4] who defines 'Caracatura' as 'the distinguishing figure of a person or thing ludicrously exaggerated, yet so as to preserve the similitude of the original'. 'Character is true Resemblance; Caracatura is exaggerated Resemblance and Outré is

---

[1] *Month. Rev.* xxiv (1760), 566.
[2] *Month. Rev.* xxvi (1762), 59. As a general term it seems frequent. 1739 in *Stanford Dictionary* and O.E.D.
[3] Dickins and Stanton, p. 63. *O.E.D.* 1779.
[4] *Month. Rev.* xix (1758), 318–20. Cp. *Spect.* (53).

exaggeration without a Resemblance.' A gentleman[1] from Worcester points out that 'caricatura' is the proper spelling and that in English it ought to be translated a charging or overloading: he defines it in the sense familiar to us.

Another art term is *Torso*, defined in 1788 (Stanford Dictionary 1722) as 'the trunk of a statue of an human figure; i.e. the body, wanting the head and the limbs'.[2] Did *trunk* require definition as much as *torso*? *O.E.D.* has no eighteenth-century examples after the first two decades.

DIALECT

Dialect words needed explanation in London as well as foreign ones. An Edinburgh *caudee*—i.e. caddy—is the same as a Black Guard-Boy in London, so Defoe[3] tells us: they run errands or light you home. It is easier for us to see how the caudee could become a golfer's caddy than how the Blackguard boy became a villain.

To us it comes as a surprise to find *donkey* described as an Essex or Suffolk word for an ass:[4] that *smash* has to be explained as 'to break in pieces', *Yule* as Christmas, *burn* as rivulet, in a list of Tyneside words,[5] and that *toddling* and *strapping* (in Burns, 'toddlan' and 'strappan') were expounded respectively as applied to denote 'the unsteady trot of children, who are beginning to walk', and 'well-grown, well-shaped, promising strength'. 'Porritch' according to the same review, is 'a mess made of oatmeal and water, boiled to the consistency of a pudding, seasoned with a little salt'.[6] We need a comment on *mess* rather than on *porridge*.

Do we need to be told that a *bumper* crop is a large one? It is a Midland word according to the *Gentleman's Magazine*.[7] Dr Johnson defines *limp* as limber, flexile, and thinks it Scots—it is of obscure origin. *To feel limp*, *limp-cover*, show that it is English enough now— these are nineteenth-century developments. *Tidy*[8] is no longer only a West of England word in its sense of neat and decent; this, whether dialectal or not, is an eighteenth-century development.

[1] *Month. Rev.* xix (1758), 606–7.

[2] *Month. Rev.* lxxviii (1788), 558.

[3] *Review* v, 21, 6.

[4] *Gent. Mag.* lxiii (1793), 1083.

[5] *Gent. Mag.* lxiv (1794), 13.

[6] *Month. Rev.* lxxv (1786), 443–5.

[7] *Gent. Mag.* xxix (1759), 271.

[8] *Gent. Mag.* lxiii (1793), 1083.

NAMES OF DISEASES

Finally, we may notice some foreign terms used of diseases: two imply
the advance of medical science, one its helplessness, and the fourth
shows how the uppermost meaning of a word can change from period
to period. In 1772, the *Monthly Review*[1] was reporting a treatise by
Dr William Heberden on 'a very singular, lingering, teazing and
dangerous disease ... which has, we believe, escaped the notice of the
faculty, nor has probably till now found a place or a name in the family
of diseases. The seat of it, and a sense of strangling and anxiety with
which it is attended, have induced the Author to give it the appellation
of Angina Pectoris.' The *Glossographia Anglicana Nova* had defined
angina as the quinsy. Dr Heberden's study placed the disease and the
name he gave it firmly before the Faculty.

Asphyxia, as the name became, was a new term used by the French—
'in Asphyxies' to denote fainting, stoppage of the Pulse, seeming
Death, so the *Monthly Review*[2] tells us in 1777. It implies that fainting
is being taken seriously.

Influenza reached us from Italy in 1743. It had long been used there
for any outbreak of an epidemic, its name suggesting some occult
'influence' not to be accounted for. When the *Gentleman's Magazine*[3]
reported it, quoting from *Common Sense*, it included the remark that it
would be no use to send to England for doctors as they were in demand
here—because *political influence* was so rife! The 1743 outbreak fixed
the name in English on the disease now so called, though it has been
applied to others of a similar kind.

It is astonishing to us to find it being said[4] in the eighteenth century
that 'Cancer, mentioned indefinitely would rather give us an idea of
the Sign of the Zodiac than of the disease.' That, sadly, is no longer true.
Our first meaning is the last of Dr Johnson's three.

TECHNICALITIES

Any new invention demands a new name. Some may be learned,
some humorous, some obviously apt. There is a touch of humour in
bosom friend[5] for 'an oblong piece of fur doubled square, to place

[1] *Month. Rev.* xlvii (1772), 257.   [2] *Month. Rev.* lvii (1777), 507.
[3] *Gent. Mag.* xiii (1743), 206.   [4] *Month. Rev.* xxi (1759), 460.
[5] *Gent. Mag.* lxii (1792), 994. *O.E.D.* 1802. Cp. Swift, *Polite Conversation*,
Dial. I, ed. Partridge (1963), pp. 89–90.

under a lady's neckerchief when she is about leaving a warm room'. It
was introduced in 1791. Apt, too, was Charles Mitchel's *Life-line*[1]—
the line he kept coiled up ready for use at Dover for the preserving of
ships and men. An obvious transfer is the use of *Hand*[2] for the larger
spreading roots of Ginger, which was reported from the West Indies in
1756. (The hand of Bananas is recorded in 1886.)

The new art of Landscape Gardening produced a more precise
meaning for *clump* and a transference of the painter's term *degradation.*

Uvedale Price[3] tells us that some disputes have arisen over the meaning of *clump*, and therefore defines it as 'any close mass of trees of the
same age and growth, totally detached from all others'. They should
be round, or at least regular. Price, however, doesn't like the Clump—
if you took away the first letter, the resulting word 'would most
accurately describe its form and effect'.

Degradation was an eighteenth-century artist's term for 'the lessening and rendering confused the Appearance of things distant in a
Landskip'.[4] It was transferred to picturesque gardening. Lord Kames[5]
asks us to visualise holly and laurel, with the holly which is of the
deeper colour nearer the eye: the degradation of colour in the laurel
makes it appear at a greater distance from the holly, and consequently
removes the object in appearance to a greater distance than it really is.
One wonders whether this sort of trickery with nature was good, and
whether she was not being degraded in the ordinary sense of the word.

Two words that bring the savage side of the eighteenth century
vividly to mind are *over-drove* and *gibbeting.* A correspondent of the
Gentleman's Magazine[6] in 1767 thinks that *over-drove* ought to mean
the creature is too weary to go further, but admits that it is a term
among butchers and drovers for violently or furiously driven, by which
the beast is enraged, and runs heedlessly on wherever chance directs.
The beast in question was an ox that had 'run on to Guildhall'. As for
gibbeting, it shows that the period had no more mercy for man than
beast. Samuel Pegge in 1789 says it 'is the hanging a notorious criminal
in irons as a public and lasting spectacle, after he has suffered death on
the gallows, for the purpose of example and of deterring others from
the like heinous offences'.[7] And he adds that it is 'a design truly

[1] *Gent. Mag.* lx (1790). *O.E.D.* 1794.
[2] *Month. Rev.* xv (1756), reviewing Brown's *Civil and Natural History of
Jamaica. O.E.D.* 1879.   [3] *Essay,* i, 20, 267.   [4] *Gloss. Ang. Nov.*
[5] *Elements of Criticism,* ii, 441.   [6] *Gent. Mag.* xxxvii (1767), 344.
[7] Quoted, *Gent. Mag.* lix (1789), 207. The word is much older.

benevolent and laudable'! The proper comment on both these words is Hogarth's series of plates the *Four Stages of Cruelty*.

In that hanging age, the definition of a word could easily be a matter of life and death if it came into court. There is a strange story[1] of an argument about a soldier accused of high treason. The defence argued that the indictment was invalid because it called him a *yeoman*. That great legal luminary Blackstone had defined *yeoman* in a way that precluded its use of a soldier; but Dr Johnson had given a definition that allowed it. It is astonishing that the Dictionary should have been given precedence over a lawyer's statement, and equally astonishing that the court should have read Johnson carelessly. His second definition says that *yeoman* 'seems to have been anciently a kind of ceremonious title given to soldiers, whence we still have yeomen of the guard'. *Anciently* was disregarded, and no-one claimed that poor James Weldon was a beefeater. To go from the particular to the general is bad logic: in this case it was also bad philology. The court also made play with Shakespeare's use of the word: they must have been more literary than historical or legal in their thinking.

Under the Coventry Act, 1671, *slitting* the nose (but not otherwise maiming or disfiguring) was a capital offence. Doctors consulted on a case of nose-slitting[2] said the wound was transverse, and that *slit* used to be used for such a wound—to *slit*, *divide* or *cut* are synonymous. A blow across the nose would be a slit, whatever the direction. Other experts contended that *slit* and *divide* were not and never had been synonymous. Every slit is a division, but not every division is a slit. It was finally agreed that 'every flesh wound, not a puncture, is a slit... [and] may be cut in a man's leg as well crossway as longway, and it cannot be denied that to make a *slit* is *slitting*'. So the jury concluded that the accused Carrol and King *did* 'slit the nose of the said Cranby'. To us it sounds like much ado about little—but two men's lives hung on the definition then.

A case which reads oddly now was one tried in 1790[3] which was 'of some importance to the commercial world'—as to whether a payment made in Bank notes can legally be deemed a payment in money. They concluded that Bank notes were 'unquestionably called money, and so

---

[1] *Ann. Reg.* xxxvii (1795), 59 (Rivington). Weldon was executed 3 March 1796. (*Ann. Reg.* xxxvi, 16, in Rivington Edition).

[2] *Ann. Reg.* viii (1765), 218. On the Act, see *Marvell's Poems and Letters*, ed. Margoliouth, 1927, ii, 123, 307.

[3] *Ann. Reg.* xxxii (1790), 196.

considered by the world'. It was left for our age to decide that stocks and shares are *money*.

AMBIGUITIES

It is well to be reminded that a word may have several meanings. Commenting on *Paradise Lost*, viii. 152 Bentley remarks that *Orb* 'sometimes means the Body of a Planet, sometimes the Orbit of the Course, sometimes a solid Ring, that wheels about with the Planet fixed in it'. He is speaking in terms of the Ptolemaic astronomy in his last clause. His list will help us to understand the lines about a medallion of Marcus Aurelius:

> Behold, my friend, to this small orb confined
> The genuine features of Aurelius' face[1]

But Bentley's logic makes him forgetful when he comes to discuss *Orient* Jewels, on *Paradise Lost*, iv. 238 and iii. 507. In the latter place it is spoken of Heaven, in the former of the primal Paradise. It is only suitable for a European—'No land is absolutely or to itself, oriental.' Richardson points out that the word need mean only 'Beautiful and rich', and Dr Pearce[2] incisively settles the problem, which he clearly feels to be of Bentley's own making: 'since (as the Doctor allows) the best gems come from the East Indies, it may be allow'd to Milton, to mean by *orient* gems no more than the *best* and *most precious* ones. Milton very frequently uses the word *orient* in such a sense. . . . Poets who write of things out of this world must use Epithets and Metaphors drawn from things in this world if they would make themselves understood'.

When we come on the word *undertaker*, we think first of 'the manager of a funeral'. The *Monthly Review*[3] feared its readers would do the same when it published a letter complaining of the hardships suffered by coal-heavers 'through the impositions and tyranny of their cruel task masters the undertakers'—i.e. 'the authorized regulators of the business of coal-heaving'. In 1747 the *Gentleman's Magazine* could speak of the undertakers of Italian operas, and the *World* could use the word in No. 152 of Magazines—'these general undertakers of learning', and three numbers later in our sense. Considering how many duties and activities we 'undertake' it is odd that the agent noun is so restricted. A combination of euphemism and frequency?

---

[1] Whitehead in Chalmers' *English Poets*, xvii, 230.
[2] *Text of Paradise Lost*, p. 98. [3] *Month. Rev.* xxxix (1768), 327.

The *Critical Review*[1] in 1792 makes an interesting if undeveloped comment on the fact that Homer prefixes the word *hero* to many names in the *Odyssey* 'on whom had he first written in English, he would never have bestowed it'. For the word 'has with us a determinate sense, and is appropriated to military characters'. 'A man eminent for bravery': and also a man 'of the highest class in any respect' says Johnson, which suggests that the *Review* was too narrow: but in the light of its statements, we can see why 'our hero' for the protagonist of a novel struck the reviewers as out of place. With the phrase, the modern technical term for the chief character, heroic or not, was well on the way. Dryden had been the first to use it, but it has become less and less tied to heroism during the last two centuries.

Occasionally it is the neatness of the definition, not its instructiveness, that strikes the modern reader. The *Critical Review*,[2] for example, puts a distinction we agree with aptly when it takes exception to 'the rearing of a youth' in reference to education—'however it may be used by writers, it does not relate to intellectual but animal improvement'. With similar clarity, it remarks[3] that the word *fowl* presents the idea of a dish upon the table, and not, as required by the translation in question, of a pet bird—and a parrot at that.

Ambiguity can exist unnecessarily—when careless speakers use only one word when two are available. Because of some likeness of form in the words, and because of muddle-headedness in the user, difficulties arise through no fault of our vocabulary. Eighteenth-century critics were never hesitant in expressing disapproval of this sort of thing. Burke[4] declares that his contemporaries confuse clear language and strong language; whereas the former 'regards the understanding, the latter belongs to the passions. The one describes a thing as it is: the other describes it as it is felt.' It is no credit to us that 'strong' language is sometimes even more different from 'clear' language now.

We do keep *contemptuous* apart from *contemptible*. Baker[5] informs us that *contemptibly* in his day was most commonly used in the sense of 'with contempt'. 'If I hear it said that one man treats another *contemptibly*, I hardly know whether the meaning is that he treats him with contempt, or that his own behaviour is contemptible.' Scholarly writer though he was, Richard Graves[6] can tell us that his Hortensius

[1] *Crit. Rev.* new arr. iv (1792), 244.   [2] *Crit. Rev.* new arr. vii (1792), 459.
[3] *Crit. Rev.* new arr. viii (1793), 387.   [4] *Sublime and Beautiful*, p. 338.
[5] *Remarks on the English Language*, xlviii.   [6] *Columella*, i, 52.

spoke contemptibly even of his chambers in King's Bench Walk. The meanings are clear in Dr Johnson's definition of the adverbs—*contemptibly* is 'meanly', *contemptuously* 'with scorn'. But the confusion was there in Shakespeare's very rare use of these two words.[1] We may thank the eighteenth century for its useful bit of clarification here.

VOGUE WORDS

We still talk of 'the biter bit', probably forgetting that the word *bite* was a fashionable slang term for a trick, deception or 'a sell'. Steele, in the twelfth issue of the *Tatler* (1709), shows us how it worked in Queen Anne's reign. A Biter is 'a dull Fellow that tells you a Lye with a grave Face, and laughs at you for knowing him no better than to believe him'. A *Biter*, says the *Spectator* (504) three years later, 'is one who tells you a thing you have no reason to disbelieve in itself, and perhaps has given you, before he bit you, no reason to disbelieve it for his saying it: and if you give him Credit, laughs in your Face, and triumphs that he has deceived you. In a word, a *Biter* is one who thinks you a Fool, because you do not think him a Knave. . . . This way of Wit is called *Biting*, by a Metaphor taken from Beasts of Prey.' 'Biting' could go further than this: Beau Nash in his youth was invited on board a naval vessel and shanghaied to the Mediterranean: he found, to use the expression then in fashion, that he was absolutely *bitten*.[2]

The term was invented by Sharpers (in the previous century?), passed to gallants and fops, and in due course was superseded by *hum*, *humbug*—and 'a variety of kindred nonsense'.[3] *Humbug* suggests hypocrisy, but not the impudence implied in *Biter*. It is interesting that the Cocker-Hawkins Dictionary does not label *to bite* in the sense 'to cheat' as cant: and that Dyche and Pardon put this meaning before the proper one. This use of the word, of course, sharpens the point of Pope's[4] epitaph for a monument at Stowe to 'Signor Fido, An Italian of good Extraction, who came into England Not to bite us, like most of his Countrymen . . . he was not a Man, but a Grey-Hound'!

'A fine fellow' sounds complimentary to us apart from sarcasms like 'Not so fast, my fine fellow.' According to the *Gentleman's Magazine*[5]

[1] C. T. Onions, *Shakespeare Glossary*, s.v.
[2] *Life of Beau Nash*, p. 19. The work is by Goldsmith though his name is omitted from the title page.
[3] *Month. Rev.* li (1774), 26. [4] Quoted in *The Art of Poetry*, p. 69, chap. VII.
[5] *Gent. Mag.* liv (1784), 173.

in 1784, it was—in 1763. Then it meant a well-informed, elegant and upright gentleman. In 1784, it meant 'one who can drink three bottles', gamble, bilk, seduce, and threaten murder!

If we look in Dyche and Pardon's dictionary, we shall find that *Flummery* is 'a cooling consistence, or sort of paste or jelly made by the boiling up of oatmeal and water together'. Lady Luxborough[1] was probably right in thinking that her friend Mr Shenstone, retired in the western wilds, would not know that in London it meant flattery and compliment, and was the present reigning word among the Beaux and Belles. She begs his pardon for telling him what his Dictionary would not have told him.

Less troublesome than the 'fine fellow' and no doubt a large consumer of 'flummery' was the fribble. The *Monthly Review*[2] noticed the persistence of the type, however the names change.[3] 'Every age has its fops. About twenty years ago we had a gentle race of fribbles. These were soon frightened away by the bolder *Bucks* and the swaggering *Bloods*; but now we are got to fribbling again, in the finicking form known by the name of Macaroni.'

Next year the Reviewers[4] were saying that to turn the *Faerie Queene* into Blank Verse was like decorating a tapestry hero with 'a maccaroni's straw hat and white apron'. Both notions of adornment betray a good deal about eighteenth-century tastes.

A term that has had a long life is noted in 1799, when the *Gentleman's Magazine*[5] remarks that *Preside* is a word now given—'not to the leader of the band, but to some distinguished performer—as "Mr. —— will preside at the harpsichord." Dr Johnson did not live long enough to insert this meaning of the word, or to enquire whether it had any.' Nevertheless, it has become a set phrase.

Another word that seemed over-employed in the later part of the eighteenth century was *line* in the sense, so familiar to us, of 'sphere of activity'. It had been seriously used in the preceding century, but when we look at its uses in our period it is hardly surprising that Dr Johnson thought it a 'colloquial barbarism'. We meet 'the military line', 'the professional line', 'the hair-dressing line', 'the clerical line', 'the fishing line' (particularly silly), 'the dramatic line, 'the venatic line'— in plain terms, hunting. It is astonishing to find that this use of the word

---

[1] *Letters*, xxxviii (1749). Quoted *Month. Rev.* liv (1776), 62.
[2] *Month. Rev.* xlviii (1773), 319.
[3] *Month. Rev.* xlviii (1773), 319.
[4] *Month. Rev.* lii (1775), 112.   [5] *Gent. Mag.* lxix (1799), 199, note.

begins with a misunderstanding of the Authorised Version of the
Bible, rendering the Greek word for a measuring-rod.[1] The bookseller
Lackington[2] seems to have thought of it as if it were the line of soldiers
on parade, for he speaks of an author's 'stepping out of his line'. So
far as we can judge, it has come to stay.

ABSTRACTS

The eighteenth-century definition of a science will show us how people
then approached it, and by implication, how far our knowledge has
moved on. *Anthropology*, for instance, according to a writer in the
Monthly Review[3] in 1767, 'is the knowledge of man—his existence, his
essence, nature, essential qualities, necessary attributes, all a priori'.
On the other hand, *Glossographia Anglicana Nova* and Bailey say it is
a 'Discourse or Description of Man or of a Man's Body', Dr Johnson,
'the doctrine of Anatomy'. The *Review*'s definition is nearer our idea
of the word than the dictionaries'. The vicissitudes of the word, as
O.E.D. reveals them, are instructive on our thinking about ourselves.

'*Psychology*', says the *Review*,[4] 'is the knowledge of the mind in
general and of the human mind in particular . . . about the substance
of which, notwithstanding every effort, it is still exceedingly difficult
to say anything reasonable, and yet more to say anything positive'.
The subject has made enormous advances since then, though it is still
possible to find a layman who feels inclined to agree with his ancestors.

Dr Johnson speaks of 'the dusty desarts of barren philology', and
Vicesimus Knox of 'the flowery paths of philology'.[5] They may not
have been talking of the same thing. George Campbell[6] holds that
Philology embraces history, grammar, languages, jurisprudence and
criticism—all the branches of learning that depend on testimony. This
is in accord with *Glossographia Anglicana Nova* which defines it as 'the
love of Discourse or Learning: the Study of Humanity, or of the
Liberal Sciences'. These are the old high senses of Philology: the
transition to the more narrowly verbal appears in Dyche and Pardon
who, though saying that Philology means universal learning, state that
it is 'especially that part that relates to letters or languages, and their
several origins, under which is comprised the art of criticism, or the

---

[1] See *O.E.D. Line*, 28. Beattie's *Third Dialogue of the Dead* laughs at a number
of these uses.
[2] *Memoirs*, p. 188.   [3] *Month. Rev.* xxxviii (1767), 517.
[4] ibid., p. 514.   [5] *Essays*, i, 300.   [6] *Phil. of Rhet.*, p. 56.

meanings and various readings of particular phrases or passages out of old authors, the customs and manners to which they often relate being wholly grown obsolete'. Whether Philology is desert or garden depends on the breadth of the philologist's interest.

Definitions of such words as *Complaisance* and *Urbanity* introduce us to the social standards of the period. 'Good-breeding is a *social virtue*; it is *Benevolence* brought into Action with all the Advantages and Beauty of Proportion and Symmetry. Complaisance . . . is its Resemblance, but it is only the Varnish.'[1] The word was going down: in the reign of Queen Anne *Complaisance* had been defined as 'a Virtue that blends all Orders of Men together in a Friendly Intercourse of Words and Actions'.[2]

Urbanity is an 'exquisite grace'—'what was most polite' according to the Latin writers, 'in the air of conversation as in the language of it'.[3] A 'Letter on Urbanity' quoted by the *Gentleman's Magazine* in 1746 had explained that '*Urbanity* is a certain impression of politeness and goodness which appears in the mind, conversation and sentiments of a person. *Homo Urbanus* was much the same among the Romans, as what we now call a man of address, probity and honour. . . . To write with *Urbanity* is to write with elegance and correctness, yet free from Art and Constraint, that is, in such a manner as without affectation shows a delicacy of mind, and a soul full of honour and virtue.'

The word was the product of the sixteenth century, but has only become common since the early nineteenth. At first *urbane* meant *urban*— the useful differentiation follows the same lines as that between *human* and *humane*. It has developed a tinge of superficiality: the *O.E.D.*'s equation with 'suave' would have surprised the eighteenth century, and the equation with 'bland' might have been ambiguous.

Another aspect of social intercourse is betrayed in Defoe's definition of *Fleering*. It is 'when a Man offers some gross Flattery to another, presuming the other has not enough Sense to see it—and then scornfully Laughing to see them (as they think) so easie to be imposed upon'.[4]

The eighteenth century, with all its learning—perhaps because of it —had a horror of pedantry and pedants. James Harris defines *Pedantry* as learned and scientific terms introduced out of season. 'The subject may have merit, the terms be precise, and yet, notwithstanding, the

---

[1] *Gent. Mag.* iv (1734), 76.   [2] *Guardian* (162).
[3] Hurd, Preface to *Moral and Political Dialogues*, p. liv.
[4] Review (VII), 89.

speaker be a *Pedant* if he talk without regard either to time or place'—like the scholar who wanted a thick pair of stockings, and told the hosier he wanted them 'of matter continuous, not of matter discrete'.[1]

The *Mirror*[2] says that Pedantry 'in the common sense of the word, means an absurd ostentation of learning and stiffness of phraseology, proceeding from a misguided knowledge of books and a total ignorance of men'. The *Tatler*[3] makes the neat point that 'Pedantry ... in Learning is like Hypocrisy in Religion, a Form of Knowledge without the Power of it.' It was suggested[4] very reasonably that the word might be applied to anyone who 'does not know how to think out of his Profession and particular way of Life'—the 'meer Man of the Town' for example. The period remembered more clearly than we do that *Pedant* had meant a schoolmaster, even if it had come to mean 'a *paltry* schoolmaster':[5] we may not find it so easy to see the connection with anything so important as pedagogy.

Some difficulties of definition are inherent in the words, because we have not sorted out related ideas, or because, though we are clear in our own personal definition in our own minds, others may be equally clear, but apply the word to something else. This is likely to happen in matters of taste, literary judgment, and morals. The words concerned belong to the philosophers rather than to the lexicographers. To define even with an unstable and temporary fence such words as *genius* or *taste*, *sentimentality* or *beauty* requires a separate study for each word, and plenty of such studies are available from the eighteenth century and from our own times. The philosophers began to distinguish Imagination from Fancy, thus sowing seeds that were to bear fruit in Coleridge's thinking. They tried to keep *astonishment* and *surprise* in separate compartments—in spite of them, we tend to be less careful, though a 'surprise packet' or 'to take by surprise' hold their ground.

Adam Smith[6] remarks that 'Wonder, surprise and admiration are words, which, though often confounded, denote in our language sentiments that are indeed allied, but that are in some respects different also, and distinct from one another. What is new and singular excites that sentiment which, in strict propriety, is called Wonder; what is unexpected, Surprise, and what is great or beautiful, Admiration.' He sums it up clearly by noting that we wonder at 'extraordinary objects' and the rarer natural phenomena, and at what we are not acquainted with, even when we have been forewarned. We are surprised at familiar

---

[1] *Philosophical Arrangements*, p. 379. [2] No. 5 (1779).
[3] *Tatler* (165). [4] *Spect.* (105). [5] *Gloss. Ang. Nov.* s.v. [6] *Works*, v, 55–6.

things met unexpectedly. And we can admire both the unexpected and
the familiar. Joseph Priestley makes the same distinction between
Surprize and *Wonder* in 1767.[1] What strikes us most is the strength of
the word *astonishment* as the eighteenth century understood it—whatever causes Astonishment may so powerfully affect the senses 'that a
Deprivation of Speech' may follow. 'The Vulgar of the Metropolis'
would say 'She was struck all of a heap', and the Peasantry 'She was
deadly frightened' or 'scared out of her senses'.[2] This is the comment
of the purist grammarian P. Withers, whom we might suspect of more
attention to literal or etymological meaning than necessary: but Burke[3]
tells us the same thing—'astonishment is that state of the soul, in
which all its motions are suspended, with some degree of horror . . .
[it is] the effect of the sublime in its highest degree'. We must admit
that there are many lower degrees.

Our critics betray an occasional impatience with the unsettled words,
without offering any stabilising suggestion—how could they, when
private or coterie opinion is so much involved? But they may incidentally throw light on the thought of their times. For example the *Monthly
Review*[4] considers *correctness* to be 'vague' and 'frequently used without meaning or precision'. The *Review* brings before us two incompatible schools of thought when it continues 'It is perpetually the
nauseous cant of the French critics and their pupils that the English
writers are generally *incorrect*. If correctness implies an absence of petty
faults, this, perhaps, may be granted. If it means that because their
tragedians have avoided the irregularities of Shakespear, and have
observed a juster œconomy in their Fables, that therefore their *Athalia*
is preferable to *Lear*, the notion is absurd.'

Priestley believed that 'the greater precision of modern philosophers
[compared with ancient ones] is owing, in a great measure, to this
circumstance, that by the previous study of languages, and a due attention to the nature and use of words, they have been better guarded
against'[5] the kind of deception we run into if we do not make an
accurate distinction of ideas because we have no accurate distinction
of words. This is a vicious circle: but Priestley is right in believing that
words indiscriminately used can mislead.

We expect dictionaries to give us objective definitions, and of course
the eighteenth-century Dictionary makes up in immediacy and the

---

[1] *Lectures on Oratory and Criticism*, p. 150. First delivered 1762.
[2] *Aristarchus*, pp. 160–3.   [3] *Sublime and Beautiful*, pp. 95–6.
[4] *Month. Rev.* xv (1756), 62.   [5] *Observations on Education*, p. 44.

order in which it lists its words for its lack of historical data. But now and then a personal viewpoint can be clearly seen—it is not only Dr Johnson who could lose his scientific detachment. Certainly we gather a good deal about him when we see him defining a *dedicator* as 'one who inscribes his work to a patron with compliment and servility'— and then telling us that 'a *Patron* is commonly a wretch who supports with insolence and is paid with flattery'. Equally forthright is his description of a distiller—'one who makes and sells pernicious and inflammatory spirits'.[1]

Much more biased are Dyche and Pardon, who seem determined to look on the gloomy side if they can find one. Was it really necessary to come down on the Beau with such a sledge-hammer? He is 'one who dresses to the top of the mode, and affects to be first in all fashions; this name is commonly applied to those whose behaviour and talk shews their whole thoughts are taken up in the pursuit of trifles, without regarding the real qualifications of gentlemen, which by their habit they would be esteemed'. Were they so near witchcraft in its sinister sense that they could not see *enchant* and *bewitch* as pleasant words? To enchant is 'to bewitch, or so blind the eyes of a person's reason, that he does things not only contrary to reason, but also hurtful to the doer'. Surely they took a limited view of *rosy*, which, they tell us is 'spoken of persons, whose spirits are much raised and their faces look very red, either with the heat of the fire, or the effect of strong liquour, etc.' We can only suppose they had never read of 'rosy-fingered dawn' in Dryden, or of the 'sweet rosie lad' in *Cymbeline*. They were scathing enough on most ecclesiastical words, and they were of their time when they gave to *cloister* the tell-tale definition 'to imprison, confine, or shut up in a religious house'. It fits an age in which it was believed that to spend six months reading Thomas Aquinas would produce an 'irretrievable derangement' of the brain.[2]

The dictionary definition may be valuable because it tells us what we should not know, since the word for us has developed another meaning. Dr Johnson tells us that 'to dragoon' is to 'persecute by abandoning a place to the rage of soldiers'—to us, dragooning is unpleasantly restrictive, but does not imply the sack of a city—the emphasis is on

[1] The proper comment is made by Hogarth's *Gin Lane*: the print was published four years before Dr Johnson's Dictionary. The quoted definitions are from the *Dictionary* (1755). One suspects some personal feeling, since *patronise* was not necessarily derogatory. See below, p. 215.

[2] Ruffhead, *Life of Pope*, p. 291.

discipline, not on its lack. An *index* is never, to us, the table of contents of a book, though there seems no reason why it should not be indication at the beginning rather than the end. *Lunch*, *luggage*, and *mechanic* have gone up in the world. We have too many occasions for agreeing with Johnson that luggage is anything 'cumbrous and unwieldy that is to be carried away'—but not necessarily that it is 'of more weight than value'. *Lunch* is a social occasion rather than 'as much food as one's hand can hold'. And a *mechanic* is not now 'a low workman'—though Johnson admits he could be 'an artificer'. I doubt whether we should expect to buy pickles from the *oilman*, as well as oil. And the dictionary may even tell us how fashions change—a *parlour* is a 'room in houses on the first floor, elegantly furnished for reception or entertainment'.[1] To us, it need not be on the first floor—it probably isn't—and if we have one, we call it the drawing-room—or, if we don't mind being 'Non-U', the Lounge. What would the eighteenth century have thought of icecream parlours, beauty parlours and milking parlours? The thirteenth-century monks who first gave us the word would be more astonished still.

[1] So Johnson. Dyche and Pardon place it on 'a lower floor'.

II

CENSURE AND PROTEST

ONE of the clearest broad statements of what constitutes badness in language is to be found in the words of a study of one branch of science—*An Essay on Chemical Nomenclature*. Its authors point out that 'poverty of language circumscribes the flight of ideas; inaccuracy of expression precludes precision of thought; equivocal words generate erroneous opinions; the associating improper accessory ideas and judgments with well-known terms diffuses and strengthens prejudices; injudicious etymologies entrap the apprehension, and figurative expressions, mistaken for actual definition, fill up the measure of confusion and inconsistency of thought that flow from the abuses of speech'.[1]

It is hardly surprising that it seems much easier to find disapproving comments on the behaviour of English than to find a welcome for new developments. 'Misusers' of words may be poets or pedants, clergymen or lawyers, business men or members of parliament, fops or females, and their linguistic sins include the misapplying of words, the use of badly formed words, of needless new ones and needless old ones, of low words and phrases, whether slang, cant or dialect, of bombast, burlesque, technicalities outside specialist contexts, foreign importations—there seems no end to them. Equally there seems no end to the protests against the vicious flood. What interests us is that so many of the protests were vain and even unjustified—the flood, to us, is more like an irrigation, for the 'objectionable' expressions have often proved their worth.

NEW, STRANGE AND MAINLY FRENCH

The most captious criticism objects to words simply because they are new. And here we must remember that often this was not true: they may have been new to the critics, however well-read, but not to the language. The dates stated in *O.E.D.* were nowhere clearly set out for them, and we wonder how far Dr Johnson was justified in his hopeful assumption that any one who referred to his Dictionary would know,

[1] Quoted *Crit. Rev.* new arr. xxiii (1798), 433.

without being told, precisely when his authoritative writers lived. But a reference to his Dictionary would have saved Dr Enfield[1] from saying that *rivality* was a new and unnecessary coinage, for Dr Johnson quotes it from Addison—it may be unnecessary, but clearly it was not new. In 1798[2] the *Monthly Review* made the same slip about *annexion*. In 1785 the *Critical Review* declared that it had never yet heard of the word *supernal*.[3] It is true that *O.E.D.* has no quotation to illustrate it from the eighteenth century, but it has plenty from earlier and later times. The period had perhaps a more earth-bound mind. Such comments often imply that a word is not a favourite with the eighteenth century, though it may have been used before or since. So the *British Critick*, ii (1793), 277, does not acknowledge *authoress*. Swift had used it, but after its quotation from him *O.E.D.* has no illustrations till the nineteenth century. Bicknell, in his *Grammatical Wreath*, ii, 66, says we do not use it, adding that *poetess* is almost obsolete too.

Any shortening or lengthening of a form strikes the reader with the irritation of an unexpected change, the reason for which he cannot see: so does the substitution of a strange ending for a familiar. This is what lies behind George Campbell's refusal to give quarter to such frivolous innovations as *incumberment, connexity, platonician, fictious, majestatic*. They are all 'good words new modelled'.[4] He includes in his list the new compound *mirror-writing*: it came into its own a century later. The *Gentleman's Magazine*[5] of 1781 had doubts about some new verbs invented or renewed by the Bishop of Lichfield, who had used them in sermons preached before the University of Cambridge. They include *symbolize* and *emblematize, solemnify* and *sanction. Solemnify* had little future; the others had one. The uncertainty of verbal criticism and linguistic prophecy is brought out very well by the list of words with 'uncommon terminations' pilloried by James Hay Beattie in his Third Dialogue of the Dead—*referral, committal* (for *commitment*), *approval* (for *approbation*), the *transferral* of property instead of its *transference*. But he goes on to say ironically that if we want to show our great learning we ought to affect Greek terminations such as *-ism* or *-ise* and use *truism* for *truth* and *agriculturalist* for *husbandman*. To us, *commitment* and *committal* have different spheres of reference: *approval* has met with our approval: a *truism* is a lesser thing than truth, and *agriculturalist* is the dignified word in a scientific age, whereas *husbandman* is in place mainly in the Authorised Version of the Bible or in

[1] *Month. Rev.* lxxv (1786), 12.   [2] *Month. Rev.* lix (1798), 431.
[3] *Crit. Rev.* 60 (1785), 318. [4] *Phil. of Rhet.*, p. 174. [5] *Gent. Mag.* li (1781), 131.

Shakespeare. Likewise, the *Monthly Review*[1] didn't like *disclaimer*—we do. In 1784[2] the *Gentleman's Magazine* was objecting to an author's use of words that are not sterling English. Having 'resided so much abroad', he appeared to have partly forgotten his own language. Of the improper words, *actual* for *present* was, as the reviewers said, a Gallicism. *O.E.D.*'s first certain example of *amelioration* is from Burke, twelve years later. *Extremity, disorderliness, distinctiveness, prosperousness*, had all been used before the eighteenth century, but *O.E.D.* has no examples from our period: its earliest example of *uninterestingness* is from 1854. Edward Gibbon was criticised[3] for the same reasons. He too used *actual* for *present* and *faculties* for *means*. *Faculties* had been used in this sense since Wiclif's day: but it is true that *O.E.D.* has no examples for this period before its quotation from *The Decline and Fall of the Roman Empire*.

Mrs Piozzi[4] felt that Fanny Burney after her marriage to General D'Arblay had lived so much with foreigners that her English suffered; she used *demand aid* and *to accord* in a way English people do not and spoke of *descending* to breakfast. *Ask, grant* or *help* and *going downstairs* are the idiomatic expressions.

The eighteenth-century critics were far too apt to jump to conclusions: it is a failing not peculiar to them. The *Critical Review*[5] is uncomfortable with such words as *appendage, foiblesse, tinted ideas, propelled, condemnable, misanthrope, tranquilly, emanate, legerity, septentrion, orient* and *occident, devastated, bilious.* 'To what language these most properly belong, the translator best knows, most certainly not to our own.' *Foiblesse* was a Gallicism, *emanate, devastate* and *to tint* were of recent growth, *legerity, septentrion* and *occident* have no eighteenth-century illustrations in *O.E.D.*, and *tranquilly* is dated by that authority 1801, though surely it is the sort of formation that anyone could make up at any time after *tranquil* had been introduced— so far as our evidence goes, by Shakespeare. (*Tranquillity* dates from the fourteenth century.) But the other six were old and established, and are all in Johnson's Dictionary—and in Bailey's (1730), apart from *misanthrope*. More reasoned is the reviewer's objection[6] to *redoubtable*, though it began as a bit of ignorance. James Grainger had used it, and had defended it by calling Pope's use of it to his support: the

[1] *Month. Rev.* xvii (1757), 306.   [2] *Gent. Mag.* liv Pt. 2 (1784), 847.
[3] *Month. Rev.* lxiv (1781), 221.   [4] *Intimate Letters*, pp. 136–7.
[5] *Crit. Rev.* 2 (1756), 340.
[6] *Crit. Rev.* 7 (1759), 149. But Chaucer seems to have introduced it.

Critical Review stuck to its guns—'even Pope's adoption will not make it a native of England'. (*Must* all our words be natives?) Pope had *terrible* and *formidable* at his command, and a great name is not enough to establish a word. So Dryden had used *fraischeur*, but that ought not to appear in the Catalogue of English words. With *O.E.D.* Dr Johnson admits *Fraischeur* but says it was 'foolishly innovated by Dryden'. (Had our reviewer been checking up?) But we should remember in Dryden's favour that the word is also one of the French affectations collected by Melantha in *Marriage à la Mode*, which suggests that Dryden had second thoughts about its value. Actually it had been used in the sixteenth century, and was not really new, though we may well agree that it offers nothing that *freshness* does not.

Uncertainty of touch in the choice of new words from abroad is illustrated by the fact that, as the *Critical Review* recalls, Lord Bolingbroke had adopted *volupté, opiniâtre*—and *develop*.[1] Even if 'he is counted one of the most elegant English writers, you will hardly affirm that these foreign words have been, or ought to be, naturalized even upon his authority'. Here we naturalise one and refuse two out of three. But the *Review* was sound in asking us to look at the words on their intrinsic merits as expression, and not only to the great names.

Even if we disagree over the particular instances, the *Monthly Review*[2] was reasonable in its reprimand to 'translators' who don't translate—why leave 'rôle . . . as it stood in the original'? *Part* would do. And why must novelists use *penchant* instead of 'the passion of love'? The 'offended ear of the unfrenchified reader sickens at the sound' and is ready to loathe the idea because of the 'uncouth' form in which it is expressed. *Penchant* has broken free from the *passion* of love, and proved useful in less romantic contexts.

To introduce French words or forms when we have synonymous ones is an affectation—*eagerness* means what *empressement* means. But it is worse to use in the foreign sense words that exist in both languages but with a different twist of meaning in each. In English we ought not to write 'the baseness of the Greeks precipitated itself at the feet of the emperor', because *baseness* does not in English convey the idea of servility and grovelling manners; nor *precipitating* the act of casting oneself at a person's feet.[3]

[1] *Crit. Rev.* 7 (1759), 149. The history of *develop* is more complicated than the *Review* suggests. See *O.E.D.*
[2] *Month. Rev.* xliv (1771), 65.
[3] *Gent. Mag.* lix (1789), 122.

George Washington was censured[1] for using *derange* for *disarrange*, *grade* for *step*, *debark* for *disembark*. It is, thought the critics, 'a vice of the times to corrupt the language by introducing foreign terms without regard to the just analogy of formation, and without any rational ground of preference for melody, or force, to genuine English words of similar import'. If *embark* means to go aboard ship, we may ask whether its opposite ought not to be *debark*. *Disembark*, which we accept, is as illogically made as *disincentive*, which still worries some of us, or *disassociate*[2] which probably worries more. Are they so far removed from the absurd type foreseen by George Orwell in his *Nineteen Eighty-four*—*ungood*, for instance?

The *British Critick*[3] disliked the new Gallic term *paralyse* and the use of *transpire* for 'arise'. (Both had been used by a University preacher.) *Egotism*[4] for *selfishness*, *replace* for *take the place of*, and *isolated* for *insulated* also are Gallicisms:[5] they are all useful and familiar now, and the last two have been given each its own work. Indeed, *isolated*, which seems so normal to us, had a hard fight for acceptance, un-English, unnecessary and foolish word that it was in the opinion of this magazine.[6] It is interesting to find that of the four senses of *replace* listed in *O.E.D.* three are eighteenth-century developments: meaning 'to put back', it probably represents a borrowing from French late in the sixteenth century.

Why should we refuse our lively native idioms? Mrs Piozzi[7] comments that the French wits have taught us to say that 'an affair was on the carpet', from their expression *sur le tapis*. John Bull used to find his business on the anvil. Unfortunately, perhaps, but naturally, he still prefers the carpet—which generally is now more part of his experience than the anvil.

Language is so much an expression of nationality that we should not be surprised to find the critics as much concerned for our national future as for the future of our language when they write scathingly about the importations from French. For example, the *Critical Review*[8]

---

[1] *Brit. Crit.* vi (1795), 237, reviewing his letters. In 1787 the *European Magazine* xi (262) commented that Dr Johnson would not have allowed *derange*—which is doubtful. Mrs Piozzi, *Brit. Syn.*, ii, 6, mentions 'Mental Derangement' as used in elegant conversation. It offers a useful distinction. See *O.E.D.*, s.v. It was commonly used in newspapers of George III's illnesses.

[2] But it came in early in the seventeenth century.

[3] *Brit. Crit.* vii (1796), 197   [4] *Brit. Crit.* viii (1796), 536.

[5] *Brit. Crit.* ix (1797), 375   [6] *Brit. Crit.* xiii (1799), 396.

[7] *Brit. Syn.*, ii, 172.   [8] *Crit. Rev.* 7 (1759), 344.

disliked the style of a biography of Gustavus Adolphus of Sweden that was 'stiffened with affected phrases, and interlarded with foreign words and idioms, which the historian contemplates with reverential awe as sacred terms of which he would not presume to attempt the translation'. Some of these are *coup d'œil, acumen, debonnaireté, sciolto viso, camisado*, of which the two last seem both unknown and unneeded, so far as we are concerned.[1] The reviewer continued: 'If English authors are not contented with their own language, which is so copious, nervous, and ductile, but proceed to introduce foreign words unnecessarily, our tongue will, in time, degenerate into a harsh medley of barbarisms. If we thus naturalize foreign words and foreign subjects, our blood, our manners, and our language will be soon alike adulterated.' Anglo-French relations in the present century may make us look at these sentiments with different eyes: but the reviewer did at least recognise that language is a reflection of life.

The patriotic critic may of course be too sweeping, or downright absurd. The claim that we don't want to borrow the word *ennui* because we never suffer from the thing, comes strangely from the age that invented 'the bore' and its relatives. When a translator rendered *ennui* by 'listlessness', the *Monthly Review*[2] noted that 'we have happily no adequate expression for it'. But this was a dissentient voice—*Ennui* in most people's opinion was a wanted word, so it will be discussed in Chapter IV under *Recommendation*.

If many felt that French words sounded elegant, one that in due course was to prove useful was blamed for its ugliness. When an author remarked 'This was his fort', the *Critical Review*[3] interpreted the word to mean 'this was what he excelled in', and commented that it was 'impossible to conceive how often ... this little hard stunted French word [had] attempted to thrust itself into the English language. It is one of those many French pretenders who, notwithstanding the repeated endeavours of the vain, haughty and presumptuous enemies of our most sacred protestant language, will never be able to establish itself here.' The *Review* protests too much: alas for knowledge and prophecy, the word had been in use since the seventeenth century, and has established itself, English pronunciation and all.

[1] 'Viso sciolto con spensiere stretti' used by Chesterfield to his son, 22 May 1749, was then proverbial. (Coxon, *Chesterfield and his Critics*, p. 84.)
[2] *Month. Rev.* lxv (1781), 229.
[3] *Crit. Rev.* 1 (1756), 73. Used by Horace Walpole in 1749.

LATINATE DICTION

In an age firmly basing its higher education on the Greek and Latin classics, we might expect to find the critics treating Latinisms more leniently than the Gallicisms. Yet a writer in the *Gentleman's Magazine*[1] would like to banish *ultimatum, sine qua non* and *facsimile*,[2] though he has no objection to *ditto* if left to the merchants, and *ad valorem* in a commercial treaty. (*Ditto* is Italian.)

In 1785 there was published *An Essay towards an English Grammar* whose author, according to the *Monthly Review*,[3] considered 'our language at present as a kind of anglicised Latin', and wished to bring it into 'some greater conformity to its Saxon original'. Arguments against Latin frequently became arguments for English. The matter is dealt with in a style at once pointed and amusing by the author of *A New Estimate of Manners and Principles*: or, *A Comparison between Antient and Modern Times in the Three great articles of Knowledge, Happiness and Virtue*. The *Monthly Review*[4] quotes the author's query why English 'might not be made . . . as good a language as the Greek or Latin' if as much care were bestowed on it. Are we not undutiful children? Every 'Coxcomb, who sticks a pen in his wig, behind a compter, if he has barely learned his *Accidence*, must have his *Items*, his *Omniums*, his *N.B.'s* and his *via Londini's*; abbreviates his pounds, shillings and pence at the top of his accompts into l.s.d.—calculates his gains at so much per cent.—and signs his receipts, "per me, Peter Stocks, Anno. Dom. etc.".' A petition to Parliament in favour of English would possibly be dated '*Die Mercurii*, Feb. 10mo. and concluded with a *Nemine Contradicente*.' Boys know more of Caesar and Alexander than of William or Elizabeth, 'and are much better able to hold a conversation with a German commentator than make a speech before an audience of their own Countrymen'. The Ancients taught 'their children to be *Citizens*, we are teaching ours to be little better than Parrots'. An equally comprehensive but more pungent onslaught comes from P. Withers[5] who contrives to hit his religious and linguistic targets with one shot—'I would as soon appeal to modern Rome for the truth of my Creed as to antient Rome for the Propriety of my Diction.' Merely personal bias, we may say: but can we seriously

---

[1] *Gent. Mag.* lvii Pt. I (1787), 212.
[2] Its usual plural at this period was *fac-similia*.
[3] *Month. Rev.* lxxiv (1786), Art. 5.
[4] *Month. Rev.* xxv (1762), 362 sqq.   [5] *Aristarchus*, p. 98.

40   CENSURE AND PROTEST

dissent from him when he goes on 'From a system of syntax so essentially different it is absurd to expect Information as to Concord and Government'? In his view, if they cannot study both the Classics and English, 'an enlightened People ought to abandon the study of Latin and Greek, and cultivate their native language'.

In view of some modern emphases on the teaching of English Grammar, it is interesting to find that in 1776 the *Monthly Review*[1] was criticising Richard Wynne for saying in his *Universal Grammar* that an active verb 'governs the accusative case, for nouns in English having no accusative termination, the verb cannot be said to govern that case'. The presence or absence of a case-ending is not the whole of the story, but the reviewer has a point that makes him a forerunner of Otto Jespersen. Earlier, this Review[2] was declaring its astonishment that in 'a matter of such allowed importance as that of teaching our language with elegance and purity... hardly any qualification is thought requisite except a little knowledge of Latin, to which tongue the English hath less affinity than most others in Europe'. The result of this discrepancy was all too apparent to the critics: 'Is it not amazing that some, who have been beyond a doubt very excellent Grecians and Latinists, have written their mother-tongue not only inelegantly, but even incorrectly and ungrammatically?'[3]

We need not, then, be surprised to find Dr Johnson being taken to task—however unsubtly and blunderingly—by Archibald Campbell in his *Lexiphanes*.[4] Campbell had found the *Rambler* heavy reading for a long voyage: he was a Royal Navy officer, not a professed linguistic critic. But he has good things to say about plain English, and he did not stand alone. All the same, we should be less likely to expect the *Gentleman's Magazine*—the periodical for which Dr Johnson wrote—to declare four years after Johnson's death that Latin words were 'his hobby-horse, and he was at great pains to pick them up with care, wherever he could find them, and give them a place in his work'.[5] The Magazine thinks that many of the sonorous words beloved of seventeenth-century taste are perfectly useless, have never been used since, and ought to be excluded from an English dictionary, or, if admitted at all, should be marked there as barbarisms!

It was all very well to argue that a dead language sets a standard because it is immutable.[6] Once a living language has borrowed vocabu-

[1] *Month. Rev.* liv (1776), 161.   [2] *Month. Rev.* xxxiii (1765), 274.
[3] Baker, *Remarks*, CLXXXVII.   [4] 1767.   [5] *Gent. Mag.* lviii Pt. 1 (1788), 7.
[6] *Lælius and Hortensia*, p. 457.

lary from a dead one, the words will be subject to change and development. Joseph Spence faced this situation in his comments on Pope's *Odyssey*. 'The *Latin sense* perhaps is one thing and the English use another. When this has obtained universally, we ought not to run back to the Latin sense of the word in our use of it. If you should, the Learn'd themselves may not readily fall into your meaning and the Unlearn'd will inevitably mistake it.'[1]

Spence dislikes 'With *partial* hands the gods their gifts dispense' (*Odyssey*, viii, 185) but the ambiguity here is due to English use rather than Latin. *Partialis* is not a classical word. Souter[2] quotes it from Gregory the Great's Epistles, but his gloss *partial* is hardly helpful— is it 'a partial recovery' or 'I'm partial to children'? The double meaning had run on for at least a hundred years in English. William Cowper (1791) translates the passage as

> Therefore the Gods
> Give not endowments graceful in each kind . . . all to one

In Book 17, l. 200, Pope wrote

> aside they lay
> Their garments, and succinct the victims slay

where *succinct* has the Latin sense of 'tucked up', 'girded'. Here Cowper says

> they fell brisk to slaughter.

According to Pope (vii, 54)

> Pallas to their eyes
> The mist objected—

she threw it literally in their way. Cowper's version is that Pallas 'dimmed their eyes with darkness'. And in book ix, 514, Odysseus describes how he clung to the ram in escaping from the Cyclops

---

[1] Joseph Spence on Pope's *Odyssey*, ii, 25. Cp. *Crit. Rev.* xiv new arr. (1795), 153, which thinks that 'liberty is the Hypothesis of democracy' is clear to a Greek scholar, but that *foundation* would be clearer to an English reader.

[2] Alexander Souter, *A Glossary of Later Latin*, Oxford, 1957. Another post-classical word in its English form was objected to—*risible*. George Campbell, *Phil. of Rhet.*, p. 193, notes a perversion of the original sense *capable of laughing* to *ridiculous*, *fit to be laughed at*. Souter shows that it meant both in Later Latin, though *laughable* was the earlier: the reverse is true in English, in which the sense of *laughable* was an eighteenth-century development. Book VIII was by Broome.

implicit in its woolly curls. Here Cowper makes the hero say he en-
folded both hands in the ram's exuberant fleece: after translating so as
to give us the literal concrete meaning that Pope intended in *implicit*,
he in turn uses *exuberant* in a literal sense where we expect it to be
figurative. The period is constantly setting us this problem: all the
Popean difficulties turn on the unexpected literal meaning of the Latin
words that have shifted to metaphorical uses in English, and dead
metaphor at that.

Even more difficult is the sudden use of a word in the wrong connection. The *British Critick*[1] noted that an archaeologist used the word
deterred in a sense totally different from common use—to mean dug
out of the earth (disinterred?) It is a properly made word—but since
we are used to *deter* from *de-terrere*, how should we associate it with
de terrā? In English we think of *deterrent*, not *interment*. And no doubt
the awkward and contradictory *dis-in-ter* is justified since clarity of
meaning is of more value than purity of structure.

Once the English meaning has been established, it must be accepted
—in common use at least—without thought of etymology. That does
not mean that we have no obligation to try to hold words to the
senses associated with them in our great writers when popular carelessness or ignorance is cutting them adrift. Some modern linguists
may be doing the language more harm than good in their all-embracing
acceptance of every usage. But there is an air of unreality about the
Critical Review's[2] insistence that the proper meaning of *celebrity* is
frequentation, and that Dr Johnson ought not to have spoken of the
'celebrity' of authors. The reviewers conceded that the word (already
over two centuries old in the offending sense, if they had but known it)
had been used in late Latin to mean 'renown', but they were still
doubtful 'whether for that reason *celebrity* ought to signify *renown* in
English'. If neither the original owners nor the present possessors can
be trusted to know how to use the word, even when they are in agreement over it, one wonders what right the Review had to set up for a
lawgiver on the point. Why should their Latin be purer than Rome's?

Many words of Latin origin are denounced as mere pedantry, with
the added drawback that they may be inappropriate. They are out of
place in letters or in common discourse, where particularly they risk
being misunderstood. And pedantry and stiffness are distasteful.[3] So

---

[1] *Brit. Crit.* i (1790), 295. Cp. Pope on the as yet unknown author of *London*
—'He will be soon *déterré*'. Boswell, *Life*, ii, 85.

[2] *Crit. Rev.* 20 (1765), 332. 21 (1766), 239.   [3] Milns, *Well-bred Scholar*, p. 49.

the *Critical Review*[1] sees no point in lengthening *habit* and *quiet* to *habitude* and *quietude*, or saying *excavated* when you mean *hollowed*.[2]

In 1798 the reviewers were commenting that Charles Cook in his *History of England* was 'continually deriving assistance from the Latin language' and seemed 'fearful of using terms which are familiar to the reader'. Among his objectionable hard words are *anticipative*, *nudity*, *quadrupeds* (horses), *reciprocation* of commercial benefit, *incipient* (applied to *reign* and *recovery*), *insurrection*, *immolation*, *Hibernian* estate, *plebeian* (friend), *senatorial* (meetings). The last two struck the *Critical Review* as particularly absurd. 'Now, fortunately, we know no such distinction in this country as those of patricians and plebeians, and Cicero would not easily discover the marks of a senator in many of our boy members.'[3]

Ruffhead in the *Monthly Review*[4] dislikes Dr Johnson's vocabulary in *Rasselas*—*excogitation*, *multifarious*, *transcendental* and '*indiscerpible* which it is difficult to pronounce with composed features'. Of these, *excogitation*, *indiscerpible* and *multifarious*[5] were already old, and *transcendental* had acquired a history both in and out of philosophy. Was Ruffhead uneasy because he was meeting them in what purported to be a story, whereas they would have been in place in a philosophical treatise?

In 1782 J. Thomson Callender[6] published anonymously an attack on what he called 'The Deformities of Dr. Johnson'. This too disliked *excogitation* (and *indiscerptibility*) as well as words that seem ordinary enough to us—*ramification*, *exacerbation*, *inanity*, *cremation*, *ratiocination*. To our scientific age, *refrigerated* for 'cooled' seems loose: but we should agree that *obtund*, *intumescent*, *nihility* and *anfractuousness* strike our ears as unnecessary Latinisms—though we don't mind *obtuse* or *nihilism*.

The *Critical Review*[7] declared that Dr Johnson, 'instead of adding to the improvement of style in modern times', had 'professed to delight

[1] *Crit. Rev.* 21 (1797), 357.
[2] This was all it did mean. As a recognised technical archaeological term, it had to wait for the next century.
[3] *Crit. Rev.* 22 (1798), 141.
[4] *Month. Rev.* xx (1759). Review by Ruffhead of *The Prince of Abissinia*, i.e. *Rasselas*.
[5] *Crit. Rev.* 17 (1764), 306, prefers *miscellaneous* to *multifarious*.
[6] See Boswell, *Life*, iv, 449, Appendix J. *Indiscerpible* and *indescerptible* are variants.
[7] *Crit. Rev.* new arr. xiv (1795), 2.

in cloathing a common sentiment in the splendour of words, and in building his fame on an inflated diction'.

Johnson's verbal splendour does not cover feebleness of thought—the common sentiments are usually the profound ones concerned with *quod semper, quod ubique, quod ab omnibus.* They can carry the weight he stands upon them. Boswell's[1] comparison of Johnson's big words to the tall caps of Frederick I of Prussia's tall grenadiers is apt—they suit. And Johnson uses his Latinate diction in the full consciousness of its etymology which he constantly elaborates into English figurative words.[2] He might have well agreed with the *Critical Review*[3] in blaming a bad poet who had had no academic education, but nevertheless had acquired the defects of one—hard words—and wrote of 'algid' rocks and 'lymphatic' zeal. We feel inclined to echo the *Connoisseur* (xxvii) which dislikes the immoderate use of 'uncouth terms' and 'words that mean nothing' which, 'provided they sound big and fill the ear, are the best succedaneum for sense'—except that by the end of the sentence we may think that the magazine is exemplifying the fault it is objecting to. Why *succedaneum*,[4] when *substitute* would do? From the contexts where we meet the word, it must have been ordinary enough. The magazine adds vividly that 'arrant nonsense' has often lain 'smugly beneath hard words, as a shallow pate beneath the solemn appearance of a full-bottomed periwig'.

Ruffhead[5] also takes to task the historian Walter Harte; he had introduced needless Latinisms, using *acumen* where *acuteness* might do as well—*operose* where *laborious* might supply its place—*eventualities* where *contingencies* or *contingent* events would be as expressive—*interferences* where *interpositions* would be more familiar—*rigidity* where *rigour* would be as intelligible—and *individuating* principle, where *distinguishing* principle would be more natural and quite as explicit. Of these, *eventuality* is not exemplified in *O.E.D.* until 1852. *Interference* is quoted from Burke in 1783, though the appropriate sense of the verb was in use—no wonder they struck Ruffhead as strange. *Individuation* was a technical term among the philosophers and may have affected the participle: *rigour* is the older word by two

---

[1] *Boswell in Search of a Wife*, p. 159.
[2] See Tucker and Gifford, *R.E.S.* n.s. viii (1957).
[3] *Crit. Rev.* new arr. xvii (1796), 463.
[4] *O.E.D.* quotes it from books on farming and cookery, as well as from scientific and philosophical works.
[5] *Month. Rev.* xx (1759), 447.

hundred years. Is there anything to choose between *acumen* and *acuteness?* *Acumen* is marked as a foreigner in Dr Johnson's Dictionary. It 'signified that acuteness of penetration which constitutes genius'[1]— surely a word with a sharp edge, deserving encouragement. *Operose* was not new, but seems to have struck the eighteenth century as it strikes us when set beside *laborious*.

The dangers of inflated language are well put by Gildon[2] who warns us against the 'great Words which are affected to heighten the Diction', but 'most commonly only make a Noise'. And he adds that a poet who 'swells into Fustian' may 'fill the Ears without touching the Heart'. We should agree with him that nothing is more ridiculous than to treat a frivolous subject in a sublime style.

The *Critical Review*[3] comes down heavily on affectation of pedantry which shows itself in the use of foreign terms where English would do better, or of fanciful phrases instead of the plain words that call a spade a spade. It commented adversely on Governor Pownall's *Antiquarian Romance* in 1796. This title was the forerunner of a long line of popularizing books on the *Romance of* this, that or the other subject, for it was a treatise on Antiquity. Why must he talk of a civil and military *imperium*, of *decadence* from the French of Montesquieu instead of plain English *fall?* Why must words in different languages have a near *agnation*, and people *locate* themselves? Our own words have 'greater strength and energy'. Next year it was Isaac D'Israeli's turn.[4] His affectations, in his *Miscellanies*, included the *amatorial passion*, to *domiciliate* a foreign idiom, the *exility* of an object, and such expressions as *evanescencies*, *orgasm*, to feast the *appetency* of the mind, to employ an ornament *artistly*.

Decadence had been used in English since the sixteenth century, but not in the sense of 'fall': *agnation* sounds as if it might have become a technical linguistic term but has not in this sense. Could we apply 'relation on the father's side' to a language? *Amatorial* was not new, but sounds more scientific than love will bear: *artistly* is here used forty years before its first illustration in *O.E.D.*—we may compare the earlier *painterly*. *Exility* may have seemed pretentious to the Reviewers, but has been widely used to cover smallness, thinness, meagreness, of such diverse things as revenues, places, pillars, learning and parts of the body. *Evanescencies* was merely a rarer and needlessly longer version of *evanescences*. *Domiciliate* has been used by Burke,

---

[1] *Crit. Rev.* 7 (1759), 344.   [2] *Art of Poetry*, p. 289.
[3] *Crit. Rev.* new arr. xvi (1796), 150.   [4] *Crit. Rev.* new arr. xx (1797), 375.

Wellington and De Quincey but with all of them it referred to literal settling in a strange place. Perhaps *orgasm*[1] and *appetency* were felt to sound pedantically learned. *Locate*, in relation to people placing themselves and not things, is primarily from the other side of the Atlantic.

AMERICANISMS

It is amusing to find that a few 'uncouth' words with which a critic happened to be unfamiliar were liable to be written off as American inventions. The *Critical Review*[2] did not like *bestowment* and *exertment* in a New England poet: neither do we, and it is true that *O.E.D.* has no example of them from near the date of the poem. For *bestowment* it shows a gap between 1754 and 1871: for *exertment* between 1696 and 1860. *Enlargedness*, *preparedness* and *lengthy* were on the list, and in the Review's opinion could not be accounted for 'on any other supposition than that of their being current in America'. The first of the three seems to have gone out in England in the seventeenth century, the second was common enough, and still is, but the third was a genuine American creation which has proved a useful tool for distinguishing what is simply long from what is longer than it ought to be. French Revolutionary language presented English speakers with an occasional problem. How should *citoyenne* be translated? *Citizeness* was the obvious calque, but the *British Critick*[3] preferred the term coined by the Americans—*Citess*. But they added 'We hope not to see any jargon of the kind adopted.' The *Anti-Jacobin* said Female Citizen. If *Citess* looks like half a word to us, we should recall the belittling eighteenth-century form *cit* which is nicely double-edged in Dr Johnson's definitions—'An inhabitant of a city. A pert low townsman'. The Rev. W. Romaine,[4] writing to a friend in January 1766, hopes he will take his letters 'according to the American phrase, for *paper currency*'. 'Paper' for 'money' was older and British, but this particular expression is first exemplified in *O.E.D.* from Adam Smith ten years later, in reference to North America. Burke uses it so in 1769.

SCOTTICISMS

Scottish usage worried English critics more than American—there were more aberrations, as the English saw it. When the Margrave of Baden-Durlach, who spoke English 'with considerable facility', engaged

---

[1] It was not new.   [2] *Crit. Rev.* 60 (1785), 300.
[3] *Brit. Crit.* vii (1796), 367.   [4] *Letters*, 16 January 1775.

a Scots tutor for his son, the *Critical Review*[1] felt that he had made an erroneous judgment 'in having recourse to Scotland for a teacher of the English language'. We still notice that Scots persist in 'confusing' *shall* and *will*, *should* and *would*, but they are now backed up by users of the language overseas, and the upholders of Southern Standard syntax are in the minority.[2] It is still a distinction worth upholding, even if it is true that, as one Englishman remarked,[3] 'our brethren north of the Tweed can master all human science more easily than these poor words'. What would he have thought of the modern catch-phrase 'I wouldn't know'?

To adduce was thought 'a verb peculiar to the Scotch dialect'[4] but we find it handy. So we do *to jot down*[5] and *to succumb*[6], the former of which can no longer be described as 'ridiculous in London', however grave it may be in Scotland. The *Critical Review* considered that the failure to distinguish between *prepossession* and *prejudice* was especially Scottish.[7] The critics waged a successful war on *timeous(ly)*, 'having some old friends' whom they liked 'much better'.[8] *Timeously* was so unfamiliar to one compositor that he misprinted it as *timorously*[9]—it was corrected in the errata.

But it betrays an unscientific, not to say conceitedly patriotic, approach to language when the *Critical Review*[10] speaks of an Edinburgh magazine being *deformed* by the peculiar idioms of its parent country, or when another magazine describes as a 'gross' Scotticism the use of *presently* to mean 'at present'.[11] If we now described it as a 'gross' Americanism, we should be equally at fault. This use is, in fact, the persistence in the North or in Transatlantic speech of an older meaning established about Caxton's time. Even some of the Scots themselves seem to have thought their language inferior. Boswell is well known for his sensitiveness on the matter, and it was a Scot, John Sinclair, who published *Observations on the Scottish Dialect*[12] which provides a long list of Scottish and English equivalents, from which the *Critical Review* (53) quoted at length. It was hardly patriotic of Sinclair to quote 'It does not apply to Scotchmen' and add that he was 'sorry to

---

[1] *Crit. Rev.* 48 (1779), 215. But English spelling defeated him. See his letter to Boswell printed in *Boswell on the Grand Tour* (*Germany and Switzerland*), p. 266.

[2] On this subject, see Fries in *P.M.L.A.* (1925), Hulbert, ibid. (1947).

[3] *Brit. Crit.* iv (1794), 431.

[4] *Crit. Rev.* 1 (1756), 228; 30 (1770), 24.

[5] *Brit. Crit.* ii (1793), 436.

[6] *Crit. Rev.* 3 (1757), 393.

[7] *Crit. Rev.* 18 (1764), 437.

[8] *Brit. Crit.* iv (1794), 431.

[9] *Brit. Crit.* iii (1794), 444.

[10] *Crit. Rev.* 64 (1787), 130.

[11] *Brit. Crit.* ix (1797), 203.

[12] Rev. in *Crit. Rev.* 53 (1782), 241 sqq.

find this phrase so frequently made use of by English writers. It would be much better to say "the observation is not applicable to Scotchmen".' Nor do we object to 'in place of' for 'instead of'. After so much touchiness, it is a refreshing challenge when we find Dr Geddes attempting to prove that broad Scots is a superior language to the English, even if, as was to be expected, the *Critical Review*[1] considered that this betrayed national prejudices 'the most gross'. National prejudices were not confined to the region north of the Border. And we are not puzzled by a *shake-down* as the *Monthly Review*[2] was when it met this term in the account of a Scottish trial.

But we can find light on our *gruesome* if we look at the adverse and question-begging comment made by the *Monthly Review* in 1759 on the Scottish idiom of a medical book—'however persons may commonly discourse, all valuable and scientific books published in Great Britain ought to be in proper English. For want of this, we were ignorant what a *grewing* and a *grewing fit* was, which occur not seldom, till a Scotch gentleman assured us it was a shivering or horror.'[3] And it is pleasant to find Dr Johnson of all people, admitting that the 'Scotch write English wonderfully well'.[4]

BOMBAST[5]

Burke did not know the word 'claptrap', or the 'gagagram' invented during this century to stand for what rouses our feelings without our understanding, but under another name[6] he points to the dangers involved. Words like *wise, valiant, generous, good* and *great* ought to be 'unoperative' unless applied to actual exemplars of these qualities— but when the 'words commonly sacred to great occasions are used, we are affected by them even without the occasions. When words which have been generally so applied are put together without any rational view, or in such a manner that they do not rightly agree with each other, the style is called bombast.' He would have certainly agreed with the remark in the *Looker-on*[7] that factious leaders can use 'language unintelligibly imposing' when they address the 'gaping vulgar'

[1] Rev. in *Crit. Rev.* new arr. v (1792), 566.   [2] *Month. Rev.* xxxiii (1765), 407.
[3] *Month. Rev.* xxi (1759), 75.   [4] Boswell, *Life*, iii, 109.
[5] 'the style of a rhetorical declaimer, a nauseous affectation of sublimity'. *Crit. Rev.* 25 (1768), 115.
[6] *Sublime and Beautiful*, pp. 318–19. *Claptrap* existed, but not in this sense.
[7] William Roberts, i, 242.

and so insinuate 'a raving philosophy'. In our propaganda-ridden age, we do well to remember that this is still more dangerously true.

LINGUISTIC SNOBBERY

Affectation of language may be pedantry—offensive, perhaps, but harmless. But there is a social affectation reflected in our choice of words, when we try to make ourselves, our work, our family, every-thing we are concerned with, sound superior to what common sense and common good manners would admit. Snobbishness, undue deli-cacy, exaggeration to impress, euphemism, singularity, chasing after something new—they all come under the eighteenth century's critical lash, which in this sort of situation needed to be—and usually was—a cat o' nine tails.

The *Gentleman's Magazine*[1] laughs, for example, at the man who has been knighted, and then, over-conscious of his dignity, tells strangers that his father was a wine-merchant in London and dealt in foreign spirits. In a sense it was true, for his father 'kept a pub'—though that is not what the eighteenth century said. J. H. Beattie[2] notices that since Boxing became a fine art, 'it is quite vulgar to call a Professor of it a Boxer. Some learned innovator, having heard of the Latin *pugil*, thought of introducing it; but *pugil* was too diminutive a name for a thing of such magnitude; and therefore clapping to it part of a Greek termination he made it pugilist, which being instantly adopted by the dilettanti (or admirers) of boxing and new words, gave rise to the adjectives *pugilistic* and *pugilistical*, as in this example—"We hear *it is in contemplation* to *run up a novel* and *superb* pavilion at Newmarket for Pugilistical exhibitions." Pugilisticism and *pugilistically* have not yet appeared, but are every hour expected.'

Apparently they have not yet arrived, but apart from these two hypothetical members, the whole family are listed here years before *O.E.D.* dates them.[3] A letter in the *Gentleman's Magazine*[4] in 1789 expressed disquiet about the future of respected names. *Lawyer* is a 'word vulgarly given to the meanest pettifogger: every farrier, little apothecary or surgeon's mate, is also commonly honoured with the title of doctor: even chimney doctors are become frequent. So that *doctor* and *lawyer* will perhaps in time undergo the same change with

---

[1] *Gent. Mag.* lvi (1786), 1105.   [2] *Dialogues of the Dead*, No. 3.
[3] *O.E.D.*'s dates in brackets: *pugilist* (1790), *pugilistic* (1811), *pugilistical* (1840).
[4] *Gent. Mag.* xix (1749), 65.

leech and pedant, though *physician* and *counsellor* still retain their
dignity.' Professional standards have stood firm, though *counsellor* in
the sense required appears to have emigrated to the United States: but
it has been left for our own day to turn the chimney doctor (or 'professor')[1] into a *flueologist*!

The butcher had become a purveyor of meat, and the poulterer was
gradually rising to become a Turkey Merchant.[2] There are Merchants
at Rag-fair, and

> Every nook, where scarce can turn a mouse
> Is call'd, absurdly call'd, a compting house.[3]

It is not surprising that all tradesmen are eminent—especially in marriage or obituary notices in the magazines—and William Woty has a
skit on the fact:

> With mincing step a hosier next appear'd
> His bob fresh-powder'd and new reap'd his beard,
> In spruce array his *Eminence* was drest,
> And the paste-buckle glitter'd on his breast.[4]

If the chemist's raw apprentice wanted to be called a pharmocopolist,[5]
there seems no reason why the lady who in plain English keeps a school
should not 'preside over a seminary',[6] except that *seminary* now has
ecclesiastical overtones. And 'it would be unpardonably vulgar to call
a milk-woman by any other appellation than that of a lady; and the
meanest artisan . . . if he happens to want an apprentice, will publicly
advertise for a young gentleman'.[7] No doubt we look back at this sort
of thing with pride in the growth of equality, rejoicing in the way class
barriers are breaking down. Chaucer's homily on 'gentilesse', voiced
unexpectedly by the Wife of Bath, who was assuredly 'not quite a
lady', would have been useful reading for the eighteenth century, as it
is at any time. But in the social circumstances of that age, it is hardly
surprising that the *Connoisseur* (lxx) should make fun of the wonderful
increase of gentlemen, who include everybody who has no trade, or is
on holiday from it. Nathan Bailey's Dictionary[8] explains *Gentleman* in

[1] *Looker-on*, ii, 36.   [2] ibid. i, 307.   [3] William Woty, *Poetical Works*, ii, 15 sq.
[4] ibid. p. 170. Cp. Boswell, *Life*, i, 310, for Johnson's ridicule of *eminent*
tradesmen. Cp. Anstey, *New Bath Guide*, Letter V ('an eminent Trader in
Cheese').
[5] ibid. p. 120.
[6] Clara Reeve, *Progress of Romance*, ii, 38.   [7] *Babler* (c), by Hugh Kelly.
[8] *Dictionarium Britannicum*, or a more Compleat Universal Etymological
English Dictionary, 1721, with many reprints. [Quoted from that of 1730.]

the historical terms of a rigid social code; but his definition comes down to earth with a swish of its ungrammatical tail: 'In our Days all are accounted Gentlemen that have Money, and if he has no Coat of Arms, the King of Arms can sell him one.' Lady Craven in the 'eighties must have been one of the old-fashioned school: she tells us that as there was no gentleman's house at Pultawa, she slept at her banker's![1]

It is hardly surprising that the 'top people' met the upsurge by attempts at exclusiveness. So we meet with comments on 'Nobody in town...' and 'though the word *Nobody*, like its fellow-vocable *Everybody*, has a great latitude of signification, and in this instance means upwards of three-score thousand people, yet undoubtedly, in a certain rank of life, one finds at this season a very great blank in one's accustomed society'. This was the *Lounger* (87) on the last day of September 1786.

The *World*—that fashionable periodical—was talking sound sense when it commented (125) on the foolish vanity that 'prompts us to imitate our superiors' and also makes us be, or pretend to be, their inseparable companions, 'or, as the phrase is, to keep the *best company*; by which is always to be understood such company as are much above us in rank or fortune, and consequently, despise and avoid us...' It is indeed a 'ridiculous affectation'.

LITERARY AFFECTATION

The critics of literary affectation are sometimes attacking social fads expressed in words, sometimes merely the hunt for unusual diction. It may be the affectations of technical writers or historians trying to write in elevated language on ordinary matters: of poets searching for striking uses of words: of novelists heightening their diction in an outburst of sentimental gush. The new uses of words may be old by now, and the interest for us lies in the fact that they were criticised—we don't think of the adjective *unique*, or *preluding*, or *averse to*[2] as affected terms, though we wonder about '*almost unique*' and '*averse from*'. But we should agree with the *Monthly Review*'s[3] dislike of 'stile memorandal', 'sons of rusticity', 'daughter of speculation', all of which occurred in a treatise on Agriculture where they must have sounded singularly out of place.

[1] *Journey*, p. 155.
[2] *Month. Rev.* lxxvi (1787), re Apthorp's *Discourses on Prophecy*.
[3] *Month. Rev.* lx (1779) reviewing Marshall's *Minutes of Agriculture*.

We view with mixed agreement and astonishment 'the far-fetched
and affected phrases of [that] present day' which young James Hay
Beattie[1] satirised in his Third *Dialogue of the Dead.* Instead of *life, new,
wish for, take, plunge,* etc. you must say *existence, novel, desiderate,
capture, ingurgitate,* etc. Mercury notices that for *reformation* everybody says *reform* 'this being French, and the other vile old English'.
As so often the old form is accepted whereas the new is thought
objectionable. Instead of 'for the future', we must say 'in future', and
beautiful or ugly 'to a degree' instead of 'to a great degree'. Now we
see a slight difference between the two ways of looking ahead—'for
the future' is more purposeful—but we must often plead guilty to the
tacit assumption of how *great* a degree. Mercury's attack includes three
phrases, of which the first, 'sporting sables', sounds frivolous, the
second, 'scouting the idea', a normal expression, and the third, 'netting
a cool thousand', slangy in all its important elements.

Other affectations are concerned with the use of proper names. James
Beattie[2] mentions *the* prefixing the name of a singer or actress—as
Horace Walpole[3] had done before him when in 1748 he referred to *the*
Clive. *O.E.D.*'s earliest example is *the* Siddons in 1786. It is an imitation
of continental use. If this emphatic and honorific use of the definite
article was noticed, so was a new use of the indefinite. It was far from
new when Beattie[4] declared it 'contrary to idiom' to say 'I was last
night in company with *a* Mr. Such-a-one.' The meaning is 'that the
person is not known, or very little known, to those who speak of him
in this manner'. This comment dates from 1783, but Horace Walpole[5]
had used it of Peg Woffington in 1741. Beattie fears that 'it will probably establish itself in the language, as it is now generally adopted'.
It has done, and now *is* the idiom.

There are fashions in proper names. Steele's Biddy, in *The Tender
Husband,* hates to have such a familiar name—'Did you ever meet with
an heroine . . . that was term'd Biddy?' How much better 'a Name that
glides through half a dozen tender syllables, as Elismunda, Cledamira,
Deidamea, that runs upon Vowels off the Tongue, not hissing through
one's Teeth, or breaking them with Consonants'. Family names like
Margery, Alice, Winifred, Joan, form a 'barbarous' list.[6]

---

[1] op. cit.   [2] *Dissertations,* p. 494.
[3] Letter of 12 Aug. 1748. Correspondence, 9, 72.   [4] *Dissertations,* p. 494.
[5] Walpole, op. cit., Letter of 22 Oct., o.s., to Sir H. Mann. Correspondence,
17, 176.
[6] Act II.

But a fanciful name may be as out of place as a plain one. In the last decade of the century, Francis Grose[1] was encouraging us to laugh at the affectation of 'romantic and royal appellations' bestowed in less exalted circles. The Joans, Hannahs, Sarahs, Rachels and Elizabeths have gone, and the Anna Maries, Charlotte Matildas and Eliza Sophias have come in. (Time's whirligig has brought the simpler names back into favour now.) 'It is next to impossible to refrain from smiling on hearing Clarissa ordered to wind up the jack, and Catherine-Ann-Maria to empty the ash-tub.' Ludicrous, perhaps, but it seems hard that even names must be an index of class-consciousness.

Romantic language is healthily laughed at whether it concerns names of people, places, things or feelings—and evidently with good reason. Richard Graves, in his *Columella*,[2] introduces Squire Milward's man Peter, reporting that the heifers had 'got into the plantation at the bottom of Aaron's Well'. ' "Aaron's Well, you blockhead," says Columella, "Arno's Vale, you mean." "Nay, nay," quoth Peter, "I know as how the right name of it is Tadpole Bottom." '

Cousin Biddy[3] may speak for all romantic high-falutin' young ladies in love. Her suitor, Humphrey, is a young gentleman that 'has . . . much kindness' for her—but how cold and inadequate! 'What a phrase is there to express the Darts and Flames, the sighs and Languishes of an expecting Lover.' Her matter-of-fact aunt tells her to 'forbear this idle Trash, and talk like other People'. She knows Humphrey will be 'true and hearty'. Bridget's ears are wounded by so homely a description—she does wish her aunt would 'endeavour a little at the Embellishment' of her style!

By 1794, the *Critical Review*[4] was launching a full-scale attack on what it calls the Arcadian Language—the fundamental rule of which is 'to express nothing plainly'. Its vocabulary is restricted—'Love, hatred, transports, desires, sighs, alarms, hopes, delights, pride, beauty, cruelty, ingratitude, perfidy, jealousy, bloom, verdure, reveries, dreams, moon, soft, tender, horrible, precious, susceptible, etc—what I cannot express, what is not to be described, above all utterance, beyond all imagination. But you must not say I love, which signifies nothing. We must say, I am the victim of love; a secret flame consumes me, I languish night and day. And no word must appear without one or more epithets: it is ridiculous to say love, indifference, regret. Tender and passionate love, cold and cruel indifference, mortal and piercing

[1] Francis Grose, *Olio*, 1796, essays of *The Grumbler*, No. II.
[2] i, 116. [3] *Tender Husband* as before. [4] *Crit. Rev.* new arr. xi (1794), 356.

regret, . . . ardent sighs, profound and bitter grief' etc. etc. and 'the more of these epithets there are in a phrase, the more beautiful and the truer Arcadian it is'.

'This little collection affords matter for whole volumes in folio, written in the Arcadian tongue.'

It was about this time that William Beckford was writing his absurd and wholly delightful prolonged skit on the whole subject of romantic love and adventure, the *Elegant Enthusiast*,[1] which satirises female authors, sentimentality of behaviour and language, idiotic situations and settings both horrific and Arcadian, in one glorious medley. Three years after its tilt at Arcadian, the *Critical Review*[2] reviewed Mrs Gunning's *Love at First Sight*, and said bluntly all that needs to be said of this kind of composition—'the wretched cant of language that pervades this species of writing—where everything is affected and nothing felt—where the same exaggerated description of distress, and the same ready-made hyperboles are introduced, whether the subject be a lap-dog, or a human being—is truly disgusting'. How many trashy magazine stories carry on the tradition?

EUPHEMISM

Euphemisms were rightly held to be affected, and in some cases morally wrong. *Expired*, for the more unaffected phrase 'died', is no improvement in a travel book, thinks the *Gentleman's Magazine*,[3] neither is 'sunk into the grave', about which the *Critical Review*[4] notes that it is 'so uniformly adopted' by the historian under review 'that amongst the great number of persons whose decease is mentioned scarce one is said to have died'. A correspondent of the *Gentleman's Magazine*[5] in 1791 tilts ironically at the fastidiousness that refuses *to sweat*—the word has 'for these twenty years past been gradually becoming more and more odious, and has indeed almost died'—it is used only of carters, coal-heavers and Irish carriers of sedan chairs! Ought we not to make Shakespeare say 'To groan, perspire', instead of 'to grunt and sweat'? Shakespeare could never have used that obsolete and disgustful term sweat. Of course, what is uncouth or gross today, will be gross and uncouth tomorrow, and must have been *so at all times*. He con-

---

[1] 1796. [2] *Crit. Rev.* new arr. xxi (1797), 43.
[3] *Gent. Mag.* lxiii (1793), 744. But why did they dislike 'the expiry of a lease'? *Crit. Rev.* 48 (1779), 330.
[4] *Crit. Rev.* new arr. ii (1790), 671. [5] *Gent. Mag.* lxi (1791), 1098 sqq.

cludes that 'we are every day growing more delicate, and without doubt, at the same time, more virtuous'. To wrap up the inescapable or the otherwise unmentionable in a Latinised blanket has been an English subterfuge for a long time. We recall Dr Johnson's[1] defiant 'Fundamentally sensible', to the company who tittered at 'a *bottom* of good sense'. There are constant complaints about the decline in moral tone that calls fast living 'sporting',[2] a vicious child 'a wicked little rogue' or 'a little pickle',[3] extravagance and dissipation 'seeing life',[4] and that makes 'an honest fellow' the highest degree in the graduation after a pickle, a lad of mettle and a dissipated dog: that applies 'man of gallantry and honour' to the high-mettled 'blood' who debauches and kills. Mr Spectator (394) had noticed that whereas the ordinary people speak of a *bribe*, the better-bred speak of a *present*. The *Looker-on* (p. 303) points out the strangely perverted use of language with which 'a false feeling of refinement . . . has turned the bent of our delicacy from things and realities to words and images; and it little purports to the chastest mind, what idea is presented, let only the medium be properly sophisticated through which it is viewed. And so a language is found to express the whole train of maladies to which humanity is exposed, that wears almost the appearance of eulogy; and crimes that call for vengeance are wrapped up in a courtesy of phrase that looks more like commiseration than abhorrence.' The essayist quotes the Naval Surgeon who talked of amputations and other *arrangements*; of a very *elegant* mode of operating; and adds a reference to the *unfortunate* gentleman who poisoned his uncle and was afterwards so unhappy as to strangle his wife. So Sir John Hawkins notes the play made with *unfortunate* as applied to Dr Dodd the forger.[5]

The *Connoisseur*[6] draws attention to the attractive advertisements which call certain violent intoxicants 'spirit of Adonis' or 'Parfait Amour'. The vulgar call them 'Strip me naked' and 'Lay me down softly'. In plain English, their basic ingredient was gin. 'Supping rich cordials' was a polite reference to dram-drinking but in the view of the essayist was no less detestable than in the vulgar idiom 'Bunging your eye'—so what does it matter whether you call it plain Aniseed

[1] Boswell, *Life*, iv, 99.
[2] *Gent. Mag.* xxv (1755), 43.
[3] *Gent. Mag.* lviii (1788), 25–6, from a Letter on Education by Beelzebub!
[4] *Universal Museum and Complete Magazine* (1766), 564–6.
[5] *Life of Johnson*, p. 232.
[6] liii. Aniseed is included among the strongest intoxicants—Gin, Brandy, Rum, Whisky, in a list given in *Gent. Mag.* lix (1789), 399.

or 'Eau de Mille fleurs'? There were, indeed, critics who preferred East End bluntness to West End fastidiousness. At a higher level, the *Monthly Review*[1] defends *Tom Jones* as against *Clarissa* by asking us to consider which is worse—'a coarse idea expressed in vulgar language in itself disgusting, or an idea equally luscious and impure conveyed in words that may steal on the affections of the heart, without alarming the ear?'

'Things are not altered by names,' says Plato in Mrs Montagu's Dialogue of the Dead.[2] 'No,' replies Diogenes—'but names have a strange power to impose on weak understandings.' It would surely have been a weak understanding that could have been imposed upon by the writer to the *Gentleman's Magazine*[3] in defence of slavery, who said 'The vulgar are influenced by names and letters. Instead of SLAVES, let the negroes be called ASSISTANT-PLANTERS; and we shall not then hear such violent outcries against the slave-trade by pious divines, tender-hearted poetesses, and short-sighted politicians.' We could find modern examples of this notion that a good name makes a radical change in a bad thing—it is one of the tricks of the propagandist. And is there not a hint of ideological things to come when the *Gentleman's Magazine*[4] remarks that it is now fashionable to term wars 'wars of principle' when 'nations fight nations in order, as it is alleged, to make them orthodox Christians and sound Legislators'?

In 1756 the *World* (166) sums it up: 'Our manners have adulterated our words; and for fear they should reproach us with our conduct, we disfranchise them and condemn them to infamy, that their testimony may be invalid, and their evidence of no credit.'

INELEGANT AND INAPPROPRIATE LANGUAGE

We have looked at the aberrations of the learned and the sophisticated. It is time to look at the language the critics disliked not because it was too pedantic or too fastidious, too fashionable or too modern, but because it was too low, too forthright, or too old. Here are the misapplied words, the inappropriate, the obsolete; here are slang, cant, commercialese, where the middle term often overlaps the other two at different points. We do not always see these expressions in the same light. But for the critics, low and ludicrous language was to be avoided at all

[1] *Month. Rev.* xx (1759), 132.   [2] No. XXX in Lyttelton's book.
[3] *Gent. Mag.* lix (1789), 334.   [4] *Gent. Mag.* lxiii (1793), 1078.

costs, and needless to say there were those who were much too per-
nickety.

Words they label comic may be a curiously mixed list. In 1756, its
first year of issue, the *Critical Review*[1] was asking 'What occasion is
there to use such an old-fashioned word as *aggrieve*, when there is no
kind of joke or humour aimed at?' On the next page it says *females* is
rather a ludicrous word, and seldom or perhaps never used by genteel
people. In Volume 3 (386) it informs us that *dumbfound* is never used
'but by the vulgar, and generally in a ludicrous acceptation'. This is not
true now, and though we may agree that *female* could be funny in the
proper context, we think it either rude or technical. But we don't
agree over *aggrieve*.

LANGUAGE AND LITERATURE

The critics offer us the kind of literary-critical comment we might
easily not make ourselves. For example, the *Critical Review* (1, 235)
wonders why none of their predecessors has taken notice of the bad
effect of the word *flambeaux* in Dryden's *Alexander's Feast*. 'Torch is
a word of some dignity and poetical import: but the flambeau is something akin to *link*, and degrades the magic *almost* to *ridicule.*' To us,
flambeau gives a period flavour, while *link* may send us to the dictionary. Possibly, our minds on our pocket electric torch, we may feel
about *torch* as the reviewer felt about *flambeau*, though if we think
about the figurative 'torch of learning' or the actual torch of the
Olympic Games, no harm will be done. Sentences such as 'Death is
hard by', 'O that I should come to this' or 'I do repent me of my fury'
sound to us literary rather than vulgar[2] or too low for the Tragic Muse.
To us *spouse* is proper to dignified language so that its effect is the
opposite of what it produced two centuries ago:

> He who is favour'd with a virtuous spouse
> Enjoys the highest state of human bliss

strikes us as formally sententious: but the *Critical Review*[3] says that
'the single word spouse turns the whole into ridicule'. And why is
'the posture of affairs' gross enough to disgrace even a prose composition?[4]

[1] *Crit. Rev.* 1 (1756), 72.   [2] *Crit. Rev.* 51 (1781), 199.
[3] *Crit. Rev.* 80 (1780), 165.   [4] ibid.

When Cowper uses the exhortation 'Courage', the *Gentleman's Magazine*[1] thinks it hardly consistent with the dignity of heroic verse —he should have put 'Take Courage'. If the Magazine could have foreseen the beer advertisements, it would have let well alone. The Magazine also disliked Cowper's phrase 'nor heed thy wrath a jot'— 'Surely this is a vulgarism not to have been expected from the elegant author of The Task.'[2] Since we hardly use 'a jot' in everyday speech, it fits into the archaic pattern of the poem. Neither do we take Pope to task for calling Telemachus the 'Mirror of constant Faith'. Spence thinks[3] the expression 'has been so often us'd in a ridiculous sort of Writings that it will sound mean to the generality of those who hear it'. We have been spared the ridiculous writings, so Pope's phrase is dignified to us. So is Dryden's line

A star-light Evening, and a Morning Fair.

This, thinks Spence,[4] might be a Bellman's poetry; but to us it is simply poetry, and not really reminiscent of the weather forecast.

The eighteenth-century background which detracted from the good effect of older poets is no trouble to us, but we cannot disregard it if we want to see how the passages struck the critics. Pope had spoken of 'the raging Pest'; 'could anything be more low and creeping?' asks Dennis.[5] 'Whoever read the word *Pest* for Plague in any good English Poet? I have heard of Pest-houses, indeed, but never of Pest alone.' No doubt we do use 'pest' lightly, but for our freedom to do so we have to thank the advance of medical science that makes the real thing unlikely. But Dennis adds a revealing social comment—'What makes the word more base and more infamous is, that it is perpetually in the Mouths of French Footmen and Taylors.'

Probably many modern readers have grown tired of Pope's too frequent use of *train* for retainers, followers, warriors. But though we find it hard to forget the railway train, we are ready to believe that the word was dignified and etymologically proper—and then we find Dennis also thinking it odd, and near to burlesque for quite another reason. 'I believe he has made use of the same word in the same Sense an Hundred times. One would swear by his Translation that Agamemnon was nothing but some Exchange-Alley Stock-Jobber, who had the Honour to command a Company of Train Bands.'[6]

[1] *Gent. Mag.* lxii (1792), 160.   [2] *Gent. Mag.* lxi (1791), 729.
[3] On Pope's *Odyssey*, ii, 142.   [4] ibid.
[5] *Critical Works*, ii, 133.   [6] *Critical Works*, ii, 131.

Spenser, using the participle like many a medieval poet, speaks of the Galaxy *powdered* with stars. Warton felt it necessary to explain this as besprinkled or embroidered, adding that it has ever 'appear'd a very mean, or rather ridiculous metaphor': a critic, quoting this in 1758,[1] offers examples of the Latinised *poudrata* in Dugdale's *Monasticon*, and recalls that in Stowe's *Chronicle* it is used of Cardinal Wolsey's robe and in the description of a Masque. Eighteenth-century readers associated powder with wigs and cookery—no wonder they needed some antiquarian instruction before they could see any dignity in the word. Their own customs stood between them and the earlier implications. Dr Johnson's comments on *Macbeth* are the best-known example,[2] and other people agreed with him. The *Critical Review*[3] thinks 'the blanket of the night'—it doesn't even bother to quote accurately—is vulgar and will lead to obscurity and debasement. It had approved of Garrick's omission of Lear's 'Pray you, *undo this button*'—'a low idea, or a vulgar expression, such as that of *undoing a button*, may unfortunately throw an air of burlesque over the most affecting incident'.[4] Upton[5] felt that Spenser's 'overshoes in blood' had become 'too mean for Epick poetry thro' vulgar use—he might have been more poetical and said o'er his greaves in blood'. Presumably so might Shakespeare. Neither could foresee eighteenth-century vulgarity, and it was a true insight that made them choose the permanent word, and not the specialised one that calls up a Roman legionary as well as an armoured knight. Did Upton notice the exaggeration that *greaves* would have implied?

Occasionally what to the eighteenth century was vulgarity, is dignity to us. Bentley considered that 'a *noble stroke* in *Paradise Lost*, vi, 189, ought to be changed to a *nimble* stroke'—vulgar use had long since made *Noble Stroke* base, and unfit for heroic poetry. J. Richardson[6] comments that 'whatever Meanness this Epithet may have contracted by Common Use', it does not appear to have had it when Milton wrote. Zachary Pearce,[7] that staunch defender of Milton's style, agrees. The objection is therefore 'frivolous'. The passing fashion does not corrupt for ever.

[1] *Gent. Mag.* xxviii (1758), 57–8.
[2] *Rambler* 168. See *Notes and Queries*, May 1956, pp. 210–11.
[3] *Crit. Rev.* 61 (1786), 77.   [4] *Crit. Rev.* 47 (1779), 447.
[5] Upton's Edn. of *Faerie Queene* I, viii, 16.
[6] The Richardsons' Commentary, p. 257.
[7] *Text of Paradise Lost*, p. 202.

An extreme case that strikes us as wilfully perverse is implied in a *Critical Review*[1] comment on Cumberland's *Battle of Hastings*. When one of its characters talks of being 'struck from out the book of hope' she is 'not indelicate, but only vulgar'. Who would not think that her royal highness had heard an Irish chairman (i.e. carrier of a sedan chair) talking of boxing one of his companions and beating him out of the book of life? Irish chairmen seem to have been considered the last word in vulgarity: but if the critic had had his mind on the Authorised Version rather than on the boxing ring, he could have found half a dozen Biblical and dignified sources for Matilda's adapted phrase.

Should we know that *glib* was a low word,[2] or that 'to make a flaming speech' was a vulgar expression?[3] Or that *glee* was always used ironically?[4] Or that in the phrase 'boards stood loaded with a rich repast' the idea is vulgarised by a single word?[5] To us *board* is literary here. The same is true of *ere*: Milton had written of 'The Discord that befell and WAR in Heaven', but Dr Bentley[6] thought *and War* a mistake for *erewhile*. His usually sensible critic Dr Pearce[7] doubts whether Milton would have used so low a word here. Should we know if Mr Jackson[8] did not tell us, that Robert and Richard are common names, and Roger and Ralph vulgar? He is suggesting the line of thought that may have led Smollett to call his hero *Roderick* Random. To *gainsay* sounds rather literary to us, but it is not fit for a conversation among the gods according to the *Critical Review*.[9]

Dr Johnson was willing to turn to common speech to throw light on Shakespeare's vocabulary. He illustrates 'sweet mouth' (*Two Gentlemen of Verona*, iii, 1, 338) by 'what is now vulgarly called a sweet tooth' and appeals to 'low language' and its use of *thwacking* or *swinging* to support Shakespeare's 'a beating oath' (*Merry Wives of Windsor*, ii, 2, 28). The 'vulgarity' of *to be sure* led the *Critical Review*[10] astray in its reading of Milton. A Grammarian[11] remarks that the infinitive cannot act as an adverb—as in Milton's 'Amaze, be sure, and terror, seized the rebel host.' '*Be sure* is an abbreviation of *to be sure*, and signifies *certainly*.' On these remarks, the *Review* comments that 'it is in

[1] *Crit. Rev.* 45 (1778), 155.   [2] So Adam Smith says, *Works*, v, 323.
[3] *Month. Rev.* lxi (1779), 472.
[4] Johnson's Dictionary s.v. But this seems arguable.
[5] *Month. Rev.* xli (1796) re *The Bruciad*, an Epic Poem, 389.
[6] re *Paradise Lost*, vi, 897.   [7] *Text of Paradise Lost*, p. 228.
[8] *Thirty Letters*, ii, 87.   [9] *Crit. Rev.* 53 (1782), 25.
[10] *Crit. Rev.* 51 (1781), 199. Cp. Dr Johnson, and *Crit. Rev.* 47 (1779), 119.
[11] W. M. Trinder, *An Essay on the English Grammar*.

reality a vulgar phrase, and ought to be exploded from all correct writing'. It is odd that neither grammarian nor critic could see that Milton's form is *imperative*. And why did they allow the wrong association to warp their judgment? The *British Critick* dislikes Pope's use of 'that extremely inelegant phrase *quite away*'.[1] It is the language of burlesque reminding the reader of how the Knave of Hearts took the tarts quite away.[2]

LOW AND FAMILIAR

Dr Johnson[3] labelled words in his Dictionary 'low' or 'ludicrous', 'familiar' or 'cant'. We should agree with him about *belabour* and *brazenface*; *confoundedly*, *cursedly*, *damnable* as intensifiers; *conjobble*, *dodge*, *lingo*, *lumping*, *nab*, *plaguy*, *shark* (greedy, artful fellow), *squabble*, *swap*, *to take in* (cheat), *tiff*, *topping*, *traipse*. He includes a fair number now out of use, like *rantipoll* (known from Hardy's Wessex characters) and *wabble* though this is really only another spelling for *wobble*. But we think more kindly of *budge*, *clutter*, *to doctor*, *doings*, *dozen*, *fiddle-faddle*, *funk*, *fuss*, *gambler*, *glum*, *hands off*, *hanker*, *by Hook or by Crook*, *in all conscience*, *lead** (in the lead), *to leave in the lurch*, *nonplus*, *shabbily* (meanly), *sham*, *slim*, *spick and span*, *splutter* (n.), *squelch*, *stingy*, *to be sure*, *for all the world*. *Posse** and *premises** (i.e. houses, etc.) strike us rather as dignified. *Snip-snap* couplets or a *tame** poem would not be out of place in our critical writing, nor *wonderment** or *blackguard* in a literary essay. *Width* sounds normal, whether used of our views or our materials. To *cajole,** to *colour* (blush) and *cheery** are part of everyday vocabulary. We accept *chitchat*, *fib* (no longer necessarily childish), *fuss** and *lad,** and our objection to *scraping acquaintance* is to the act, not the phrase. It may be that *flirtation* and *frightful* (unpleasing) are still feminine favourites, but they are not so restricted as to be stigmatised as 'female cant'. The *British Critic*[4] objects to phrases used in a sermon—'Nor can the scribes and pharisees *gravel* him' . . . 'a groping after God' . . . 'The covetous are *glued* to the world.' The speaker was a Scot; and the magazine remarks that the 'plainest audience in *England* would be offended at such low expressions'. A twentieth-century audience would see nothing wrong with *groping*, would regard *gravel* as archaic or literary, and be amused at

---

[1] *Essay on Criticism*, 117.   [2] *Brit. Crit.* iv (1794), 592.
[3] Words asterisked are noted in the same way in Kenrick's Dictionary.
[4] *Brit. Crit.* x (1797), 199.

glued, in this context, though present-day speakers would talk of being 'glued to the Telly' if they disliked the habit. Was Dr Gillespie deliberately trying to shock his audience with this word? There is no reason to suppose so. To *glue* has been used figuratively by Chaucer, Shakespeare, Dryden and Smollett, and applied to such unlikely words as *name, concord, friends, lips, life* and *eyes*, all of which imply a transfer every bit as violent as in 'glued to the world'.

'Low' expressions are the stumbling-blocks in older English, for as we have seen, words travel up and down the social scale, and the eighteenth century was often woefully unaware of the status of words in earlier days. It is enough for them that an expression is low in their day: and of course there is a real and urgent practical problem here when the books concerned are Elizabethan plays to be acted in a theatre, or the Bible and Book of Common Prayer to be read in church. They may easily give a false impression.

PROBLEMS OF MODERNIZATION

As a result of the dual objection to the low and the archaic, eighteenth-century scholars made several attempts to bring the King James version of the Bible up to date, to modernise the Prayer Book, and to 'improve' Shakespeare. Their comments and proposals throw a good deal of light on English and their attitude to it. The Biblical translators sometimes went to extremes. There was the glossy polish of Dr Edward Harwood's[1] 'polite version' and there was the commonplace method that retells the Biblical narratives in the language of the street or market-place. The latter probably represents the original Greek fairly enough—but it comes as a shock even to the modern reader who knows his Moffatt, Knox or New English Bible, as well as his Authorised Version or his Rheims-Douai.

A reasonable comment comes from the *Monthly Review*[2] in its account of Benjamin Blayney's New Translation of *Jeremiah* and *Lamentations*. It finds in this 'some particular terms and modes of expression . . . that are of too modern a cast to be venerable, and equally detract from its dignity and simplicity'. Among them are *paramour, regency, insulation, atoms, extricate, species, commanding, affixes, privy council, purloin, legitimate, convoked, courier, inarticulately, annihilation*. The reviewers feel rightly enough that of these expressions some are

[1] 1768. [2] *Month. Rev.* lxxi (1784), 162.

too modern, some too refined, others too vulgar, and others 'too obscure for a translation that is adapted to general use'. (We wonder which are the vulgar words in the list.) Blayney should have admitted no words but those 'generally intelligible: and such as would convey no idea that might destroy the effect of the sacred text by any improper association'. If he was bent on accuracy, a periphrasis would have been better than 'a word that is low or ludicrous, pedantic or obscure'.

The *Monthly Review*'s principles are sound. It takes a generally conservative attitude to the attempts at translation or modernisation, though it approves of changes made to help understanding, or to fall into line with current grammatical usage. In 1770 John Worsley of Hertford published his translation of the New Testament from the Greek 'according to the present idiom of the English tongue'; he thought that 'the continual change of English' meant that we need a new revision made by public authority 'at least once in a century'. 'Where the common version speaks of a *mote* in the eye,' the Review[1] reports, 'the word is here changed for *chaff* or *splinter*; instead of the awkward phrase, we do you *to wit*, we here read, *we make known to you*; and where *shall* is used for *will*, *should* for *would*, or the contrary, they are altered.' Likewise, the *Monthly Review*[2] approved of Joseph Priestley's *Harmony of the Gospels* in which his corrections were in general 'just and judicious'—'take no thought' becomes 'be not anxious', 'declare' a parable becomes 'explain' it, 'living' becomes 'livelihood', 'occupy' 'trade', 'message' 'embassy'. But he ought to have altered *lay a dying*, for it is a very inelegant expression.

In 1736, the *Gentleman's Magazine*[3] had remarked that the literal translation of idioms may produce nonsense, and that poetry suffers specially if this is done. To find a Hebrew Psalm capable of being rendered into English word for word would be the greatest of all miracles. By 1763, the *Monthly Review*[4] had a critic who was not so sure. He thought that William Green's *New Translation of the Psalms* showed a caution in avoiding Hebrew idioms that was 'no advantage at all . . . since these Hebrew idioms, having been so long used in former translations, are become as familiar as English ones and, in general as well understood'. And did he not flatten the spirit, without clarifying the sense, when he replaced the concrete by the abstract—the

[1] *Month. Rev.* xliii (1771), 11.
[2] *Month. Rev.* lxiv (1781), 87 on a version of Psalm 68.
[3] *Gent. Mag.* vi (1736), 509.
[4] *Month. Rev.* xxviii, 267–9.

metaphorical by the proper—when for example, he wrote 'asperse my reputation' for 'turn my glory into shame' or 'look graciously upon us' for 'lift the light of thy countenance upon us'?

In 1749, the *Monthly Review*[1] was commenting on some 'Free and Candid Disquisitions relating to the Church of England', which included a plea for modernising the Bible. 'They observe very justly, and with a becoming concern, that . . . we deal with no book as we do with our *bible*; that since the improvement of our language, and the refinement of our taste in literature, we have seen beautiful versions bestowed on other books of antiquity, their sense clearly exprest, their spirit preserved, and their matter and subject adorned with all the elegance and grandeur our language can afford; but that our *sacred* books are denied this favor, and have not even common justice done them—tho' they so loudly demand it, and the times make it absolutely necessary they should have it.'

Unfortunately, what constitutes elegance to one may suggest pretentiousness to another. One cannot but agree with the *Monthly Review*'s[2] comment on Dr Harwood's 'liberal' translation of the New Testament. Here Dr Hirons points out that Harwood in his search for an elegant *polite* version, loses simplicity. 'We are surprised that Dr. Harwood should take pains to modernize expressions and introduce what may be thought more polished words and phrases, but which sometimes rather degrade than add any real grace or dignity to the style and sentiment. We cannot think he improves the text when he says we should *immolate*, instead of *sacrifice* . . . or when he speaks of a *certain opulent gentleman* instead of a *certain rich man*.' The *Monthly Review* has no patience with alteration for alteration's sake, especially when it merely lowers the style.

A quarter of a century later, the *Gentleman's Magazine*[3] summed up this translation as a version 'for gentlemen'; the *Critical Review*[4] attacked it for its *frivolous embellishments*. We, however, should not call the phrase 'burst into a flood of tears' *fantastic*—it is a cliché to us.[5]

A version which by no means catered for gentlemen appeared under the title of *The Christian History*, by William Williams. The *Critical*

[1] *Month. Rev.* i (1749), 199.
[2] *Month. Rev.* xxxviii (1768), 217.
[3] *Gent. Mag.* lxiv (1794), 146.
[4] *Crit. Rev.* 25 (1768), 108, 115. The book exemplifies Harwood's 'nauseous affectation of sublimity'.
[5] Johnson, at this phrase, threw the book down, exclaiming 'Puppy!' (See G. B. Hill, *Johnsonian Miscellanies*, ii, 429.)

Review[1] found it 'low, familiar and inelegant', though the author had hoped elegance was one of its qualities. He made a dashing attempt to break away from language hallowed by antiquity or religious associations.

Some of its wording, stigmatised by the *Review* as 'vile, plebeian language' does not seem so shocking to us. A great *squall* of wind; *startled* at the sight; the *lad* Jesus; he *set off* to the festival; a Levite *slipped* away: they wanted to *arrest* him, but he escaped out of their *clutches*—all these seem middle-of-the-road English. *In a terrible fright, chop it off, slapt her face, ramble* from house to house, the period he had *picked* out, press and *squeeze, screamed* out through fear—these do sound colloquial, and so does the angel's *Don't be afraid,* where the abbreviation must have then sounded socially inferior as well as undignified. No doubt 'the angels shall sally out' sounded too much like an earthly military manœuvre and more so then than now, and 'this man receives reprobates and *messes* with them', strikes us in the same way. We should prefer a *penny* or a *denarius* to Mr Williams' *denary*. But when the *Gentleman's Magazine* takes exception to 'not apparently but incognito' we are more bothered by the Latin sense of *apparently* than by the inappropriate atmosphere of *incognito*. At times this version —to us—is very lively. Perhaps the Prodigal Son's elder brother really did say the Aramaic equivalent of 'This son of yours has consumed your substance among *wenches*.' The untrustworthy servant who began to *lash* his *comrades* and to *junket* and *carouse* with *sots* is a vivid figure: 'thou fool' and 'Raca' (untranslatable as the King James translators felt it to be) come out strongly when rendered 'fie skum!' and 'out scoundrel'. And there was something to be said for 'Begone from me, ye hackney'd villains', as long as we read *hackneyed* in its old sense of 'inveterate'.

Harwood and Williams are poles apart, and we should find neither any real improvement on the Authorised Version, even if that, in the opinion of the *Critical Review,*[2] contains ideas 'meanly and imperfectly expressed'. But the reviewers underlined its preference for native words. '*Make* is better than *constitute*; and *look into* than *inspect.*' Again, technical terms should be avoided—*horseman* is a more timeless word than *cavalry*, and *number* than *muster*. As between varieties of the foreign words we cannot avoid, the more familiar and less technical should be used. *Trade*, they considered, is better than *traffic, get* than *acquire, fine linen* than *muslin*, a *meat offering* than a *donative*, and the

[1] *Crit. Rev.* 43 (1777), 391–2.   [2] *Crit. Rev.* 25 (1768), 108.

Tabernacle of the Congregation than a *Convention Tent. Skipover* for *Passover* is certainly 'very ridiculous'.[1]

Dr Symonds,[2] one of the most scholarly of the revisers, considered it 'the business of a translator of the Bible to avoid a diction too much modernized, for though it may lie open to the level of all capacities, it may possibly have an air of littleness, incompatible with the grave simplicity of the Scripture'.

The usual objections to the Authorised Version itself are that it is antiquated and incorrect, but the standing difficulty of modernisation lies in partial change, so that a style results which is a linguistic patchwork. When Gilbert Wakefield offered *A new translation of the New Testament*, the *Critical Review*[3] welcomed the idea, because 'nearly 200 years [had] elapsed since the publication of the old translation', and 'because the English language has undergone an almost total change, both in words and in the construction of sentences'. Wakefield set out to alter 'only some low, obsolete or obscure words, some vulgar idiom, some coarse or uncouth phrase, some intricate construction, some harsh combination of terms, or some misrepresentation of sense' —but this partial treatment only produced 'a motley style, in which quaintness and refinement are united'. But if, in the opinion of many divines, the style of the Authorised Version was uncouth, obsolete and vulgar, there were worse attempts at reform than Wakefield's. Two years earlier, the *Critical Review*[4] had reviewed a version of 'the Actions of the Apostles' by a Mr Willis which it pronounced confusion worse confounded, disgusting and displeasing. *High roads* for *ways, an angel of divinity* for *an angel of the Lord* were bad enough, but did Mr Willis really think that 'to make an ejectment' is more familiar to the reader than 'to lighten the ship', and did he imagine that there was more simplicity and beauty in 'Claudius Lysias to his excellency governor Felix sendeth compliments' than in 'Claudius Lysias to the most excellent governor sendeth greetings'? But the critics approved on the whole of a version by Nathaniel Scarlett[5]—*tax gatherers* is better than *publicans*, *demons* than *devils*, *happy* than *blessed*, *favour* than *grace*, *love* than *charity*. The last two are echoes of Tyndale and look forward to later

[1] *Brit. Crit.* iv (1794), 7ff.

[2] *Gospels*, p. 98. He realises that the Translators 'adopted the same words and idioms that were employ'd by the best writers of the age' even if to later ages they appear mean and vulgar. (Ch. vi.)

[3] *Crit. Rev.* new arr. v (1792), 309.

[4] *Crit. Rev.* 69 (1790), 172.

[5] *Crit. Rev.* new arr. xxiv (1798), 66.

versions: but Mr Scarlett stuck to *bishop* and *church* unlike his famous predecessor. The *Review* thought *dip* better than the old *baptise* or the new *immerse*.

It should be noted that not all translators of the Classics treated their authors as respectfully as the Biblical Critics sometimes claim.

ARCHAISM

If trying to be too modern sets traps, so does trying to revive the obsolete or obsolescent elements of the language. For us, the interest lies in the words that are said to be out of use, for the twentieth century does not always see eye to eye with the eighteenth about their status.

George Campbell's *Philosophy of Rhetoric*[1] states the general principles and points the uncertainty. We ought to avoid words no longer understood by any but critics and antiquaries, such as *hight, cleped, uneath, erst, whilom*; also, 'when writing in prose and on serious subjects', those terms that 'all writers of any name have now ceased to use', such as *behest, fantasy, tribulation, erewhile, whenas, peradventure, self-same, anon*—to the modern mind, an odd mixture of the living and the embalmed. We feel much the same when Samuel Pegge[2] includes *mischievousness* among words worn out for some time, though we should agree over *plenteousness* and *grievousness*. We may, too, agree with Warton when he thinks *blood-guiltiness* would be obsolete but for the Book of Common Prayer, but we don't feel the same about *blood-thirsty*. Dr Johnson, coming on *right now* in 2 *Henry VI*, III, ii, 40 tells us it means 'Just now', 'even now'—we have learnt as much from America. He also tells us that *gear* was a general word for things or matters. Shakespeare used it more widely than we do, but do we not recognise one of our meanings when in Julius Mickle's *Syr Martyn* it is glossed as 'furniture, tackle'? Mickle also glosses *ruthless, semblance, strain, tenour, fay, fairy, fray* and *bale*. We know *baleful* and our *fray* is hardly more than part of a cliché—when we join the fray, we are not likely to meet the heroes of chivalry and we don't find it *bathetic*.[3] We don't need to be told that *murk* means dark.

Spence[4] thinks that antiquated words may be grotesque or rough in sound. He mentions *seneschal, viands, beverage* and *ireful*. They are all still recognisable and *beverage* has fallen into the hands of the advertisers. It is surprising to be told[5] that *seeing that* for *since* is obsolete

---

[1] p. 171. [2] *Anecdotes*, p. 212. [3] Melmoth, *Letters*, p. 202.
[4] On Pope's *Odyssey*, ii, 24. [5] Symonds, *Epistles*, p. 56.

and that *lack*, both noun and verb, is gone into disuse.[1] *Lack* is laughed at in *Columella*,[2] when the visitors are asked by Mrs Betty the house-keeper 'what they pleased to lack'—they *lacked* to see Mr Milward. But the point here is that she was using *lack* to mean 'desire' as though it had the double meaning of *want*—Betty, however, always murdered the King's English, and nearly failed to marry her master in consequence. *Astounded* seems the odd man out in a list of unintelligible archaisms that include *ween, erst, gan* and *whilome*.[3] *Scant* seems equally out of place among *besprent, chosen imps* and *pensive eld*. We observe the same survival, against the feeling of the time, in many words listed as obsolete or obsolescent by Johnson and Kenrick—*aback, abut,* the adjective *advertising* (with a new lease of life), *in case, dell, gleeful, hurtle, jeopardy, inthrall, languorous, lovesome, niggardliness, olden, ruination, sensuous, serenitude, troublous* ('An elegant word but disused,' says Johnson), *unkempt* (though with no thought of the *comb*), to *war*. Neither have we altogether forgotten *divers* (=diverse), *fell* (=skin), *eschew, mavis* (with a new lease of life as a girl's name), *meet* (=fit) and *paramour*.

How far archaism is a help in liturgy and poetry was, and is, a matter of debate. The would-be modernisers of the Bible and Prayer Book were more vocal than the conservatives, but these make their points. James Beattie[4] dislikes the habit of saying 'Our Father *who* art in Heaven'; 'he pardon*s*'; 'through all eternity', for 'world without end'. 'These old modes of language, in writings consecrated to religious use, should never be altered until they become unintelligible, or ludicrous, or likely to occasion a mistake of the sense.'

The danger of mistaking the meaning through the use of old words that live in a sense far from the one implied in their etymology, is noticed by the *Monthly Review*[5] in a comment on a translation of *The Philosophical and Mathematical Commentaries of Proclus*. The Translator had used *fanatic* in a good sense—and he was not foreseeing our reduction of the word to 'fan'. Custom had made the etymological meaning opprobrious—would Mr Taylor on the same principle like to be called a 'wiseacre', even if it did once mean a prophet?'

The eighteenth-century reformers wanted to alter the Prayer Book's *prevent*, and wondered[6] why the more go-ahead Americans had not

[1] Symonds, ibid., p. 67.   [2] Graves, *Columella*, i, 43.
[3] *Crit. Rev.* 23 (1767), 365.   [4] *Dissertations*, p. 340. Swift had said the same.
[5] *Month. Rev.* lxxxi (1789), 336–7.
[6] *Gent. Mag.* xix (1749), 413. *Month. Rev.* lxxx (1789), 389.

changed it when they brought out a liturgy adapted to their independent status. Theophilus Lindsay altered *indifferently* to *impartially* in
his Unitarian liturgy.[1]

Archaism *has* a proper place in poetry but it is not enough of itself.
The *Monthly Review*[2] thought that some would-be poets believed it
was. A Seaton Prize Poem in 1754 was, in the reviewers' opinion,
merely an imitation of Milton—its author was 'one of those mistaken
bards who think that in order to write like Milton, little more is required than to select certain peculiar, now exploded words, used by
that great poet, and familiar to the times in which he lived, as *nathless,
caitiff, erst, ken, governance*'. One wonders why *governance* was not
acceptable from its use in the Prayer Book but the eighteenth century
was not to know that 'Beyond our Ken' would be the punning title
of a popular B.B.C. programme 200 years later. Any modern critic
who is inclined to hold Milton responsible for bad eighteenth-century
blank verse, should find it salutary to recall that a satirist of the time
could laugh at pseudo-Miltonic diction as the choice of 'those

> Who can't write verse and won't write prose'.[3]

MISUSE

What were regarded as careless misuses of words were handled firmly.
The meaning objected to is often the one we feel most at home with,
but these old critics have something to say to us if we are being hasty or
thoughtless, and the argument often makes us see how the change took
place. The dislike of a new use, as of a new form, may be simply that
it is new, and there may be no real ground for complaint; but it may be
because a new metaphor has been made, which can be good, or because
someone is betraying a confusion of ideas, which is bad. It may be a
philological misapprehension, an illogicality, a false analogy, or a piece
of plain ignorance. It may be that some one is using a term objectionable because of its implication of social or religious bias, or one
divorced from its usual meaning through mere carelessness.

The *Gentleman's Magazine*[4] disliked *generate* as applied to motion—
produce is preferable, and it would have been better to have left
generate 'to the noble purpose whereunto it originally belongs, for by
applying one word to different Significations, our Language is likely to
degenerate into confusion. The moderns have for some time attempted

---

[1] *Gent. Mag.* xliv (1774), 222.   [2] *Month Rev.* xii (1755), 159.
[3] *Connoisseur*, lxvii.   [4] *Gent. Mag.* xxix (1759), 127.

to *propagate* notions, and now they seem to *generate* motions; we are in danger of generating and propagating a race of confounded people.' Actually, we have been *propagating* ideas since the seventeenth century, and now we commonly *generate* power—what would the *Review* have thought of our Generators? But *O.E.D.* shows that the use it deplored was a late eighteenth-century, and nineteenth-century, development. All the same, the critic was too much bound by his etymological knowledge.

Lord Kames[1] considers that *dignity* and *meanness* are words inapplicable to anything inanimate: 'the most magnificent palace that ever was built may be lofty, may be grand, but it has no relation to dignity: the most diminutive shrub may be little, but it is not mean. These terms must belong to sensitive beings, probably to men only.' That modern English does not agree is plain from our phrase 'human dignity'. Nevertheless, a mean hovel or a mean trick would hardly be significant, unless they were seen in relation to a human being. *Dignified* and *mean* can act as transferred epithets from the man to the thing he is considering. But that does not excuse Lady Peckham, that upstart Cockney, for talking of the *magnanimous* buildings in London![2]

Samuel Pegge[3] felt that few words were as misapplied in the public prints as *premature*. The word is so common now that we are unlikely to reflect as Pegge did, that its original picture is that of fruit falling or being gathered before it is ripe. If left to itself, it would ripen—and therefore we ought not to apply the word 'to anything that is not certain to happen in due order of time'. This is the etymological fallacy: the word had been in use for 'before the proper time, over-hasty', during the previous two centuries.

It is surprising that Pegge should have let himself be caught out when he objected to *ill success*.[4] He and his time thought as we do, that success must be good, though we have only to look back to Shakespeare to be reminded that success originally is merely what *follows*. But it would do us no harm, in these days when *win* so often means no more than 'be lucky', to recall the comment of the *Gentleman's Magazine*[5] on Gray's line 'she wins her easy way'. 'To win is to

---

[1] *Elements of Criticism*, i, 356.
[2] Thomas Holcroft, *School for Arrogance*, 1791.
[3] *Anecdotes*, p. 226.
[4] ibid., p. 213.
[5] *Gent. Mag.* li (1781), 569. Contrast the muscular context of Charles Wesley's 'Clearly he sees and wins his way . . . And more than conquers all' (Hymn, 'Light of the World, Thy beams I bless').

gain with a contest, and implies labour and hazard: to win one's way, therefore, is to make way through obstacles with force and difficulty.' Indeed, 'there could not have been a more unfortunate combination of terms than *winning* an *easy way* by *gliding*'.

An equally proper comment is made by the *Monthly Review*,[1] that *transpierce* is no word to use of a pistol-shot, since it should imply a pointed instrument.

John Dennis[2] may have been a captious critic, but he was right when he took Pope to task for making *Murmur* mean a great noise, in comparing the murmur of moving hosts to old Ocean's roar: this is to give it 'a Meaning directly opposite to that which Use has given it.' In English use, 'it is always for a soft, a gentle, an agreeable sound'. Dennis was negatively right, but his positive definition is wrong—the murmuring of an *angry* crowd is far from agreeable, and the word had that sort of connection from medieval times.

The *Critical Review*[3] had a logical point when it laughed at a *Compleat* treatise to which an appendix was soon to be published. But with our human limitations, can we be sure anything is complete? It is this striving after what we hardly hope to reach that encourages us to say '*more* perfect', '*more* universal', illogical expressions often attacked then as now.[4] They really mean *more nearly* perfect, *more nearly* universal, and this usage is now being recognised in grammatical handbooks.[5]

Lassitude, remarks the *British Critick*,[6] is erroneously used for indolence, when actually we are plain lazy. This is a more innocent example of the frame of mind that uses *arch* for 'obscene'.[7]

Not dangerous, but absurd, is the habit of which Grose[8] tells us, and which he believes to be a purely English trait—the application of *delightful* and *charming* to shrouds and coffins, as if we envied the person for whom they were provided. I do not know whether we have given up this inappropriate talk: but we have not improved upon the lady who expressed dissent by declaring she was 'not agreeable'. This confusion of active and passive was noticed by Pegge[9]—a 'compassionate' case ought to be a *compassionable* one. The language has refused,

1 *Month. Rev.* xx (1759), 517.
2 *Critical Works*, ii, 155.
3 *Crit. Rev.* 42 (1776), 43.
4 e.g. *Gent. Mag.* lxvii, Pt. 2 (1797), 567, noting them in Gibbon and Blair. Cp. N. Bailey's title for his Dictionary.
5 B. M. Strang, *Modern English Structure* (1962), §111, n. 3.
6 *Brit. Crit.* xi (1798), 55.
7 S. Richardson, *Familiar Letters*, clviii.   8 *Olio*, iii.   9 *Anecdotes*, p. 220.

and 'compassionate leave' has become a Services technicality. After all the *World* (29) had used the word in this sense in 1753.

False orthography: to *enjoy bad health*: to *reason ill* are etymological (or actual) inconsistencies, but the language has accepted them. *Cacography* seems remote, and *graphy* alone insufficient as a neutral word. Why not *bad* or *good spelling*? The Romans too enjoyed bad health, if their derivatives from *valere* are evidence: and even if you reason badly at some point, you reason well at others—unless you are qualified for a lunatic asylum.

Those innocent of etymological knowledge adapt old words to new uses by analogy or by inventing new forms on the basis of some wrong association, or abstraction of meaning from an accidental circumstance. Grose[1] tells us that a Westminster election was to be celebrated by a *cavalcade*, by way of triumph, which led an Irishman 'to offer to bet a crown that it would be only a foot cavalcade'. The eighteenth century might have liked the metaphor which gave Noel Coward the title for his play dealing with the procession of recent history, but what would have been said about *Motorcade*?

TECHNICAL TERMS

Good authors and speakers ought not to interlard their books or conversation with technicalities, which, as James Beattie says, 'have something of a vulgar appearance' and are likely to be unintelligible.[2] The last part of this comment is unfair so far as books go—conversation is quite another thing because it may not be our own choice. But if we have enough interest to read a specialist's book, we should be ready to do some work. If such nautical terms as *starboard, mainmast, mizzen* or such military ones as *counterscarp, palisade* or *bastion* are thought to throw an 'impenetrable mist' over a work, readers should try something simpler.[3] How far such technicalities are good in poetry is more debatable. Addison disliked Milton's array of architectural words and his scientific ones—*Doric pillars, Cornice, Architrave* or *Ecliptic*, stars dropping from the *Zenith*, Rays *culminating* from the *Equator*.[4] The *Monthly Review*[5] had doubts about James Grainger's *The Sugar Cane*— 'the modern names of trees and herbs and fruits are unpleasing even to the eye'. Botanical names are more classical and incomparably more harmonious.

[1] *Olio*, pp. 188-9.   [2] *Dissertations*, p. 651.   [3] *Connoisseur*, xxvii.
[4] *Spect.* (297).   [5] *Month. Rev.* xxxi (1764), 106.

But William Whitehead in his verses on *The Goat's Beard* disagrees:

> The flaunting woodbine revell'd there,[1]
> Sacred to goats; and bore their name
> Till botanists of modern fame,
> New-fangled titles chose to give
> To almost all the plants that live.

Attitudes to the Linnaean nomenclature vary. It struck the Latinists as barbarous, but it would be frivolous to let linguistic purism prevent us from studying Nature. And now that we have a fixed English botanical language, it should be strictly adhered to, for consistency is better than accuracy.[2]

The *Critical Review* was objecting, in 1786, to a writer on Ferns who invented his own technical words.[3] Jackson of Exeter thought the Linnaean terms too pompous, and too much based on the idea of 'animal' properties, and indeed Erasmus Darwin's *Loves of the Plants*[4] shows what can be done if you think of the sex characteristics of plants imaginatively. The *Critical Review*[5] even took exception to the observation that often plants *close* their leaves at evening. An English reader might find it affected, and the author in fact apologised for it by saying he had 'only adopted it from Linnaeus' who first used it. The intransitive use—'the leaves close' is as old as Chaucer.

We may agree that there is no 'more difficult task than to write at once for a profession and for the public; on the elegance of a polished style to engraft the harsh and unmanageable vocabulary of technical language'.[6] But technical terms, as the subject to which they belong grows more popular, have a way of entering into common use by way of metaphor, as Dr Johnson remarked.[7] It needs a large dose of eighteenth-century decorum (or snobbery) to feel as shocked as the critic who disliked reading that 'the whole spirit of the jest was allowed to evaporate' when the jest had been made by the court fool at a small German court, and had been translated—badly, it seems—for the benefit of an English visitor. The *Critical Review*[8] was 'sorry to find' that the author had fallen 'into the impropriety of alluding to any

---

[1] Cp. the Greek-based *tragopon* and *tragacanth*. Neither was new. Chalmers' *English Poets*, xvii, 233.
[2] *Crit. Rev.* 61 (1786), 16.
[3] ibid.
[4] 1789. Cp. the *Anti-Jacobin*'s satire *The Loves of the Triangles*, 1798, i, 168–74.
[5] *Crit. Rev.* 4 (1757), 227.   [6] *Crit. Rev.* new arr. viii (1793), 1.
[7] *Plan for Dictionary*.   [8] *Crit. Rev.* 48 (1779), 216.

chemical process, in describing the conversation at the hospitable entertainment of the prince palatine'.

The transference of terms from one walk of life to another lies behind the *Monthly Review*'s[1] implicit disapproval of the fine gentleman who blames his mistress for making his rival happy without any *demurrage*, and the lady who *swears* she never saw people so exactly alike. These are uncouth expressions, doubtless all right in their place—in commerce and law.

Professional language, in the view of the eighteenth-century scholar and gentleman, was tainted. Even Parliament was subject to blame. Indeed, why 'should not Ministers speak as plainly and intelligibly as the Rest of their countrymen' and give a plain Yes or No in their replies? Why not get rid of 'Preliminaries, Congresses, Conventions, Interpretations, Explanations, References, Mediators'? So the *Craftsman*[2] asked, in a discussion of the language of treaties and negotiations. In our conference-ridden age we are still asking why—but Sir Winston Churchill's dictum that Jaw, jaw is better than War, war is true, though the eighteenth century would undoubtedly have thought it inelegant.

In 1783 the *Gentleman's Magazine*[3] was quoting from an evening paper which considered that Parliamentary orators had 'taken hold of several strange, vulgar, quaint, and pedantic expressions'. Business is not discussed *on* Monday but *as* Monday: if a Member wants to have a matter brought before the house speedily 'he will request that some *short* day may be appointed for that purpose'. Can business be done only round about Christmas? And, of course, no M.P. can confess, deny or say anything—he is now *free* or *bold* to do these things, and that is servile and 'inelegant if not ungrammatical'. 'One great orator ... declared that he was not yet *ripe* to say so and so. A most ridiculous expression! especially as, from the personal appearance of the member who used it, one would have concluded he was *ripe* for anything.' But this 'monstrous phrase' did not come into vogue. Hawkins,[4] discussing a plan to bring Dr Johnson into Parliament, thinks that his oratory might have 'prevented the introduction ... of a great number of words, phrases and forms of speech, to which neither dictionaries, nor the example of any English writer of authority, have given a sanction'.

---

[1] *Month. Rev.* xliv (1771), 91. Cp. Anstey, *New Bath Guide*, Letter VI ('the Lawyer may choose to Demur'). But both senses had run parallel since the seventeenth century.

[2] Quoted in *Gent. Mag.* ix (1739), 608–9.

[3] *Gent. Mag.* lii (1783), 415.   [4] *Life of Johnson*, p. 227.

COMMERCIALESE

Commercial language, so cultured eighteenth-century circles were inclined to think, ought not to come out of office or warehouse. They laugh at the Stock Jobber who, on being asked how he is, tells you that he is 'cent per cent better': or says a friend is 'above or below par' (why are we always below it?) and declares 'he would not underwrite' a person in a dangerous situation.[1] Mrs Piozzi[2] thinks *cash* is always pert and pedantic, unless used on its native soil, the banker's shop, where it means coin, opposed to notes. She was not to foresee the time when it would often mean ready money—hard or paper—opposed to credit. It is noticeable how *cash* has come into a wider sphere than her other examples—*ready rhino, chink, corianders,* which have gone or are still 'nothing better than a mere jargon of schoolboys, 'prentices, etc. ... excluded civil society'.

The general style—as apart from the specific vocabulary—of business letters was under fire then as now. In the seventy-eighth number of the *Tatler* we find Mr Lemuel Leger writing to Mr Bickerstaff begging him not to forget Alderman Whittington: 'If you want any further Particulars of Ditto Alderman, Daughter, or Cat, let me know and per first will advise the Needful.' On which Mr Bickerstaff observes 'how wonderfully this Sort of Style is adapted for the Dispatch of Business, by leaving out insignificant Particles: Besides that, the dropping of the first Person is an artful Way to disengage a Man from the Guilt of rash Words and Promises.'

It is amusing to find Mr Bickerstaff opposing in 1709 the same sort of thing Sir Alan Herbert was objecting to over 200 years later[3]—'the Favour of your Letter' (why not 'Honour', or just 'Letter'?) and to such flowery endings as 'I am with great Truth and Esteem your humble Servant'—Why not just 'I am'? But he prefers 'your most obedient Servant' to 'your faithful Servant', whereas we see little difference between them.

No wonder the *Critical Review,*[4] commenting on a travel book, objects to its frequent 'cant phrases'—does not 'twenty florins for *self* and man' resemble a shop-keeper's style, who signs receipts for Self & Co.?

[1] Grose, *Olio,* xx.   [2] *Brit. Syn.,* ii, 35.
[3] e.g. in *What a Word.*
[4] *Crit. Rev.* 33 (1772), 304–5.

THE PROFESSIONS

Henry Fielding's periodical the *Champion*[1] notes how 'every particular Profession seems to have laid violent Hands on some certain Syllables which they use *ad libitum* without conveying an Idea whatsoever'. The essay laughs at Merchants, Doctors and Lawyers—the mercantile favourites are 'very cheap', 'lowest price', 'get nothing by it': with the Physicians it is 'out of Danger, safe Prescriptions, infallible Method': with the Lawyers, 'Sounds peculiar to themselves, without any Meaning—learned in the Law, dispatch, reasonable'. Fielding was a lawyer! These are of course not technicalities, but professional patter, and fair game for the satirist. So are the easy phrases of the Great Man—the potential patron with an appointment in his gift—'upon my Honour, believe me, depend on me, I'll certainly serve you another Time, etc., etc.' The Great Man, it is insinuated, has no honour, is unworthy of belief and has no intention of serving anybody but himself. Was Fielding thinking of Sir Robert Walpole?

The *Tatler*[2] has a similar suspicion of the Critic. 'He is Master of a certain Set of Words, as Unity, Style, Fire, Flegm, Easie, Natural, Turn, Sentiment, and the like; which he varies, compounds, divides, and throws together ... without any Thought or Meaning.' Not all these critical counters survive, but there have been replacements.

Actual legal technicalities struck the critics as low and unnatural, as French rather than decent and proper English. But surely the profession had a right to *Indictment* or *snap judgment*, and we a right to borrow 'common parlance' from it.[3]

Mrs Sealand[4] in *The Conscious Lovers* may well be expressing a popular view, but one most unfairly misconceived, when she says, with Lawyers particularly in mind: 'Tis a wonderful thing Sir, that men of Professions do not study to talk the substance of what they have to say in the Language of the rest of the World.'

We have an advantage she had not—we can read Dr Johnson's sane paper on Hard Words in the *Idler*[5] and should realise that every Art must have its proper terms.

Johnson adds that the expert need not always be using them—it is a problem of communication, and there was a natural breakdown when a Doctor[6] asked a man with a pain in the head about his cephalick

---

[1] i, 197–8. [2] *Tatler* (165). [3] *Brit. Crit.* ix (1797), 478.
[4] Produced 1722. [5] *Idler* (70). [6] *Month. Rev.* iv (1751), 365.

symptoms. No doubt the breakdown was intentional and perhaps kindly, when another Doctor tried to elude a sick man's questions 'with a slow profusion of Latinised evasions'.[1]

We should hardly expect the eighteenth century to take kindly to the specialist language of scholastic Theology and Philosophy–for them 'the idle jargon of school divinity' which 'obscure[s] and perplexe[s] even the learned'.[2] But it is condemning thought to stand still when objections are made to theologians who would take upon them to define what revelation does not, and to coin terms not made use of in Scripture, to express their 'imperfect conceptions'. Constant attempts at definition are a sure way to clarify thought. Whether philosophers were always wise in their approach to language was a moot point. Joseph Priestley[3] notices justly that as 'minute differences in the significance of words are sometimes of considerable use to Philosophers', they will 'refine upon the vulgar language' as well as upon vulgar sentiments. Priestley feels there is danger in the dichotomy between the ordinary use of words and the philosophical—it may make all the difference between a serious and a frivolous reading of a poem: he quotes Pope's lines

> Who sees with equal eye, as God of all,
> A hero perish, or a sparrow fall;
> Atoms or systems into ruin hurl'd;
> And now a bubble burst, and now a world.

Not improbably, 'many of Mr Pope's readers may affix ludicrous ideas' to these lines, which in Pope's 'own conception, and that of his more philosophical readers, were very sublime'. For 'Sparrows, atoms and bubbles do not make the same figure in the eye of the generality of mankind that they do in that of a philosopher.' Priestley, scientist though he was, was not to foresee that because of the march of discovery, the word *atom* would set off a new train of thought in both the general reader and the philosopher, and that the word would be so immensely strengthened for us that Pope's intended contrast between the infinitesimal and the vast would be hard to hold.

But with the recognition that philosophers, of all specialists, are under the necessity of definition, there was a suspicion that they—and the prescriptive grammarians—sometimes forgot that everyday language is to be interpreted by common-sense and circumstance rather

---

[1] *World* (195).   [2] *Month. Rev.* i (1749), 296.
[3] *Oratory and Criticism*, i, 153.

than by technical logic and first principles. It is a charge of treason against English idiom that Reid is bringing when he points out[1] that

In all languages, there are phrases which have a distinct meaning, while at the same time, there may be something in the structure of them, that disagrees with the analogy of grammar, or with the principles of philosophy. And the reason is, because language is not made either by Grammarians or Philosophers. Thus we speak of feeling pain, as if pain was something distinct from the feeling of it. We speak of a pain coming and going, and removing from one place to another. Such phrases are meant by those who use them in a sense that is neither obscure nor false. But the Philosopher puts them into his alembic, reduces them to their first principles, draws out of them a sense that was never meant, and so imagines that he has discovered an error of the vulgar.

WOMEN'S USAGE

I suspect that eighteenth-century critics would have put women speakers low down in the scale in comparison with philosophers. It was not that they were uneducated, but that they had particular vogue words. When we read that a woman should never profess to understand a technical word (even if she does?) but should apply to a man for enlightenment,[2] perhaps we should admit that she should be excused for her own inventiveness and fads. No doubt it was undramatic of Dr Johnson to make the princess in *Rasselas* 'speak in the same lofty strain with the philosopher, and the waiting woman harangue with as much sublimity as her royal mistress'.[3] But surely it was not only the ladies who were puzzled by the strangely mixed vocabulary in the English translation of Isaac Hawkins Browne's Latin poem on the Immortality of the Soul, on which the *Critical Review*[4] remarked: 'There is great inattention ... to separate words, as I *ween,—dazzling sheen—mendacious—incarnate* as applied to a bone, when it has long acquired a peculiar sense from its use in theology—*inhume—nathless—microcosm*, where little world suits the verse just as well, ... *portents,—doffing* these mortal spoils; for we must remind our translator that he sets out with a determination of being peculiarly agreeable to the fair

[1] *Intellectual Powers of Man*, i, 354.
[2] Grose, *Olio*, p. 149.
[3] *Month. Rev.* xx (1759), 381.
[4] *Crit. Rev.* new arr. xiv (1795), 271. Cp. Z. Pearce, *Text of Paradise Lost*, pp. 298–9, pointing out to Bentley that *incarnate* can go with *Devil*; and *Gloss. Ang. Nov.* which gives the technical sense in medicine.

sex, and he ought not to give them the trouble of searching through a
dictionary for the meaning of a word, when he might easily have saved
them this labour, and joined to a greater perspicuity more harmony of
versification.'

Obviously, this was no language for ladies whose main ornaments
to their correspondence were an ah! and an oh![1] But even the well-
educated woman with literary interests could develop tricks of style
that annoyed the critics. Mrs Piozzi, says the *Critical Review*,[2] was
possessed by those linguistic demons *such*, *so* (without the corresponding part of the sentence), *somehow*, and the indefinite *one* which was
rightly felt to be unmanageable. She had indulged in these words so
much in her *Observations and Reflections made in the Course of a Journey
through France, Italy and Germany*, that the reviewer ended his comment in a burst of sarcastic imitation—'Really Madam, one cannot
read ten lines without feeling *somehow* such disgust, *so one* is tempted to
lay down a book where *one* meets so many inelegancies, *such* colloquial
barbarisms, which *one* must always feel *somehow* unpleasant.'

Indeed, they were hardly suitable for 'even the conversation' of
elegant and well-educated women. There are plenty of modern women
who must plead guilty to *so*, *such* and *somehow*. *One* may be also used
by men—but it pinpoints a deficiency of English, a singular common
gender pronoun corresponding to *they*.

The over-use of a favourite and loosely applied epithet or adverb is
also charged on the ladies. The *Critical Review*[3] rebukes a novelist for
the indiscriminate use of *fine*—'the true criterion of a female pen'. The
hero must be a man of *fine* sense, *fine* accomplishments, *fine* eyes, in
every scrawled love-scene: 'fine passions', 'a fine sense of honour',
'fine accomplishments' should have been avoided; the 'fine sense of
honour' wedged in between the passions and the accomplishments
accentuates the danger of carelessness. Does it mean 'fastidious',
'scrupulous'—'to find honour in a straw'—or is it merely, as *fine* often
is, a mere enthusiastic but uncritical equivalent of *beau*? And are the
passions delicate and full of sensibility, or merely those we generally
approve of?

Gildon[4] had been inveighing against the feminine fondness for *fine*
over seventy years before—'that Sex has a mighty *tendre* for *fine Things*
and *fine Language*, as they call it'. Some women still have. The *Critical*

[1] *Crit. Rev.* 65 (1788), 149.
[2] *Crit. Rev.* 68 (1789), 104.
[3] *Crit. Rev.* new arr. iv (1792), 270.   [4] *Art of Poetry*, 224.

Review[1] rebuked a woman novelist in 1797 for an affected use of *mentally*—' "Alas!" cried she, *mentally*—'she *mentally* preferred' or 'persuaded herself of that'. This is a seventeenth-century school term, for which there is a gap in *O.E.D.* until the nineteenth century. It is useful and common enough now—we could well be grateful to the lady for helping to make it so.

CANT

The 'idioms of cant' form 'a jargon introduced by ignorant or affected persons, and which the most perfect acquaintance with every good author in a language, would not enable one to understand'. So says Dr Beattie in 1783,[2] and it may amuse us to find that of a baker's dozen of expressions he damns as vulgarities of the lowest order, over half are quite intelligible to us and in use, even if sometimes in a slightly modified form. We can say 'He's a bore', 'he's in liquor' (or 'half-seas over'), 'he's beat(en) hollow' or 'he's check-mated'—though not 'has received check mate'—and that 'it's down in black and white'.

'Clipping the King's English' is an apt description of a man too drunk to speak plain, but it is a low phrase according to both James Beattie and *The Town and Country Magazine*.[3] The Magazine adds 'corporation' for a man's body—still not unknown—which may well be an inferior kind of drollery as the critic says, but the *Concise Oxford Dictionary* calls it *colloquial*.

Though cant words are hasty productions, and so often short-lived, 'sometimes they get firmer hold and by degrees gain a settlement in the language and become part of it'. *Bore* has filled a real gap; so has *humbug*, which is not to us, as it was to the *Connoisseur*,[4] part of 'the uncouth dialect of the Huns, or the rude gabble of the Hottentots'. Dr Johnson[5] says that *privateer* and *auctioneer* illustrate a 'cant termination'. We feel that it is a handy bit of machinery, usually derogatory, though not of pioneers and engineers—and *to engineer* is no exception. *Racketeer* and *black-marketeer* show that the suffix is alive and useful.

An expression can work clear of slangy association and restriction. *Good Company* says the *Connoisseur*[6] is one of the vaguest of phrases in

---

[1] *Crit. Rev.* new arr. xxi (1797), 356, reviewing *Anzoletta Zaboski*, a novel by Mrs Howell.

[2] *Dissertations*, p. 651. Cp. *Gent. Mag.* xl (1770), 559–60 (list of slang words for drunkenness).   [3] *Town & Country Mag.* xiii (1781), 365.

[4] xlii.   [5] Note to *I Henry IV*, II, i, 84.   [6] lvii.

modern conversation. People of fashion modestly explain it to mean only themselves, and one indispensable requisite in a good companion is Mimicry, to which they have given the appellation of taking-off. Now we stress the *good* more than *the company*, and J. B. Priestley's novel would make enlightening reading for eighteenth-century 'good companions'.

Ash's Dictionary says *Bristol Milk* is a cant term for a kind of sherry —we should call it a trade name, but that to the eighteenth century would have been a distinction without a difference.

In all these instances, the critics are using *cant* to cover slang and trade terms. It was used for two others kinds of language—one is the underworld secret jargon of the habitual criminal, the other, the kind of language that now goes by the name—lofty and sentimental expressions that cover (or are thought to cover) insincerity.

In 1781 the *Critical Review*[1] had before it a book called *A View of Society and Manners in High and Low Life*. Low Life seems to have been its main interest, and it gave dozens of such names as readers would never have heard of before—the cant names for every sort of cheat and sharper, the activities of whom are all explained. Kiddy-nappers, carrier-pigeons, jigger-dubbers, evening-sneaks, shore-tumbrils, do at least encourage the reader to investigate. There would be no two opinions about the nefariousness of the activities and the lowness of the names, which are appropriate for that reason.

But cant in the common modern sense does raise questions. It is easy to accuse people of hypocrisy if you don't like their theology or politics or their particular ritual. Cant, said Mr Spectator,[2] signifies 'all sudden Exclamations, Whinings, and unusual Tones'. It is here suggested that the word derives from an ignorant Presbyterian preacher, one Andrew Cant—but this is like deriving Cabal from Charles II's five ministers whose initials happened to spell the word. Any deviation from the style of the *Book of Common Prayer* was apt to produce the cry of 'Cant', any use of unctuous language particularly so. The *Critical Review*[3] declared that it had the 'utmost aversion' to 'a certain nauseating and canting style' displayed in a certain clergyman's discourses, in which he used such phrases as 'Notes of *mellifluous* gratitude' and '*Love-exalting* page', and spoke of past, present and future 'sweetly linked together'.

[1] *Crit. Rev.* 52 (1781), 299.
[2] *Spect.* (147).
[3] *Crit. Rev.* 61 (1786), 111.

POLITICAL LANGUAGE

In view of the hard things said about English as used in Parliament, it is interesting to find the speakers at the time of the Civil War being praised for the polishing their disputes afforded to the language— 'since both parties endeavoured at strength for the good of their cause, and at perspicuity for the sake of being universally understood . . . and these two principles go near towards making a perfect style'.[1]

Perhaps eighteenth-century politicians had less clear-cut causes, and believed in themselves more than in such causes as there were. They certainly multiplied their own names. Dr Wendeborn[2] tells us that Whigs and Tories, Highflyers, and Jacobites were not very common in his day—the fashionable words were Patriots and Courtiers, Ins and Outs. The *Critical Review*,[3] discussing a pamphlet on the 'reputed principles of Whigs and Tories', remarks that these are distinctions which have been so often falsified that they no longer deserve any attention. 'This ridiculous language is now nothing more than the jargon of politics, and serves only to expose the prejudice of those who use it.' But we need to remember that all political parties must move with the times, so that what is Conservative in 1960 may have been Liberal in 1910 and would have been Labour—if they had known the term or the party—in 1860.

'Patriotism is the last refuge of a scoundrel,'[4] declared Dr Johnson in the famous dictum that is so easily misunderstood when quoted out of its historical context. An apt comment comes from Charles Johnstone's *The Reverie*[5]—those rambling reflections on things in general. The Guiding spirit explains that a Patriot 'in the original and proper sense of the word, is the noblest title which can be given to man, and includes every virtue moral, social and civil. But so entirely is the use of words changed with the course of things, that, stripped of every idea which can deserve respect, it implies only a factious opposer of the measures of the court, who pretends a regard for the public welfare, to gain the confidence of the people, and make himself of sufficient consequence to be admitted to a share of the spoil which he declaims against.'

[1] Jackson, *Letters*, i, 81.
[2] *View*, i, 51.
[3] *Crit. Rev.* 55 (1783), 145.
[4] Boswell, *Life*, ii, 348. Cp. n. 8, p. 174, in Boswell's *London Journal.* Johnson's pamphlet *The Patriot* (1774) used the word seriously.   [5] 1762.

Four years later, the *Gentleman's Magazine*[1] quotes from *A Constitutional and Political English Catechism*—
'What are the qualifications to constitute a man a patriot?'
'He must be insolent without measure, of a voluble tongue, or ready at his pen, a bare-faced liar, a man of abandoned principles, incapable of blushing, and in fine, he must be proof against any bribe but a large one.'

Comments on *Excise* reveal an attitude of mind, and show also how a word can be extended for emotive use. *Tax* is bad enough, but it 'grows nauseous, especially if it swells itself into an EXCISE';[2] the Excise, for *Common Sense* in 1738, was 'one of the most destructive schemes to our Properties and Liberties'.[3] Five years earlier, the *Craftsman* (343) had noted that 'Robbing of the Highway is term'd *Collecting*, or *Excising*', that 'the Test Act is an *Excise* upon Conscience' and that 'the late Epidemical Distemper which cut off so many' had been called an *Excise Plague*.[4] Dr Johnson was not idiosyncratic when he defined *Excise* as 'a hateful tax levied upon commodities, and adjudged not by the common judges of property'.

ADVERTISEMENTS[5]

Political misapplication, with its twisting of emotive words, comes at one end of the linguistic scale. Lower down, being concerned with more ordinary matters, comes the language of advertising. All the familiar tricks of the men simply out to sell are there—exaggeration, pseudo-science, vulgarity, careless structure: some of it funny, some pompous, some stupid. But a modern reader misses the puns, the clever twist to familiar word-patterns, the alliteration, rhyme or juggling with spelling, the adaptation to the language of various kinds of reader that enliven the good modern advertisement.

Francis Grose[6] notices the careless wording that is symptomatic of conceit in the keeper of a madhouse who 'does not take in lunatics': his 'more comprehensive mansion lodges and boards lunacy itself'. Likewise, he notices a chimney-sweep who 'does not, like his brethren, put out the fire in chimneys, but, acting on a larger scale, extinguishes the chimneys'.

---

[1] *Gent. Mag.* xxxvi (1766), 235.
[2] *Craftsman*, quoted *Gent. Mag.* iii (1733), 229.
[3] *Common Sense*, quoted *Gent. Mag.* viii (1738), 28.
[4] Quoted *Gent. Mag.* iii (1733), 71.
[5] Cp. *Tatler* (224), *Mirror* (80).   [6] *Olio*, pp. 244, 252.

A full and entertaining skit on the art of puffing is to be found in William Woty's poem *The Auctioneers*. He claims to have 'retained and concentrated in one grand striking point of View THE CURIOUS, LARGE, RICH, GENUINE, ELEGANT, CAPITAL, MAGNIFICENT, VALUABLE and DESIREABLE BEAUTIES' of auctioneering language.[1] Two proficients in the art contend for the prize of a hammer, which is to go to him 'whose oily tongue affords

> The best assemblage of the choicest words'.

Woty wickedly quotes the actual advertisements in his footnotes. There is 'the ground composed by Nature in a bold and great Stile' or the place where 'Nature hath shaped the ground with elegance': you could buy a house in a 'vicinage truly respectable, commanding prospects replete with beauty'—or where the 'elements conspire together, in social harmony, to render the prospect complete', or where the 'adjacent country . . . portends abundance of field sport', and in the offices 'Utility and Neatness reciprocally meet'. Woty deftly fits all this into heroic couplets and tells us how

> The hills and vales, which give to pleasure scopes,
> Rise in acclivities and sink in slopes . . .

or how

> Itinerant objects on the Thames display
> A prospect truly picturesque and gay.

How can one sell a house near a brick-kiln?

> The mansion's use what mortal can define
> Built on an incombustible design!
> In sweet Vicinity, on yonder lands,
> The Nostril's treat, a fragrant Brick-kiln stands.
> The smoke ascends voluminously fair,
> And scents, like Musk, the circumambient air.

After that, it is child's play to dignify a kettle as 'this culinary utensil' and to describe its layer of soot 'Black as black velvet, and almost as soft'.

SAILORS' LANGUAGE

Sailors' language evidently struck the landsman as *sui generis*. They are notorious for clinging to it on shore, but references to it are made more out of interest than in disapprobation. Indeed, it made the interest of

---

[1] *Poetical Amusements*. Preface to *The Auctioneers* iv sq.

characters like Commodore Trunnion. But when it seemed nonsensical the critics noticed. It is 'gibberish' to talk of a man-of-war or a merchantman, especially when the vessel is referred to as *she*.[1] It doesn't worry us, and we are not content to leave this sort of talk 'to mariners'. Writers, also, should be careful in their use of nautical terms. The *Monthly Review*[2] points out that if the landsman says 'loudly roars the gale', a sailor would inform him that the moment when the gale begins loudly to roar, it becomes a *storm*. This is technically still true, and Dr Johnson's Dictionary was clear—'A wind not tempestuous, yet stronger than a breeze'. Yet we may doubt whether the 'gentle gale' beloved of eighteenth-century poets was any more exact: to us it seems a contradiction in terms.

LEVELS OF LANGUAGE

So far we have found the eighteenth-century critics objecting to words as 'low' because they thought their users were. But sometimes the dislike arises from the blunt meanings of the words rather than the social status of their users, though a complete separation of word and man is not feasible. The *Critical Review*[3] is shocked at the down-to-earth language of a religious writer who says that Jesus 'appeared as a *young carpenter*, and *sweat and laboured* . . .' For the reviewers, 'Elegance of sentiment and language is perfectly consistent with ease and perspicuity. But this representation is coarse and vulgar'. We wonder how they would have expressed the hard facts: after the style of Dr Harwood? No wonder they wanted to re-write Dr Blair's 'the run of our composition' as 'the modulation of our periods'.[4]

The retreat from the 'low' could be carried too far, and eighteenth-century critics could be as well aware of it as we are. There is an anecdote of a 'nice' clergyman whose unrecorded name must surely have been Collins, who, in offering thanksgiving for the recovery of the great lady of the parish, 'thought it too familiar and even bordering upon rudeness, to say 'O Lord, save this woman thy servant', altered it to 'this Lady' . . . and instructed his clerk to respond 'Who putteth her Ladyship's trust in thee'. We laugh at this with the Magazine:[5]

---

[1] Campbell, *Phil. of Rhet.*, p. 315. Boswell, however, wanted to refer to a fleet as *she* (*Boswell in search of a Wife*, p. 319).

[2] *Month. Rev.* lxxix (1788), 433.

[3] *Crit. Rev.* 56 (1783), 160.   [4] *Crit. Rev.* 56 (1783), 273.

[5] *Gent. Mag.* xxiv (1754), 210. Cp. *Spect.* (312).

ought we also to be amused at Dr Johnson's two definitions of Matron
—'An elderly lady: an old woman'?

Just what was in the mind of the contributor to the *World* (175) who
thought that 'there is a distinction and subordination of style, as well
as of rank', and that an 'affectation of talking above our level is as bad
as dressing above it'? In its context, this passage suggests irony. To
have a better command of language may be the means of social advancement and to wish for both is not necessarily snobbish.

Dramatically, speech and appearance should match. It was when the
bailiffs (disguised 'as officers') in Goldsmith's *The Goodnatured Man*
began to talk on a level out of keeping with their appearance—below it
—that the hero's subterfuge was betrayed and the play wrecked by the
too fastidious audience. A dramatist and critic like Arthur Murphy
might think it true humour, 'but the upper gallery was too delicate
and hissed furiously'.[1] No wonder Goldsmith felt that *low* is enough
to damn any style, however indiscriminately the word is applied. 'By
the power of one single monosyllable, our critics have almost got the
victory over humour among us. Does the poet paint the absurdities of
the vulgar, then he is *low*, does he exaggerate the nature of folly to
render it more thoroughly ridiculous, he is then very low.'[2] The
opposite fault of being too lofty is easy in an age that is afraid of the
normal middle way of clear plain words. Why should cups and spoons
be too low for poetry, as Ruffhead says in his Life of Pope?[3] Warton
bids us observe the many periphrases and uncommon appellations
Pope has used for *scissors*—Fatal Engine, Forfex, Shears, Meeting
Points. Scissors would 'sound too vulgar'. Must we credit Pope with
only this notion, and rob him of his mock heroic and fanciful bril-
liance?[4]

James Beattie[5] has some sound sense on this matter. 'Those words
are not mean, which are so necessary at all times, that it is impossible
to speak without them on any subject. Words are not mean because
they are plain; nor elegant, because none but men of learning understand them; on the contrary, everything in style is blameworthy, which
is obscure or ambiguous to an attentive reader. 'Let there be light, and
there was light' is a much more elegant sentence than 'Let light irradi-

[1] Murphy to Mrs Thrale (1792). See Dunbar, *The Dramatic Career of Arthur
Murphy*, p. 199.
[2] *Present State of Learning*, Ch. XI.   [3] p. 117.
[4] Warton, *Essay on Pope*, I, 241.
[5] *Dissertations*, p. 656.

ate the universe and instantly light flashed into existence.' We should agree with Beattie that this version is 'affected and ill-chosen'.

He notes too that in a translation of poetry dealing with other times, modern common form politeness is out of place. 'How ridiculous would it be, if a translator of Vergil were to make Eneas introduce himself to Dido in these words:

> Madam, your majesty beholds in me
> Your most obliged, obedient, humble servant,
> Eneas, prince of Troy.'

A fit illustration of this, says Beattie, would be a figure in a wig and feathered hat, in the posture of a minuet bow.

The fear of colloquial phrases could lead to unreasonable dislike of stylistic features that help to keep our language living, vigorous and supple. Godwin, in his discussion of English style,[1] dislikes concrete metaphors and muscular adjectives and adverbs, such as *by dint of* memorials, *cramp* the ministers, *trim the balance* of Europe, *choak canals* of censure, *pursue one's game*, *set one's heart upon*, *grow full* of dissimulation, *staunch* to the minister, *hearty* in his cause, *heartily* sick, *boldly* quarrel, *bury their heads*—even the word *hard* when it means difficult. He may have found them too colloquial, but they are better than Latinate abstractions. Why did he dislike the old idioms, *broad sunshine, to stand one's ground, use one's understanding?*

He is franker than most in demonstrating that he has no historical sense, for the essence of his detailed analytical criticising of the great writers of the past is that they lived when they did, and could not take advantage of the later eighteenth-century polish and enlightenment. But he had had his predecessors: seventy years earlier the *Guardian* (25) had accused 'my Lord Verulam' of abounding 'in low phrases beneath the dignity of History'. It is a failure of historical knowledge and imagination that it has taken years of patient accumulation of proof to shift from impressionistic minds. John Upton[2] put it well when he pointed out that to be a critic of an old poet, you must know about the 'customs and manners' ... the 'grammar and construction' of his period: 'the knowledge of these is presupposed: to be caught napping here is an ominous stumble at the very threshold and entrance upon criticism; 'tis ignorance which no guess-work, no divining faculty, however ingenious, can atone and commute for'. The critic's business

[1] *Enquirer*, Essay XII.
[2] *Critical Observations on Shakespeare*, pp. 131, 238.

is not to 'presume to judge what Shakespeare [or any other] ought to have written' but to 'endeavour to discover what he *did* write'. The eighteenth century needed this warning. It is surprising how quickly their historical knowledge could be blurred, though it is hard to escape from the impression that a dogmatic belief in their own rightness was the root cause. George Campbell[1] notes that *human* and *humane* are not to be confused—'the only authorized sense' of *human* is *belonging* to *man*, and of *humane*, kind and compassionate. And then he tells us that Pope had confused them when he wrote

> Tho' learned . . . Modestly bold and humanly severe.

The differentiated spellings, pronunciations and senses, were only just coming in when Pope was writing this: here the eighteenth century made us a good new tool, but it was hardly on the market in 1711.

Campbell also objects[2] to Dr Burnet's phrase, 'the invention of truth', for which he ought to have said 'discovery'. Warton betrays the same attitude in his *Observations on the Fairy Queen*—*invention* is 'one of Spenser's Latinisms'. *O.E.D.* makes it clear that *discovery* was one of the normal meanings of the word from the fourteenth to the seventeenth century.

After this, it is not surprising that the *Monthly Review*[3] should jib at *invention* used technically and traditionally. Reviewing a Dictionary of Painters, it noted that the work contained 'much of the cant of the connoisseur, of which the reader is left to make English as he can. The supposed discovery of the cross on which Christ suffered the Author calls the invention of it.' The Festival of the Invention of the Cross was 1100 years old even then, and in English the word had had this technical use since the fifteenth century. Characteristically, the only eighteenth-century example quoted in *O.E.D.* refers to a continental ceremony. It is true that the *Monthly Review*'s staff were largely nonconformist, but they could have found the phrase in any Anglican prayer-book. If the critics could be ignorant of the uses of ordinary English, only a century or so before, it could hardly be expected that they should bother about anything out of the general run. And so, when Milton mentions a *cry* of hell-hounds, Bentley blandly and unrepentantly admits 'I may be ignorant of the Hunter's language'.[4] He was.

---

[1] *Phil. of Rhet.*, p. 191.　　　　　[2] ibid., p. 193.
[3] *Month. Rev.* xliii (1771), 25.　　　[4] Note to *Paradise Lost* ii, 564.

SHORT-CUTS

Eighteenth-century critics tend to regard abbreviations as vulgar. Swift laughed at them in 1710,[1] and the *Monthly Review* was still objecting in the 'seventies.[2] The *School for Wives* was a 'genteel play' —all the more reason to rebuke the author for using such ill-looking, uncouth, barbarous and vulgar forms as *isn't, wouldn't, won't*, etc., especially as he puts them into the mouths of people who are supposed to have enjoyed the advantages of education. The criticism is purely social or snobbish—the shortened forms suggest the affected style of a 'mincing milliner' or a 'coxcomb valet'. It was agreed that they are destructive of language—*often* is better than *oft*, and *'tis, it's, there's, sha'n't* are unnatural. The more general opinion was that they are all too natural—'Englishmen are much prone to clip and curtail their words, both in conversation and writing, especially in verse, and to use I've for I *have*, and I'll for I *will*.'[3] But not every critic had made up his own mind. One nobleman wrote a Poetical Epistle to another: after his death it was printed with 'corrections by the Author of Night Thoughts'.[4] Edward Young altered 'Why don't they trust?'to 'Why trust they not?' In view of Young's own practice throughout the *Night Thoughts*, this is odd—*can't, won't* are constantly intruding on his pompous blank verse. But if eighteenth-century plays are any evidence, this was how people talked. Even Dr Johnson does so in Boswell's *Life*. On the other hand, it is noticeable that the only people in Jane Austen's world who do so, are the flighty and underbred. A sensible comment comes from J. Mason[5] when he says that 'running two words into one may be all very well in conversation or in reading familiar Dialogues, but is not so decent in grave and solemn subjects'. One must have a sense of occasion: it is surprising to find a Preface full of abbreviated forms prefixed to an *Art of Rhetoric*.[6]

Of a different kind are the short-cuts *ult., incog., extra*, which George Campbell[7] fondly believed to be affectations that had gone out of fashion. He noted that *mob* had not. Now that we have invented the verb *to mob, mob-law, mob-violence*, we can see that however bad Latin

---

[1] Letter to the *Tatler* (230). [2] *Month. Rev.* l (1774), 42, review of the play.
[3] *Month. Rev.* xl (1769), 84. *Oft* is *not* an abbreviation.
[4] *Crit. Rev.* 41 (1776), 230.
[5] J. Mason, *An Essay on Elocution and Pronunciation*, p. 18.
[6] John Holmes, 1739.   [7] *Phil. of Rhet.*, p. 179.

mob may be, it is useful English, as Campbell foresaw. The others too are very much in evidence, and probably *ult.* is the only one we might question—outside business use. Campbell also mentions *hyper* (critic) which did die—but its Latin relative *super* has had a new lease of life in schoolboy slang and in certain professions. We might question its usefulness since it stands for *supernumerary*, *superfine* and *superficial*: but context is all important.

All the grounds for objection—wrong application, wrong users, wrong form, are to be found in Mrs Piozzi's comment[1] on the misfortunes of *acute*. It is 'vulgar to call any one an ACUTE fellow by way of saying he is a sharp-witted one: it having been a practice lately among low Londoners, to say, when they like a boy, how "cute he is"! So that the word would now shock a polished circle for its grossness.' The word has been unusually resilient: *acute* is now dignified, and 'cute' is playful rather than low, and commoner in the United States than here.

[1] *Brit. Syn.*, i, 13.

III

APOLOGY

A WRITER who slips in an apology for a word is making a linguistic self-criticism.[1] He may feel he has invented a new form, suggested by already-existing words—he is then applying a piece of freely available machinery. He may know he has borrowed from abroad and be uncertain how the foreigner will be received. He may think his new bit of figurative language is startling.

The new use of old tools may be careful or blundering: in either case, the new invention may prove good in practice. Once Pope had popularised the Sylphs, it was easy for the *Adventurer* (93) to coin *sylphish*. The suffix had been available ever since English was English. But there is more to this than obvious word-building—there often is, when the eighteenth century makes a new word. The inventions are not exercises in morphology so much as experiments in meaning. 'The images, customs and employments of his SYLPHS, are exactly adapted to their natures, are peculiar and are appropriated, are all, if I may use the expression, SYLPHISH.' The essayist wants the adjective to describe something *sui generis*—the ending has the full meaning it originally had: not the neutral sense of 'like' or the specifically English sense of 'somewhat' but the basic idea of 'having the nature of' its noun.

A similar stress on the full meaning of a word can be felt when Addison, discussing *Paradise Lost* in the *Spectator* (321) says that 'our first Parents seldom lose sight of their happy Station in any thing they speak or do; and, if the Reader will give me leave to use the Expression, that their Thoughts are always *Paradisiacal*'.

So, when Duff is writing in his *Essay on Original Genius*[2] about early man, he remarks that in this 'primitive state of Nature ... the manners, the sentiments and passions are (if we may use the expression) perfectly original'. He adds[3] that the 'undisturbed peace, and the innocent rural pleasures of this primaeval state, are, if we may so express it, congenial to' the nature of Genius. The basic sense of original and the connection of *congenial* with *genius* are really emphasised.

[1] Cp. Society for Pure English, Tract 48, *On Linguistic Self-Criticism*.
[2] 1767, p. 269.   [3] ibid., p. 271.

But the most interesting words which call forth apologetic asides
are those to which their users are giving (or think they are giving) an
extended meaning—the metaphors and new applications. Many have
become accepted usage, so that we should not notice them if they were
not being so tentatively introduced: some are individual and more
vivid for that: some will strike us as inappropriate. They all raise the
questions, Who first thought of using these expressions in the new way?
Why did they strike people as strange?

Adam Smith is not sure whether he may speak of a scientist 'enlarging the *precincts* of some species in order to make room for it',[1]
when confronted with a singular plant or fossil. He thinks that when
we contemplate irregularities among the phenomena of the heavens,
we cannot wonder that the imagination of the first enquirers should
slur over[2] such disturbing features. And can one talk of a Planet's
'natural inertness, *encumbered*, if one may say so, and clogged in its
flight'?[3] Mr Bickerstaff, thinking also of the night sky, confesses 'I
could not behold a Scene so wonderfully adorned and lighted up (if I
may be allowed that expression) without suitable Meditations.'[4] Should
such sublunary phrases be used of the heavens? More noteworthy
phrases are Vicesimus Knox's reference to the *embers*[5] of literature, and
the comment[6] that Dr Swift in his verses on his own death had 'dissected' the human heart, or the 'bold metaphor' as Campbell calls it of
cementing ideas.[7]

It is to be noted that the authors are sometimes too wary, apologising
for expressions already established. Dr Wendeborn[8] was not sure
whether he ought to speak of the Ashmolean Museum being *eclipsed*
by the British Museum: the metaphor was normal—but English was
not Dr Wendeborn's native tongue. Why, however, did Adam Smith
hesitate over *temperate* joy and realm of thought?[9]

The technical terms of one walk of life may be transferred—with
apologies—to another. George Campbell[10] is not sure about a *group* of
passions: Hurd[11] has the same doubt over his use of it in his description
of Kent's landscape gardening which 'consists in grouping his ground
and objects if I may use the term, in so easy a manner, that the careless

[1] *Works*, v, 69.
[2] His italics; ibid., p. 101 (*O.E.D.*, 'usually of words or music').
[3] ibid., p. 140.   [4] *Tatler* (100).
[5] *Essays*, p. 130, 'if we may venture to use that expression'.
[6] *Art of Poetry*, ii, 106, 'if I may so express myself'.   [7] *Phil. of Rhet.*, p. 83.
[8] *View*, ii, 166.   [9] *Works*, v, 281.   [10] *Phil. of Rhet.*, p. 130.
[11] *Moral and Political Dialogues, with Letters on Chivalry and Romance*, iii,274.

observer, though he be taken with the symmetry of the whole, discovers no art in the combination'. They are taking a term that at first belonged to the painter or sculptor, and then to a crowd of people, and transferring them, Campbell to psychology and Hurd to the picturesque improvement of country seats.

Defoe[1] uses a military metaphor to describe the depredations of 'a new gang of Rakes—who have lately *taken the field*, as we may call it, against Mankind, and who are, very deservedly, whoever gave them that name, call'd Mohawkes'.

So in Duff's *Essay on Original Genius* we meet with 'the evolutions of Genius (to use a military phrase)'[2] applied to the varying manifestations of that elusive quality: Duff spoke also of the symptoms[3] of genius, admitting this to be a 'physical' term—a medical one, that is. There is an apology for speaking of the *line of demarcation*[4] between the fine arts and the Belles Lettres. Military manœuvres, medicine, and the law are all pressed into service.

In a Latin-conscious age, 'Fitzosborne'[5] could have no fear of misunderstanding when he spoke of the quantum ('if I may so express it') of human merit. His use was not complicated by the quantum theory: but the exactness of philosophical language may seem pedantic to the man in the street and so Mr Spectator (628) admits when he says 'if I may use the philosophical terms, we may apprehend a *Potential*, though not an *Actual Eternity*'. The word sounds much more like our popular use when the *World* (120) remarks 'I make no doubt but there are potentially (if I may use that pedantic word) many Bacons, Lockes ... and Marlboroughs at the plough-tail.'

'Folly', says the *Looker-on* (p. 99), 'has splendid temples ... and whole hecatombs of human victims, if you will allow the expression, swell the honours of her *red-letter day*'. Is this uncertainty over *hecatomb* or *red-letter day*? The latter seems half-way between the strictly liturgical and that modern colloquial use of which the first clear example is to be credited to Coleridge in 1811. On the other hand, Dr Johnson defines *hecatomb* as the sacrifice of a hundred *cattle*, so it could have been the human victims that seemed inappropriate. Much wider deviations from the Greek meaning had been in use, so there was

---

[1] *Review* (viii), 613. *O.E.D.* 1831 (figurative sense).
[2] p. 85.
[3] ibid. *O.E.D.* 1771 from Burke.
[4] *Literary Mag.* v (1790), 212. *O.E.D.* quotes Burke in the same year.
[5] Melmoth, *Letters*, p. 22.

no call for worry here, and Johnson was being far too strict: Bailey, and Dyche and Pardon agree that we need not be etymologically exact.

The river of life is almost an obsession with Dr Johnson, but other metaphorical rivers are tentatively brought forward. The situation of Bologna, '(being in the very heart of Italy) makes it a continual river of foreigners—if I may use that term for their certain coming and short stay'. Lady Pomfret[1] has hit on a lively picture. Much more interesting is Dugald Stewart's conception: 'By means of the Association of Ideas, a constant current of thoughts, if I may use the expression, is made to pass through the mind while we are awake. Sometimes the current is interrupted and the thoughts diverted into a new channel.'[2] The modern idea of the 'stream of consciousness' lies in that remark.

The -*ize* suffix is capable of more than one meaning, and it is the misapplication—real or apparent—that troubles some critics. Dr Johnson defines to *humanize* as to soften; to make susceptive of tenderness and benevolence. But it is only by a considerable stretch of meaning that we can use the word of spelling. The *Gentleman's Magazine*[3] 'thinks that at long last we are beginning to follow the example of Spain, Italy and France, and humanize our orthography . . . if the term may be allowed'. Presumably this means 'to make less hard', to render more fit for human use. Campbell sounds to us needlessly wary when he speaks of 'an original incapacity of classing and (if I may use the expression) generalizing their perception'.[4] It is an eighteenth-century use—the passage is *O.E.D.*'s second illustration: the intransitive verb came in the nineteenth century.

When Sir Joshua Reynolds contemplated Rubens,[5] he remarked that he 'had not been dead long enough to be canonized, as he may be said to be at present'. The evidence collected by the *O.E.D.* shows that the application of *canon* to the authoritative texts as principles of other than religious matters happened earlier than the similar transfer of *canonized*. Reynolds was widening a technical term. Saints can do little wrong, books in the canon are to be accepted, and a painting can be set up as an unquestioned standard for his art. The sense is quite clear.

Remembering the eighteenth-century horror of being incorrect, it is amusing to see writers trying to have the best of both worlds—to keep

[1] Hertford-Pomfret Correspondence, iii, 173.
[2] *Elements*, p. 289. *O.E.D.* 6, but the phrase is not given. See G. H. Vallins, *The Best English*, Ch. V.
[3] *Gent. Mag.* lix (1789), 315.   [4] *Phil. of Rhet.*, p. 48.
[5] Reynolds, *Journey to Flanders*, ii, 253. *Works*, ed. Malone, 1809.

their upright dignity, and yet to bend down and pick up some lively expression. Squire Squeakum's voice makes Mr Spectator (205) think him 'cut out for an Italian singer'—if the expression may be used. The *Guardian* (126) talks of sagacious men who cannot see the wood for the trees, while admitting this to be a vulgar saying. *Glib* is a 'very low' word—but Adam Smith[1] can't restrain himself from twice using it in half a dozen pages. The *British Critick*[2] thinks Hunter's celebrated Museum is certainly unique, if an exotic expression may be allowed. Many commentators on the word, noun—'an unique'—or adjective, were sure it might not.

Is the apologetic spirit a sign of grace or gracelessness? It is good to have standards, to watch our words; but if we never deviate, the very standard can become a barrier to the imagination. And how often the new use proclaims its meaning as it comes. We know well enough what was meant by the man[3] who said William Hogarth's features were *uneducated*, just as we appreciate the negative verb when Ralph Griffiths[4] castigates an author for taking 'pains to perplex his diction, and unpolish his stile, if we may use the expression'. For this, *O.E.D.* quotes *Clarissa* five years before, and interestingly enough does not give a literal example before the nineteenth century.

We speak (not with approval) of 'talking like a book', and King Alfred could speak of Book-language, meaning Latin. It is the more surprising that a neat phrase of Lawson's[5] has not caught on; he is protesting against pulpit and stage voices, and the teaching of children to read unnaturally, and he dislikes 'this formal Stiffness and the Uniformity of this, if I may so call it, Book utterance'.

It is hard to believe that any modern introducing new words or new applications would feel he must apologise for them. The hand of authority does not hold us in its grip to anything like the same extent as it held our ancestors.

[1] op. cit., pp. 323, 326.
[2] *Brit. Crit.* v (1795), 269.
[3] Quoted from *Anecdotes of William Hogarth* by *Crit. Rev.* 52 (1781), 205.
[4] *Month. Rev.* viii (1753), 188.
[5] *Oratory*, p. 417.

IV

RECOMMENDATION

The Progress of a language towards perfection may be considerably accelerated by the labours of persons who give their attention to it, if they study the analogy of the language, recommend phrases that are agreeable to it, and detect and expose those that are improper. While literary critics keep within these bounds, their opinions are left to recommend themselves by their own weight; they do a very important service to a language: but when their decisions have the sanction of any authority, and forms of speech are adopted because recommended by them, and not on account of the reasons that might be alledged in their favour since all men, and all bodies of men, are fallible, the interposition of their authority is in danger of contributing to establish phrases and constructions which the more mature judgment of after ages would see reason to correct.

Priestley, *Universal Grammar*, pp. 180–1

NEW WORDS, WANTED WORDS

DRYDEN,[1] discussing foreign importations, remarked that he pro-posed the adoption of a loan-word by using it himself. It is the most practical form of recommendation. Unlike the correct or timid innova-tors we have just been considering, there are the more self-reliant and volatile spirits who invent new words with complete freedom. They may toss them off on the spur of the moment: they may be serious or frivolous, finding needed terms for some matter of permanent value or for a passing fad. The period has its large quota of neologisms, whether new forms or new meanings, for new things of every kind, from the *tea-things* to the *electric-battery*, from *landscape-gardening* to the *Turf*, from *persiflage* to *insubordination*, from *brochure* to *villa*, *white lie* to (industrial) *strike*, *Methodist* to *alarmist*.

John Dennis,[2] disagreeing as usual with Pope, remarks that to refrain from coining words 'is directly contrary to the Improvement of Languages, for if *Chaucer* and succeeding Authors had had this Advice given them, and had been weak enough to take it, how could our Language have improved in Purity, in Force, in Grace or in Harmony?'

[1] Dedication of the *Æneid*.
[2] *Critical Works*, i, 407.

The case for new words is well put by Samuel Pegge:[1] 'New Words, well-formed and well-distinguished, enrich a language; while one and the same word with remote senses betrays a mean economy, and tends to embarrass and impoverish the diction.' He adds that a little periphrasis is better and more intelligible than a fine word with but half a meaning, or than a too compact phrase. Some of his own suggestions have not caught on, though it is not always easy to see any reason in logic or euphony to account for it. Why should not -*ist*, which we use in *druggist*, be extended to *bookist* and *hattist*? A trumpet*ist* or a drum*mist* would do as well as a trumpet*er* and drum*mer*. So Pegge argues, and indeed we have invented *trombonist*, *harpist* and *stockist*. To say that -*ist* is Greek and is therefore unsuitable as an ending for non-Greek words is obviously no answer, since many of the accepted -*ist* forms are not based on Greek (including the examples here given). On the other hand, he goes too far when he argues for more use of -*ize*. A hairdresser powderizes (in those days of wigs, he did), while a chemist or apothecary pulverizes. 'Why may not an author authorize —and why may not I (as such) blunderize?'[2] We can only reply, that it is blunderizing to forget that *authorize* means 'to provide authority' and *not* 'to be an author'. What would Pegge have thought of *slenderize*, *tenderize*, *hospitalize*, *finalize*? Of one -*ize* word the *Critical Review*[3] tacitly approves. It notes that an author commenting on the French Revolution had represented the French as *demonized*, making a new word—'and indeed the utmost powers of language has (*sic*) scarcely force enough to describe their atrocity'.

Naturally there must be new terms for new inventions, even for possible new inventions, and there are two kinds of literature particularly in need of linguistic innovation whether for renewal or novelty—poetry and the technical presentation of science. Spence, writing on Pope's *Odyssey*,[4] puts the case for poetry: 'One of the greatest Sources of raising as well as enlarging the Poetical Language, is by inventing New Words, or importing Old Ones from a foreign Soil. Words when they are us'd vulgarly, grow mean: Like other Fashions, when their use is once got among the Populace, they soon begin to be rejected by the politer Part of the World. This it is (as the Gentlemen of Port Royal very justly observe) which necessitates the introducing of New Words into every Language; it occasions a continual Decay and demands continual Supplies. Thus whoever has a Felicity this way is

[1] *Anecdotes*, pp. 212–13.   [2] op. cit., p. 255.
[3] *Crit. Rev.* new arr. x (1794), 279. 1864 in Webster (*O.E.D.*).   [4] ii, 9.

a Benefactor to the Publick: he adds so much to the Bank,[1] and gives his Assistance in supporting the present Credit of Language among us.' Spence approves of *ever-shady*, *ill-persuading*, *serpent-mazes*, none of which needed any special skill to invent.

The formation of adjectives from Proper Names is a measure of the impact made on the times by the thought or action of the people whose names have been so extended. The *Annual Register*[2] thinks that the new method of husbandry, called the horse-hoeing, would be more justly called the Tullian husbandry after its inventor Jethro Tull. It is noted[3] that many foreign publications on the subjects of electricity apply to it the terms Franklinism and the Franklinian system, in honour of Benjamin Franklin's discoveries. The *Critical Review*[4] approves of calling new plants after famous naturalists. With *Rousseau-istic*, *Johnsonian* and *Gibbonian* we come to an impressive trio, though none of these adjectives was intended to be complimentary.

Johnsonian[5] corresponds to *Lexiphantic* (after the name given to Johnson in Archibald Campbell's skit) and implies an over-Latinised vocabulary. *Rousseauistic*[6] implied then a whole system of absurdity, sentimental and enthusiastic. And *Gibbonian* was hopefully suggested by the *Critical Review* with an explicit guide to meaning—'that sneering infidelity, which after times, perhaps, will distinguish by the epithet of *Gibbonian*'.[7] There is no such word in *O.E.D.* but any reader of Gibbon knows what is meant. On the other hand, the *Critical Review*[8] seems to look askance at the poet who wrote of

> The holy vestments light and corregiesque.

Where, asks the *Review*, could this great sketch-painter pick up the word *corregiesque?* The adjective still serves.

In all these examples, the adjectives are wanted because of the new contributions to knowledge or national culture, or because of the individual characteristics of the great men concerned. A whim of fashion or the social sense of the period may produce similar naming, but then the neologism does not become established. Franklin was favoured in France more for his politics than his science, one supposes,

[1] Dryden had used the same sort of commercial metaphor (Dedication of the *Æneid*).
[2] *Ann. Reg.* vii (1764), Chronicles, p. 27.
[3] *Literary Mag.* vi (1791), 13.   [4] *Crit. Rev.* 41 (1776), 145.
[5] Monboddo, *Origin and Progress of Language*, IV ii. 6 (1789).
[6] Reviews of his works, *passim*.
[7] *Crit. Rev.* new arr. xi (1794), 60.   [8] *Crit. Rev.* 17 (1764), 311.

and we are told that as ambassador he was the *ton*, the fashionable topic of modish conversation; the ladies had hats *à la Franklin*.[1]

Trial, error and unconscious forecast are all involved in the question of how to name the planet discovered by William Herschel in 1781. According to the *Monthly Review*[2] the astronomer wanted it to be called Georgium Sidus, 'an appellation that will conveniently convey the information of the time and country where and when it was brought to view'. The twentieth-century Georges were far in the future, so Herschel was accurate as far as he could go. But the magazine thought the proposed name uncouth. 'Why not *Georgii Sidus* or barely *Georgius*[3] according to the nomenclature of other planets?' Why should it not be Herschel?[4] In the same year the *Gentleman's Magazine* was referring to 'the newly discovered (or Georgian) Planet',[5] and Erasmus Darwin introduces it as the Georgian Star in *The Loves of the Plants*.[6] A writer of lessons in Geography and Astronomy for young ladies noticed by the *Critical Review*[7] in 1787 was blamed for omitting the new planet, the Herschel: and Mr Jackson[8] tells us that the constant practice of foreign astronomers suggests the propriety of calling it after its discoverer. But Jackson noticed that 'Great George's name' dissatisfied all Europe, that Sidus is not the Latin for planet, and that the rest of them all have names of the same house—Mercury, Venus, etc. etc., and the new one might not improperly have taken that of Neptune. The *Critical Review*[9] earlier had thought the same— referring to the Georgium Sidus, or, as it ought to be called, the Neptune. The foreign scientists, however, had decided on Urania, as the *Gentleman's Magazine*[10] informs us. By 1802 it was Uranius, and by 1822 Uranus (proposed by Bode) was almost universally adopted. And Neptune had to wait another 65 years when the name was given to the more remote planet of the solar system discovered by Galle in 1846.

[1] *Ann. Reg.* xxxii (1790), 202.
[2] *Month. Rev.* lxx (1784), 257.
[3] Did they realise the danger here? Maryland had a plan, reported in the *Gentleman's Magazine* for 1745, to reform weights, measures and time. There were to be thirteen regular months—the *Georgian* account—each known by number. 'But', asks the Magazine, 'if we have July, why not call the 13th month Georgy in honour of King George?' It hardly sounds a serious proposition to us now. (*Gent. Mag.* xv, 378.)
[4] *Month. Rev.* lxx (1784), 257.   [5] *Gent. Mag.* liv (1784), 86.
[6] ii, 54.   [7] *Crit. Rev.* 64 (1787), 239.
[8] Jackson, *Four Ages* (1798), p. 51, n.
[9] *Crit. Rev.* 56 (1784), 237.   [10] *Gent. Mag.* lxiv (1794), 887.

Words like *punyism*,[1] *womanette*,[2] *prentice-cide*,[3] to *Lillebullero*,[4] to *peerage*,[5] to *Robinson Crusoe*,[6] to *prude*,[7] *puzzleation*,[8] *squeakation*,[9] *puppybility*,[10] show how easily any one can invent a new word if he feels he needs it, and has a set of affixes ready to hand to form it. People who talk of their *don't-know-howishness*[11] or their *wanting-to-be-diverted*[12] spirits, or of one of the strangest *out-of-the-wayest*[13] men are playing about with compounds less dignified than Shakespeare's *world-without-end* (hour), less normal than *never-to-be-forgotten*, but they are taking advantage of the liberty English affords. We cannot say we do not immediately understand them—unless we don't know that the song *Lillebulero* is said to have driven James II out of three kingdoms, or have not been brought up on *Robinson Crusoe*, or know nothing of the abuses of the eighteenth-century apprenticeship system. The difficulties lie in the facts behind the words, not in the words themselves.

More interesting uses are the sudden quirks of application, analogical inversions or parallels—to be henpecked would seem to be not an infrequent state, but how many people have been *grimalkined*?[14] Yet *catty*—or *feline*—women do exist. With our modern notions of the equality of the sexes, it may seem an over-refinement to say you have seen fashionable people displaying their clothes in a very masterly and *mistressly*[15] manner, but the word sharpens the picture. And was it not a dryly humorous contrast in the *Gentleman's Magazine* to pair off such *watering* places as Margate with such *dusting*-places[16] as Coxheath? Beau Nash 'was so fond of the small sort of potatoes that he called them English pineapples, and generally eat them as others do fruit after dinner'.[17] He would have been an asset to any firm of advertising copywriters.

[1] Invented by Tom Paine: see *O.E.D.*
[2] See E. Turner to Sanderson Miller (1754), Dickins and Stanton, p. 242.
[3] *Anti-Jacobin*, i, 35.
[4] A. Collins, *A Discourse Concerning Ridicule and Irony*, 1729, p. 35. *O.E.D.* calls it a nonce-word, quoting Sterne, 1762. It may well date back in popular speech to the Revolution, the period of the song.
[5] Woty, *Poetical Amusements*, p. 4. [6] *London Mag.* (1768), 543.
[7] Henry Carey, *Poems*, p. 67.
[8] *Crit. Rev.* 24 (1767), 424 (six years earlier than *O.E.D.*'s one example).
[9] Horace Walpole, *Correspondence*, 13, 97.
[10] Evans, *Warburton and the Warburtonians*, p. 231.
[11] *Gent. Mag.* iii (1733), 307.
[12] *Month. Rev.* xii (1755), 120, quoting satire on female loquacity.
[13] Lounger (65). [14] Lord Chesterfield: see *O.E.D.* s.v. [15] *Lounger* (76).
[16] *Gent. Mag.* xlix (1779), 316. [17] *Life of Beau Nash*, p. 231.

When Lady Craven[1] visited Constantinople in 1786, she found the cemeteries beautifully laid out, but was horrified to consider that 'it is pestiferated earth we tread on; that every new made grave may contain a body rotting with the plague'. *Pestiferated* is not recognised in *O.E.D.*, but if Lady Craven invented it, she made a good word for her purpose. Cowper appears to have invented *cross-eyed* which, the *Critical Review*[2] says, it has never met—a statement which *O.E.D.* supports. The *Review*[3] also thought *to horrify* was new in 1796— actually *O.E.D.* has an example from 1791: it is, unfortunately, a useful word.

However much eighteenth-century critics disliked the encroachment of technical terms on everyday usage, they felt that there were principles to be followed in the invention of these terms. The *Essay on Chemical Nomenclature* already quoted has a clear-cut programme for the formation of new names required by growing science: Ancient names which express the same combination of ideas as we have occasion to employ should be preferred to new ones, unless they have grown obsolete, but every name ought to be applied as nearly as possible in the sense which general use has annexed to it. New names ought not to convey hypothetic distinctions. They should fit into 'the language into which they are introduced, and ought to correspond with the genius of the language from which they are respectively derived'. And they ought to be derived from Latin.[4] The *Critical Review* prefers Greek— it is 'more euphonious, and runs more easily into compound words'. On the whole, modern scientific nomenclature has agreed with the *Review*.[5]

Another point of view is represented by Michaelis, and made available to the ordinary English reader by the *Annual Register*:[6] if we teach the Sciences in Latin, it 'prevents the modern languages from acquiring such a degree of perfection' in scientific discussion as the oriental tongues have acquired by depending on their own capacities'. A classical vocabulary of technical terms seems a half-way house, and the *Critical Review*[7] wanted to have the best of both worlds. Commenting on Thomas Martyn's *The Language of Botany* in 1793 it explains that the author 'wishes to Anglicize the Linnaean terms, where custom has

---

[1] *Journey*, p. 219.   [2] *Crit. Rev.* new arr. iv (1792), 566.
[3] *Crit. Rev.* new arr. xvi (1796), 238.
[4] *Crit. Rev.* new arr. xxiii (1798), 434–5.
[5] T. H. Savory, *The Language of Science*, 1953.
[6] *Ann. Reg.* vii (1764), 208.   [7] *Crit. Rev.* new arr. ix (1793), 85.

not already established a synonymous English one, or where the new denizen is not too harsh and inharmonious'. 'We greatly approve this plan,' says the *Review*, 'for it will give, in some measure, an universal language, with little difficulty as the Anglicized term is as easy to learn as a new corresponding English one.' Yet is *corymb* any greater help to the English student than *corymbus*?[1]

Occasionally, the eighteenth century looked abroad wistfully: the French had made such advances in chemistry that 'those who would pursue the science were obliged to follow it in a new language—or to be guided by it in English'. Some years earlier the *Review*[2] had said *à propos* of a volume of *Annales de Chemie*, 'The neglect of employing a technical word for *light* has occasioned a little indistinctness and awkwardness: the French employ the word clarté which, to avoid words applied indiscriminately, we have translated *luminousness*.' Dugald Stewart,[3] in his *Elements of the Philosophy of the Human Mind*, thinks the 'new nomenclature which has been introduced into chymistry' a 'striking illustration of the effect of appropriated and well-defined expressions, in aiding the intellectual powers'; and he looks forward to the not too far distant period 'when similar innovations will be attempted in some of the other sciences'.

Samuel Pegge[4] notices some less serious technicalities that he thinks worth preserving in the dictionary. 'How otherwise is the next generation to understand what is meant by the *Lyceum*, The *Eidophusicon*, Sir Ashton Laver's *Holophusicon*, Walker's *Eidouranion* or the *Panorama*? *Ranelagh*, the *Pantheon*, *Vauxhall*, may perhaps survive some time longer; but of the others some are already gone, and the rest will probably die with their sponsors.' Ranelagh still stirs ghostly memories in the lover of the period, though Vauxhall and Pantheon have other stronger associations. The other words—all 'entertainmatic'[5] ones—show their devisers' combination of advertising flair and capacity for classical word-building. We can read about the Eidophusicon in Austin Dobson's[6] vivid account of that amazing spectacle. Now we have our own more marvellous invention, and *Panorama*, so far from being dead, has received a new lease of life to cover views more extensive than were ever dreamt of by Loutherbourg.

---

[1] *Crit. Rev.* new arr. xxiii (1798), 483.
[2] *Crit. Rev.* new arr. xiii (1795), 540 n.
[3] 1792, p. 202.   [4] *Anecdotes*, p. 250.
[5] The *Champion*'s word for Rich of the pantomimes, ii, 127.
[6] *At Prior Park*, pp. 111–17, 277–81.

The eighteenth century had a keen sense of gaps in its vocabulary. Everything in nature that is distinct and different from all others should have a name whereby it may be distinguished without a tedious enumeration of its properties and adjuncts. Words are wanted to make clear developing distinctions, to name new discoveries, to answer to the particular writer's awareness of experience. Some were suggested, but failed to be accepted: some were both suggested and accepted; and some gaps were not filled until the nineteenth century, though the observant knew they were there. On the one hand, it is often clear that we may have the thing without the name, and on the other, how much easier it is to marshal our thought and convey our meaning when we have the word. We can see an amusing and striking example of this last proposition if we look at the *Gentleman's Magazine*[1] for 1773. Opposite page 320 is a plate depicting what the running title calls a 'Nondescript Animal', that the article illustrated describes as 'nearly approaching the Mus genus', with its 'head like a Fawn's, lips and ears like a Hare's', and 'tail like a greyhound's'. Sydney Parkinson, draughtsman to Mr Banks the Australian explorer, has in fact drawn a picture of a beast we all recognize and name as soon as we see it—a kangaroo. The impact of the verbal description is nothing like as sharp. By 1793 the new animal is a *gam-garoo*.[2]

In 1781, the *Town and Country Magazine*[3] published a letter dated 1777 from a Mr S. Scott, who says he cannot distinguish between green, pink, and pale blue; a full red and a full green are the same to him; purple and dark blue baffle him; and he thought 'black' an inappropriate colour for his prospective son-in-law's wedding suit, whereas it was really 'very genteel, rich claret'. Obviously he was suffering from colour-blindness—but nobody had thought of the word. It was not even as yet Daltonism, the name given it in 1841 after Dalton who first described it scientifically in 1794.

The archaeologist Stukeley discerned 'the perfect vestigia of a temple as easily discernible in the corn as upon paper'. He saw it at Chesterford in Essex and described in a sentence what the modern archaeologist in a neat compound calls a *crop-mark*.[4] If the eighteenth century had thought of *Romanesque architecture*, would its discussions on Gothic have been less confused than they are? It did not come till early the next century. But of course, if they had thought of the term,

---

[1] *Gent. Mag.* xliii (1773).   [2] *Gent. Mag.* (1793), 531.
[3] *Town & Country Mag.* xiii, 230. (*O.E.D.*) *Colour-blindness*, 1854.
[4] Piggott, *William Stukeley*, pp. 52-3.

it would imply that they had their historical thinking straight. Here thing and word are intertwined.

In their differing degrees, *Kangaroo*, *Colour-blindness*, and *Romanesque* are names of things. To find exact names for ideas and attitudes would be a much deeper problem and the *Gentleman's Magazine*[1] was handing Mr Herbert Croft[2] a heavy task when it suggested that 'a proper person or committee be appointed to ascertain all such words as are wanting in our language to convey clearly and precisely such ideas as naturally arise in the mind of every man; or, in other words, to point out such ideas as we have not at present any words which convey a proper sense of and, at the same time, suggesting such words either formed of our own compounds, or from any other either dead or living languages, to remedy and supply all such defects.'

Much as the patriotic critics disliked French words, there were people who felt that some were needed. Any that would afford real improvement 'ought not to be contemptuously or neglectfully omitted' says the *Gentleman's Magazine*.[3] Joseph Priestley[4] states roundly that 'the convenience' of borrowing from other tongues 'will soon establish such words notwithstanding all the clamour that is made against them'.

ENGLISH FOR FRENCH

Addison[5] had laughed at the way the victorious English armies during Marlborough's campaigns defeated the French and then wrote the news home in despatches and private letters full of French technical language. It seemed unpatriotic, and it was cluttering up the art of war with new affected words when there were well established old ones available. Not even Addison could stop them.

The argument goes a step further when an Englishman is ready to *invent* English terms instead of the French technicalities; or at least to use ancient loans instead of the current jargon. Notwithstanding the fact that French treatises on military matters had carried French terms all over Europe, a treatise discussed by the *Critical Review*[6] in 1759 demonstrates how we could replace them by English technicalities. The types of formation suggested, and the relative merits of the terms

[1] *Gent. Mag.* lviii (1788), 947.
[2] He was proposing an *Oxford English Dictionary*.
[3] *Gent. Mag.* lviii (1788), 947, as above.   [4] *Universal Grammar*, p. 286.
[5] *Spect.* (165).   [6] *Crit. Rev.* 8 (1759), 177–8.

existing and proposed, are worth some consideration. Certainly *car-casse* and *cavalier* were ambiguous if they could be replaced by *fire-ball* and *mount*. *Crow'sfoot* for *chausetrappe*, *turn-spike* for *chevaux de frise*, *blocking-guard* for *bivouac*, *flanking-fire* for *enfilade*, are good compounds, though *tree-felling* for *abattement* and *bold stroke* for *coup de main* sound insufficiently technical. *Operation* for *manœuvre* is more complicated, since, as it has happened, an operation is normally greater than a manœuvre, and the manœuvre by no means confined to military matters. *Parley*, suggested for *chamade*, is also a word of wider application, but does serve. *Crow'sfoot* is quoted by *O.E.D.* from a military manual of 1772: it was still in use at the end of the next century, and is an interesting example of the widely different forms a metaphor can take. The shape of the bird's foot is visible in both the wrinkles round the eyes and the caltrop. If *turnspike* had been adopted (it is not in *O.E.D.*), the history implied in *Chevaux de Frise* would be dimmed— for 'Frisian Horses' on its gallant though savage level is linguistically like *Welsh-rabbit*—the name of the real thing you haven't got applied to the substitute with which you must make do. *Bivouac* (*biovac* in the article) is another vivid word, originally the picture of a night-patrol keeping watch. It was an eighteenth-century word, probably from Switzerland. French, German and the local dialect appear to be together responsible for initiating the extraordinary variations of spelling in which the word is dressed. At this period it was purely military: it began to be used of peaceful encampments in the nineteenth century.

The Reviewers could not understand why *ricochet* had been omitted. They evidently considered it a needed term, for they proceeded to define it as a process and by a familiar phrase. It is 'a method of cannonading, invented by Vauban' (best known for his complicated fortresses). 'To fire *en ricochet* is to level the cannon in such a manner that the ball shall rebound from the earth in a succession of plunges, like a bit of thin slate skimmed along the surface of the water, making what is called Duck and Drake.'

The date of the *Review* is 1759, ten years earlier than *O.E.D.*'s first quotation for *ricochet*[1] and thirteen before *crow'sfoot* appeared in the text book.

On the whole question of enlarging the language by loans, William Godwin[2] thought that it is of 'no great moment whether our language

---

[1] The transitive verb (= to subject to such firing) is first given in *O.E.D.* from 1841: but there is an example quoted in *Gent. Mag.* (xxviii), 387, which is from 1758—'to ricochet the works of the town'.   [2] *Enquirer*, pp. 379, 478.

be German or French in its structure and phraseology, provided it be uniform, simple, copious, impressive and energetical'. But, he adds, expanding his thesis at a later stage, 'it must have an idiom. . . . Those Gallic modes of speaking, which have been introduced by our best writers, ought not probably to be rejected, merely because they are Gallic. Even new and unauthorized forms of expression may be introduced into a living language, provided it be done sparingly, provided that they be decisively beautiful or expressive, and provided that they do not so depart from the genius of the language into which they are introduced, as to stand out from the substance into which they are meant to coalesce. Let us dare to enrich the language in which we write; but let us not debauch it by inadvertence.'

On the whole, this is a fair expression of eighteenth-century practice.

FOREIGNERS

We have seen that foreign words met considerable opposition from purists and patriots. But there were some that filled obvious gaps; in English there was no way of saying the thing so precisely and succinctly —or politely. Or even if, rarely, there was, critics could be found who preferred the foreign expression.

Edward Bysshe[1] remarks that there are words 'such as are never met with but in the Mouth of the Vulgar, and never us'd, either in Conversation or Writing, by the better and more Polite sort of People. The French call them *Des Mots Bas*, but our language scarce allows us a term to distinguish them by.' In an age that was to be so free with 'low', it is hard to see why Bysshe was worried. George Campbell[2] is on surer ground when he defends *encroachment* and *purport* because 'we have no single words in English' to express their precise meaning perfectly. These two had been English for centuries—indeed they were Anglo-French by origin. It is likely that they were disliked not because they were 'French' but because they were legal terms that had strayed into general use.

A gentleman calling himself Peter Pikestaff who furnishes the *Town and Country Magazine* in 1781 with an amusing list of fashionable French affectations, approves of *à propos* because 'it cannot be done into English with tolerable success'. We seem to agree.

A reviewer for the *British Critick*[3] discussing Barruel's *Memoirs of*

[1] *Art of English Poetry*, 27, iii.
[2] *Phil. of Rhet.*, p. 164.   [3] *Brit. Crit.* x (1797), 162.

Jacobinism suggests that *Philosophism* and *Philosophist* might be 'very happily adopted from this work to designate the doctrines and persons of the Deistical sect; and thus to rescue the honourable terms of Philosophy and Philosopher from the long abuse into which they have fallen. *Philosophism* may be interpreted the love of *Sophism*, and thus completely describes the sect of Voltaire: a *Philosophist* is a lover of *Sophists*.' This last definition is hardly fair or by analogy: the whole suggestion was a more specific recommendation than the one made five years before that *Philosophism* should be used to mean any abuse of Philosophy. The depreciatory senses had begun in France: it is a useful distinction, though of course one man's *philosophism* may be another man's *philosophy*.

A French word adopted despite some protest is *Presentiment*. Baker[1] says it is wrongly translated as pre-sentiment, for that has no meaning. 'It ought to be translated (as it is by some few) "pre-sensation" which word would be very useful in our language, and ought therefore to be adopted. The French word does not signify a fore-knowledge, but an unaccountable fore-feeling of what will happen.'

When we think on any meaning *sentiment* has ever had in English we can see that this is fair comment. *Presensation* perhaps stresses the physical feeling too much. *Foreboding* implies only a sense of disaster. *Presage* can mean also an omen. It is not surprising that we accepted the new French word. Baker[2] also felt that we wanted a word to answer to the French verb *ménager*, where it signifies *to treat with tenderness or caution, from the fear of giving offence by a rougher behaviour*. As he says, *manage*, used by some in this sense, will not do, because its ordinary English senses obtrude themselves. The *Critical Review*[3] independently agreed—*ménager quelqu'un* is improperly rendered by to *manage*; indeed, there is no one English word which expresses the idea. Baker wonders whether there is 'no word in Greek or Latin which bears the sense of this French verb, and no other sense, and which word ought to be Anglicized'. It seems as if there is none to be found.

Aeronaut[4] (what would they have thought of *cosmonaut*?) and *aerostat* were taken over bodily. The *European Magazine* used them in 1784, the year after the first balloon ascent. A French inscription to

---

[1] *Remarks*, LIV.   [2] ibid., CXLVII.

[3] *Crit. Rev.* new arr. xxi (1797), 159, *à propos* of a translation of Mme de Montier.

[4] *Aeronautics* was virtually in existence in 1753. *O.E.D.*'s quotations for this word make astonishing reading in the 1960's.

the memory of some unfortunate pioneers of air travel who were killed when they tried to reach England 'dans un aerostat' was translated in this Magazine in 1786, but the words for men and machine were left as they stood. About the same time, the *Critical Review*[1] was pointing out that *aerostation* was a badly formed word—it ought to be *aerostatation*. From *aerostat*, according to analogy, the substantive is formed, not by adding *tion*, but *ation*. *Aerostation* must be derived from *aerost*, which has no meaning.' This is true; it is, says *O.E.D.*, an improper formation—but as long as we used the word, we left it at that.

Naiveté was welcomed: it was one of Melantha's strange collection, but it came into its own in the eighteenth century and fills a gap, particularly as *ingenuous* could hardly then serve as a base for a noun, owing to contemporary confusion with *ingenious*.[2] The *Critical Review*[3] calls it 'elegant and expressive', and perhaps as difficult to translate as the *simplex munditiis* of Horace. Dennis[4] had defined it as 'a charming simplicity, dictated by pure Nature'. Shenstone[5] thought *naive* was used by the French 'in such a sense as to be explainable by no English word; unless we will submit to restrain ourselves in the application of the word sentimental. It means the language of passion, or the heart; in opposition to the language of reflection and the head.' Hume[6] tells us he has borrowed *naivety* to describe Sancho Panza—it 'is wanted in our language'. Lady Mary Wortley Montagu had used it in 1725. It has come a long way since the *Glossographia Anglicana Nova* (1707) defined *naif* as what 'looks quick and natural, a Term apply'd to Jewels'.

When we are told[7] that the famous actress Mrs Pritchard 'has been in figure more than what the French call "embonpoint"', we feel that a more forthright English description might have been lacking in gallantry, even if the original saving clause had followed—'yet she never lost either her ease or vivacity'.

The phrase 'what the French call' this or that is a sure signal that some Englishman is about to do the same: the English language has often benefited by the theft. How else should we describe the kind of composition that is now summed up as *recherché*?[8] Or that particularly dramatic quality which produces what the French call 'a happy

---

[1] *Crit. Rev.* 59 (1785), 340.   [2] See below, pp. 119–20.
[3] *Crit. Rev.* 53 (1782), 343. Goldsmith had said much the same in 1765 (Essay XII).
[4] *Critical Works*, ii, 161.   [5] *Works*, ii, 275.
[6] Footnote, p. 194, 1742 edn. of Hume's *Essays*.
[7] *Ann. Reg.* xi (1768), Characters, p. 35.   [8] *Crit. Rev.* 24 (1767), 124.

coup de théâtre'?[1] Or a *platitude*?[2] But why did the *Critical Review*[3] refer to 'that warmth of expression and a devout sense of religion, or what the French call *onction*'? We already had *unction* and it had not so far been spoiled—'anything that excites piety and devotion' says Johnson, and this may be the key. For *onction* is wanted to express the *response* to the excitement, and the eighteenth century was not to know that the nineteenth would have cause to grow tired of pseudo-excitements and the inevitable insincere responses. This one did not catch on. Nor did *Enflure* (as the French call it) which Spence[4] used of Pope's 'profusion of Glitter and Embroidery in the Language'. It seems a word hard-packed with meaning but there is no recognition of it in *O.E.D.* or the *Stanford Dictionary*. Another word that did not find acceptance, but might well have been useful, appears in the remark about a German art collection that contained 'more trash and remplissage' than any the visitor had ever seen. It is a good word for 'things-put-in-merely-to-fill-up'.[5] A word that enables us to make a real distinction is *verbiage*. Ruffhead accusing Pope of what the French call *Verbiage* in his 'Alps on Alps arise' passage notes that he would not use the word if English had one as expressive.[6] George Campbell[7] tells us that *verbosity* is an offence against vivacity, verbiage against perspicuity.

The varying estimate of the worth of French words can be clearly seen in the *Critical Review*'s[8] comment in 1775.

'We are obliged to the French for a great number of terms and phrases, some of them used by men of taste and learning; others only by the *coxcombs* of both sexes, who *affect* to speak à la Mode de Paris.' The list includes *connoisseur, premier, etiquette, vis à vis, tête à tête, fracas, bon mot, billet doux, bagatelle, manœuvre, je ne sçais quoi, jeu d'esprit, mauvaise (honte), éclaircissement, à propos, bon ton, rouge, dishabillé, ragoût, fricassée, tour, route, levée, finesse, foible, caprice, douceur, embonpoint*. Not all of these were new, and most of them seem to have come to stay, having proved useful in some sense or other.

Tête-à-tête is innocent enough now, and does *not* even mean what 'laying heads together' means. There is no intrigue, amorous or other, in it now. This is no thanks to the *Town and Country Magazine* which

---

[1] *Crit. Rev.* 27 (1769), 80.
[3] *Crit. Rev.* 27 (1769), 78.
[5] *Gent. Mag.* lxv (1795), 38.
[7] *Phil. of Rhet.*, p. 115.

[2] *Month. Rev.* lxxviii (1788), 315.
[4] On Pope's *Homer*, p. 60.
[6] *Life of Pope*, p. 81.
[8] *Crit. Rev.* 39 (1775), 49.

gave it a peculiar twist unrecognized by O.E.D. or the *Stanford Dictionary* despite the reference in *The School for Scandal*. The periodical ran a series of articles describing the amours of certain ladies and gentlemen, miniatures of whom, identified by initials or nicknames, preceded the stories *tête-à-tête* (or *vis-à-vis*). Apparently these pieces of scandal were popular—it is easy enough to guess in what publications we should find their modern counterparts—and the Magazine's own comment has a familiar ring. 'With respect to the History of Têtes à Têtes,' says the Preface to Volume ii, 'we shall only remark that it was not undertaken to gratify malignity, or to indulge impertinent curiosity, but to hold up a mirror to the *offending parties*; by which they might see their own likeness reflected in such a manner as to force them to renounce the *fashionable vices* of the age.'

We tend to associate *ci-devant* primarily with the fate of the people of the Old Regime under the new, but this handy expression appears in English with no such connotation.[1] Burke was speaking in 1790 of a *ci-devant* friend, and nearer the end of the century two witnesses in a prosecution for gaming were described as Lady B's *ci-devant* servants.[2]

It was all very well for satirists to laugh at *Bon Ton*, that 'cant phrase . . . for the fashionable air of conversation and manners' but the definition, however sarcastic, that Mrs Montagu[3] gives it in itself shows we cannot convey the idea as well if we do not use the phrase. 'In conversation, it is not wit; in manner, it is not politeness; in behaviour, it is not address; but it is a little like them all. It can belong to people of a certain rank, who live in a certain manner with certain persons, who have no certain vices, and who inhabit a certain part of the town.'

Was *Belles Lettres* really wanted? The *Monthly Review*[4] thought it a 'frippery French phrase' and that we are under no necessity of resorting to it while 'polite literature' is good English. This was in 1777: by 1781 the *Review* had a section headed *Belles Lettres*, in reference to the Royal Academy of Berlin, and was referring to the progress of the belles-lettres and sciences in Germany. *Polite* has changed from polished and elegant to merely mannerly, so there might have been misunderstanding if the earlier phrase had been kept. *Amateur* and *Connoisseur* have proved their worth, though the former has shifted its ground from lover to the inexpert and the latter has become compatible with

---

[1] *O.E.D.* s.v. [2] *Ann. Reg.* xxxix (1797), 17 (Rivington).
[3] Lyttelton, *Dialogues of the Dead*, xxx. The 'cant phrase' quotation is the *Annual Register*'s footnote to its reprint of Mrs Montagu's contribution, iii, 262.
[4] *Month. Rev.* lvii (1777), 405.

scholarship. *Critique* was a useful distinction from *critic* on the one side and *criticism* on the other. *Silhouette* and *platitude* fill obvious gaps. 'Je ne sçais quoi'[1] which the eighteenth century discussed at length and with every degree of seriousness or lack of it, is still a useful phrase. Even Peter Pikestaff approved of it: 'I do not know what to substitute in the room of . . . these four words.' 'Words to be felt, never to be translated,' said a story-teller in the *Town and Country Magazine* in 1770. Spence[2] thinks it is really the equivalent of grace: a face may have no good feature in it and yet 'have a very taking Air', because of 'the Sensibility of the Eyes, the general good-humoured Turn of the Look, and perhaps a little agreeable Smile about the Mouth. And these Three Things . . . would go a great way toward accounting for the *Je ne sçais quoi*, or that inexplicable Pleasingness of the Face (as they choose to call it) which is so often talked of, and so little understood. . . .'

Hogarth[3] states that the expression is 'become a fashionable phrase for grace'.

Uvedale Price thinks it is 'not precisely beauty', but that it is something that produces 'striking and pleasing effects'.[4]

The opposition thought the phrase a modish substitute for hard-thinking in the critic, or good character in the subject of praise. The *Gentleman's Magazine*[5] will sum it up—it is 'the cant of all ignorant pretenders to taste and delicacy and an excellent phrase for those who can assign no reason for their opinion'. It is still true, nevertheless, that we cannot always put our finger on exactly what it is we find attractive or impressive.

The *Monthly* Reviewers claimed[6] that they were not fond of using Gallicisms, but admitted that now and then, when our language seems to fail, they were tempted to transgress their own rules. In 1788 they spoke of the '*toute ensemble* of a play, which, notwithstanding one or two tolerable scenes, and a few good passages', was what the French call a platitude, and they noted[7] a little later that 'we want a better term than *whole* to express the French *Ensemble*'. *Ensemble* or *toute ensemble* was a succinct term that could be applied to the total effect made by a complex structure, such as the Duke of Argyll's castle at Inveraray,[8] or

---

[1] For its origins, see R. L. Brett, *The Third Earl of Shaftesbury*.
[2] 'Sir Harry Beaumont', *Crito*, p. 31.
[3] *Analysis of Beauty*, vii.   [4] *Essay*, i, 87.
[5] *Gent. Mag.* lxv (1795), 24.
[6] *Month. Rev.* lxxviii (1788), 215.
[7] ibid., p. 555.   [8] *Literary Magazine*, v (1790), 273.

a mountain view,[1] or a complicated literary work.[2] The nineteenth century extended it to musicians, and the twentieth to ladies' dress and mathematics.

Cordon (used of men) and *Dénouement* have proved to be useful technicalities. So in its smaller way has *chenille*, which the *Annual Register*[3] defined as the silk twist used in tambour work, *à propos* of the punning epitaph on a lady who preferred tambour work to cards—

> Stretch'd in my frame, I'm compass'd now
> With worms instead of lively snails—

the snails being the English version of 'chenille', though the word really means a hairy caterpillar. Either way, it is perhaps best left comfortably in French.

Carte blanche, débris, deficit, egotism, maraud, nonchalant, persiflage, reconnoitre, sortie, are other useful words that we owe to eighteenth-century users and popularisers who were undeterred by adverse comment. *Ennui* deserves a closer look, partly because of the state of mind the discussion reveals—it is a curious mixture of national pride and unreality. The *Monthly Review*[4] considers *lassitude* a bungling translation, for that implies the 'state of debility and dejection which succeeds hard labour'. But *ennui* has no connection with labour of any sort and has been known 'even among kings, princes, lazy lords and fine ladies. According to our Author's definition, *ennui* is that languour and stagnation of body and mind which proceed from inactivity and the absence of all lively sensations that give us an agreeable information of any existence and well-being.' *Listlessness* was another version and so was 'weariness of life'. A writer in the *Gentleman's Magazine*[5] remarked that '*ennuy, ennuyeux, ennuyer, s'ennuyer*, are familiar with the most illiterate French, and yet surprising it is that we cannot express their meaning without great difficulty and circumlocution, notwithstanding we often feel their influence more than any other nation'. Eleven years later, the same Magazine[6] was again commenting on 'that singular word *Ennui*, so expressive, so emphatic, so current, . . . for which we have no synonyms or equivalent. It is hard for us to have the malady so exactly from the French without the power to express it, which surely is an aggravation of the evil. We are, in fact, perishing of the thing for which we have not a name.'

[1] *Month. Rev.* lxviii (1788), 555.   [2] Spence, on Pope's *Homer*, ii, 110.
[3] *Ann. Reg.* xvi (1773), 124.   [4] *Month. Rev.* lv (1776), 144.
[5] *Gent. Mag.* lvii (1787), 118.   [6] *Gent. Mag.* lxviii (1798), 663.

It seems clear that however much the word was wanted 'the generality of Anglo-Gallic Philosophers' who believed we have 'no word of
our own to express[1] it, were wrong. Mrs Montagu[2] says that her father
suffered from it, but in his time it was the 'hyp' or 'the vapours'.[3]
She adds that 'it is a distemper so well bred as never to come but when
people are at home and at leisure', for it is 'the disease of an idle imagination'.

TECHNICALITIES, DISTINCTIONS AND ABSTRACTIONS

The most fertile fields of verbal invention lie in the realms of
technical terms, fine distinctions and abstractions. Literary critics,
philosophers, politicians, physicians and observers of the social scene
are frequently full of a sense of the inadequacy of the vocabulary at
their disposal. 'Questions purely verbal are frivolous,' says Gerard,[4]
but goes on 'Yet it is often of importance to ascertain the precise
meaning of words, because impropriety in the use of them may occasion confusion of thought, and errors in reasoning. This holds true
especially of those words which denote the leading ideas on any
subject, for these ideas, set in a wrong light, would necessarily introduce improper modes of expression, and even false conclusions.'

If we have *solidity* and *fluidity*, why not *vaporosity*? The question is
mooted by the *Monthly Review*[5] in 1788. Actually the word had been
used early in the sixteenth century and was to be used early in the
nineteenth—but the eighteenth thought it had no authenticity. But the
Review rightly concluded that if science wanted it, it must be used.
Other wanted scientific words are *infiltration, Family of Languages,
Plit, Puddling* and *Trimestre*. In 1779, the *Monthly Review* (lxi, 499)
was conveying the findings of the Royal Academy of Sciences at
Paris, and describing how the 'void spaces in lava are often observed
to be filled up by infiltrations', and implied that the reader should
pardon this term, which is expressive and wanted. This was seventeen
years before the first illustration in *O.E.D.*, whose article shows that
the word was to have a useful future in several scientific senses, as well
as in military and political contexts.

Joseph Priestley[6] suggests that the Eastern tongues related to
Arabic could be called a family rather than a genus—he anticipates

[1] *European Magazine*, xi (1787), 253.   [2] *Letters*, p. 11.
[3] *Letters*, p. 30.   [4] *Essay on Taste*, Appendix.
[5] *Month. Rev.* lxxix (1788), 587.   [6] *Universal Grammar*, p. 117.

Whitney, whom *O.E.D.* credits with this useful invention, by over ninety years. Marshall, the agriculturalist, feels we want a word for the soil turned by the plough: the furrow is the trench—what is the ridge of earth? He thinks *plait* or *fold* sounds like a word for milliners or laundry-maids rather than ploughmen. Why go to Greek or Latin if we can find a word agreeable to English analogy: it *is* English if it conforms to this condition. 'A spade is a hand-plow; a plow is a spade worked by cattle. The portion of earth turned by a spade is, in English, a *spit*; and the writer will not hesitate to call the portion of earth turned by the plow, a plit.'[1] It is an interesting example of the deliberately made word, and it was adopted. The *Monthly Review*[2] defends the technicality *puddling* used by 'that great engineer' Mr Brindley—the process of making watertight by means of a clay lining. 'We have no other term in the English language to express the idea conveyed by it.' *Trimestre*[3] struck the same Review as a useful word to cover a space of three months, the time covered by a quarterly publication. With the spelling anglicised to *trimester*, it came eventually early the next century.

Lord Kames comments in his *Elements of Criticism*[4] on a figure of speech, 'which, among related objects, extends the Properties of one to another', and he notes that it has not yet been dignified with a proper name because it has been overlooked by writers. His examples include giddy brink, jovial wine, daring wound, dim religious light. His index enters this under 'Attributes transferred by a figure of speech from one subject to another.' It is well on the way to our simpler name Transferred Epithet. Gerard in his *Essay on Genius*[5] notes 'What is called an *experimentum crucis* in philosophical enquiries': it is strange that the English *crucial experiment* had to wait till 1869.

Uvedale Price[6] is in difficulty how to sum up that *want* of form, that unshapen, lumpish appearance, which, perhaps, no one word exactly expresses. We wonder what is wrong with *formlessness*. It is in Bailey's Dictionary, but not in Johnson's, and *O.E.D.*'s first examples are from Coleridge and Carlyle. Or *shapelessness?* For this, *O.E.D.* has no quotations between Golding in 1587 and a newspaper of 1872. We must sympathise with Price's comment that we can indeed explain what we mean by a few more words; but whatever enables us to convey our ideas with greater precision and fidelity must be a real improvement to language. From this point of view the language has benefited

---

[1] Quoted *Month. Rev.* lx (1779), 254.   [2] *Month. Rev.* lxxviii (1788), 371.
[3] *Month. Rev.* lxxvii (1788), 154.   [4] p. 268.   [5] p. 92.   [6] *Essay*, i, 205.

by the welcome given to *acme* and *nemesis* as technical terms—indeed *acme* is popular now. Goldsmith[1] was still using them as obvious foreigners in their original Greek dress.

Edward Young[2] was not satisfied with Blank Verse, because '*blank* is a term of diminution; what we mean by blank verse is verse unfallen, uncurst; verse reclaim'd'. He begs his friend Richardson 'to crown it with some nobler name' and not 'let the greatness of the thing be under the defamation of such a name'.

A literary technicality they seem to have forgotten is *quatrain*—Jackson[3] of Exeter in 1798 tells us he assumes the word 'to save the trouble of frequently using the long term of the four-line stanza'. The word is in Johnson, but *O.E.D.* has no eighteenth-century examples. 'I wish', says Jackson,[4] 'we had some word in our language to express the same idea in poetry as *Crescendo* does in music; *swell* is applied to many other purposes, that it has not the effect of an appropriated term.'

Among the useful technicalities introduced at this period are the archaeological word *trilithon*[5] and the political *cede*. Mrs Piozzi[6] thought Dr Johnson would not have thought well of using *cede* as a transitive verb—his dictionary recognises no such verb transitive or otherwise. The evidence of *O.E.D.* shows that it was in general use by the mid-century; it had been applied to land in 1762. What Mrs Piozzi said of it is fair comment: 'it is so neat a word, so elegant, so easily understood as being of Roman original . . . Speaking of islands given up by one nation to another, when peace is made, what word can be so proper to call them by, as the islands newly ceded to Great Britain.'

But it is in our more complex thought that we feel the need to be more and more precise, and the difficulty keeps pace with the necessity. Should a man 'undetermined in his opinions' be called a sceptic? Eighteenth-century philosophers in England agreed with the *Gentleman's Magazine*[7] that *speculatist* would be a proper word. The Magazine had in mind Mr Henderson, a correspondent of Mr Priestley, and considered that where his opinions seemed to be fixed, he was, if such a word may be used, a *credulist*. (It had been used a year previously, *O.E.D.* tells us.) *Sceptic* to the philosopher and to the man in the street

---

[1] *Essays* 1765, xii, xiii.   [2] *Conjectures on Original Composition*, p. 27.
[3] *Four Ages*, p. 321.   [4] *Thirty Letters*, ii, 26.
[5] Invented by William Stukeley to describe Stonehenge.
[6] *Brit. Syn.*, ii, 40. *O.E.D.* gives 1798 for ceding land, but see Bute to Bedford in the Bedford Correspondence, iii, 152.
[7] *Gent. Mag.* lix (1789), 497.

certainly conveys very different totals of meaning and emotion. In the eighteenth-century a valiant attempt was made to keep *free-thinker*[1] colourless—neither a smear-word to the orthodox nor a rallying-call to the unbeliever, but emotion is usually too strong for philosophic dispassionateness. It was generally observed that there are not enough names for our emotions. Ought there not to be a word for the good emotion that corresponds to Remorse? We can be glad to have done good actions. If we feel shame when we give way, what do we feel when we resist temptation?[2] I suspect that a medieval moralist would have found the name among the twiglets of Pride on the Tree of the Deadly Sins, and not thought it a virtue at all.

Hume[3] was right linguistically as well as psychologically when he pointed out that English does not exactly fix the boundaries between virtues and talents, vices and defects. He might have added that there is a penumbra where virtue may easily pass into vice. And for many people one man's virtue is another man's vice. Party politics, self-interest, a lack of firm standards, could produce complete confusion of terms even if we had them nicely differentiated. Hume, however, after admitting that *Pride* is 'commonly taken in a bad sense', argues that it is an 'indifferent' sentiment, good or bad according as it is well or ill-founded, and according to the other circumstances which accompany it.

Dugald Stewart[4] draws attention to the dual use of *Memory*—a 'retentive' memory means the capacity to 'treasure up and preserve for future use the knowledge we acquire'. A 'ready' memory means the power of recalling our knowledge when we want to use it. He suggests that we should appropriate *recollections* to this latter idea. Wordsworth's 'emotion recollected in tranquillity' illustrates this precisely.

Mr Spectator[5] wonders why we have no name for the 'very contrary

---

[1] e.g., definition quoted in *Gent. Mag.* iv, 541. 'A Free-thinker is one who is *free* or *ready*, to enquire into the Meaning and Truth of any Proposition that merits an Examination.' And contrast *Month. Rev.* xiii (1755), 134, which claims to be using the word in its best sense 'not in the vulgar acceptation which generally implies a compound character, made up of ignorance, infidelity and profligacy'. Cp. Ambrose Philips' Magazine, *The Free-Thinker*, 1718–21.

Sceptic in the philosophers' sense dates from the late sixteenth century, and began to be more widely (and more superficially) used in the seventeenth. See *O.E.D.* s.v.

[2] F. Hutcheson, *Passions and Affections*, p. 66.

[3] *Enquiries concerning the Human Understanding*, Sections 261–2–3.

[4] *Elements*, p. 397.   [5] *Spect.* (374).

of Procrastination: not being too anxious to hurry on, but being too anxious to look back'—since 'most of us take occasion to sit still, and throw away the time in our possession, by Retrospect on what is past, imagining we have already acquitted ourselves, and established our characters in the sight of Mankind'. No doubt this is what is now known as 'resting on our oars'—or even, 'on our laurels'!

At times, our critics want the language to be more precise than common sense requires. 'A statue between every pillar' is illogical, though we are in no doubt as to what it means. What's wrong with 'between every two pillars'? But that is not enough for Mr R. Baker[1]— 'it does not convey neatly the idea intended, which is that there is one statue and no more between every two pillars that are next to each other'. He thinks *proximate* would not be an improper word in the required sense. Later he advocates *priorly*—it 'seems a wonder we have no such word', and it would be 'a very useful one'.[2] 'I had like to have done' or 'I am like to do' struck him as very awkward and uncouth phrases and he wishes some respectable writer whom the rest of the world would not disdain to follow, would invent some other concise, and better phrase, to signify the same thing. 'I nearly did it' satisfies us for the past tense: but how do we express nearness to a contingency in the future? 'I shall probably do it'? 'I expect I'll do it'?

CONFUSIONS AND DISTINCTIONS

Some critics put their energy into advocating distinctions between similar words. It may be that the forms are subject to easy confusion like *lie* and *lay*, *fly* and *flee*, or their meanings, like *mutual* and *common*. The *lie–lay* muddle the eighteenth century did disentangle and brought us back, much against the grain, to the original distinction of function as it existed in Anglo-Saxon. Much the same applies to *sit* and *set*. Well-educated people confused these pairs. But in other instances, it is chastening for the modern critic to notice how the critics of this period tried to keep useful words sharp when people were blunting them by indiscriminate use, and to reflect how often we go on contentedly with the damaged words. It would have been useful if we had remembered Withers'[3] dictum that *fly* and *flee* both 'imply MOTION, but the Modes of Motion differ as an Attack differs from a Retreat'. Of course we

---

[1] *Remarks*, CLXV. *Between*, of course, does not make *two* tautologous in our usage.
[2] ibid., CCVII.   [3] *Aristarchus*, p. 211. Cp. Baker, *Remarks*, XXXVIII.

have other uses for *fly*. We often prefer *propose* to *purpose*, making as little use of the latter as they did then. Withers puts the distinction neatly: 'We PROPOSE Doubts, Questions, and Projects to Others. But PURPOSE is not dependent on external will.' Much the same is true of the old *mutual-common* problem, about which Baker[1] says sensibly 'It must be owned, after all, that there are places where the word *common*, though more proper in respect of its sense, would sound awkward, and where, for want of an easy-sounding word in the language of the same import, *mutual* must be borne with.' It is the possibility of a social misunderstanding that makes *common* suspect. The eighteenth century tried to save the connection of *demean* with *demeanour*, but *mean* in the sense of *low* was too much for it.

In 1796 the *Critical Review*[2] makes an observation interesting in view of recent developments, that the French 'very incorrectly use consommer and consommation for consume and consumption. Words of obviously different meaning and etymology.' It seems to be a growing habit of the English to pronounce *consummation* as if it were *consumation*—even a good actor may be heard declaiming 'Tis a consumation devoutly to be wished.'

The distinction between *hanged* and *hung* was stressed. The *Monthly Review*[3] says that *hanged* is the more solemn word. It should be 'adopted in all cases where it denotes strangling'. To use *hung* in this sense 'is a sort of modish modern phrase which occasions a needless ambiguity. We would naturally say that a man *hung* by a branch, meaning that he voluntarily laid hold of it or was accidentally caught by it'. But if he was *hanged* on a tree, it would mean 'he was strangled by being suspended from it by the neck'. Some years later the *Gentleman's Magazine*[4] illustrated the difference neatly—it is 'a common vulgarism' to say 'highwaymen were *hung*'. It is correct to say that 'he was hanged, and afterwards hung in chains'.

The attempt to distinguish the naval *engagement* from the land *battle* or *fight* strikes us as wire-drawn. The *Monthly Review*[5] condemns any confusion of these terms as ignorance or negligence, and Trusler agrees. Dr Johnson lays no restrictions on *engagement*, but he does define a battle as 'an encounter between opposite armies'. *Particular* and *pecu-*

---

[1] *Remarks*, XLIII.
[2] *Crit. Rev.* new arr. xvii (1796), 542. The French have semantic excuses that we have not. See Alfred Ewert, *The French Language* (1947), § 586.
[3] *Month. Rev.* lx (1779), 173.   [4] *Gent. Mag.* lxvii (1797), 567.
[5] *Month. Rev.* xlvi (1772), 460. But why do we restrict *army* to the land?

CONFUSIONS AND DISTINCTIONS   119

liar, says Blair,[1] are often confounded. The former stands opposed to
general, the latter to what is *possessed* in common. This is still true of
peculiar in some technical and limited contexts, but the connotation of
odd that *peculiar* now carries most strongly[2] did not enter into his mind
—there is no hint of it in Johnson, and *particular* had not then acquired
any idea of fussiness (a nineteenth-century development). What it
could do was to serve in the modern colloquial sense of *peculiar*. The
eighteenth-century recommendation here holds good in literary English rather than in colloquial.

The eighteenth century made an effort to clear up the all-too-pos-
sible confusion between *ingenious* and *ingenuous* at least so far as their
nouns were concerned. The confusion seems to have been widespread.
The Cocker-Hawkins Dictionary defines *ingenious* as 'ready-witted'
and *ingenuous* as good-humoured, well-born and bred—not our idea
of the word[3]—and says these two words are often confounded. One
who did not confound them was Vicesimus Knox who refers to an
'ingenious and ingenuous boy'.[4] Mrs Piozzi[5] puts *ingenuity* with
candour, openness and sincerity, explaining that 'time has taught us
however to annex meaner ideas to the word ingenuity, made peculiar
in these late days to petty contrivances and subtleness of skill, in the
mechanic arts particularly, and from these taken up, half-figuratively,
to express the operations of the mind'. Francis Grose[6] notices the
muddle—'ingenious is often substituted for ingenuous. Come, be
ingenious and tell the truth, is an exhortation frequently used by
justices' clerks to culprit poachers.' It seems they need not have been
descendants of Dogberry or Verges. Baker[7] was right in thinking it a
'blemish in our language that the word *ingenuity* has two senses; for
hereby it often becomes unintelligible'. Is it the noun of *ingenious* or
ingenuous? The context does not necessarily help since the word
signifies 'two excellent mental qualities, *ability* and candour' and so
we are at a loss to know which is meant. He suggests that the noun
for *ingenious* ought to be *ingeniety* (with the accent on the *ni*)—it
would 'be both useful and ornamental'. 'I have known', he adds,
'some persons, who, to avoid ambiguity, have made use of the word
ingeniousness. This is not a word much authorised by custom, yet, as

---

[1] Blair's Critique of *Spect.* 411 (Lecture 20).   [2] 'mod. coll.' *O.E.D.*
[3] Contrast *Month. Rev.* xxxvi (1767), 521, which translates *L'Ingenu* as 'The
Man of Nature'—'We are not quite pleased with it ourselves, but it was the best
word we could think of.'
[4] *Essays*, ii, 296.   [5] *Brit. Syn.*, i, 318.   [6] *Olio*, xxii.   [7] *Remarks*, x.

the sense of it cannot be mistaken, I would not condemn anyone that
should employ it.' Pegge agreed over *ingeniety*, and wanted *ingenuosity*
(like *impetuosity*) for *ingenuous*.[1]

We assume that *ingenuity* goes with *ingenious*, and that *ingenuousness*
is the word that goes with *ingenuous*. The former is badly made, and it
isn't easy to see why the latter suits us when *ingeniousness* is less
popular. But at least we have our solution, though not on eighteenth-
century lines. Here, historically, the period was trying to clear up an
inherited confusion. It produced another of its own when it shifted
nervous from the idea of *strength* to that of *weakness*—via 'nervous
diseases'.

When Dr Cheyne in 1734 published his study, *On Nervous Diseases*,
it was a disordered state of the nerves that he was dealing with, medical
treatises being naturally on defective states of the body. Pegge,
following Dr Johnson, calls the word 'medical cant' and notes that it
used to mean muscular strength, a strong and forcible style, but is now
'used only in a contrary sense' to express a man whose nerves are
weak, and even absolute enervation. He suggests '*nervish* man' and
'*nervish* disorder', bidding us note *waspish, devilish, feverish*—all expressive of bad qualities or disordered habits.[2] It would have been a
useful word: the amazing thing is that *nervous* could live so long with
double and contradictory senses. It is a good example of the technical
term being taken to the public's heart—the nervousness of the 'genteel'
and even of those who weren't, became a subject for satire and a standing joke. As the *Looker-on*[3] remarked, 'Porters complain of the weakness of their nerves, and chairmen [i.e. carriers of sedans] are not
seldom affected with lowness of spirits. Not a snug party at tea but
some lady feels somehow she don't know how.' It was left for the
twentieth century to use *nervy* to mean 'jumpy'.

In social matters there are suggestions for new words to cover a
variety of things, from frivolous to serious. There ought to be a different word[4] for a visit of fifteen days from the one for that of fifteen
minutes. Starting with *visit* for the norm, why not *visitation* for the
unduly long, and *vis* for the unduly short? It seems a good idea. And
would not a gentleman called a 'Town Usher'[5] be a good institution
to attend on awkward country cousins, to show them the sights 'and

---

[1] *Anecdotes*, pp. 212–13.

[2] op. cit., 213: but his comparisons seem irrelevant—it is the nouns *wasp, devil,
fever* that mean something bad, not the *-ish* ending. The trouble with *nerve* is
precisely its ambiguity.   [3] iii, 323.   [4] *World* (62).   [5] op. cit. (164).

instruct them how to wonder and shut their mouths at the same time'?

Two other words connected with social intercourse may be added, one that did not catch on, and one that did.

Mrs Piozzi[1] knows that in public schools a dull boy is called a *blunt* and she thinks the term 'so good' that she 'sighs for its removal into social life, where blunts are exceedingly frequent, and we have no word for them'. We can indeed speak of Joan Blunt—but she may well be sharp.

Lord Kames invented *dissocial* (1762) as *O.E.D.*[2] confirms. Kames considers it well made—it is perspicuous, and it is in the tone of the language. But does it add very much to the older *unsociable?*

Lord Chesterfield, always interested in the social scene, thinks we ought to have a word for *les mœurs.*[3] 'Manners are too little, morals too much.' What sums up 'A general exterior decency, fitness, and propriety of conduct in the common intercourse of life'? Decorum? The word was not new, but he is giving a very special colour to it. *Decency, seemliness*, says Dr Johnson of *decorum*, with no suggestion that the decency need be only an external thing. It is a much more serious matter when, in the same essay, Chesterfield tells us that the French accuse us, perhaps too justly, of having no word in our language which answers to their word *police*, which therefore we have been obliged to adopt, not having, as they say, the thing.[4] The word in eighteenth-century English has a meaning that no longer springs easily to the mind: we think of 'the police' as the officers of the law, not of the system of control they carry out. The responsibilities of the police then included affairs that come under Highway and Housing Committees now such as cleanliness of the streets and demolition of unsafe houses. The *Critical Review*[5] states that 'The English Language can yet hardly be said to have naturalized the word *Police*, which is a plain proof that the thing itself is but little understood among us. Of late indeed, we have seen it used with great parade, in the narrow and confined sense of thief-*catching*: whereas it not only includes the punishment of villainy, but the maintenance of order, uniformity, and neatness in cities and public buildings, and the regulating of the lower class of the people, the idle and indigent, in such a manner as to prevent them from being a nuisance to society; at least this is the sense in which

---

[1] *Brit. Syn.*, i, 176. [2] See *O.E.D.* s.v.
[3] *World* (189), 1756.
[4] ibid. [5] *Crit. Rev.* 16 (1763), 30.

it is used by our neighbours in France.'[1] A definition enlightening in more ways than one.

The history of how a distinction was made between the sublime and the beautiful can be read in Francis Hutcheson, Hume and Burke, and their modern editors and commentators—it is a philosophic question rather than a linguistic. But the attempts of Burke (and of Alison) to impose new definitions on *Delight* are interesting examples of how the language of common use will resist even a great man's well-meant effort to channel it where the main stream of the language is determined not to go.

Burke was troubled by the use of *Pleasure* for both a positive and a relative feeling. 'Whenever I have occasion to speak of this species of relative pleasure, I call it Delight.'[2] He admits that this is not the common use—but thought 'it better to take up a word already known, and to limit its signification than to introduce a new one which would not perhaps incorporate so well with the language'. He uses *Delight* 'to express the sensation which accompanies the removal of pain or danger'. The *Critical Review*[3] disapproved of this attempt to define delight in connection with grief. We may ask what is wrong with *relief*, a word used of removal of anxiety in the fourteenth century—it is first noted in John Gower, 1390, and in the sense of freedom from pain in the seventeenth. Alison,[4] on the other hand, wants to relate *Delight* to *Taste*, and to make it 'signify the peculiar pleasure which attends the Emotions of *Taste* or which is felt *when the imagination is employed in the prosecution of a regular train of ideas or emotion*'.

The *Critical Review*[5] notices that in English 'we have but one adjective to distinguish what relates to policy and politics: the word political is ambiguous'. The modern world has solved this problem by simply using the noun *policy* as an adjective, so that we can speak of a policy statement, which may or may not be political: this use is not recognized even in the Supplement to the Oxford Dictionary, or the 1964 *Concise Oxford Dictionary*.

TASTE AND COLOUR

It is not only the niceties of thoughts and attitudes that clamour for exact expression. So do physical complexes. 'There is in some flowers

[1] See Charles Reith, *The Police Idea* (1938).
[2] *Sublime and Beautiful*, pp. 53, 54.   [3] *Crit. Rev.* 3 (1757), 361.
[4] *Essays*, i, Conclusion, Sect. V.   [5] *Crit. Rev.* 63 (1787), 256.

an exquisite scent, and in some fruits a delicious flavour, to express which no language has a name.'[1] The eighteenth-century critics were far too fond of telling us what every language, or no language, did, on the basis of a very limited knowledge even of European languages: but here Knox is putting his finger on a point where the English language does fail. Is it that *de gustibus non est disputandum* partly because there are no words for the discussion? Yet the language can be made to work even when no appropriate name is forthcoming. Dr Armstrong[2] speaks of the 'crisp' pineapple's 'poignant sweets', which is as far as we can reasonably go. Likewise Spence[3] notices how 'infinitely deficient' are our names for colour. He himself gives the reason—'the different shades and degrees under each of the principal colours are innumerable, and as to the most common of them, it has been doubted by some whether any two leaves, even on the same tree, are exactly the same green'. There must be millions of shades, and all our colour words put together, he reckons, hardly reach fifty. The Anglo-Saxon stock would amount to fewer than a quarter of the fifty—we have increased it by borrowing from abroad, and by taking the names of things that exemplify a colour—cream, orange, cinnamon—and using these as colour words. These three are among those that have become permanent parts of the language. Others, made on the same principle, come and go as Fashion decrees. The modern world has seen battleship-grey, aluminium, clove-carnation, for shades in silk stockings and dress materials, and the eighteenth century could do as much. A lady and a philosopher will tell us about it. Mrs Piozzi[4] seems less impressed than she might have been at the 'dubious and composite colours' that 'strive for the distinction of a season, under appellations unheard of before perhaps'. She mentions 'the emperor's eye' and 'the boue de Paris'. They 'fade and shrink from fashion's train, however—while the primitive tints vary not name or nature so long as the sun endureth'. If *boue de Paris* had been named 'London Mud' it would probably have faded even more quickly.

Dr Alison[5] a few years earlier remarks that a 'plain man would scarcely believe that the Colours of a glass Bottle, of a dead leaf, of Clay, etc. could ever be beautiful: yet within these few years, not only these, but some much more unpleasant colours, that might be mentioned, have been fashionable and admired'. *Filemot* (the dead leaf)

[1] Knox, *Essays*, ii, 99.   [2] *Art of Preserving Health*, ii, 336–7.
[3] Spence on Blacklock, xlvi. Cp. Alison, *Essays*, p. 219.
[4] *Brit. Syn.*, i, 309–10.   [5] *Essays*, pp. 214 f.

and *clay-coloured* were seventeenth-century names, so presumably there were revivals or variants in the 'nineties. *Bottle-green* is Coleridge's invention in 1816, according to *O.E.D.*—one wonders whether he was recalling a term fashionable in his youth.[1]

ART TERMS

Landscape gardening, says Mr Jackson of Exeter in 1798,[2] is an English Art. The term was invented by one of the great exponents of it, Humphry Repton,[3] and it fills the gap noticed in 1755 by the *World* (118) in its comment on the 'modern art of laying out ground (for so we must call it, till a new name be adopted to express so complicated an idea)'—'In an age so liberal of new names, it seems extraordinary', says the periodical (119), 'that these universal connoisseurs have as yet obtained no title of honour or distinction.' After all, they have to be experts in optics, hydrostatics, mechanics, geometry, trigonometry ... is there not a satirical sting in this list, which seems pretty remote from the soil? Against this, Repton in 1795 (ten years before *O.E.D.*'s date) tells us in his *Sketches and Hints on Landscape Gardening*:

To improve the scenery of a country, and to display its native beauties with advantage, is an art which originates in England, and has therefore been called *English Gardening*; yet as this expression is not sufficiently appropriate since gardening in its more confined sense of *Horticulture* has been likewise brought to the greatest perfection in this country, I have adopted the term *Landscape-Gardening* as the most proper, because the art can only be advanced and perfected by the united powers of the *Landscape-Painter* and the *Practical Gardener*.

The new art gave a peculiar twist to the old agricultural words *improve* and *improvement*.[4] (The ornamental estates of England that we so much admire are largely the result of the improver's hand.) But there is a story of a man who wished to die before that other Landscape-Gardener 'Capability' Brown—he felt he would like to see Heaven before Mr Brown had had a chance to 'improve' it!

[1] Cp. Iris Brooke, *Dress and Undress: the Restoration and Eighteenth Century*, p. 123, where bottle green is mentioned with grey and brown as one of the soberer colours towards the end of the century.
[2] *Four Ages*, p. 78.   [3] Quoted in the *British Critick*, vii (1795), 65.
[4] 'the present custom of improving (to use a short though often inaccurate term)', Uvedale Price, *Essay*, i, 2.

The cult of the picturesque was a concomitant, and the word *picturesque* widens and deepens in its connotation. Its complicated history must be read in Christopher Hussey's study: some eighteenth-century comments will illustrate it here. Sir Joshua Reynolds[1] uses it as might be expected of 'all the tricks of art' and speaks of Luca Giordano's 'picturesque compositions': it could be used simply to imply 'giving a picture'—Jackson[2] says a drawing should be 'a *picturesque* view, not a mere outline for the use of navigators: and he finds *The Bard* picturesque—the hero 'is a subject as proper for painting as poetry'. The connection with pictorial composition is frequent: Mason in *The English Garden*[3] advises a choice of colours and plants to give the effect of the foreground, middle distance and background of a painting, referring to Claude and Salvator Rosa. It is the picturesque principle. The *Annual Register* in 1764 was speaking of Landskip, or picturesque gardening—an anticipation of Repton. Richard Jago describes Edge Hill, Scott of Amwell describes his village, and Pope describes a swan gilded by the sun on the Thames in terms of the picturesque—they would all look well in a picture. This application of the word should be the proper one, thought the *Critical Review*[4]—'we would confine it to the principles of the landscape-painter in the arrangement of his objects, the judicious selection of those which ought to be more prominent than the rest, the harmony of grouping and colouring, and the breadth of light and shade'. The Review was discussing Uvedale Price's *Essay on the Picturesque as compared with the Sublime and Beautiful; on the Use of Studying Pictures for the purpose of Improving Real Landscape* (1794). His title stresses his main purpose—to tie the meaning of Picturesque to something opposed to both *beautiful* and *sublime*—'a certain playful wildness of character, and an appearance of irregularity'. He thinks *piquante* means much the same and argues that it applies to music as well as painting or scenery. The word was indeed widely applied. Alison[5] considers the sound of a hunting horn extremely picturesque in seasons of gaiety. We hear of picturesque travellers, the picturesque eye; picturesque hair-styles; no wonder Price thought that 'there are few words whose meaning has been less accurately determined'. Between them, its users shifted its meaning from 'constructed like a picture' to 'suitable

[1] *Journey through Flanders*, pp. 312, 386.
[2] *Letters*, i, 116. *Four Ages*, p. 218.
[3] i, 179–255.   [4] *Crit. Rev.* new arr. xxiii (1798), 427.
[5] *Essays*, p. 154.

for making into a picture'.[1] A comic thrust at the confusion, in which nature could so easily be subordinated to art, is dealt in Graves's *Columella*.[2] The hero's friends admire his 'natural' cascade, and are told that it 'was only copied from a cascade on a much larger scale belonging to Mr. B— ... well known for his skill in painting'. The innuendo surely is that Mr B— arranged his waterfall to look like a picture, and then Mr Milward imitated that.

[1] Cp. John Steegman, *The Rule of Taste*, 1936, p. 14. He calls it 'this unhappy word'.
[2] i, 125.

PART TWO

THE TWENTIETH CENTURY LOOKS BACK

Languages, like most great cities, are of progressive growth under unskilful hands, more attentive to present convenience than to method and uniformity: they do not come under the regulations of grammarians, architects, and surveyors, until they are too far advanced to be new modelled, and will only admit of occasional emendations: where they will not bend to rules, rules are bent to them.

The *Monthly Review*, lii (1775), 393.

V

THE UNKNOWN

THOMAS REID[1] remarks that what is 'peculiar to a nation in its customs, manners or laws, will give occasion to complex notions and words peculiar to the language of that nation. Hence it is easy to see why an *impeachment* and an *attainder*, in the English language, and *ostracism* in the Greek language, have not names answering to them in other languages.'

We of the present day have to bear in mind that our own language in another period must represent its peculiar customs, manners or laws, that now belong to history rather than experience. The words may be unknown to us until we meet them in some old book. Even if we have met them, words 'may be remembered as sounds, but cannot be understood as signs, whilst we remain unacquainted with the things signified'.[2] On the other hand, we may have the thing still, but under a different name.

We have all met people who 'unfortunately solicit a share of our time and attention', but we do not know them by the name of '*mumpers*',[3] 'fashionable' or not. We know what 'junketings' are, but we don't get invited to a 'Junket' as Mr Spectator[4] was (unless perhaps it were the main dish at a West-country party). We eat pullets, but we should hardly know that the Florence[5] he couples with them was wine from that city. We may buy things by the gross, but we do not speak of the 'gross of an audience'[6]—strangely enough, we can speak of the *bulk* of an audience and buy in *bulk* as well. Nor do we speak of the 'Heap[7] of an Army, utterly out of all Prospect of Rising and Preferment'. We know *fantastic, phantasm* and *fantasia*, but we should not call a whim a *Fantasque*.[8]

We may wear a suit of clothes, but we should not 'sort a suit of Ribbons'.[9] We can use walking sticks or canes, but not Jambees and

<hr>

[1] *Intellectual Powers of Man*, ii, 144.   [2] Campbell, *Phil. of Rhet.*, p. 142.
[3] *Lounger* (8).   [4] *Spect.* (298).
[5] *Spect.* (372). Dr Johnson said it neither pleased the taste nor exhilarated the spirits. (Boswell, *Life*, iii, 381.)
[6] *Spect.* (502).   [7] *Tatler* (87).   [8] *Tender Husband.*   [9] *Spect.* (10).

Dragons.[1] Since it is no longer the universal fashion for a gentleman
to wear a wig, we no longer take any interest in the varieties he used
to be able to choose from. Beau Nash 'had seen flaxen bobs succeeded
by majors, which in their turn gave way to negligents which were at
last totally routed by bags and ramilies'.[2] There are of course parallels
in modern ladies' hats to 'the progress of bonnets from the Quaker to
the Shepherdess and Kitty Fisher, and then to the Werter, the Lunardi,
and Parachute'.[3] A Tyburn hat began as a small round one worn by
pickpockets, but was later adopted by ladies and gentlemen.[4] We
know the pork-pie hat—our ancestors knew the chitterling shirt-frill
from the sixteenth century on through this period—a vivid term if you
look at the edible kind.

We need the dictionary to tell us that bishop was a drink made of
wine, oranges and sugar, or that when wine was *prickt* it was sour.
Field peas sound unattractive under the name of gray peas.

Now that we are no longer given to duelling, we no longer know
the phrase 'to go to sharps'.[5]

Games in fashion vary from age to age. 'Shilling Whist' and 'loo',[6]
if not 'chicken loo', would still be possible, but one would not now
play *Crimp* or *Basset, Passage, Rolly Polly* or *Marlborough's Battles.*
Passage was a dicing game dating from the fifteenth century; *Rolly
Polly* is the English name of Roulette. An act of 1745 forbade them
both, describing Rolly Polly as a 'pernicious' game. Ombre, the most
famous from the literary point of view, needs to be explained for most
readers of *The Rape of the Lock.*

We should not now fall in with a 'return chaise' if we were hitch-
hiking and if we met any vehicle with a vacant seat we should not agree
with the driver for a *cast*[7] or accept a *set-down.*[8] The cast would take
us to the next fare-stage, and the set-down, by a curious inversion, is a
lift, to us.

When we read that one William was a *faggot* in the first regiment of
Guards,[9] we need the dictionary to tell us that he was a Mrs Harris—
a soldier numbered in the muster-roll, but not really existing.

We are familiar with the Buffs and the Scots Greys, so we might
suppose that the regiments of *Ultramarines*[10] mentioned in Fielding's

---

[1] *Tatler* (142).   [2] *Life of Beau Nash*, p. 74.   [3] *Lounger* (79).
[4] Whitehead in Chalmers' *English Poets*, xvii, 240.
[5] Collier, *Of Duelling*, p. 131.   [6] *Tatler* (250).
[7] Thompson, *Sentimental Tour*, p. 20.   [8] *Looker-on*, p. 318.
[9] *Connoisseur*, cii.   [10] *Champion*, i, 290.

paper wore uniforms of that colour. But the *O.E.D.* tells us that in the military sense the adjective means literally 'from beyond the sea' —it has no record of the noun.

It is interesting to come on expressions unknown today, but in their context quite recognisable. We wonder why they went out. In reference to materials or features, fine is the opposite of coarse: why should not the opposite of a fine day be a coarse one, as it often was in the meteorological reports of the eighteenth century? In 1773, for example, July 4th was a cloudy coarse day, the 14th was a coarse day with some showers, and the 17th ended in a coarse evening. Another term no longer in use was *churlish*—in 1774 there was a churlish cold day in February and, our weather running true to form, exactly the same phrase was used of a day in June.

We keep comfortably to the beaten track, but we do not treat of beaten subjects:[1] we prefer the Latin equivalent *trite*.

The first issue of the *British Critick* in 1773 informs us that the *Monthly Review* had set out with the intention of lessening the influence of the established Church and 'blanching' the bigotry of less orthodox writers. We should say 'whitewashing', but *blanch* in this sense was old. It seems to have been little used at this period, or for the greater part of the next century, and is now commonest in various technical senses—apart from the cookery book's 'blanched almonds'.

If we use *callous* figuratively for any sort of hardness of heart or mind, there seems no reason why we should not talk of callous hearers[2] who 'feel' nothing in music but kettle-drums and trombones, but we should speak of their 'feelings' rather as appreciations or perceptions. Another figurative use occurs when a writer[3] on punctuation talks of the *higher* pointing proper to serious works—'that is to say' they might be 'divided into more members than . . . Pieces of mere Wit and Humour'. A look at such a page will confirm us in our preference for *heavy*.

Why, since we talk of a man wearing his 'regimentals' or 'academicals', do we not still speak generally of appearing in our 'formalities'? When Sir Humphrey Edwin, Lord Mayor of London, went to a Presbyterian meeting-house soon after the passing of the Act of Toleration, in his formalities,[4] he may have been imprudent, considering the temper of the times, but the description of his act is clear. So is that of

[1] e.g. Warton on *Essay on Criticism*, i, 101.
[2] Uvedale Price, *Essay*, i, 172.   [3] J. Burrow, *Essay on Punctuation*.
[4] *Month. Rev.* xli (1769), 298. Inherited from sixteenth century.

a ship, as Bolingbroke[1] describes her—'the galley was in all her
Formalities, Colours flying, the oars shipp'd, Slaves all aboard, and
Soldiers in their Posts'. Similar uses of adjectives as nouns that have
not become fixed are 'the ornamentals of life'[2] and 'volatiles' for
writings of transient interest.[3]

Sometimes the earlier use of a familiar word gives us a reminder of
its original or older sense when we have restricted it to a special mani-
festation. In 1775, according to the *Annual Register*,[4] died one Peter
Garden, at the extraordinary age of 131. He had lived under ten
'sovereigns' from Charles I to George III. And so he had, if you count
Oliver and Richard Cromwell, the Protectors, who were undoubtedly *superani*. Historically, *sovereign* means the person at the top, who
need not be king or queen. The mayors of several Irish boroughs
were *sovereigns*.

We still *tax* opponents with whatever bad qualities and acts we
believe them to be guilty of, but we should not talk of a 'Tax on
Religion'[5] unless money were involved—*tax* and *taxation* are indisso-
lubly tied to our pockets. We can also take an opponent to task. In
fact *task* is a metathesised form of *tax*, and the money sense was the
earliest one. Context makes it clear that when the eighteenth century
uses *cartel* it is not thinking of big business—that is a twentieth-
century development. Dr Johnson defines it as 'a writing containing
stipulations', which would cover a large number of activities, including the basis of our own. The two leading earlier senses are given
by *Glossographia Anglicana Nova* as a challenge to a duel and an
agreement between parties at war for exchanging and redeeming
prisoners.

Often our difficulty springs from the fact that our ancestors were
using a word of Latin derivation where we prefer an English one, or,
with the usual perverseness of English, the other way round. We are
used to books provided with a key—whether they are text books
with exercises, allegories or *romans à clef*. But, despite the French
phrase, we don't expect the key to be called the *clavis*.[6] On the other
hand, when we meet 'any Footsteps of this Expression'[7] we should

[1] Quoted in the *Daily Courant*, 5 Sept. 1712.   [2] Collier, *Concerning Clothes*.
[3] *Crit. Rev.* 6 (1758), 518.   [4] *Ann. Reg.* xvii (1775), 57.
[5] *Lælius and Hortensia*, p. 527. An early reader of the University of Bristol
Library copy thought it puzzling and wrote *attacks* in the margin.
[6] *Month. Rev.* x (1754), reviewing *The Dreamer*.
[7] Atterbury, *Vindication* (1709), 27.

be happier with *vestiges*. *White gold* seems an imaginative name, but we prefer *platinum*.[1]

At times, we have shifted or specialised the Latin word so far that an earlier wider meaning worries us. We soon grow accustomed to the eighteenth-century use of *Natural Philosophy* for what we call *Science*; it would not hurt us to remember that *Science* was at first knowledge in general; its present restriction implies a different stress in our interests and values. But we should talk of a man's *ignorance* of the middle ages and so his *inscience*[2] of them is unfamiliar. We cannot move easily from Science to Inscience.

Sometimes the strangeness is due merely to unexpected distribution. New versions of the Bible 'may be attended with the most violent con-cussions'[3]—*commotion* would be better, we think. But when a hurricane struck the carriage of a Swedish prince 'he received a most violent commotion, and was almost suffocated, but soon recovered'.[4] Obvi-ously it was not a concussion in the medical sense, though it easily might have been. I suspect we might use *shake-up* in both these in-stances—if we did not think it too colloquial.

The general public now is familiar enough with *topical* matters, comments, jokes: in this period it was a medical term for treatment at a particular part of the anatomy—we have to think back to the literal sense before we recognise it. *Destiny* and *Destination* now go their separate ways, encouraged by the growth of travel. *Glossographia Anglicana Nova* tells us that *Destination* means an Ordaining, Pur-posing or Designing, and this will gloss the *Monthly Review*'s[5] remark that William the Conqueror was called to the succession by the destination of Edward the Confessor.

There is no inherent reason why *longitude* should be mainly re-stricted to its geographical sense. We allow ourselves much more latitude with *latitude*, its twin. In the eighteenth century it was still possible to write of a painter, that critics have 'measured the value of his works by the length of his beard, and conclude as much in favour of the excellency of the one as the longitude of the other'.[6] But this

---

[1] *Gent. Mag.* xxxv (1764), 128. The eighteenth century also said *platina*.
[2] *Crit. Rev.* new arr. ix (1793), 162.
[3] Knox, *Essays*, i, 226.
[4] *Ann. Reg.* xii (1769), 136.
[5] *Month. Rev.* xlv (1771), 39.
[6] Shebbeare, *Letters*, ii, 44. Cf. Collier's remark (ii, 79) that a body 'will have Longitude, Latitude, and Profundity, in spight of Fate'. T. L. Peacock still punned on this type of word.

example suggests that the jocular quality of the word in this literal sense was well on the way.

The literal meaning of Latin words of course is frequently found. A lapdog may have a *pendent* ear, trees may *impend* and stretch their *extravagant* arms. Lamps may *depend* in rows: a savage may *deject* his head. Glover writes of implicated[1] shields and Philips[2] in his *Cyder* of turgid fruit, and Mason[3] in *The English Garden* of fluent oil and of a 'rustic balustrade Of firmest juncture'.[4] Diaper[5] makes his whales

Discharge their nostrils and refund a Sea

and Blacklock[6] makes a sportsman 'display *latent* nets'—though surely the words contradict each other. These words are in place now in figurative language but not in literal.

Again, the eighteenth century used words of Latin origin in etymologically defensible senses that are nevertheless strange to us because of some later specialisation. We should not call snails *reptiles*,[7] though certainly they creep. Shoots cannot now 'Condense and interweave their prickly boughs',[8] because *condense* has gone over to the scientists. People are not now of ductile dispositions,[9] because *ductile* has gone to the metallurgists. A parrot is not one of the Volatile[10]—it is we ourselves who are volatile—and (with a difference of pronunciation) we may stand in need of sal volatile. We are all too often 'perplexed with errors'—but when the *World*[11] used that phrase of a grove it meant that it was full of crooked walks—as indeed the periodical adds. It is odd that we still call the woodbine the con*volv*ulus, though we no longer, like Dr Johnson, say that its leaves in*volv*e the flower.[12] And why may we ply the oar, ply a task, knit three-ply wool or use four-ply plaster-board, but not speak of a word that will not *ply*[13] to the quantities of English verse? They are all varieties of bending.

Several verbs, indeed, common enough in particular uses, look strange in others. We do not *saunter*[14] away our time, or *shear*[15] wheat, as well as sheep, or *waft*[16] over into our country from abroad. We know the pedestrian or the student who *plods* but we do not use the verb to

[1] Chalmers' *English Poets*, xvii, 184.   [2] *Cyder* (1709), p. 54.
[3] *English Garden*, ii, 377.   [4] ibid., ll. 351–2.
[5] *Oppian's Halieuticks*, i, 578–9.   [6] Blacklock, *Desiderium Lutetiæ*, l. 149.
[7] Philips, *Cyder*, p. 26.   [8] Mason, *English Garden*, ii, 293–4.   [9] *Adventurer* (77).
[10] *Tatler* (27).   [11] *World* (15).
[12] Note on *Midsummer Night's Dream*, iv. i. 45.
[13] Thomas Parnell, *Works*, p. 198.   [14] *Gent. Mag.* xlix (1779), 21.
[15] *Ann. Reg.* (1776), p. 158.   [16] *New Universal Mag.* x (1756), 179.

mean to study closely and dully as Ash's Dictionary defines it, and as Shebbeare[1] means when he says the Dutchman plods how he may draw some personal advantage.

Vicesimus Knox[2] observed that people go to see the player rather than the play: 'It is not Shakespeare's Hamlet or Lear whom they admire, but some name which stands in rubric characters on the walls and on the play-bills.' *Rubric* is here simply 'printed in red', with far from ecclesiastical associations such as the word often has. 'The rubric' may now mean the instructions—on an examination paper, for instance—with no regard to the colour of the type. But red for danger and impressiveness is explanation enough.

It is at once exciting and frustrating to come on the occasional word about which *O.E.D.* tells us nothing. Mr Sylas Neville[3] confides to his Diary how he found out the name of an attractive young lady because she brought a 'small caravan' with her out of the coach with 'Miss Scott' written upon it. The caravan as a vehicle was known—but it was used in socially different circles then. The *Connoisseur*[4] is clearly shocked that any man should 'have his family dragged to his country-seat like servant maids, in the Caravan'—it is as far from the gypsies as from the members of Caravan Clubs. But it could not have been any sort of carriage that Miss Scott brought out of the coach. Was it a carry-all?

The *Critical Review*[5] in 1765 remarks that it has been held actionable to call a counsellor 'Daffa-down-dilly', which Eric Partridge[6] defines as a fop, dating it from 'before 1841', as it emphatically is if the same sense is implied. It seems a fairly mild term hardly justifying court action. Does this throw light on *Daffodil*, applied to a character in the play *The Male Coquette?*

We know a plant called Honesty, but what was *Jealousy?* St Vincent's stone-crop, according to the *English Dialect Dictionary*, in Shropshire and Kent—but the *Universal Magazine*[7] bewilders us with a variety of names when it gives a description of Amaranthus Tricolor, or Variable Amaranthus. 'Some call it the variable amaranthus, some jealousy, and others the viola tricolor, or three-coloured violet. The botanists call it symphonia . . . because a sort of pipe was made of the

---

[1] *Letters*, 88. [2] *Essays*, i, 111.
[3] *Diary*, p. 115. [4] *Connoisseur*, xxv.
[5] *Crit. Rev.* 20 (1765), 46. Dorothy L. Sayers makes the same remark in *Unnatural Death*.
[6] *Slang*, p. 366. [7] *Universal Mag.* xiii (1767), 117.

stalks of this plant which was used in concert with the Voice.' The classical amaranth was no real flower—it grows only in the Elysian fields—and nothing O.E.D. says about more mundane uses of the name agrees with this, nor is a stonecrop a violet.

Lady Pomfret writes to Lady Hertford that the 'town-house' of Innsbruck had a portico whose *shed* was covered with gold.[1] The context shows that the *shed* is not the kind of building we should call by that name: does it mean the ridge, as in watershed? Or a shed-roof—i.e. a roof with only one slope? The latter term was as old as 1736 in America, but dated from 1805 by O.E.D. for England. But the building—the town-house of the Duke of Tyrol built in 1500—is still there. It is known as Das Goldene Dachl, and has a *shed-roof* of gilded copper.

The *Anti-Jacobin*[2] declares that we all know *Forging of Eclairs* to be a bad thing, though forging Gentlemen's Letters is still worse. *Eclairs* were forged for the Stock Exchange. We do not know *eclair* in any such sense.

In 1766, the 'bells in most churches rang from morning to night, particularly St. Michael's, Cornhill, which did not finish till near twelve o'clock and concluded with forty-five platoons'.[3] *Platoons* must be a transferred use of *volley*—itself a transfer from the artillery salvo. The celebration was in anticipation of the repeal of the Stamp Act—but, regrettably, in America, more platoons in the military senses were involved in the end.

---

[1] Hertford-Pomfret Correspondence, iii, 255. I am indebted to Dr Estelle Morgan for details of the building.

[2] *Anti-Jacobin*, ii, 45, 118. No suitable sense in any French Dictionary I have consulted.

[3] *Ann. Reg.* ix (1766), 68.

VI

THE ENLIGHTENING

EIGHTEENTH-CENTURY ATTITUDES

(1) *Life*

EIGHTEENTH-CENTURY verbal uses can enlighten us in two ways. They may tell us about the attitudes of mind then prevalent, or they may tell us what was meant historically by words and phrases we use in figurative or weakened senses. Much social and intellectual development is held in the circle of these expressions.

Eighteenth-century attitudes may be revealed by one tell-tale word. We are a long way off, scientifically, from the Dictionary[1] that could define a dragon as a 'kind of serpent, *perhaps* imaginary', or from the remark that Wilkins entertained an *extravagant* notion of the possibility of man's flying.[2] Aesthetically, we are a long way from the age when it could be said that Switzerland is 'for the most part mountainous, *but* there are some places that are very pleasant',[3] or that could talk of purling streams and *horrible* cascades.[4] These incidental words[5] are the linguistic expression of a frame of mind as different from ours as that betrayed by Sir William Chambers when he said the Parthenon would be improved by a steeple![6]

It is true that *accident* once meant any event, and then any unexpected one, but it is clear from such period dictionaries as Bailey's, Dyche and Pardon's, and Dr Johnson's that the idea of chance was as normal then as now, though the result could be more easily good in the eighteenth century than in the twentieth. Dyche and Pardon make a clear distinction between the accidental death of a man hit by a falling tile, and that caused by the murderous throwing of it. The *Spectator* (315) illustrates the first sense when it describes as 'very surprizing Accidents' Ulysses' ship being turned into a rock and Aeneas's fleet into a shoal of water-nymphs. The possible pleasant nature of an accident can be illustrated from one of Samuel Richardson's *Familiar*

---

[1] Kenrick's Dictionary.
[2] Ruffhead, *Life of Pope*, 383.
[3] *New Universal Mag.* (1756), 188.
[4] *Art of Poetry* (1762), p. 36.
[5] My italics in this paragraph.
[6] *Brit. Crit.* vi (1795), 3.

Letters[1] where a needy man is given a part in a play—an 'accident' which offered him 'present bread'.

At Northampton Assizes[2] in 1735 one Mary Farron, aged 20, was condemned to be burnt for 'poysoning' her husband (aged 17) to whom she had been married for only six months, 'by putting white Mercury into sugar sops which she gave him. . . . Her criminal Affection for a young Man occasion'd this Accident.' It was hardly 'an unforeseen occurrence', as Ash defines the word. On the other hand it certainly was an accident that nearly killed two men who had eaten what the wife of one of them believed to be a pudding flavoured with ground ginger. 'This Accident happened by the mistake of a Girl whom she sent for beaten ginger, which proved yellow Arsenick.'[3] Surely it was the mistake of the shopkeeper: and we appreciate the approving surprise of Lady Craven[4] who finds at Vienna that 'you cannot buy a Drug at the apothecaries without an order from a physician—A very prudent caution against the madness of those who choose to finish their existence with a dose of laudanum, or their neighbours with one of arsenic.' Or indeed, to prevent Accidents.

Any modern Temperance Movement would be surprised at finding small beer in a list of permissible drinks along with water and milk—even more so at finding that cider, perry, wine, porter and strong beer deserve the title of 'temperance' drinks 'when taken in moderate quantities at meals'.[5] Proportion enters into it, and the incidence of drunkenness in the eighteenth century, particularly as a result of drinking spirits, would horrify the most rabid anti-teetotaller as well as the staunchest abstainer of our age. Hogarth's 'Beer Street' is the healthy and happy contrast to his 'Gin Lane'.

Attitudes towards people and their behaviour, individually or generally, come out in a variety of verbal ways. We probably all like 'to figure' in some affair; but the word has lost the social colouring Knox[6] recognises when he talks of families 'figuring, as it is called, in all the profusion of emulous extravagance at Bath or Brighthelmstone'. The word conjures up of itself the gay life of the eighteenth-century watering-place. No doubt there were fops at both towns. And a *fop*

---

[1] 1741, xlvii.   [2] *Gent. Mag.* v (1735), 386.
[3] *Gent. Mag.* i (1731), 128.
[4] *Journey*, p. 112. N. Wraxall, Jr., was struck with the same arrangement in St Petersburgh in 1774. *A Tour*, pp. 256–7.
[5] *Gent. Mag.* lix (1789), 399.
[6] *Essays*, ii, 136.

is 'one who has not the honour to be a coxcomb; there is not stuff enough in him to reach that character'.[1]

It is a sad comment on the practical 'jokers' of the time, that that pleasant word *frolic* which 'formerly signified nothing more than a piece of innocent mirth and gaiety' should have grown much more lively and spirited because the Mohocks and the members of the Hell-fire Club 'introduced these elevated Frolicks and struck out mighty good jokes from all kinds of violence and blasphemy.... Whatever is in violation of all decency and order, is an exquisite piece of wit; and in short, a Frolick....'[2] This is a word we have reinstated.

We have not been able quite to reinstate *knowing*, which by the end of the eighteenth century is leading a double life, sometimes serious, sometimes slangy. They could be knowing in the art of painting,[3] for example (we should say expert, or knowledgeable); they could couple the polite and the knowing,[4] the knowing and the judicious,[5] contrast the ignorant and the knowing,[6] or speak of a man knowing in the scriptures and devoutly disposed,[7] of knowing and sober divines,[8] of 'so knowing a person as Chrysostom',[9] of the Romans being more knowing than the Greeks,[10] of civilised and knowing nations,[11] of an upright, knowing and diligent magistrate.[12] In all these the participial adjective is firmly tied to its verb. But the slang use was an eighteenth-century invention. Mrs Piozzi[13] says it is a vulgar word, belonging to 'a pedantry in use among gamesters, horse-jockeys etc.' and a writer to the *Connoisseur*[14] says he supposes a Connoisseur is only another word for a knowing one—'So write me a few papers in defence of cards, dice, races and gaming in general.' Knox[15] concludes that a hunting parson will pass for a knowing one—*not* in Dr Waterland's sense—and comments elsewhere[16] that 'the knowing ones consider church attendance, to express their own ideas in their own language, as a cursed lounge'.

Do we think peevishness mainly a childish failing? And that to be 'peeved' is suitable for adults, the short word implying a less permanent state of mind? The eighteenth century paid it more respect. Mrs

---

[1] *Month. Rev.* ix (1753), 468, quoting *A Dictionary of Love.*
[2] *Connoisseur*, liv (1755).   [3] Gerard, *On Taste*, p. 99.   [4] ibid., p. 112.
[5] Waterland, *Doctrine of Eucharist*, p. 7.   [6] Gildon, *Art of Poetry*, p. 236.
[7] Waterland, op. cit., p. 156.   [8] ibid., p. 466.   [9] ibid., p. 583.
[10] Ferguson, *Civil Society*, p. 48.   [11] Dennis, *Critical Works*, i, 262.
[12] Cole, *Sketches of the Life of Soame Jenyns, Esq*, p. xvii.
[13] *Brit. Syn.*, ii, 267.   [14] *Connoisseur*, ii (1754).
[15] *Essays*, i, 240.   [16] op. cit., ii, 151.

Piozzi[1] thinks *peevish* 'best expresses female frowardness, and delicacy worn too thin to endure the handling'. Dr Ferguson[2] calls it the reverse of patience, which tends to make imaginary evils real (*realise* is his word) and to increase real ones. Is it a difference in medical theory or in the stresses of the times that has caused *relaxation* to change from suggesting often an undesirable state to one we would all enjoy if we could? In the eighteenth century we find *relaxed* in company with faint, pale, low-spirited. 'Melancholy, dejection, despair, and often self-murder, is the consequence of the gloomy view we take of things'[3] when in a 'relaxed' state of body.

They did consider a pleasant country house as 'an easy and useful Relaxation',[4] and Sir Joshua Reynolds[5] thought his students should relax by going to the theatre. Burke[6] speaks of the agreeable relaxation which is the characteristic effect of beauty. Henry Carey[7] tells us

> I now a measure of contentment find,
> Can labour or relax whene'er I please.

But the bad sense may be just round the corner. 'How', asks Lord Lyttelton,[8] 'may men with minds relaxed by the enervating ease and softness of luxury, have vigour to oppose tyranny?' Reynolds[9] thought also that the return to scrupulous labour is difficult after the relaxation of the mind by delightful trifles. Boswell[10] reported on Sir Joshua that he had been kept on so low a diet that he was quite relaxed and desponding. Nowadays,[11] to be told that a sick man is relaxed, encourages hope for his recovery—though 'relaxed throat' serves to remind us of the older usage. We need to make some adjustment when we read in Pope's[12] *Homer* of the hero who tumbles to the ground with limbs relaxed, or when Thomson[13] describes with regret the Golden Age in which

> Sickly damps and cold autumnal fogs
> Hung not, relaxing, on the springs of life.

In an age when 'relaxation' may be the strenuous playing of games, we need a great deal of adjustment to the eighteenth-century idea that

[1] *Brit. Syn.*, i, 89.   [2] *Institutes*, p. 257.
[3] Burke, *Sublime and Beautiful*, p. 254.   [4] Lawson, *Lectures*, No. 16.
[5] Quoted Hilles, *The Literary Career of Sir Joshua Reynolds*, p. 209.
[6] *Sublime and Beautiful*, p. 299.   [7] *Poems*, p. 108.
[8] *Dialogues of the Dead*, iii.   [9] Hilles, op. cit., p. 47.   [10] *Letters*, ii, 441–2.
[11] cf. BBC Bulletin on Gen. Eisenhower (4 Oct. 1955) which said he was comfortable, relaxed and cheerful.
[12] *Iliad*, vii, 18.   [13] *Spring*, pp 328–9.

it produces languor. Uvedale Price thinks that the 'passion excited by beauty ... acts by relaxing the fibres somewhat below their natural tone, and this is accompanied by an inward sense of melting and languour'.[1] And Ruffhead equates the relaxation which for him is the effect of exquisite beauty with 'that enervate tremulous sensation which we experience when we contemplate any object of distress or pity'.[2]

From this exquisite sensibility decline was easy, and Ferguson wants a more active frame of mind. 'If that time which is passed in relaxing the powers of the mind, and in with-holding every object but what tends to weaken and corrupt, were employed in fortifying these powers, ... we should not, at the years of maturity, be so much at a loss for occupation.'[3]

The eighteenth century spoke of *bracers* where we speak of *tonics*— and even *O.E.D.*'s definition of *tonics* strikes oddly on the non-medical ear—they are any medicines producing tension. As if we needed help to produce that now!

Our world is full of projects if not of projectors. The eighteenth century ruined *projector* for us, because the word became the reflection of a sceptical attitude towards innovations. It is 'a reproachful name' says the *Monthly Review*,[4] 'usually bestowed by the ignorant on all those who attempt any thing new for the service of mankind'. The *Critical*[5] agreed, for it regretted the title chosen by an author— 'Observations on the Commutation Project.' The word suggested that a 'political plan of great magnitude' was being treated 'with disrespect', if the degrading term of a 'project' was given to it.

When the *Universal Spectator*[6] said in 1735 that the word *King* in most parts of the world served only to convey an 'Idea of an absolute, despotick National Bully'—but not in Great Britain—we see the attitude of the patriotic Englishman, and perhaps, the reason why kings are so rare in our own day. We need no mental adjustment here, but in our changed times, with their changed symbols, it is interesting to read an effusion of nearly 200 years ago—

> Illustrious RED! Magnificently bright
> By Newton found the strongest beam of light,
> Prime of all colours! on the Monarch's throne
> In robes majestic is its lustre shewn.

[1] *Essay*, i, 104.   [2] *Life of Pope*, p. 439.
[3] *Civil Society*, p. 50.
[4] *Month. Rev.* viii (1753), 233. N.B. our modern mechanical kinds.
[5] *Crit. Rev.* 61 (1786), 387.   [6] Quoted in *Gent. Mag.* v (1735), 9.

It is from a poem called 'Rubrella, true Beauty',[1] rejoicing that 'Britain's RED FLAG commands the subject main.'

The eighteenth century had moved a long way from the medieval or even the Elizabethan concept of the nature and relation of Church and State when a Dictionary[2] could define *Church* as 'a voluntary Society of Men joyning themselves together of their own Accord in order to the publick worshipping of God in such a Manner, as they judge Acceptable to him, and effectual to the Salvation of their Souls'. This is wide enough to include the Society of Friends and the Salvation Army. Of course not everyone in the period would have found it satisfactory—but the High Churchman Dr Johnson says 'the collective body of Christians' and Dyche and Pardon make the word the excuse for some acid remarks on ecclesiastical controversy. Thirty years after the *Glossographia Anglicana Nova*, the *Old Whig* (89)[3] was offering a historical disquisition on *Church* which would have delighted the heart of William Tyndale: 'the *Ecclesia* rendered CHURCH denotes any Assembly of either Men or Women, met together, as well in Civil as Religious accounts. In this sense it is used by *Aristophanes*. In the New Test. [*sic*] also it signifies an Assembly of Men met together for *merely civil* Purposes, Acts xix. 39. Hence it is applied to the Collective Body of Christians, throughout the world: but *never once* to the Clergy, in opposition to the *Laity*. If this word was always translated CON-GREGATION instead of CHURCH it would appear that the *Authority of the Church* is nothing more than the *Natural Power* that resides in the Laity, and the *Rights of the Church* the same with the *Rights of the Christian People*.' Out of such ideas, religious toleration was bound to come.

That observant German Dr Wendeborn[4] had his eye on English ecclesiastical divisions; he tells us that the 'parochial churches alone bear the name of *Church* throughout England. The other religious buildings are called *Meeting-houses, Chapels, Preaching-houses'*— which is no longer always true. On the other hand the eighteenth century could speak of the regular clergy, whether dissenters or of the establishment.[5]

---

[1] *Gent. Mag.* xxxviii (1768); by Dr Clancy.

[2] *Gloss. Ang. Nov.* Cf. *Guardian* (80).

[3] Quoted in *Gent. Mag.* vii (1737), 37.

[4] *View*, ii, 330.

[5] op. cit., i, 261. But not Dr Johnson, who spoke of a dissenting teacher (*Life*, iii, 33). Gibbon uses *clergy* of Julian the Apostate's priests.

Wendeborn notices the ambiguity of *high* and *low*[1] as applied to churchmen, and defines the high as those who wanted to make the bishops almost independent of the state, and the low as those who wished to extend the power of the king in ecclesiastical matters. He recognizes another meaning for 'low churchmen'—'those who contended that the difference between the Episcopal and other Protestant Churches, was of no great moment'. He does not think of ritual as playing any part in the distinction—that came in with the Oxford Movement.

The eighteenth-century attitude to bigotry is a reaction from the bigotry—or the convictions—of its more strenuous predecessors. Lord Shaftesbury[2] makes the interesting point that you cannot translate the word *bigotry* into either Greek or Latin—which shows 'how peculiar a Passion it Implies'. (I am not sure that you could translate 'Common Market', 'Iron Curtain', 'space-woman' or 'closed shop' very easily— the test is not really relevant to the usefulness of the word, of course.) But if this was the cool disapproval of a philosopher of dubious orthodoxy, we can add two Dictionary definitions. *Glossographia Anglicana Nova* has two senses—a Bigot is either a Hypocrite, or 'one that obstinately adheres to his own Opinions and Humour'. For Bailey, bigotted (*sic*) is the same as *superstitious*.

It is not easy to see why certain expressions should have been felt as sectarian: they throw light on those who used them. In the seventeenth century, people had described their religious experiences as God's dealings with them: the *Monthly Review*[3] tells us that about 1730 Mr Whitefield revived it. It does not sound very odd now, but before the Evangelical Revival, the period was little concerned with mystical experiences.

Nowadays we are used to the spread of this or that doctrine, religious, aesthetic, political, so it seems strange to be told by the *Monthly Review*[4] of 1775 that 'the spread of religion and virtue' is a phrase 'much used by the Dissenters'. In the previous year, the *Gentleman's Magazine*[5] says it is 'a favourite Unitarian phrase'.

[1] op. cit., ii, p. 278.
[2] *Works*, iii, 81. This is an excellent example of the relation of word to thought. My colleague Mr S. J. Tester points out that *charity* and *humility* will not go into classical Latin either. He suggests that *bigot* could be rendered 'cui rationibus suaderi non potest ut suam pervicacem de religione opinionem permutet'—'a very long way round, though Cicero might have understood what one was driving at'.
[3] *Month. Rev.* xxiii (1760), 254.
[4] *Month. Rev.* liii (1775), 262.   [5] *Gent. Mag.* lxiv (1774), 345.

In 1783 a Constant Reader informed the *Gentleman's Magazine*[1] that he could not understand the term *Liberal* 'in its fullest extent, as understood amongst us at present and as first introduced among us by writers of the dissenting persuasion'. Evidently he had his own ideas, for he goes on, 'What the liberal-mindedness of the present age amounts to may be in part learned from the plans of education held forth by the Warrington Academy, by Dr Price's political plans, by Dr Harwood's translation of the New Testament, and by Dr Priestley's last publication on religious subjects.'[2] It may be that these gentlemen could not have reduced their ideas to a definition as he demanded; but the liberal politics and liberal theology of the next century and a half were implied in his examples.

The critics kept a watchful eye on what they considered the misuse of words appropriated to religious ideas. The *Monthly Review*[3] dislikes the application of *divine* to Shaftesbury's eloquence—it is 'truly admirable: but there is nothing divine in the case'. Years before, the *Guardian* (4) had commented on a new style which 'is above the Sublime and may be called the Celestial; that is, when the most sacred Phrases appropriated to the Honour of the Deity, are applied to a Mortal of good Quality'. *Divine* in the sense of 'excellent' (given in *Glossographia Anglicana Nova*) is as old as the fifteenth century, and for the *Guardian's* comment, all we can say is that the eighteenth century was not on the whole in the habit of reading medieval love poetry.

The *Monthly Review*[4] considered 'the illustrious author of Nature' inadequate: from our standpoint, do we not consider the *Guardian's*[5] description of God as 'the great Superintendant of the World' equally inadequate?

Fashion, says the *Gentleman's Magazine*[6] in 1789, denominates everything serious '*fanatical*', and adds that every one, 'according to his own system of indulgence, terms the person observing a pure system of conduct a fanatic'. Smear-words do betray the speaker. So thought the *London Magazine*[7] of 1768 when it remarked that 'religion is so totally banished from all polite conversation that any person who brings in the subject with that zeal as if his life was animated by the precepts of the gospel, needs no other qualification to be termed a methodist'.

[1] *Gent. Mag.* liii (1783), 938.   [2] *Gent. Mag.* lviii (1787), 870.
[3] *Month. Rev.* xxxiii (1765), 545.   [4] *Month. Rev.* xxvii (1763), 41.
[5] *Guardian* (117).
[6] *Gent. Mag.* lix (1789), 1071.   [7] p. 29.

Discussion about the term *Good Nature* is a window into many aspects of the eighteenth-century mind—patriotic, dogmatic, kindly or cynical. Some, like Shaftesbury, thought it a mark of the English character, 'a Quality so peculiar to the English Nation that no other Language hath a word to express it. . . . Neither the *Philanthropy* of the Greeks nor the *Humanity* of the Romans can raise in us such a lively and amiable Picture as that beautiful Expression *Good Nature*.'[1] It was all very well to define it as the healing Balm for all our Sores, and the powerful Charm for all our cares, or the cement of love, the bond of society, the rich man's pleasure, the poor man's refuge,[2] or as that disposition which partakes of the felicity of all mankind,[3] or even to equate it with Charity in St Paul's sense.[4] As early as the *Spectator* (525) the identification of Good Nature with a species of folly had been noticed. The degradation is noticed throughout the period. Would one suppose that a man of honour was a deliberate murderer, 'a careful Man a Thief, an honest Gentleman only a Whig or Tory, according as the Person is who gives him the Character; or that a very honest Fellow meant nothing but a very drunken One, and a very good Sort of Man, or a very good-natur'd Man, meant either nothing at all, or meant a Fool?' 'Every Man is the best natur'd Man alive'[5]—and that is the root reason for the bad sense: the word is too widely used. Goldsmith's *Good-natur'd Man*, according to the *London Magazine* of May 1768, demonstrates the madness of good-nature, and is calculated to show the dangerous consequences of that benevolence, which is indiscriminately showered upon the worthy and undeserving. The *Adventurer* (30), though granting that the term often means 'that flexible imbecillity of mind which complies with every request', proceeds to give an account of the ideal quality that could hardly be bettered. 'In true good Nature, there is neither the acrimony of spleen, nor the sullenness of malice; it is neither clamorous nor fretful, neither easy to be offended, nor impatient to revenge; it is a tender sensibility, a participation of the pains and pleasures of others; and is, therefore, a forcible and constant motive, to communicate happiness and alleviate suffering.'

Two great writers offer us comments on Good Nature to which most of us will find it much harder to adjust our thinking. 'Good Nature',

[1] *Gent. Mag.* iii (1733), 513 quoting the *Free Briton*.
[2] *Universal Mag.* xiii (1767), 109.
[3] Lyttelton, *Persian Letters*, p. 33.   [4] *World* (126).
[5] Quoted from *Common Sense* in *Gent. Mag.* viii (1738), 117.

says Defoe[1] with devastating logic if you accept his doctrinal premisses, as a term 'is Nonsense and Contradictory, Nature being in its Constitution Corrupt.' And Henry Fielding,[2] who was to become a Justice of the Peace, tells us that 'to bring a *real* and *great* Criminal to Justice is, perhaps, the best-natured Office we can perform to Society'. It is the attitude which led Samuel Pegge[3] to describe hanging on the gibbet as 'benevolent' in intention, and Dr Johnson to regret the abolition of public executions. It is difficult to believe that the strongest supporters of capital punishment would use quite such frank adjectives now.

In an age of luxury goods which we all want and luxury hotels where we enjoy a holiday, should we feel amused or chastened at *Glossographia Anglicana Nova*'s definitions of *luxury* and *luxurious*? (The eighteenth century of course did not use *luxury* as an adjective—it is not quite the same as *luxurious*.) *Luxury*, says the dictionary, is 'all superfluity and excess in carnal Pleasure; sumptuous Fare, Riot': *Luxurious* is 'Riotous, given to Excess and Debauchery.' Dr Johnson mentions only Delicious fare, which is too narrow, but, to our way of thinking, on the right lines: he does not allow anything but plants to *luxuriate*. Evidently there was an austere attitude to luxury, akin to the Elizabethan tone of the word, and a more indulgent one as well. There is a hint of the older meaning of lecherous in Langhorne's *Letters on Religious Retirement*[4] (1762) when he speaks of indulging in the luxurious songs of Solomon.

Defoe[5] believes Luxury to be a good thing, but admits that the word implies it isn't—he speaks of the 'Pleasures and Conveniences of Life, commonly included in that ill-natured term, Luxury'. No wonder Bishop Warburton[6] called it 'this ambiguous term', holding that 'there is no word more inconstantly used and capriciously applied to particular actions'. He inclines to the bad view, that 'Luxury is the using the gifts of Providence, to the Injury of the User ... or to the Injury of any other'. Jonas Hanway[7] agrees—it is 'a vicious excess, particularly such as prevents individuals from doing their duty to the public'. That is a side of the question we do well to remember, though we must remember also that one man's luxury is another's necessity, and that the same applies to the generations. A cup of tea was a luxury to Mr Hanway's mind. It is characteristic of eighteenth-century class consciousness that luxury could be defined as 'that kind of expence'

[1] *Little Review* 6, 22 June 1705.   [2] *Champion*, ii, 40.
[3] Quoted in *Gent. Mag.* lix (1789), 207. See above, pp. 21–2.   [4] Letter III.
[5] *Review*, vi, 135.   [6] *Divine Legation*, i, sect. 6.   [7] *Journal*, ii, 237–8.

which is 'above the rank' a man holds in the nation.[1] The *Town and Country Magazine* in 1777[2] quotes a comment on national luxury that pin-points the difficulty of definition in such a 'point-of-view word'— 'It seems to be, indefinitely, the pleasures arising from the gratification of artificial wants; and it will be found extremely difficult to draw a line between the artificial wants that should be admitted, and those that should be rejected.'

The practical down-to-earth spirit of the period is well conveyed by its uses of the word *visionary*, which for us too implies that the thing is impracticable, but, also, that we wish it were not. 'Where there is no vision, the people perish,' said the prophet: the eighteenth century was more inclined to think that vision led to disaster. What they believed or hoped to be visionary throws a flood of light on the age. The *Anti-Jacobin*[3] declares that the principles of the Jacobins rested at first on a new theory of government, false, visionary and impracticable. The twentieth century has seen that a system may be false but far from either visionary or impracticable. The writer on Slavery[4] who thought it a visionary plan to convert the slave into a hired servant would not have had to wait long to see it come true. Rousseau's system of education might appear 'romantic and visionary',[5] but it has influenced our educational theory and practice. Ferguson[6] thought that 'when the merchant forgets his own interest to lay plans for his country the period of vision and chimera is near, and the solid basis of commerce withdrawn'. What would he have thought of modern state controls in war and peace? On the other hand, it was easy to say then in that Age of Enlightenment that for 'the same darkness which once overspread ancient Greece and Rome' to cover modern Europe is 'an event too improbable to be apprehended, but by the visionary'.[7] If so, we are all visionaries in our pessimistic moments—but what we see is a nightmare.

Eighteenth-century views on Art-forms are given incidentally or at length, and are often not ours. We do not require an opera to have a happy ending as the *Monthly Review*[8] says it should. The initial unsympathetic ignorance of the middle ages is concentrated in the

---

[1] *New Universal Mag.* (June 1759), 219.
[2] *Town and Country Mag.* xiii (1777), 318.
[3] *Anti-Jacobin*, i, 23.   [4] *Crit. Rev.* 66 (1788), 342.
[5] *Crit. Rev.* 56 (1783), 267.   [6] *Civil Society*, 241.
[7] Knox, *Essays*. No. 79.
[8] *Month. Rev.* xv (1756), 153.

Tatler's[1] contemptuous remarks about the bore who tells a 'long Canterbury Tale of two Hours by the time he is three score'. True, this was a legacy from the sixteenth century, but it helps to explain why Pope could not take Chaucer seriously.

It took a long time for *Romance* and *Romantic* to work clear of derogatory connotations. They are parallel to *vision* and *visionary*. Bentley writes off one of Milton's finest passages—*Paradise Lost*, i, 580 sqq. —as 'Romantic Trash' which 'even when he wrote was obsolete and forgot'. It 'clogs and sullies' the poem. Even John Upton,[2] sympathetic as he was to Spenser, tells us that Romances are made up of 'exploits founded on false notions of love, gallantry, and mock honour, and in a word are no better than downright madness or Quixotism'.

The anti-romanticist in Clara Reeve's *Progress of Romance*[3] defines the genre as 'a wild, extravagant fabulous story'—and the eighteenth century would never have used the word *fabulous* as a general term of praise. He says later that when people talk in an affected manner, and still more when they utter improbabilities, it may without impropriety be called 'Romantic' at any time. Ruffhead's[4] comment on Ariosto's world represents a widely held view—however 'grotesque the picture of humanity, it was a true one of the times he lived in; which were extravagantly depraved, by the romances of chivalry and the legendary tales of the saints'. With that we may compare Bishop Lavington's[5] sneer about the 'romantick Life of St Bernard', which is *not* meant as a compliment.

At times they saw everything as romantic if it was difficult or unlikely. Hanway,[6] who disapproved of the time and money lost in teabreaks (though that word had not then been invented), nevertheless felt that it would be romantic to expect people to drink herb tea unsugared. More seriously, the Project of sending a great fleet to the Turkish archipelago struck the *Town and County Magazine*[7] as an enterprise bordering upon Romance. We should not have applied the word to the Gallipoli expedition of the First World War.

As for the romances beloved of the young, the stern Aunt in Steele's *Tender Husband* speaks for all moralizers when she describes them as a 'parcel of improbable lies . . . fit to corrupt young Girls, and fill their Heads with a thousand foolish dreams of I don't know what'. Bernard

[1] *Tatler* (132).   [2] Re *Faerie Queene*, VI. VI. xxxv.   [3] i, 5, 67.
[4] *Life of Pope*, p. 453. Does he mean 'to judge by', or 'because of'?
[5] *Enthusiasm*, ii, 58.   [6] *Journal*, ii, 231.   [7] *Town & Country Mag.* ii (1770), 5.

Mandeville[1] considers the writers of Legends and Romances 'to have been the greatest enemies to Truth and sober Sense the world ever produced'.

Dyche and Pardon's tirade[2] in their Dictionary is in full agreement with both the lady and the moralist.

Even when the word is not exactly derogatory, it may suggest that it was applied more widely than now. We should hardly choose *romantic* to characterise the *Spectator*'s (611) grim story of a murderer who takes refuge in a Madrid church and finds there a murderess who has plucked the heart of her betrayer out of his corpse.

But as time goes on, romantic scenery makes its appeal, whether it is man-made like the elegant and romantic retirement afforded by a grotto,[3] or the romantic and sequestered regions of the Savoy glaciers.[4] And naturally, for the readers of Romances, *romantic* meant nothing but good. James Usher[5] may speak for them—there is a passion characterised by 'heroic sentiments, a contempt for life, a boldness for enterprise, chastity and purity of sentiment. People whose breasts are chilled with vice or stupified by nature call this passion romantic love: but when it was the mode, it was the diagnostic of a virtuous age.'

The visit to London of that famous South Sea Islander Omiah inspired a poem put in the mouth of the Queen of 'O'Taheiti', and called 'The Injured Islanders, or the Influence of Art upon the Happiness of Nature.' 'If Omiah had heard,' says the *Critical Review*,[6] the line

And glean'd the Gothic relics of the storm,

would it 'have presented to him the idea meant to be conveyed, or indeed any idea, till after a very long and minute explanation'?

Faced with *Gothic* as the period used the word, we surely feel very much as Omiah would have felt. *Gothic* is a touchstone of prejudice and changing taste. There is the non-technical use, inherited from the seventeenth century in which the word means simply 'barbarous' at

---

[1] *Enquiry*, p. 48.

[2] *Romantick*: mad, frenetical, silly, idle trifling, belonging to, or favouring of a romance.

Romance: a feigned story . . . wherein abundance of enthusiastical flights are introduced, which renders the reading of them in general prejudicial, by mispending of time . . . giving false images of life [and generally brings the young to irrecoverable misfortune].

[3] Ruffhead, *Life of Pope*, p. 197.   [4] *Crit. Rev.* 41 (1776), 373.

[5] *Clio*, p. 82 (1778).   [6] *Crit. Rev.* 47 (1779), 224.

worst, or 'old-fashioned' at best, and generally that the speaker doesn't approve. Here what interests us is the kind of thing to which it is applied. Duelling is Gothic and absurd:[1] to 'compel King Augustus to surrender Gen. Patkul to his implacable enemy was a most barbarous thing, and to the last degree Gothick'.[2] The Gordon rioters who could so easily have burnt down the British Museum were 'Gothic incendiaries'[3] to Dr Wendeborn, and he applies[4] the same adjective to the law which ordered that women guilty of petty treason—i.e. murdering their husbands—should be burnt alive (as in this period they still could be). Not barbarous to this degree, but still *Gothic*, were the prejudices that prevented St Paul's from being decorated with paintings, again according to Dr Wendeborn.[5] John Dennis[6] remarks with more historical sense than most people, 'if that is truly the most Gothick, which is the most oppos'd to Antique, nothing can be more Gothick than an Opera'. It is a Gothic servile custom at our Universities 'of the poor scholars waiting on the others at table'.[7] To convert the fields in front of the Royal Crescent at Bath into kitchen gardens was a Gothic design.[8] More lightly, to be acquainted with the names of one's own family is 'thought preposterously Gothic'.[9]

The old-fashioned formal garden with straight lines and trim alleys, box hedges, parterres, terraces and labyrinths, was a Gothic arrangement;[10] and an old-fashioned chaise and one is made upon the Gothic plan compared with a phaeton.[11]

In Law and Politics *Gothic* is usually complimentary, though elsewhere it was for long a smear-word. Defoe in his *Review*[12] briefly explains what he means by Gothic principles of Government—'That the Nobility and Commons . . . always either Collectively or Representatively, had certain reserv'd Rights which the Kings were sworn to Maintain as the Postulata of Government.' Lyttelton[13] thinks that a system of this sort was produced not in a cabinet, but in a camp—he is describing what he knows of Anglo-Saxon Law and Custom. This was an inheritance from the seventeenth-century antiquaries.[14]

---

[1] *Month. Rev.* l (Dec. 1773–June 1774), 11.
[2] *Review*, vi, 237 (1709). Johan Reinhold Patkul, a Livonian noble quartered alive in 1706 for conspiring against Sweden.
[3] Wendeborn, *View*, i, 325. [4] ibid., p. 427. See above, p. 138.
[5] ibid., p. 348. [6] *Critical Works*, ii, 391. [7] *European Mag.* xi (1787), 320.
[8] *Month. Rev.* xlix (1773), 229. [9] *Babler*, c.
[10] *Crit. Rev.* 44 (1797), 312, on Mason's *English Garden*.
[11] Warton, *The Oxford Sausage*, p. 44. [12] *Review*, vii, 274.
[13] *Persian Letters*, lviii. [14] Samuel Kliger in *M.P.* xliii (1945).

Gothic was equated with feudal or medieval: the *Squire's Tale* was Gothic,[1] baronial haughtiness[2] was Gothic, and so were tournaments in the reign of Henry III.[3] These were the ages of Gothic ignorance and superstition. It is not surprising that 'Gothic' architecture was equated with medieval of any date, and that for so long the classically-conditioned eighteenth century disapproved.

The basic aesthetic reason for disapproval was the intricacy of the style, which they saw as 'bittiness'—and obviously capitals ought not to be carved with the leaves of 'Thistles and Coleworts'![4]

Dyche and Pardon say (ungrammatically) that *Gothic* means 'rude, inartificial, rustick, after the manner, or like to the *Goths*, whose architecture was very heavy and rude, like most of our old churches which are built in their manner'. It would be hard to pack into one sentence more errors of fact or failures of artistic perception. One longs to ask the critics when and where they suppose the Goths to have lived. Bailey says the style was introduced 'after those barbarous People the Goths and Vandals made their irruptions into Italy', which is true—but 'after' can imply a long time, and Bailey's words suggest not so much 'after' as 'when'. To him it is 'a licentious and fantastical Mode, wild and incorrect', and with lamentable imagery. But he goes on to admit that it can be strong, rich and pompous (in a good sense) as in some English Cathedrals. He distinguishes Ancient Gothick—by which he means something like Romanesque—massive, heavy and coarse—and Modern Gothick—bright, delicate and rich to an extreme, full of whimsical and impertinent ornaments—like Westminster Abbey. *Impertinent* here means irrelevant, and perhaps some Gothic ornaments are, from the religious point of view. Nevertheless, the more we know of this background, the less irrelevant they become.[5] Whether they are valid artistically, is another matter.

As early as 1748 Mrs Montagu[6] was describing the beautiful appearance of that 'finest' of Gothic buildings, King's College Chapel. By 1776 a Lincolnshire antiquarian[7] was calling his Cathedral 'the noblest Gothic structure in England', and expressing surprise that such a building had ever been thought the production of a rude people; he remembers that it used to be the fashion to use *Gothic* of every irregular

---

[1] Hurd, *Letters on Chivalry and Romance*, iii, 264.
[2] Lyttelton, *Dialogues of the Dead*, xxv. *Life of Beau Nash*, p. 24.
[3] Scott of Amwell, Chalmers' *English Poets*, xvii, 464.   [4] Bailey's Dictionary.
[5] See D. W. Robertson, Jr., *A Preface to Chaucer* (1963).
[6] *Letters*, i, 257.   [7] *Month. Rev.* lvii (1777), 266.

or disproportioned building. Gilpin,[1] his eye on the picturesque, thought Tintern Abbey elegant, and that the 'awful solemnity' of Gothic buildings makes a more lasting impression on the mind than all the studied exactness of the Grecian models. Uvedale Price,[2] in the same spirit, speaks of Gothic splendour and magnificence, instances of which were noted by others in Somerset churches and Salisbury Cathedral;[3] but he too stresses the intricacy of the style—'plain simple Gothic is almost as great a contradiction as plain simple intricacy and enrichment'.

Gerard[4] deplores the bad taste that prefers the Gothic profusion of ornament—it 'may please one who has not acquired enlargement of mind sufficient for conceiving at one view their relation to the whole'. Shenstone[5] took no pleasure in the laboured carvings and futile diligence of Gothic architecture, though he had a 'Gothic' alcove with a pseudo-medieval inscription. It sounds like Strawberry Hill Gothic in miniature.

The dual appeal and repulsion of Gothic that characterises so much of the period can be found early in one man—Addison.[6] When he visited Siena, he found the Cathedral extraordinary, but said a man may view it 'with pleasure after he has seen St. Peter's, though it is of quite another Make, and can only be looked upon as one of the Masterpieces of *Gothic* Architecture'. If only our Forefathers, who put so much money and effort into 'these Barbarous Buildings' had been 'instructed in the right way', what 'Miracles of Architecture' they would have achieved! Hogarth[7] found consistent beauty in Gothic, and was particularly impressed by 'the famous steeple at Strasburg'. The artist saw more clearly than the literary men; Warton[8] considers that Gothic architecture is for the most part 'founded neither in nature nor reason, in necessity nor use', and is therefore 'fantastical'. To revert to Gothic is to lose all the advantages of acquired taste and revert to the days of ignorance.[9]

The effect of a Gothic building could vary at polar extremes. At the beginning of the century, Addison[10] says that a classical structure like the Parthenon fills the imagination 'with something Great and Amazing'. The 'Inside of a Gothick Cathedral', though five times

[1] *Observations on the River Wye*; cp. p. 14, of Gloucester Cathedral.
[2] *Essay*, ii, 262.   [3] *Gent. Mag.* liii (1783), 551; lix (1789), 214.
[4] *Essay on Taste*, p. 111.   [5] *Works*, ii, 351.   [6] *Remarks on ... Italy*, p. 224.
[7] *Analysis of Beauty*, pp. 48, 55.   [8] *Essay on Pope*, ii, 21.
[9] Jackson, *Four Ages*, p. 427.   [10] *Spect.* (415).

larger, makes little impression because of its 'Meanness of Manner'. Knox,[1] towards the end of the period, disapproves even of the 'meretricious' staining of the glass.

Mason[2] challenges the adverse critics at the central point, when he writes of those rich cathedral fanes,

> (Gothic ill-nam'd) where harmony results
> From disunited parts, and shapes minute,
> At once distinct and blended, boldly form
> One vast majestic whole.

But what about Gothic considered religiously rather than aesthetically? Its power was felt, but in different ways. Some thought that Westminster Abbey was 'nearer to converting one to Popery than all the regular pageantry of Roman domes. Gothic churches infuse superstition, Grecian admiration.'[3] Yet on the other hand, William Woty[4] would like to build a church in the Gothic style

> With length'ning ayles, and windows that impart
> A gloomy steady light to chear the heart,
> Such as affects the soul, and which I see
> With joy celestial, *Westminster!*, in thee.
> Not like Saint PAUL's, beneath whose ample dome,
> No thought arises of the life to come:
> For tho' superb, not solemn is the place,
> The mind outwanders o'er the distant space,
> Where 'stead of thinking on the GOD, most men
> Forget his presence to remember *Wren*.

That certainly reads into 'Si monumentum requiris . . .' what Wren would not have wished, and is unfair to St Paul's: but for some temperaments and moods there is a great deal in it.

The *Annual Register*[5] for 1758 quoted a remark from Montesquieu's *Essay on Taste* which declared that 'a Gothic building is a kind of ænigma to the age, and the soul is embarrassed, as when she is presented with an obscure poem'. Contemporary critics, presented with an obscure poem, promptly thought of Gothic architecture. So, when

[1] *Essays*, i, 346.

[2] *English Garden*, iv, 69 sqq.

[3] George Vertue, *Anecdotes of Painting*, ed. Walpole, quoted *Ann. Reg.* v (1762), 257.

[4] *Poetical Amusements, Church Langton* (Pt. II).

[5] *Ann. Reg.* i (1758), 313. This was the basic trouble—medieval thought *was* an enigma to the eighteenth century. It is not crystal clear to the twentieth.

used of literature, *Gothic* suggests that its user disapproves of complication, disproportion, and needless ornament. Rhyme is that iron Chain

> Forged by the hand of some *rude Goth*, which cramps
> The fairest feather in the Muse's wing
> And pins her to the ground.[1]

This comes from a poem in praise of 'those who have written in Blank Verse', but it is not an isolated judgment. Edward Young[2] wishes Pope had resisted the temptation of that 'Gothic dæmon rhyme which modern poesy tasting, became mortal'.

When Lawson[3] enlivens his *Lectures concerning Oratory* with allegory, he sees a Gothic building with 'a Superfluity of Ornaments' crowded without Unity of Design or Elegance, fitted by the Help of Varnish and Gilding to dazzle the unskilful Eye'. It was the Temple of False Eloquence. Or, as Isaac Hawkins Browne[4] said more compactly,

> Beauty, when best discern'd, is most compleat
> But all is *Gothic*, which is intricate.

So an unharmonious sentence is 'a Gothic arrangement'[5] and writing that lacks simplicity can be described as made up of 'contrasted phrases, affected conceits, the mere trappings of composition and Gothic minutiæ'.[6] 'Tasso's poem, like a piece of *Gothic* architecture, is decorated with many little affected prettinesses that gratify the fancy at the same time that they do violence to the understanding.'[7] The comments on Tasso suggest that the period thought of him as medieval. They had no word *Renaissance*, and such remarks—and some on Shakespeare—make it clear that they had no such idea either.

But here, too, there were defenders. When they used Gothic for medieval, they were ready to justify both form and content. Hurd[8] argued that just as Gothic architecture proves on examination to have its own rules and merits, so does Gothic poetry—he too is thinking of a Renaissance poet, Spenser. Clara Reeve[9] puts it in a nutshell when she surmises that Spenser may owe his immortality to the 'Gothic imagery that gives the principal graces to his work.' Alison[10] considers that there are 'many beautiful Compositions both in Prose and Verse' based on Gothic manners and adventure.

[1] Quoted in *Gent. Mag.* xliii (1773), 34.   [2] *Of Original Composition*, p. 26.
[3] *Lectures on Oratory*, p. 68.   [4] *On Design and Beauty*, ll. 63–4.
[5] Melmoth, *Letters*, p. 64.
[6] *Ann. Reg.* vii (1764), 187, quoting an Essay on Simplicity in Writing.
[7] *Art of Poetry*, ii, 356.   [8] *Letters on Chivalry and Romance*, viii.
[9] *Progress of Romance*, i, 52.   [10] *Of Taste*, ii, 393.

For Hurd[1] there is 'something in the *Gothic* Romance peculiarly suited to the views of genius and to the ends of poetry'. He does *not* mean the Gothic romance as a horror tale—a development that was to owe more to novelists like Mrs Radcliffe and 'Monk' Lewis than to the critics. Even the mere trifling fancies have their supporters. The *Critical Review*[2] in 1791 agreed that if the lighter Gothic superstitions are forgotten, our poetry will degenerate into cool criticisms, didactic morality, or harsher satire.

The history of *Gothic* as a value word must take account of all these varying ideas, moods and judgments.

'You sure gave us an elegant time,' wrote an American student, a statement that would have sounded more British in the eighteenth century than it does now. *Elegant* seems characteristic of certain aspects of the period, and we need be in no doubt what they meant by it. Shenstone[3] tells us that it 'excludes the glare and multiplicity of ornaments on one side, as much as it does dirt and rusticity on the other'. It would, he thought, translate Horace's allegedly untranslatable 'simplex munditiis'. Burke[4] used it of 'any body . . . compounded of parts smooth and polished without pressing upon each other, without shewing any ruggedness or confusion, and at the same time affecting some regular shape . . . It is closely allied to the beautiful, differing from it only in this regularity.'

At times they saw an older, fuller meaning in a word than we do. Phrases like 'at the bottom of a regular climax'[5] or the 'settled climax of subordination'[6] are not so much unknown, enlightening or misleading, as just puzzling: we have come to think of the climax as the highest part, forgetting that the word is Greek for a ladder, and that ladders have a bottom rung as well as a top one. Our misuse of what was a rhetorical figure began in the late eighteenth century, and was, as *O.E.D.* points out, the result of ignorance of the proper meaning of a learned term.

We tend to think of temper (without a qualifying adjective) as anger—the kind of temper likely to make the deepest impression at first. But the eighteenth century will remind us that *temper* used to mean self-control—we still speak of even-tempered people and of keeping or losing our temper—as it clearly does when Hurd[7] talks of keeping an opponent in temper and avoiding the heat of altercation, or

---

[1] op. cit., Letter I.   [2] *Crit. Rev.* 70 (1791), 635.   [3] *Works*, ii, 275.
[4] *Sublime and Beautiful*, p. 227.   [5] *Gent. Mag.* li (1781), 131.
[6] Knox, *Essays*, i, 240.   [7] *Moral and Political Dialogues*, i, 104.

when the *Spectator* advises treating those guilty of error 'with the greatest Temper and Humanity' (389). The hero of *Columella* had naturally a 'most amiable temper' (he would be 'sweet-tempered' now) and we are told that Molière could never speak of physicians with temper after they had treated him too severely.[1] To be *in temper* then and *in a temper* now is more than a difference of English idiom concerning the indefinite article.

Do we now connect *Generous* and *Generosity* with *generate* and *generation?* There is social history in the fact that most of us do not, but there is some interest in being reminded that it is 'a sort of Family Excellence and hereditary Quality of Blood and Preheminence of Nature, to take all opportunities of doing that which is Fit and Right, Good and Respectable'—and doing it 'from a free, bold, innate Principle of goodness and from the Reasonableness of things'. Even a generous horse is one of the best breed—generous wine, of the best sort. So says an Essay[2] on Generosity. The author goes on to describe the disposition we now call generosity in whatever social class it is manifested. 'Moral Philosophers call any one generous who does good unconditionally . . . and him ungenerous and degenerate, who by his inhumanity . . . obscures the Lustre of his Progenitors, though descended of the best Families.' The coupling of *ungenerous* with *degenerate* throws light on the origins of both words. But how did *generous* come to emphasize giving and forgiving in particular? Our essayist explains—'a generous Person gives without Asking, rewards beyond Desert, does good freely, requires no Gratuity, speaks his Mind openly, pities the Miserable . . . hates to be covetous, scorns to be Revengeful'.

Occasionally we are shown a glimpse of some unexpected episode in the life history of a word. Mrs Piozzi[3] tells us that *dubious* was popular some twenty-five or thirty years before—roughly in the 'sixties—but was made ridiculous through being ill-pronounced in the mouth of a clown in a popular though paltry drama, which caused people to be afraid of uttering the word. She remarked truly that 'such mean impressions wear away by time, leaving only the half-effaced head and fool's cap to puzzle antiquarians'. In this case, we might not see even the faint outline of the fool's cap if she had not told us. She observed too how *droll* had been a common verb, but that now 'we do not say a man DROLLS upon his neighbour's foible, but how DROLL he

---

[1] Graves, *Columella*, i, 125: *Lælius and Hortensia*, p. 146.
[2] Quoted in *Gent. Mag.* viii (1738). [3] *Brit. Syn.*, i, 172 (1794).

is when he so entertains the company'. That is still true of our idiomatic usage, but our meaning is kinder—drollery is more delicate than 'coarse buffoonery'.

The *Gentleman's Magazine*[1] for 1789 exemplifies the word *Follower* in the sense of 'lover' about fifty years before the quotation from Dickens which *O.E.D.* gives as its first illustration: the Magazine is offering a draft certificate of servants' characters, which includes the statement that they are free of 'improper connexions and unallowed followers'. Having read our Victorian novels and our *Punch* jokes, we see nothing odd in this: but there is a hint in the *Spectator* (573) that the word has left the drawing-room for the kitchen—it is a lady speaking who says that all her 'Followers' were attributed 'to the inevitable Force' of her charms.

We feel that *insanity* is a word any one might use—unless he prefers the modern 'mental illness': we could apply it to the policies of politicians if we disapproved of them. So we may be puzzled when the *Gentleman's Magazine*[2] in 1768 objects to 'Insanity overthrew her lovely mind', because 'the image of insanity overthrowing a mind is not happy' (did they not recall 'O what a noble mind is here o'er-thrown'?)—and indeed the word Insanity itself is more fit for a lawyer than a poet. The quotations in *O.E.D.* show this latter statement to be true: up to the *Junius Letters* at least, all the quotations are legal. Mrs Piozzi says it is medical: but of course the two departments merge when it is a question of whether a man is in his right mind, since his liberty, property or life may be at stake.

Even the occasional bias or detail of a dictionary entry may throw light on the eighteenth-century taste. *Sunburnt* was no more a compliment then than in Elizabethan times—it applies to 'harvesters and sailors'. People in this period would not have wished to buy sun-tan lotions.

They define *Marmalade* as made of 'plumbs', apricots and quinces, though certainly citrus fruits were used. And our White Sauce seems dull beside their exposition of it as 'a sauce made of blanched Almonds and the Breasts of a Capon pounded together with Cloves, Cinnamon etc.' They took, also, a kinder view of a Carousal than many a modern —it was 'a grand feast or act of mirth and jollity' such as a prince's installation or marriage, or a Lord Mayor's banquet.

It casts a curious light on their society that *Vixen* could be defined (by Dyche and Pardon) with no reference to its proper meaning—

[1] *Gent. Mag.* lix (1789), iv.   [2] *Gent. Mag.* xxxviii (1768), 133.

indeed, *she-fox* was in use—but only as transferred to peevish women and children.

We do not now refuse to say we are 'very sorry' to read of the death of an acquaintance. The *Gentleman's Magazine*[1] in 1793 regarded it as a 'fashionable' expression—the fashion has become something of a fixture. We should most of us have sympathy for the gentleman who wrote to the Lord Bishop of Ferns to explain he had been unwell—we easily could be. But the *Monthly Review*[2] in 1767 when it quoted the letter, felt constrained to note that the word is commonly used in Ireland[3] for ill or indisposed. We tend to use it euphemistically, but there is much to be said for Lord Chesterfield's distinction when he declares himself 'neither well nor ill, but *unwell*'.[4]

For English speakers of the early modern period, it was a question of grammar whether they answered *Yes* or *Yea*. By the eighteenth century it had become a social matter. James Buchanan[5] says *Yes* is 'more genteel' than *yea*, 'which is seldom used but by the People called Quakers'. 'We use *I*,' he adds, 'as an Answer in a familiar, careless or merry way; as I, I, Sir, I, I; but to use *ay* is accounted rude, especially to our betters.' We envy his freedom of spelling (*I* was the earliest version) and wonder why 'Ay, Ay, Sir' joined the Navy and the third spelling variant 'Aye' entered Parliament.

No department of usage reflects social ideas more faithfully than the modes of address and reference in use on different occasions. We can see our own conventions growing up, find some of our own debates beginning, and receive some surprises where our usage has noticeably deviated from theirs.

Mamma, it seems, was middle-class. The *Monthly*[6] in 1769, reviewing Mrs Charlotte Lennox's comedy *The Sister*, says it is never used among people of fashion, at least out of the nursery, and is not suitable for an Earl's daughter to use to her mother. On the other hand, a letter[7] of the same decade complains of the suburban boarding schools where *Miss*, whose *Mamma* sells oysters, tells *Miss* whose Father deals in small-coals, that her *Governess* [Mistress is 'vulgar'] shall hear

---

[1] *Gent. Mag.* lxiii, Pt. 2 (1793), 610.

[2] *Month. Rev.* xxxvii (1767), 399.

[3] A reader notes in the margin of the University of Bristol Library copy 'And in England, too'.

[4] Letter in 1769—Willard Connely's *Chesterfield*, 1939, p. 451.

[5] *English Syntax*, Sect. IV.

[6] *Month. Rev.* xl (1769), 249. The dictum seems doubtful.

[7] *Lond. Mag.* xxxvii (1768), 651.

of it, if she spits in her face, or does anything else unbecoming a young lady!

Miss was the subject of enquiry and comment. A writer[1] in 1781 wonders when it was first used as an appellation to single ladies. He could not remember it in the Spectator, or in any comic writer of that period. Miss is injudicious in addressing unmarried ladies, says the Monthly Review,[2] but does not make it clear whether the objection is to Miss X or to Miss alone. Mrs continued to be written of single ladies. In 1768, the Annual Register[3] recorded the deaths of Mrs Jane Lipscomb and her sister Mrs Elizabeth Lipscomb. 'They were both maiden ladies.' The Connoisseur (xliv) wishes there were 'some middle term between Miss and Mrs to be adopted at a certain age by all females not inclined to matrimony'—Miss conveys the idea of youth and beauty if not of 'a bib and hanging sleeves'. However, 'every unmarried woman is a Miss, every married one by the same courtesy is a Lady'. Dr Wendeborn[4] is surprised, not to say shocked, at the way two washerwomen call each other Madam.

What is polite to the living may be out of place of the dead. À propos of a history in which Anne Boleyn is prefixed with Miss, the Critical Review[5] asks whether one could help laughing if he thought of Henry VIII making his addresses to Miss Nancy Boleyn, Miss Jenny Seymour and Miss Kitty Howard. We should feel that what makes it funny is the pet names even more than the title.

The extent to which eighteenth-century logic could go even here is demonstrated by the query to 'Mr Review',[6] which asked whether it was not absurd for a community to address the Queen as Madam. Why not Notre Dame? To which Defoe gives the two proper answers—Madam is English 'legitimated by custom', and Notre Dame would be absurd, since even in French it is appropriated to the Virgin: to use it 'would be a Banter upon the Queen, and you would be thought to be going to say your Prayers to her'. It must have been a similar logical doubt about the pronoun that led a grammarian[7] to say that 'My Lord Hawke' suggests 'some degree of familiarity' and is 'only proper to the stile of a king, whose lords they originally were'. We are told[8] that the Scots addressed strangers with Friend, like the French, and said 'My dear Sir' by way of calming argument.

[1] Gent. Mag. li (1781), 64.
[2] Month. Rev. lii (1775), 361.
[3] Ann. Reg. xi (1768), 90.
[4] View, i, 20.
[5] Crit. Rev. 5 (1758), 70.
[6] Review, I, 352.
[7] Bicknell, Grammatical Wealth, ii, 65.
[8] Crit. Rev. 42 (1776), 89.

Men's titles of course raise more complicated questions than women's. As with the historical ladies, it was felt affected[1] to use *Mr* of the great of the past: 'we do not say Mr Shakespear or Mr Dryden; a great poet rises far above all *Misters*, and his name alone becomes the most honourable title by which he can be called'—these are names of dignity enough to dispense with 'all these *Misters*', though both these comments are made in criticism of writers who did not share the journal's view. Why do we now so often say Dr Johnson? Because we think of him as a friend as well as an author? It is interesting to notice that he could use pet names for his circle and yet address them as *Sir*, a form in much wider use then. (The Quakers are reported not to have used it.)[2] It would hardly be used now as it is in the anecdote from the *Margate New Guide* of 1799[3] about a young lady asking for a book: ' "Pray, Sir," said she, "have you Man as he is?" "No, Ma'am," replied the assistant (wishing to accommodate her, and with no other meaning) "but we have Woman as she should be." '

If the eighteenth century could be snobbish, it recognized breeding and position when it saw them, and used the social forms accordingly. The *Annual Register*[4] of 1766 writes of the visiting chiefs 'and their ladies' precisely as it would have written of any European visiting nobility: one would like to believe the same attitude was prevalent everywhere today. It is a sad comment on our civilisation that the eighteenth century would not have understood the word *colour-bar*— its slave-holding notwithstanding.

It is also refreshing to find a critic who thinks it childish to say *noble authors*—'I cannot see what a man's nobility has to do with his authorship.'[5]

There were complaints that *esquire* was being applied to every one —even to vagabonds[6]—and indeed there were those who thought *Mr* too indiscriminately used. *Mr* was then as now vague, 'equally claimed by the son of a *peer*, or a *porter*, an opulent *merchant*, or the master of a green-stall'.[7]

[1] *Brit. Crit.* ii (1793), 58; v (1795), 652.
[2] James Beattie, *London Diary*, 4 June 1773.   [3] *Brit. Crit.* xiv (1799), 184.
[4] *Ann. Reg.* ix (1766), 122. We may remember that Boswell writes to the ex-slave Francis Barber, who became Dr Johnson's servant and residuary legatee, as 'Dear Sir': letters to his factor Andrew Gibb, begin simply 'Andrew' for they are from master to servant. And he tells Andrew not to write to him as Good Sir —the adjective is improper to a master.
[5] Baker, *Remarks*, xxxix.
[6] *Crit. Rev.* new arr. xxi (1797), 460.   [7] *Month. Rev.* xxxiii (1765), 248.

They were concerned about double titles: 'is it not awkward to say Admiral Lord Howe, General Sir Guy Carleton'?[1] Others disapproved of calling officers Mr So and So, 'a manner of speaking which makes our officers of the army and navy too often to forget their station and has a tendency to cause them to drown the employment in the idea of a gentleman'. Why not call them 'what they are, in order to distinguish them for their acquired desert'?[2]

Likewise, there were those who doubted whether affectation or humility was the cause of the omission of 'the Reverend' before 'Mr' in the addresses of the clergy.[3] In the 'nineties correspondents in the *Gentleman's Magazine*[4] were arguing whether you should write 'The Rev. Mr Jones' which one of them thought 'bad heraldry' and absurd. If you don't know the Christian name, put a dash. Another argued[5] for 'The Rev. Mr A.E.'—you say 'The Rev. Sir A.E., The Hon. Mr A.' —the contrary practice is 'an affectation of very recent date'.

The *Guardian* (137) had objected long before to 'the impertinent (i.e. out of place) use of titles and a paraphrastical way of saying *you*'. An amusing illustration comes from the *Annual Register*[6] of 1774, when it reports how a man gave much offence to an auctioneer who happened to be a magistrate, and whom he failed to address as 'Your Worship'. The magistrate jailed him for contempt. On his release, the victim went round to the sales bidding 'Threepence, your worship, sixpence, your worship' until his worship paid him ten guineas to stay away!

In 1794 the *Annual Register*[7] reported that a Mr Wilcocks in New York had proposed that 'the titles of *excellency, honourable, esquire*, and all other characteristic designations not warranted by the constitution and inconsistent with the plainness and real dignity of republican manners, be abolished'.

It is interesting to find that republican America negatived the motion, and has since found her own special applications of 'the honourable'.

This objection to the common forms was political. Others were moral—or cynical. Fielding's *Champion*[8] asks what idea a man can have who says to another, 'Sir, I am your most obedient servant, I

---

[1] *Gent. Mag.* lx (1790), 1189.
[2] Gemsege [Pegge] in *Gent. Mag.* xxvi (1756), 486.
[3] *Crit. Rev.* new arr. iii (1791), 221.   [4] *Gent. Mag.* lx (1790), 1189.
[5] *Gent. Mag.* lx (1790), 1189.   [6] *Ann. Reg.* xvii (1774), 150.
[7] *Ann. Reg.* xxxvi (1794), 9.   [8] i, 196.

am heartily glad to see you . . . you might as well say *Barababatha* as most obedient servant.' Indeed, 'no ideas are attached to Captain, Doctor, Esquire, Honourable, Rt Honourable'.

If that was true, it is a sad reflection on the age. But the *Looker-on*[1] was talking sense when it said that the language of politeness is 'perfectly consistent with truth. . . . A lie is not locked up in a phrase, but exists in the mind of the speaker. In the common compliments of the day, we have no intention to deceive; and there is a secret compact between the parties to understand them as words of course' [i.e. conventional words].

(2) *Letters*

Eighteenth-century comments on poetic language are enlightening in their exposition (or betrayal) of ideals, of verbal associations and all too often of the critic's insensitiveness and his fear of any flight of the imagination.

A poet's words should be rational. Johnson,[2] it will be remembered, dislikes Gray's 'honied Spring' on morphological grounds—he disapproves of 'giving to adjectives, derived from substantives, the termination of participles, such as the *cultured* plain, the *daisied* bank', and he was sorry to see a scholar like Gray speaking of the *honied* Spring.

A letter to the *Gentleman's Magazine*[3] objects to the *sense*: honey is the product of June and July, so honied Spring 'might do very well in a true London poet'. One doubts whether Gray meant anything more definite than 'sweet', or at the most that flowers bursting in Spring will provide nectar in due course. The correspondent claims that he had told Warton that *fragrant* is not a suitable word for poppies: they are 'faint' as a Londoner would say—'making faint' that is, and they add to the disagreeableness of gleaning. *Flagrant* would be better.

We should find *Flagrant* a misleading personification: it means merely 'red' here, not 'strikingly vicious'—or 'caught red-handed'.

Bentley[4] disliked Milton's 'wandering Mazes' on the rational ground that mazes and labyrinths 'do not themselves wander'—*winding* would be better. In the same spirit, he dislikes 'floury Brooks'— 'Floury Banks is vulgar; but floury Brooks, as if the Flours grew in

---

[1] iii, 30–1.
[2] On these words, see G. B. Hill's edn. of *The Lives of the Poets*, iii, 434.
[3] *Gent. Mag.* li (1781), 319.   [4] Re *Paradise Lost*, ii, 561.

the Water, are not easily met with.'[1] One feels that Bentley had made no close study of any brook: but what worries us is the incongruous picture of banks (or brooks) coated with flour, for which the undifferentiated spelling for the flower of the field and the flour of the wheat is responsible.

Bentley was not alone in betraying ignorance of nature in his verbal criticism. Apart from *skirtings*, which apparently did not bother the eighteenth century, it is hard for us to see what is obscure[2] in Mr Polwhele's verse describing how

> The foliage *lash'd* the forest steep,
> Then *shrunk* into a gloom more deep ...
> O'er dun skirtings of the dale,
> The brooding spirit of the gale
> In pitchy darkness hung
> Where, on a lofty crested oak
> Sudden, the forked azure broke ...

It seems hardly to need the detailed defence offered by 'A Southern Faunist'[3] (i.e. Naturalist) who points out that in his district they say that saplings must be thinned because they lash each other; if Dryden could make leaves dance, why should not Polwhele make them shrink? In personifying the storm, the conversion of the verb *brood* into an adjective is only an expressive poetic paraphrase on the common expression 'there's mischief brooding'. And by forked azure 'what can we understand but lightning?' What, indeed? We may well be happier with the verses than with the explanation at one point, for we speak of mischief *brewing*. Did not Polwhele have at the back of his mind Milton's rendering of a Biblical phrase—the Spirit's 'brooding wings' in *Paradise Lost*, xii, 235?

Perhaps the most prosaic example of over-rational comment is the scientific objection[4] to the *swan-song*. From the ornithologist's point of view this time-honoured expression is an 'idle conceit' for their 'organs undoubtedly are not formed for that purpose. It is time to explode' an expression 'too trite and absurd to be admitted into modern poetry'.

Langhorne[5] was perverse in his depreciation of a Cambridge poem when he picks out metaphorical words and interprets them in their most prosaic sense. The poet has said 'No more stern winter *whitens*

---

[1] Re iii, 30.   [2] *Gent. Mag.* lxii (1792), 833.   [3] ibid., p. 878.
[4] *Crit. Rev.* 47 (1779), 314.   [5] *Month. Rev.* xxix (1763), 39.

every plain'—so Winter is 'a white-washer': 'nor spreads the fetters of his frosts around'—so now he is 'a gaoler'; Spring is 'a blacksmith', for his breath 'breaks the icy chain', and then 'a taylor' for he clothes in 'fertility's green robes the ground'. This method would turn the laugh against some of the best poetry in the language.

Hume[1] was offering a true defence of the poet against this literal-mindedness, when he wrote

Many of the beauties of poetry, and even of eloquence, are founded on falsehood and fiction, on hyperboles, metaphors, and an abuse or perversion of terms from their natural meaning. To check the sallies of the imagination and to reduce every expression to geometrical truth and exactness, would be the most contrary to the laws of criticism.

On the other hand, the critics dealt faithfully with the absurdities of the poetasters, with incongruous images or far-fetched vocabulary, especially with new and strange compound epithets.

The unwary author of 'an heroic ballad' was accused by the *Criticai Review*[2] of 'great impropriety' in his use of personification. He had portrayed Despair assailing the gates of Virtue's breast, and had converted Candour into the base of Virtue's throne (which betrayed 'a very Gothic talent' for poetical designing), had described Surprize as resembling a Merry Andrew, and represented Sympathy as bestriding a Sigh! Would not the author be 'shocked with the ridiculous fancy of a painter who should, if possible, represent Sympathy riding at full gallop upon a sigh to lay hold of the heart of Virtue in which, that the rider might have the more commodious access, the artist had placed gates in her breast'?

Whether a poet's word picture can be turned into the artist's pencilled picture is a sound test of its integrity and consistency, provided we remember that some words originally figurative have lost whatever pictorial quality they once had. Priestley[3] puts this situation well:

When a figure is become absolutely evanescent, and long use hath made the metaphorical term more familiar than the proper name of the thing, or circumstance denoted by it, it is pains employed to very little purpose to trace out the long-forgotten allusion, in order to show its *latent inconsistency* with anything it is connected with. Who can expect that such phrases as these, *fallen into an error*, to *spend time* upon a thing, to be *incensed* at a person, etc., should be used with any regard to the latent figure they contain? It is

---

[1] *Essays*, i, 269.   [2] *Crit. Rev.* 41 (1776), 403.
[3] *Oratory and Criticism*, pp. 191–2.

impossible however for any person to construct many sentences without exposing himself to the same censure; terms which are ultimately figurative abound so much in all languages, all our intellectual ideas are expressed in terms borrowed from sensible things; but who, in using them, attends to the sensible images they suggest? Or, whoever attends to the ideas of *local position*, which every preposition implies?

Warburton[1] says much the same, when he argues that similes die into metaphor and the metaphor becomes an epithet, which soon loses all the colouring of the original figure. *Decrepid* and *capricious* are his examples. It is of course an easier process if the word is a foreign loan —an Englishman innocent of Latin cannot connect *capricious* with *goats capering*. If, like Touchstone, he can, the word becomes the more interesting. But this is punning, not etymology.

These are salutary caveats to critics. Difficulty arises, however, when there are different views of the deadness of the metaphor. Dr Johnson[2] criticised Addison sharply for treating his Muse as if she were first a horse and then a ship, and confusing the attributes of both. A defender[3] of the lines argued that both *launch* and *bridle* had lost their metaphoric quality. It is certainly true now, when people often say they '*launch* a *campaign* to *raise money*' with no thought of the etymology of the four main words. To say that Mr X has an unbridled tongue (or desire, or temper) does not really mean we see him as a horse. It is doubtful whether the defence should stand, since Addison's own *Spectator* (595) is hard on mixed metaphors—'I have known a Hero compared to a Thunderbolt, a Lion and the Sea; all and each of them proper Metaphors for Impetuosity, Courage, or Force. But by bad Management . . . the Thunderbolt hath overflowed its Banks; the Lion hath been darted through the Skies and the Billows have rolled out of the Libyan Desart.'

The trouble with Addison's lines is that the apparently dead metaphors are proved to have been only dormant when they are put together: they get up and fight when brought into each other's company.

Even the faulty juxtaposition of a metaphor and a straight word can make us uneasy. The *Monthly Review*[4] remarks that *embrace*, used figuratively, should imply a choice—a martyr may embrace death, but

---

[1] *Works*, iv, 139.   [2] *Lives of the English Poets*, ed. G. B. Hill, ii, 128.
[3] Arthur Browne, Fellow of Trinity College, Dublin, quoted in *Crit. Rev.* xxiv (1798), 88.
[4] *Month. Rev.* xl (1769), 242. But Mr Hoyle's 'saw' was a technicality of whist (=*see-saw* or *cross-ruff*).

one cannot embrace inevitable doom. It continues 'The immortal Mr Hoyle, in his excellent treatise on the game of whist, advises his pupils to *embrace* a *saw*. Perhaps there are few things upon earth that a man could be admonished to embrace with less congruity than a saw!'

The ease with which incongruity can occur can be seen from two remarks of the *Critical Review*.[1] It blamed an author for 'losing himself in a mist of discordant metaphors': is not that itself another? Whether you think actually of jarring sounds or etymologically of a disunion of hearts, it is difficult to see how *discord* can produce a *mist*, and indeed, how a *blaze* can be *blunted*, though the same *Review*[2] apparently thought it could when it observed that 'the blaze of sublime description with which the Messiah of Pope is gloriously invested, has not been essentially blunted or impaired'.

Poetry should not indulge in new-fangled diction. There are frequent adverse comments on unheard-of compounds, and it must be granted that some sound very odd—*gain-insidious*, *genius-kindly*, *ardour-drunk*, *death-dew-dropping*.[3] Lloyd[4] thinks the diction of Elegy, provided it is not mean, cannot be too simple: 'Compound epithets have a harshness rarely suitable to the English Language, and are to be used very sparingly.' Not all English poets have acted on this principle[5]—the effectiveness of the epithet depends on the imagination of the poet. Some of those adversely criticised here are surely acceptable —*time-corroded*, *brown-brow'd*—though it may well be that *saint-encyphered* and *time-unlettered* 'cost the Author much more pains than they are worth'. We might on the whole, however, apply more widely the comment of the *British Critick*[6] that many of our modern poets have 'an appropriate language [i.e. one of their own] very like English, but somewhat less intelligible. The perfection of this seems to consist in bringing words together, which nature and common sense never intended to meet.'

If occasionally the critics' response to a word they felt unfamiliar was strangely out of touch with the past, naturally they could not be expected to have any inkling of the future. 'What idea can we have of a breathless calm?' asks the *Critical Review*[7] in 1782 when it meets the phrase in the poems of the Rev. William Bagshaw Stevens—another who 'abounds in strange affected unintelligible epithets' such as

[1] *Crit. Rev.* new arr. vi (1792), 559.
[2] *Crit. Rev.* new arr. xv (1795–6), 32.
[3] *Gent. Mag.* lix (1789), 1020.
[4] *Month. Rev.* xxv (1762), 328.
[5] See S. P. E. Tract 49.
[6] *Brit. Crit.* ii (1793), 437.
[7] *Crit. Rev.* 53 (1782), 463–4.

wealth-puffed insolence, *sphere-inspiring* worth, *bounty-blessing* scene, *coarse-throng'd* way, *religion-lifted* thought. These may all be too harshly compressed, but they are not unintelligible. 'Breathless calm of soul' is much more interesting. *O.E.D.* says that the original sense was the plain 'without breath', whether dead or gasping, and that 'holding one's breath with awe, expectation or excitement' is first found in Wordsworth's sonnet of 1802 ('breathless as a nun'), and that the sense 'unstirred by breath of wind' is again from Wordsworth in 1815. Whichever idea Stevens had in mind, he was a humble precursor of a greater man. It is interesting also to find the views expressed in the *Preface* to the *Lyrical Ballads* anticipated by the *Gentleman's Magazine*[1] in 1765. True, the subject was a prose work—Hervey's *Letters on the eloquence of the pulpit*—but Hervey was incapable of writing prose as it should be written. The reviewer says that a man 'must know very little of language indeed who is still to learn that a bold, an elegant, and figurative stile may be formed of words familiarly known to the meanest peasant, which, with all the advantages of perspicuity, will have all the force of rhetorick'.

The *Critical Review*[2] came on a line about 'blooming vales and ever-fadeless groves': *blooming* caused no qualms, but the reviewers took *fadeless* to be a word of the poet's own coining and hoped it would never be current. Actually it can be found as early as 1652; it had been used by Isaac Watts and was to be used by Coleridge. In a high-flown mood, we should accept it for figurative or celestial flowers, and in our mundane mood we should go in search of fadeless fabrics.

The language plays strange tricks. In the 1760's the *Monthly Review*[3] objected to the expression 'a rude arch curtained door-wise'; in the 1960's *-wise* has made a fashionable come-back, if not quite in this sense. And if the reviewers had not drawn our attention to the words, we should see nothing odd in *curly* tresses or a rivulet *jumping* from precipice to precipice. *O.E.D.* dates this use of *curly* from 1772, and this use of *jump* to 1860. No wonder the reviewers found both un-familiar.

Poetry should not use undignified words—too archaic, too techni-cal, too every-day. Much of Bentley's uneasiness with Milton springs from this principle. *À propos* of 'a cloudy Chair' (*Paradise Lost*, ii, 930) he remarks that 'a *Chair* is too mean a *Carriage*'—and certainly a Sedan Chair would be incongruous in its period colour. But Bentley

---

[1] *Gent. Mag.* xxxv (1765), 288.
[2] *Crit. Rev.* 52 (1781), 234.   [3] *Month. Rev.* xl (1769), 372.

wants us to substitute *carr*—and what cleared the eighteenth-century difficulty immediately produces one for us.[1] Bentley dislikes *ground*—if Adam and Eve are to 'possess the spatious ground' of Paradise (*Paradise Lost*, v, 367) 'it implies that they were to dig and delve' there as 'afterwards they did in common Earth'. *Ground* is 'too low a word'. What else Milton should have said does not appear. And when Milton used the nautical technicality *larboard*, for Bentley it was 'in Heroic Stile . . . abominable'. Dr Johnson[2] thought the same of Dryden's naval words in his *Annus Mirabilis*.

For us, *larboard* has the dignity of the unfamiliar: perhaps we should feel differently about its modern substitute *port*.

In 1783[3] a lesser poem borrowed Dryden's title and ran into the same criticism. Badcock, reviewing it in the *Monthly*, thinks that *guns* 'hath a most un-epic sound'. The poets, he thinks, have over-used *cannon*; but even *guns* was better than *tubes*, which would have been the choice of 'nicer [i.e. more fastidious] poets who affect an uncommon chastity of expression'. Badcock gives a reasoned explanation of his dislike— 'Recent events, familiar names, and familiar circumstances ill accord with the dignity and solemn tone of the heroic Muse. They have somewhat of the air of burlesque.' This is tantamount to saying that you cannot write an epic poem on a piece of modern history, as if all heroes had lived in the classical past.

Poets should not be imitative, either of archaic vocabulary and syntax, or of older poems. The Monthly Reviewers[4] in 1789 felt fatigued with *groves among*, *what time*, *grayflies* and *gadflies* and their *sultry horns*, *twilight grey* o'er the *dark* mead throwing her *dusky mantle*; with, 'in short, all the paraphernalia of the ancient Muse; whom we recollect on these occasions only by her old clothes'. By implication, it seems things would go hard with *Lycidas*.

There are dissentient voices: a writer in 1735[5] thinks it a pity we neglect Chaucer and Spenser, and introduce unsuitable words; and another quotation in the *Gentleman's Magazine*[6] suggests that shortage of words 'may be abundantly supply'd by a *Revival* of *antiquated* words, which are confess'd to give a *venerable* Air as *Poetical* Descriptions'.

---

[1] Cp. comment on Glover, below, p. 195.
[2] *Lives of the English Poets*, ed. G. B. Hill, i, 433.
[3] *Month. Rev.* lxviii (1783), 121.   [4] *Month. Rev.* xxxi (1789), 81.
[5] Quoted from *Fog's Journal*, *Gent. Mag.* v (1735), 466.
[6] ibid., p. 252.

But what if the eighteenth-century reader did not understand his Chaucer, Spenser or Milton? It seems clear that many did not, when we look at the lists of words in Spenser or Milton that the critics in the period thought in need of explanation. The Richardsons' list—in the order in which they occur in *Paradise Lost*—included for example the following: *hideous, weltring, Arch-Enemy, dreary, forlorn, beach, sheer, affront, orgies, fanatic, Crete, palpable, uncouth, dint, purlieus, torrid, behests, rues, prowling, clustring, lithe, askance, abash'd, clime, swerve, mould, silvan, pondering, havoc, spume, jocund, promontory, tepid, dank, lair, brake, supernal, incur, tortuous, murkie, portentous, texture, bevy, gulph, seal* (='sea-calf'), *carol, brand* (=sword).

Forlorn, uncouth, behests, askance, swerve, bevy, and *brand* are explained also by John Upton in his edition of the *Faerie Queene*, and so are *Ado, affray, aloof, array, baleful, bent* (=propensity), *betide, counter-stroke, debonaire, doff* and *don, doughtie, dreare, fare, fay, fell* (adj.), *glade, glee, glen,* to *gore, guerdon, guise, hurtle, lament* (n.), *lay* (n.), *meed, quarry, riven, score* (=reckoning), *seare, seemely,* to *shrill, sods, sway* (n.)., *tenor* (of voice), *thrall,* to *vaunt, unkempt, unrest.*

All this implies a serious narrowing of the poetic vocabulary or of common knowledge.

It is also of interest to find that certain words we can use any day were poetic words in Dr Johnson's view.[1] For him, *Abundance* is chiefly poetical, and so is *dreary*. *Lad* belongs to pastoral language, and *each*, meaning 'every one of any number' is poetic—it is the prevailing modern sense. *Ruddy* means pale red, and also yellow, and if used at all, only in poetry in such a phrase as 'ruddy gold'. This second meaning sounds like a false contextual deduction. The eighteenth century used it of the complexion: we should hesitate to do so now, for the word in its degenerate sense is in all too common use, but it does not strike us as poetical.

The *Tatler* (32) describes a lady who uses poetic language as an affectation—her blue clothes are 'her Azure Dress', her scarf her 'Pinions', her chariot her 'vehicle'. We think *vehicle*—that blanket term in traffic regulations—the prose word, and *chariot* the poetic. Transport terms seem particularly tricky. But we sympathise with the other lover[2] who almost lost his English as a result of adapting himself to his lady's style—'at least to speak such as any body else does'. He had called a cave a grotto for years, and even asked one of his father's tenants come to pay the rent whether there were any shepherds in the

---

[1] Notes s.v. in his Dictionary.　　　　　[2] *Tatler* (107).

'Flowry Meads' at home. The craze for pastoral poetry in pastoral language seems to have been a standing joke in Queen Anne's reign. The best comment is the 'advertisement' in the *Tatler* (143)—March 1709—according to which a coach from London would travel to Dorchester via Basingstoke, Sutton, Stockbridge, Salisbury and Blandford, at 'all which Places there are Accommodations of Spreading Beeches, Beds of Flowers, Turf Seats and Purling Streams for happy Swains, and Thunder-struck Oaks and Left-handed Ravens, to foretel Misfortunes to those that please to be Wretched; with all other Necessaries for pensive Passion'—such as 'opening Buds, Flowring Thyme, Warbling Birds, sporting Lambkins and Fountain Water' all of which can be sent to London for those who can't go to the country.

LIGHT ON OUR VOCABULARY

(1) *Reminders of the origins of terms now dulled*
An occasional word unexpectedly used will remind us of meanings long since dead. We *seethe* with anger, but we no longer *seethe* the meat as fifteenth-century cookery recipes instruct us to do, and though we keep *sodden* it has lost any sense of connection of form with *seethe* or of meaning with boiling. The remark in the *Guardian* (139) that Androcles, after having *sodden* some flesh in the sun, gave it to his lion, shows the half-way stage—the heat is there, but not the wet. *Recipe* was still a medical prescription then; it was Horace Walpole who used it first as we do.[1] This explains Collier's[2] remark about a disease which is in the mind, and therefore cannot be reached with a recipe. We talk of *scrubby* people, but forget that there used to be a noun *scrub* used of persons. A *Turkey-Stone*[3] explains the 'turquoise', *Italian characters*[4] 'italics', and *Pinchbeck's metal*[5] what we call simply 'pinchbeck'. We can see how cordials got their name when a character in a play asks the maid to 'bring something cordial' to the lady. . . . 'Enter Tattlaid with bottles.'[6] We don't use penknives for trimming quill pens, but it is a good reminder of their use when we read of the unlucky schoolmaster who 'dropt his penknife, and catching it between his thighs, it pierced so deep that it killed him'.[7] We know the colour Venetian Red, but may not know that at Venice the 'floors are of a kind of red plaister, with a

---

[1] In 1743 (*O.E.D.*).   [2] *Essays*, p. 127.
[3] Hertford-Pomfret Correspondence, ii, 142.
[4] *Champion*, i, 57.   [5] *World* (67).
[6] Steele, *The Funeral*, p. 55.   [7] *Ann. Reg.* xii (1769), 106.

brilliant glossy surface'.[1] We talk of 'old junk'—any sort of rubbish—but there was a more exact sense, as the precise list 'pitch, tar, rosin, old junk' reminds us: they were all inflammable substances that encouraged a fire at Limehouse.[2] 'Pieces of old cable' says Dr Johnson.

(2) *Special and General*

What we regard as a general term may then have been exact. A *dismal ditty* is no longer especially a cant term for the psalm sung by the criminal at the gallows.[3]

Garbage—especially in the United States—can be any household rubbish (and moral rubbish by transfer), though for Dyche and Pardon it was the entrails of any creature, fat, tripe, guts. Of course it may work the other way. School and Post Office were both defined by Dyche and Pardon as 'public houses', and there is no inherent reason why the term should be restricted to the tavern. Entrance to a school may be a problem, but not to a Post Office.

Trash is no longer *especially* perished or bad fruit (s.v., Dyche and Pardon).

Restriction of a word's meaning—theirs and ours—throws light on our respective customs. For them a *carol* would have been the proper description of 'Happy Birthday to you'—it is 'a song of joy, or salutation at a feast or birthday, or any publick or private banquetting or merriment'. A *cage* to us is for birds or beasts, or people going down a mine shaft: to them it was also a place of confinement for thieves and vagrants that are taken up by the watch in the night-time. Modern organizers of billeting have not restricted themselves to inn-keepers, ale-houses, brandy-shops etc.—though of course *etc* covers everything in theory if not in practice. Raffling is no longer associated with the 'quality' at Tonbridge, and we do not think of cockfighting when we *spar*—the sense of 'the fighting or striking of a cock with his heels and spurs' was a special eighteenth-century restriction.

Why should we not use *youths*[4] of young women, and why don't we think of tulips as gay *vegetables*?[5] The basic sense of 'young folk' and 'growing plants' would allow both. And why do we feel that only faults can be *glaring*, so that it sounds strange to read of the virtues of a great and good man that were 'too glaring in his life to be forgotten at his death'?[6] The 'humble airs' of children in the *Spectator* (380)

---

[1] *Ann. Reg.* xxiii (1780), from Dr Moore, *View of Italy.*
[2] *Ann. Reg.* xvii (1775), 102.   [3] Dyche and Pardon s.v. *ditty.*
[4] *Spect.* (514).   [5] *Tatler* (218).   [6] *World* (173).

reminds us that 'to give oneself airs' is only one possibility. And since *stark* meant 'strong', why not 'stark love and kindness'?[1] Why should the adjective *laboured* suggest that the labour has been largely misapplied? The eighteenth century could speak approvingly of a 'laboured and finished performance'.[2] And, *per contra*, why does *facile* now imply 'too easy by half'? When people *decamp* we are inclined to suspect that their departure was furtive and unauthorised: but 'Leonidas' Glover[3] talks of an army that will 'decamp

> To choose a friendlier station'.

(3) *Literal and Figurative*

There are too the words which were commonly literal then but seem figurative to us. They could speak of the *unctuous* lotos, *unctuous* pitch, *unctuous* mist;[4] of the sun *enlightening*[5] some part of the world or of *enlightened* and *darkened* objects.[6] We can *thwart* an opponent's progress, but we don't say a fox *thwarts*[7] the path when he goes across (or athwart) it. The *fag-end* is hardly likely to be the 'latter or hindmost End of cloth'. We may *bristle up*, but Dyche and Pardon's definition may give us something of a shock—'to erect the hairs upright upon the back, like an enraged hog'. We may be case-hardened —so could they—but they knew better than we that the verb means 'to render iron or steel so hard as to be capable of resisting any edged tool'.

Frequently an eighteenth-century comment on a phrase, or a description of a situation to which we owe some idiom, will show us how we got the expression, which we may well be using with no idea, or a false idea, or a weakened idea, of its origin.

'It's a flash in the pan,' we say, perhaps with no clear picture in our minds of the meaning of the elements in the phrase, though we know that as a whole it means a sudden brilliant effort that doesn't last, or a promise that is not fulfilled. It begins with a shot that failed—the powder explodes without sending off the bullet. It becomes vivid when we read how a 'servant belonging to Major Congreve of Charlton, in Kent, was robbed by two highwaymen. The alarm being given, two

---

[1] Collier, *Essays*, p. 51.   [2] *Looker-on*, ii, 258.
[3] Chalmers' *English Poets*, xvii, 177.
[4] Glover in Chalmers' *English Poets*, xvii, 103; Brooke, ibid., p. 346; Jago, ibid., p. 301.
[5] *World* (118).   [6] *World* (117).
[7] Brooke in Chalmers' *English Poets*, xvii, 437.

men went in pursuit ... meeting with the patrols, who also received information of the robbery, they mistook each other, and one of the men levelled his piece at the patrols, which fortunately *flashed in the pan.*'[1]

An epigram by John Byrom[2] gives it allegorically:

> The specious sermons of a learned man
> Are little else but *flashes in the pan;*
> The mere haranguing upon what they call
> Morality, is *powder* without *ball;*
> But he who preaches with a christian grace
> *Fires* at our vices, and the *shot* takes place.

We talk of people who are *cut out* for one another: the *World* (151) throws light on one origin of this when it says that 'the Men and Women of Fashion fit like tallies, are made of the same wood, and are cut out for one another'.

We say we are 'working like a galley slave', and indeed the *Monthly Review* remarks that the 'labour of a galley-slave is become a proverb'. It quotes[3] a description of that labour and the conditions in which it was done from the memoirs of a French Protestant, which shows us precisely what the phrase meant in its literal and harshest application.

We metaphorically 'pour oil on troubled waters'. In 1776 a report from Leyden published in the *Annual Register*[4] stated that a citizen of that place had offered a prize to whoever should 'most effectively try the experiment of appeasing [i.e. quieting] the waves which surround a ship in a storm, by pouring oil into the sea'. Later, the *Philosophical Transactions* of the Royal Society described the case of a ship sailing from Texel to Jutland. Six barrels of oil were poured slowly on each side of the ship, the waves were by degrees abated, the ship soon began to answer her rudder, and soon afterwards entered the port in safety. This experiment followed papers by Benjamin Franklin published in 1774 after having been read at the Royal Society that year.

If we call some one a *blockhead*, do we think of hats? Vicesimus Knox[5] reminds us—people 'who live only to display a pretty face, can scarcely rank higher than a painted doll, or a blockhead, placed with a cap on it in a milliner's window'. This is much older than the eighteenth century, in both senses, but Knox illustrates it effectively.

---

[1] *Gent. Mag.* lix (1789), 366.   [2] *Poems,* ii, 224.
[3] *Month. Rev.* xviii (1758), 449.
[4] *Ann. Reg.* xviii (1775) but published in 1776, p. 173.   [5] *Essays,* i, 162.

Fielding[1] has some enlightening and amusing remarks on what he calls the 'strange Lignification'[2] of the English. According to some writers, he says, 'a *Wooden Age* succeeded that of Lead; the Symptoms of which ... evidenc'd themselves ... even in their Language. Not only single Words, such as *Blockhead, Logerhead,* etc. becoming characteristic of the Change, but whole Phrases, such as a *Special Stick of Wood,* to signifie a good-for-nothing Fellow; a *Chip of the old Block* that Father's own Son is no Changeling; *Heart of Oak,* a Man true to his Trust (this is rarely us'd); to *go against the grain,* a Point carried in spite of one's Teeth; and a *wooden Piece of Business,* a Blunder of the first Magnitude'.

It may come as a surprise to find an exaggerated phrase taken literally, or a technical one taken at face value. The *Annual Register*[3] for 1778 reports a blackmail case: the victim 'lost all memory and recollection, being reduced to the condition of an idiot and dying suddenly, a jury sat on the body, and brought in their verdict *died of a fright'*. But was there any real justification for the other coroner's jury that investigated a sudden death, concluded that it was due to over-indulgence in food and drink, and brought in a verdict of Felo de Se?[4] Literally logical, no doubt, but no attention was paid to motive.

A surgeon called as witness in a murder trial had occasion to be careful with his words. Before he was sworn, he had 'vaguely said the rheumatic tincture had mercury enough in it to *kill a horse'*;[5] he explained that he used this expression merely figuratively, without meaning to infer more from it than that it was a very violent medicine.

'Give a dog a bad name and hang him' we say, without really thinking of dogs. Soame Jenyns[6] reminds us that the 'social and friendly dog is hanged without remorse if, by barking in defence of his master's person and property, he happens unknowingly to disturb his rest'.

Nowadays the Chancellor of the Exchequer *introduces* his Budget. In the eighteenth century, which invented the term Budget in the financial sense, he *opened* it, which reminds us that it could be thought of as a literal bag. As late as 1777 it was felt to be an odd phrase. Dr Price's *Additional Observations on Civil Liberty* had dealt with some remarks on Lord North's speech 'at opening the budget', and the *Monthly Review* commented:[7] 'The Doctor has not scrupled to repeat

---

[1] *Champion,* i, 115.   [2] ibid., p. 113.
[3] *Ann. Reg.* xxi (1778), 205–6.   [4] *Ann. Reg.* xl (1798), 20.
[5] *Ann. Reg.* xvii (1775), 236.   [6] *Works,* iii, 158.
[7] *Month. Rev.* lvi (1777), 214.

this tinker's term; he perhaps thought himself countenanced by those who introduced it into the House of Commons.' The *Gentleman's Magazine*,[1] referring to the same procedure, spoke of Lord North opening 'what is called the budget'. The statesman who introduced the phrase, in a pamphlet, was Sir Robert Walpole in 1733: it seems to have taken a long time to win approval.

We talk with no linguistic regrets of our fortunes being 'at a low ebb', unaware that the purists[2] once thought it an absurd metaphor. The phrase is as old as Queen Anne's reign, but later critics argued that 'lowest ebb' used for 'greatest depth' was misleading—the lowest ebb of distress ought to mean abatement of distress. Do we not think of the ship waiting for the tide, rather than of the tide itself? J. H. Beattie also disliked the frequent use of *hold out*—'every imaginable conception of the human mind is now supposed to have hands and arms for holding out something'. We have no mental picture of outstretched hands now.

To *launch into Eternity* may strike us as bombastic, or as a cliché. *O.E.D.* quotes it from 1812 in the sense 'to put to death' but it is surely an eighteenth-century phrase in this sense as well as in that of *to die*. In 1779, the *Gentleman's Magazine*[3] reports the speech of an American judge passing the first sentence for High Treason there, and admonishing the prisoner before he launches into eternity. It occurs again in reference to a criminal in 1785.[4] It is the suddenness of violent death: is there also the age-old idea of the voyage to another world? The phrase occurred with terrible appropriateness on the monument to the *Royal George* at Portsea, an engraving of which appeared as frontispiece to the May issue of the *Gentleman's Magazine* in 1783: 'On the Twenty-ninth day of August 1782 his Majesty's ship, the Royal George, being on the heel at Spithead, overset and sunk: by which fatal accident about nine hundred persons were instantly launched into eternity.'[5]

We say 'we won't have any hank with it', meaning 'nothing to do with it'; it is another way of saying we have no patience with it. The word is commonest as the hank of yarn, rope or wool—it implies a coil, and by transfer an entanglement, a hold. Garrick[6] in a prologue wrote some lines that show us a love-lorn swain with a *positive* hank—

[1] *Gent. Mag.* l (1780), 180.   [2] J. H. Beattie, *Dialogues of the Dead*, No. 3.
[3] *Gent. Mag.* xlix (1779), 14.   [4] *Gent. Mag.* lv (1785), 314.
[5] The inscription has now been removed to the wall in the south-eastern corner of Kingston Churchyard and a modern cross erected in memory of the victims. The Cemetery has been cleared.   [6] Quoted, *Gent. Mag.* xxxv (1765), 288.

O the charms, the enchantments of love,
On my heart it has got such a hank,
If I talk, eat, sleep, think, sit or move,
Each thought, dream and word is Miss Pank.

No poet: but he could hardly have done better when the lady had such a prosaic name.

The social standing of figurative and conventional phrases is sometimes noted. According to 'the Tyburn phrase'[1] criminals *die hard*: to *make up one's mind* was fashionable in 1796:[2] to be *laid on the shelf* is vulgar.[3] So is *to crack a joke*:[4] to *put a boy into a good way* is 'a traders' term'[5] and *to do better for someone* is a Smithfield phrase.[6] *Do you see*, is 'unpolite'.[7] To wish people a Merry Christmas and a happy New Year is to use the phrase of 'barbers, taylors, shoemakers' and other tradesmen: we all do it now.[8] *To have a good mind* to do this or that is Cockney.[9]

A comment in the *Monthly Review*[10] for 1769 shows a seventeenth-century French phrase 'On lui a donné son sac et ses quilles' rendered into English as 'they have given him his sack and his pens'. The Review thought the metaphor should have been translated by its English equivalent 'They have sent him packing' or by the plain statement 'they have dismissed him from their service'. *O.E.D.*'s first examples of 'to be given the sack' and 'to get the sack' come from the nineteenth century.

(4) *Variants*

Now and then the eighteenth century was using a phrase which has lasted in part only or which has been replaced with a parallel. We 'talk of the devil' but do we still hear tacked on 'and his imps appear'?[11] Concerned as at least we pretend to be if it rains on St Swithin's Day, do the younger generations keep up the old saying 'that it is the saint christening the apples'?[12] And when did 'Hear him, hear him', give way completely to 'Hear, hear'?[13] The eighteenth century used both versions.

[1] *Gent. Mag.* liv (1784), 19.   [2] *Gent. Mag.* lxvi (1796), 204. *O.E.D.* 1821.
[3] *Gent. Mag.* lxviii (1798), 510.   [4] Withers, *Aristarchus*, p. 138.
[5] *New Letters to the Tatler and Spectator*, p. 188.
[6] *Connoisseur*, cxxlv.   [7] Withers, op. cit., p. 138.
[8] *Connoisseur*, xlviii (1754).   [9] Pegge, *Anecdotes*, i, 233.
[10] *Month. Rev.* xl (1769), 221.   [11] *Gent. Mag.* lxi (1791), 217.
[12] *Gent. Mag.* lxii (1792), 884. I have met an old lady of over eighty who does.
[13] Jackson, *Four Ages*, p. 340. Cp. *Oyez, Oyez*.

Accidents may be ascribed to Mr Nobody: but in Steele's time, 'in every Family in Great Britain, Glasses and Cups were broken and Utensils displaced, and all these faults laid upon Mrs How d'ye call'.[1] 'One who has a head of glass should never engage in throwing stones.' Chaucer had said it (with French *verre* instead of *glass*) and the eighteenth century was still saying it.[2] Something deceptively like our phrase was recorded by George Herbert with 'house of glass' instead of *glasshouses*. But there was no reference to greenhouses, as I think there is for us, since that specialised sense is nineteenth-century. Perhaps morally the proverb would also be true if we took *glasshouse* as military slang.

We may get into hot water: apparently eighteenth-century people *lived*[3] in it—they invented the phrase in the 'sixties.

We speak of people as inseparable as Siamese twins: then it was Hungarian ones, as the *Tatler* (118) says.

William Roberts (the Looker-on) states in his Introduction to his essays that he will keep the denominations of good and evil 'at polar distances': we say more simply 'poles apart'.

To us, the bull in the china-shop is proverbial, though according to the *Oxford Dictionary of English Proverbs* it dates only from 1834. Roberts speaks of 'clerical Goths'[4] who don't appreciate learning and should no more be admitted to a good library than 'a blind bullock into a glass manufactury'. In 1769 Boswell[5] noted that fastidious gentlemen thought Dr Johnson, in genteel company, 'like an ox in a china-shop', because he overturned everything.

When a sudden pause occurs in our talk, during which we look seriously at each other, somebody is likely to break the tension by a reference to an angel's wing or a Quaker meeting. Dr Wendeborn[6] tells us that the English knew this sort of thing is peculiar to themselves, and 'call therefore this short silence an *English conversation*'. It is a characteristic irony.

There is much to be said for the conclusion of a correspondent of the *Gentleman's Magazine*[7] in 1791 who argued that discussion of the etymology of phrases was not below the dignity of that periodical. They 'may be inelegant from the fluctuation of language and fashion, yet they throw a light on old customs they allude to'.

---

[1] *Guardian* (64).
[2] Grose, *Olio*, p. 281.
[3] Hanway, *Journal*, ii, 249.
[4] *Looker-on*, ii, 259.
[5] *Boswell in Search of a Wife*, p. 288.
[6] *View*, i, 405.
[7] *Gent. Mag.* lxi (1791), 217.

(It would indeed be useful to know why a giver of advice that cannot be followed was a dealer in bearskins[1]—because of the danger of getting the skin from a bear? And what sort of sallies were sometimes called White Bears?)[2]. Are Bears on the Stock Exchange involved?

Now and then, our enlightenment may be formal. We think of *stronghold* as one word—until we hear of an attack on the 'strongest hold of society'.[3] We may know that *boddice* is really *bodies* (like *pence, pennies*) but it is hardly as obvious to us as it was to the composer of a punning epitaph[4] on a stay-maker—

> Reader, this tomb a body chang'd contains,
> Who many *boddice* form'd with won'rous pains.

(5) *Enlivening our Words*

Eighteenth-century writers, aware of the older, more pictorial senses of words of Latin origin, used them as the starting point of metaphors, sometimes extended so far as to become little allegories. Their alertness and care should encourage us to see more in these words than we sometimes do: they *need not* become dead metaphors, even though that is so often the fate of such words, and when that has happened there is not much point in raising their ghosts. 'Every deviation from the plain Road of Custom' shows the figure of going 'from the way' in miniature. At greater length, it is clear in Gerard's[5] picture of a man after a *few steps following* an association however *trivial* or *devious*, and finding that these *bye roads lead* to rich and unexpected *regions*. He does the same sort of thing when he remarks that when an ingenious *track* of thinking presents itself, imagination *darts* along it, with very great rapidity, and by this rapidity its *ardor* is more *inflamed* and may reach to an astonishing degree of *fervour*.

Mrs Piozzi[6] is remembering her Latin in her etymologically tautologous remark about drawing up the *eyebrows* into a *supercilious* sneer. Spence in his *Crito*[7] had quoted from Le Brun 'who published a very pretty Treatise, to shew how the Passions affect the Face and Features' and who said that their principal seat was in the eyebrows. 'Old Pliny' had said much the same, and that is why the Romans used *supercilious* to mean proud and arrogant. (The stress now is rather on contempt and assumed indifference.)

[1] *Crit. Rev.* new arr. x (1794), 99.   [2] *Brit. Crit.* xiv (1799), 99.
[3] Melmoth, *Letters*, p. 227.
[4] Grose, *Olio*, 308. A *body* for a *boddice* was in use within living memory.
[5] *Essay on Genius*, Pt. I, 49, 54, 67.   [6] *Brit. Syn.*, i, 317.   [7] p. 24.

The *World* (86) speaks of *eradicating* prejudices, follies and vices, with the care so requisite to cleanse a garden from weeds. As it requires more pains to extirpate some weeds than others, 'so those faults will be found the most difficult to be suppressed which have been of the longest growth and taken the deepest root'. Their gardening metaphor may not be exactly ours. Knox[1] talks of the metropolis of a great Empire being 'the hotbed of manners, in which any plant shoots up with forced luxuriousness'. We use *hot-bed* rather of undesirable growths, preferring *forcing-house* for the good, though we usually distrust the process.

As *hot-bed* shows, the enlivening of words is not confined to Latin. *Hackneyed* wakes up when we find it coupled with ideas of careless travelling on a beaten track. The eighteenth century used it more widely than we do. You could speak of people 'hackneyed in the ways of men,'[2] children hackneyed in the ways of the world,[3] of how novels 'hackney youth in the ways of wickedness'.[4]

Favourite modern phrases, regrettably, are 'I haven't a clue'—'He's quite clueless.' I suspect that *clue* suggests cross-word puzzles or detective stories, in which case it is vivid, but no help to reading any eighteenth-century author. They knew it in its literal sense of a ball of thread, and when they used it figuratively they were remembering that most famous of all clues, the one given by Ariadne to Theseus, which led him into the Cretan Labyrinth and safely out of it again. In this period, the word was used in full consciousness of its origin. A good example of the basic literal sense occurs in Glover's *Athenaid*:[5] Soldiers are climbing up to take a rock citadel

> —mazy still
> We trod through dusky bowels of a rock
> While our conductor gather'd as he stepp'd
> A clue, which careful in his hand he coil'd ...
>   We attain'd
> An iron wicket, where the ending line
> Was fasten'd.

It is easy to find examples of *clue* linked with *maze* and *labyrinth* in metaphorical expression. Indeed Mrs Piozzi[6] says that *maze* and *labyrinth* are used only in a figurative sense.

---

[1] *Essays*, i, 6.   [2] *Month. Rev.* xxiii (1760), 158.
[3] Clara Reeve, *Progress of Romance*, ii, 59.
[4] ibid., p. 89.
[5] Chalmers' *English Poets*, xvii, 142.   [6] *Brit. Syn.*, ii, 18.

Smollett's *History* of 1757 was a 'round, firm compacted clue of composition, which may be gradually unwound, without being unravelled or disordered'.[1]

Adam Smith[2] speaks of the clew (both spellings were in use) 'that is most capable of conducting us through all the labyrinth of philosophical history'.

Erasmus Darwin[3] speaks of how the blood

> Maze within Maze, its tortuous path pursues,
> Winds into glands, inextricable clues.

The *Craftsman*[4] spoke of 'the clue to that crooked *Maze* of Policy' in which they had been wandering: Punctuation[5] is a 'clew to guide the reader through the mazy labyrinth' of meaning: the Ruling Passion[6] is 'the clue to lead us into the true characters of men and to unravel all the intricacies of their conduct'. We have moved away from the Greek myth with Soame Jenyns'[7] conviction that Christianity is 'the only clue, which can guide us through the pathless wilderness of this world', which, says Godwin[8] on the other hand, 'is full of enigmas', not 'a labyrinth' of which some men assert they hold the clue. His reference to enigmas is an unconscious pointer to the puzzle clue, but it is hard to believe that any eighteenth-century writer or speaker would have talked as moderns will of 'the clue *behind* the situation'.

Where we talk of the thread of our discourse, they could talk of the clue, as on the occasion when poor Mr Drake, M.P. said 'Behold, Sir, another feature of the procrastinating system. Not so the Athenian patriots—Sir, the Romans—Sir, I have lost the clue of my speech—Sir, I will sit down.'[9]

Thread was in use too: another anecdote[10] tells of a lawyer, who could never plead unless he had a piece of pack-thread to twist about his thumb and finger—wags called it the thread of his discourse, because he was not able to utter a word without it.

Our attention may be focused on a word if someone makes a joke of it. 'Capability' Brown 'began the reformation of those zig-zag, corkscrew walks' in gardens. He 'used to say of them with very great ridicule, that you might put one foot upon zig and the other upon zag'.[11]

---

[1] See L. F. Powell, *M.P.* xxxiv (1936), 179.   [2] *Works*, v, 82.
[3] *Botanic Garden*, iii, 553–4.   [4] Quoted *Gent. Mag.* xiii (1743), 29.
[5] Burrow, *Essay on Punctuation*, p. 12.   [6] Ruffhead, *Life of Pope*, p. 274.
[7] *Works*, iv, 17.   [8] *Enquirer* (1797), 22.   [9] *Gent. Mag.* lvi (1786), 53.
[10] *Spect.* (407).   [11] Uvedale Price, *Essay*, ii, 179 n. i.

We can *outdo* one another, using *do* very generally. It becomes much more lively in certain eighteenth-century uses for good and bad doings. Mrs Montagu[1] tells us that the actor Quin was so good in the 'seven stages of man' passage that he 'outdid his usual outdoings'. On the other hand, the *Craftsman*[2] reports with gusto that Lady Lye one night 'even *outdid* her usual out-*doings*, and added Theft to Imposture'.

We know about 'alarm and despondency' and 'alarms and excursions', but an 'alarm clock' does not call us to actual arms. Neither did it 200 years ago, and it would be unfair to a poet if we thought ludicrously of one when we read that 'Conscience rings her loud alarum'—we ought rather to think on Macduff's cry 'Ring the alarm bell'. We should think *alarum* a poetic variant, whereas the *Monthly Review*[3] tells us that it is 'a poor and vulgar extension used only by mechanics, and beneath the dignity of the muse'. The *Review* may have been wrong on both points.

The literal and figurative senses of *alarm* are neatly illustrated in an item of news from Montreal reported in the *Gentleman's Magazine*[4] of 1784. A number of savages broke into a barn to steal sheep: three men who lay in an adjoining house, being alarmed in our sense by the noise arose and went out to know what occasioned it. One was stabbed, one had his throat cut, but the third made his escape; and 'alarmed' the neighbourhood, no doubt in both senses. 'The Savages, when they found the inhabitants alarmed [literally?] made off.'

Await, says Dyche and Pardon's dictionary, is 'to watch privately for a person, to lie in ambush to surprize him': it throws considerable light on 'Awaits alike the inevitable hour'. Gray was surely seeing the hour of death as the enemy lying in ambush to snatch all that heraldry, power, beauty and wealth had ever given.

Since early last century we have spoken of amalgamating peoples or organisations or ideas. In the eighteenth century, as their dictionaries remind us, *Amalgam* still meant 'metals reduced to fine powder' and *amalgamate* meant chiefly 'to mix quicksilver with gold or some other metal'. The Amalgamated Engineering Union does not have to decide whether some of its components are gold and some base metal.

Catcalls are now made often enough, but by the unaided human voice. The *Gray's Inn Journal*[5] could be quoted in reference to modern hooliganism when it informs us that the 'Board of Criticism will meet ... during the Winter Season, where all Persons, who are willing to

[1] *Letters*, ii, 47–8.   [2] Quoted *Gent. Mag.* xiii (1743), 26.
[3] *Month. Rev.* xii (1755), 159.   [4] *Gent. Mag.* liv (1784), 867.   [5] 21 Oct. 1752

furnish the Critics with Apples, Oranges, Catcalls and other Imple-
ments of Criticism, are desired to send in their Proposals.' But the
catcall was originally as tangible as the misused fruit—'a strange
instrument' that could be bought at a 'toy-shop'. The *Spectator* (361)
provides full details, and another essay in that periodical shows that
the name was soon transferred to those who played on it, for in No. 602
we read of 'a notorious Rake that headed a Party of Catcalls'. A man
who so behaved now would be *eccentric*, if nothing worse. Eighteenth-
century comment shows us this 'term in the Ptolemaick Astronomy'
(*Glossographia Anglicana Nova*) assuming its metaphorical sense, not
without protest. In 1750 the *Monthly Review*[1] quotes comments entitled *Reflexions on Conversation*, whose author asked 'if a man who
affects some astronomical learning has occasion to speak of some uncommon steps in life, or of some odd proceedings of his neighbour,
what would you think, if he told you, *That his neighbours conduct rolls
all in excentric movements?* How ridiculous soever anything of this
kind may be in a pedant, why shall it be more allowable, in a beau or a
fop, to run into whimsical *cant terms?*' The transfer from the behaviour
of the heavenly bodies to that of human ones had been made in the
previous century, but the *O.E.D.*'s lack of illustrations before the 1770's
may suggest that the *Review* expressed a general attitude: at least it
explains the origin of the word for us. We talk of being out of our
sphere, and Cowper[2] brings the two figures neatly together when he
addresses the clergy—

> ... while your orbit is your place,
> Lights of the world, and stars of human race,
> But, if eccentric ye forsake your sphere,
> Prodigies ominous and view'd with fear.

The *sphere* also is the sphere of Ptolemaic astronomy. The notion
that it is eccentric to be off the beaten track can be seen literally applied
in the tale of the man who was fatigued with the length of the way
because the house he was seeking was 'fashionably eccentric'.[3]

Eccentric people may exercise their own secret *fascination*. The
eighteenth century used the word for the art by which the rattle-snake
can 'ogle' a hare into its formidable jaws, and also to describe how we
feel when tempted to do the very thing we view with the utmost
horror—of Caligula striking off his lady's head, of the effect of Dover
Cliff, of a lady who jumped to a shark. They used the word as we

[1] *Month. Rev.* iv (1750), 417.   [2] *Progress of Error*, l. 96.   [3] *Mirror* (34).

commonly do, and we can use it in the bad sense. 'Launcelot Temple's' *Essay Of Fascination* (whose examples, bridging the gap between Evelyn and Cowper in *O.E.D.*, I have quoted) is a useful exploration. Dr Johnson says that one of the meanings of *fascination* is influence in some 'wicked and secret manner'. That is not what we normally mean when we say 'It's fascinating'.

We think of 'a forlorn hope' as a hopeless enterprise: form and meaning unite to make us forget that it began, in Dutch for what modern servicemen would call 'a suicide squad'. The eighteenth century remembered that *hope* is here our *heap*. The *Connoisseur*[1] recalled that 'a suicide has always been compared to a soldier on guard deserting his post', but considers it more like those 'desperate men who rush on certain death, as a body of troops sent out on the Forlorn Hope'. Presumably the troops are not necessarily volunteers, which somewhat spoils the simile.

We talk of 'garbled reports', implying that they have been muddled or made tendentiously, so it is surprising to find that garbling was originally done for the protection of the consumer. *Sifting* or *Screening* would be the words now. Defoe[2] explains that the 'Garbling Office is an ancient Thing'—it was as old as the fifteenth century—'practised in the first Ages of Trade and confirm'd in the Mayor and Commonalty of the City of *London*, by the Statute I Jacob. and is to appoint Inspection to be made into several Sorts of Foods, more particularly subject to frauds, Mixtures and false Package, in order to cleanse them and make them Merchantable. . . .' He notes that the Dutch garble spices, and wonders whether we could 'garble' the political parties and get rid of strife, ambition and separate interests. *Glossographia Anglicana Nova* says to garble is 'to purifie or sort out the bad from the good, 'tis borrow'd from the Druggists and Grocers, who are said to Garble their spices, that is, to cleanse them from Dirt and Dross'. The eighteenth century spoke of garbling and new modelling the army.[3] The bad modern sense had run parallel: it is only in the last hundred years that *garbling* has become to mean an essentially unfair treatment.

Sophistication seems to be moving in the opposite direction. According to *Glossographia Anglicana Nova* it means 'counterfeited, debased, or adulterated, usually spoken of Wines, Chymical Preparations *etc.*' It is 'a villainy of many chemists and druggists' which militates against

[1] 1 (1755).   [2] *Review*, iv, 635.
[3] *Gent. Mag.* ii (1732), 645.

improvements in physic.[1] The present use of *sophisticated* as applied to a person is not necessarily disapproving. We mean 'helped by art' rather than 'artificial'; if there is falsification, it is not really meant to deceive. It implies some 'savoir faire'. Even the Supplement to *O.E.D.* and the *Concise Oxford Dictionary* (1964) recognise none of these things,[2] yet many a young woman would feel complimented if you said she was sophisticated.

When we feel 'stigmatised' or talk of 'carrying a stigma', we hardly have the literal sense in mind, but we know it from the story of St Francis on Mount Alvernia, and we may think of the botanical stigma as well. Remembering the saint, we may wonder, as Mrs Piozzi[3] did, why the word has a bad sense when used figuratively. But the eighteenth century will remind us of ancient history, and of something not so ancient. 'Caligula branded and condemned many respectable citizens, and among the early Christians many carried this disgraceful stigma.' The mark was generally indelible 'as the wounds of the iron were stained with a black liquid'.[4] *Glossographia Anglicana Nova* has more modern examples—to stigmatize is to 'mark with a hot Iron, as we commonly do Rogues at a gaol delivery'.

Bailey says 'Stigma is a Mark with a Hot Iron, such as Malefactors have when burnt in the Hand.' Shebbeare[5] refers to the practice in 1755. The *Monthly Review*[6] uses the word metaphorically with full awareness of its literal meaning when it remarks of a satirist that there are plenty of characters 'for the bountiful *stigma* of an author who seems to take particular delight in the exercise of the branding-iron'. The word should suggest the varying histories of *mark* and *brand*.

If eighteenth-century usage helps us to remember history, it also helps us to remember myth. We tend to use *synopsis* for any summary. It is amusingly brought home to us that the word by origin means what you can take in by a look, when the *Monthly Review*[7] takes an author to task for a much too complicated synopsis: it could not be synoptical 'to an Argus'—who had 100 eyes.

We take up our 'points of view', and may be surprised to find that the phrases once had a literal sense—you could go to 'the prettiest points of view in the park'.[8]

[1] *Month. Rev.* iv (1751), 365.
[2] The *Penguin English Dictionary* (1965) admits 'refined, subtle'.
[3] *Brit. Syn.*, i, 69–70.   [4] *Crit. Rev.* new arr. iv (1792), 525.
[5] *Letters*, Dedication, xxii.   [6] *Month. Rev.* xxxiii (1765), 87.
[7] *Month. Rev.* lxxvii (1789), 373.   [8] *World* (1755), 127.

We *precipitate* matters, act *precipitately* and use the word scientifically: the eighteenth century reminds us of earlier concrete uses—a cascade precipitates[1] on a remarkably fine sheet of water. Dyer hears

> disparting towers, Tumbling all precipitate down-dashed,
> Rattling around, loud thundering to the moon—[2]

which reminds us of Pope's more English phrase 'headlong hung the steep'.

We use *Progress* figuratively: so did they, as the *Rake's Progress* shows. It was not new. Bunyan's *Pilgrim's Progress* was both literal of Christian's journey and figurative of his spiritual development. But Royal Progresses were still remembered, and so Clara Reeve calls her study *The Progress of Romance through Times, Countries and Manners* —she speaks of 'progress through the Land of Romance' and makes one of her characters arrange that they shall meet every Thursday 'till the progress is finished'. College officials and Judges still made Progresses in the eighteenth century.

We feel that *stamina* means staying power, physical strength, 'guts'. It has weakened its connection with the learned phrases *stamina vitae* or '*prima stamina* of all animal and vegetable bodies'[3] so that such phrases as 'the internal stamina of the bones'[4] or 'the End of my Stamen,[5] which was sixty years' strike us strangely, though to look into them is to see the origin of our meaning. In botanical use they called *stamens* by the Latin plural *stamina* and you could talk of the 'stamina, threads, vulgarly the Chives'[6]—*not* onions. The word had been used of fabric, as well as of thread-like stamens. So Priestley[7] spoke of 'declensions, inflections of verbs, and syntax' as 'the stamina of a language'. Godwin[8] calls the cardinal interests of a human being the stamina of his happiness, Junius[9] speaks of the stamina of government and Johnson[10] allows that 'Pope may have had from Bolingbroke the philosophical *stamina* of his Essay on Man.'

We often 'feel thrilled', but probably not with any real physical sensation, like the one experienced by the eighteenth-century schoolboy who said[11] it seemed to pass through his body. Ash defines it as

[1] *Gent. Mag.* lix (1789), 517.
[2] Dyer, *Ruins of Rome*, 40–3.
[3] *Month. Rev.* iv (1750), 59.
[4] *Gent. Mag.* xxxix (1769), 5.
[5] *Tatler* (46).
[6] *Month. Rev.* xxiii (1760), 213.
[7] *Universal Grammar*, p. 277.
[8] *Enquirer*, p. 350.
[9] ii, 12.
[10] Boswell, *Life*, iii, 403.
[11] *Lælius and Hortensia*, p. 96.

'Piercing, boring, penetrating', where we should think *boring* ambiguous and unhappily chosen.

We may take umbrage—we dislike being put in the shade. The eighteenth century reminds us that the word once meant literal shadow —trees afford an Umbrage, the 'garden's umbrage mild' is 'beauteous'[1] —or, rather differently, Thomson[2] speaks of 'flowering umbrage'. There are dunces who shelter their idleness and ignorance under the umbrage of such a name as Shakespeare's.[3] Another sort of transfer is seen when *umbrage* is used where we should say *adumbration*. Mysteries may be wrapped in clouds or 'hid in Umbrages',[4] and Scripture gives 'little Umbrage'[5] of any superiority of one Apostle to the rest. Our meaning was being prepared for—*Glossographia Anglicana Nova* says *umbrage* is a Shadow, a Covert, a Suspicion; Bailey, a shadow, Jealousy, Pretence or Colour; Dr Johnson, Resentment, offence, suspicion of Injury, as well as screen of trees.

Etymologically, an umbrella should be a protection against heat or sun, and so it sometimes was. Hercules attended Omphale like a slave, with 'her umbrella to keep the sun from her'.[6] *Sunshade* came in 1852. One suspects that English weather has defeated good linguistic intentions.

(6) Changed Reference

The period often throws light on words whose use we have restricted. A *Continent* could be any land mass in relation to islands or peninsulas. The Isle of Man[7] could be said to lie west of 'that part of the British continent called Cumberland' and a new volcanic island was mistaken 'for the "continent" of Iceland'.[8] We should say *mainland*, and they could have done so. And why should *strata* be restricted to Geology and by metaphor to Society? Our ancestors could speak of sleeping on strata of hemlock leaves[9]—the word basically means layers. It is odd to find an eighteenth-century critic explaining the *Lair* of an animal by referring to the *Lairs* (i.e. layers) of potted meat![10] We *garnish* the

[1] Smart's *Song to David*, stanza LXXVIII. [2] *Summer*, l. 626.
[3] Upton, *Critical Observations on Shakespeare*, p. 15.
[4] Shaftesbury, *Characteristics*, iii, 322.
[5] Atterbury, p. 32. *Adumbration* at this date could mean literally a rough sketch.
[6] Spence, *Polymetis*, p. 127. Cp. Ash s.v.
[7] *Ann. Reg.* viii (1765), 71 (Characters).
[8] *Gent. Mag.* liii (1753), 661.
[9] *Month. Rev.* xxix (1704), 172.
[10] Pearce, *Text of Paradise Lost*, p. 257.

meat with parsley etc.—but the *Gentleman's Magazine*[1] spoke of the Russians garnishing their caps with sheepskin.

Magazine suggests first to most of us a periodical, then an ammunition store. When we recall the Magasins across the Channel, we see that the word was once much wider. In the eighteenth century we meet Magazines of meal and oats, hay and straw, words, etymologies, fish, herbs, plenty, circumstances, plants, teeth, marble, science, health, thoughts, snow, projects. The military sense is sometimes clearly at the back of the figurative use. The *World* (188) is a satirical plea for female soldiers whose bright eyes would provide magazines of lightning. The joke looks shabby after the work of the Women's Services in two world wars. It was the *Gentleman's Magazine* that focused attention on the periodical magazine: Sylvanus Urban would probably rejoice at his grandchildren the Radio Magazines.

It has regularly been noted that words whose meanings were once non-committal or good often settle down to bad ones. Uvedale Price[2] admits that 'irritation is generally used in a bad sense; rather as a source of pain, than of pleasure; but that is the case with many words and expressions which relate to our more eager and tumultuous emotions, and seems to point out their distinct nature and origin'.

The eighteenth century could speak of the *duplicity* of a word, and the *duplicity* of fable in a two-fold plot. In people, duplicity is not richness of character. We may recall the gentleman[3] who saw a play that was said to turn on a *double entendre*—he thought it as *single* an entendre as ever he saw in his life.

On the whole, *effluvia* to us means nasty smells. Richardson explains *odours*—Milton's word—as 'Effluvia exhaled from Flowers or whatever is Sweet-scented'. It was possible to speak of 'horrid' effluvia or 'delicious' effluvia.[4] And the period reminds us that the word earlier meant any sort of outflowings—it could describe the cosmos as the effluvium[5] of the majesty of God, or speak of a man mixing in good society catching its elegance 'by the contagion of invisible effluvia'.[6]

And neither was *contagion* necessarily any more tainted than *contact* then.

We distinguish between the physical or metaphorical *ascent* and the theological *Ascension*: at this period they spoke of the *ascension* of a

---

[1] lvi (1786), 548.   [2] *Essay*, i, 146.   [3] *Lounger* (80).
[4] Thompson, *Sentimental Tour*, pp. 244, 278. He thinks the word is singular.
[5] *New Universal Mag.*, April 1756.
[6] Knox, *Essays*, ii, 58.

balloon.[1] *Quietism* to us is a particular kind of religious outlook, not the general 'perfect tranquility' of Ash's definition, which explains the wish 'Peace be to the quietism of the admirers of any poet.'[2] We think of *transcend* as figurative only, but it was possible to write of a huge rock that was 'difficult to be transcended'.[3]

The Mansion House to us means primarily the official residence of the Lord Mayor; for the eighteenth century it could be the Manor house: in *Columella* it refers to Stourhead.[4]

[1] *Ann. Reg.* xxvii (1784–5), 227, 230.
[2] P. Stockdale, *Inquiry*, p. 99.
[3] J. Holmes, *Art of Rhetorick*, ii, 16.
[4] Graves, *Columella*, ii, 5. Cp. *Lælius and Hortensia*, p. 47.

VII

THE UNDEVELOPED

THERE ARE many words from 200 years ago that now call up at once a more vivid or impressive picture than they did then. *Advertisement* began merely as 'the turning of attention to something'. Sir Joshua Reynolds[1] could still describe a picture as showing 'St Joseph advertised by an Angel' which to us sounds very incongruous behaviour for either a Saint or an Angel. It had begun to mean trade notices, and there were, as we have seen, complaints about Advertisement English, but the whole battery of hoardings, press and television has taken possession of the word now. We shall hardly remember that *Advertisement* was once the 'fashionable' word for a preface.[2]

Slump and *Inflation* had no economic connection in the eighteenth century. Dr Johnson does not even admit the former—the verb 'to slump' implies for Bailey slipping or falling 'plum down into any wet or dirty place', and for Johnson *inflation* is merely flatulence.

The commercial use of *relations* came in the late 'nineties and is now the accepted term; where Ruffhead[3] found a translator from French saying literally that 'the reciprocal damage belligerents do each other, turns to the advantage of neutral powers whose merchants extend and multiply their *relations*', he commented that an English reader might be at a loss to conceive what is meant—'but they who are conversant with the original know that the French word *relations*, in this place, signifies correspondences; which the merchants of neutral states must multiply of course' [i.e. naturally].

To a reader, an appendix is an addition to the main text of a book: in our unliterary moments it is that part of us that may cause appendicitis. For both reasons we need to be reminded of an earlier less specialised sense when the *Tatler* (18) talks of an 'Appendix of proper Apartments furnished with Pen, Ink and Paper', to be added to Chelsea Hospital for decayed war-correspondents. An asylum to us is a hospital for lunatics; asylum in the abstract is any refuge. The old historical

[1] *Journey*, p. 258.
[2] *Month. Rev.* xxv (1762), 507; xxxvii (1767), 105.
[3] *Month. Rev.* xviii (1758), 39.

sense is there in *Glossographia Anglicana Nova*'s definition of it as a 'Sanctuary or Place of Refuge for Offenders': something on the way to our general use appears in the remark[1] that Caledonian ports seem designed as *asyla*, though the Latin plural shows how foreign the word was felt to be.

Conscription then was any sort of enrolling or registering, which is what the Roman 'Conscript Fathers' implies. The sense of compulsory calling up for National Service came into use about 1800, from France. The *Monthly Review*[2] objected reasonably enough to *Old Veterans*— had anybody heard of young ones? If the reviewers had lived in the present century, they would have often met them, since we use *veteran* for an experienced service man (with transfers to other walks of life), and the U.S.A. more technically for a demobilised man.

The eighteenth-century idea of a Code was purely legal: the nineteenth extended it to ciphers and non-legal rules. *Peculation* then was theft of public money, as it still may be: but it was the nineteenth century that extended it to the money of small traders. An *absentee* was a non-resident Irish landlord, or some one who failed to appear at a public assembly—the absentee workman had not the name as yet. A *refugee* was only a French Protestant or a fugitive from justice: the eighteenth century might well have been shaken from its belief in the rationality and humanity of man if it could have foreseen our need of the word. *Electorate* to them concerned the German Electoral princes, not citizens capable of voting. A *Friendly Society* existed to provide fire insurance. *Mortuary*, in our usual sense, and *mortuary chapel* were not invented till the nineteenth century—the word still referred to death generally and in particular to the feudal dues payable when a tenant died. The only *pet* one would normally have was a lamb and a civilian did not wear *gauntlet* gloves. Even *jujubes* were 'a sort of Italian prunes'—the sense of pastille came in the nineteenth century. The eighteenth century called pastilles *loʒenges*.

Other special applications still to be developed concern *flimsy* and *aʒure*, *normal* and *sub-normal*.

That useful eighteenth-century invention *flimsy* is included in George Campbell's list of low words ennobled by good use.[3] It sprang from the 'cant of the manufacturers' and was soon to be used in the figurative sense, often as a literary critical term—'a very feeble, flimsy,

---

[1] *Crit. Rev.* 42 (1776), 171.
[2] *Month. Rev.* xxxiii (1763), 322.
[3] *Phil. of Rhet.*, p. 168.

poem'[1]—'flimsy epithet'.[2] It came into poetic use as in Dr Armstrong's 'trite invention and a flimsy vein',[3] or in Erasmus Darwin's[4] *Botanic Garden*—

Fine as the spider's flimsy thread.

Lawson[5] joins it with *thin-spun* and *wire-drawn*. The technical office use of 'a flimsy' dates from the nineteenth century, which also used the noun slangily for a bank note.

To the eighteenth century *azure* was a poetic word for blue, as it still can be. Which blue, depends on context. It is used of the sky at midday and at midnight, of the sea, of mountain tops, of the eyes, of ashes, of smoke. 'Stars sparkle in their azure ground' says the *Guardian* (49). Glover[6] talks of an azure flood, and of 'the transparent azure of autumnal skies'. Mason's *English Garden*[7] speaks of an azure coil of smoke and of 'that deep azure grey'

Form'd from the calcin'd fibres of the Vine

which his editor glosses as *blue black*. Jonas Hanway[8] notices the azure sky in day-time, and Pope writes of the azure brightness of the eyes of Pallas. Mrs Piozzi[9] indeed thought that Minerva's azure eyes so often mentioned in Pope's exquisite translation had fixed these two words for ever to each other, as long as our language lasts. That is no longer true, and we should not now laugh at a foreigner who said 'sapphire eyes' instead. It would be pedantic, she thought, to use *azure* or *sapphire* of furniture or dress. Now the British Colour Council lists azure in their Standard Dictionary under the name Larkspur, matching it to the heraldic colour azure.

The reference to azure smoke and Kenrick's definition 'faint blue', which are quite unlike the heraldic colour, suggest that the writing paper known as azure has a justification for its name.

Normal and *subnormal* are so often applied to people that it surprises us to find that the eighteenth century had not thought of either. *Normal* is exact, according to rule or square, and the transference and the modification did not come till the nineteenth century. *Average* was still a commercial term not used of people. Nor was *truculent* applied to writings or *dense* to the unintelligent.

[1] Warton's Pope II, 199, re Mallet's *Verbal Criticism*.
[2] Graves, *Columella*, i, 132, re 'respectful compliments'.
[3] *Taste*, p. 204.   [4] ii, 169.   [5] *Oratory*, p. 376.
[6] Chalmers' *English Poets*, xvii, 109.
[7] ii, 371.   [8] *Journal*, i, 199.   [9] *Brit. Syn.*, i, 33.

Many an eighteenth-century word was to change its sphere with changing times. A *cruise* in the following period was to be more for pleasure than war, a *smack* was to lose her connection with fighting. *Dormitory* was to be connected more often with schools than convents, and 'dormitory towns' were far in the future. *Repertory* was to suggest specifically theatrical or other entertainment and not a general storehouse—and an *Emporium* was to descend from a mart or commercial city to become a shop. A *saloon* was to be in place in a hotel or on board ship, a *buffet* was to be no longer a side cupboard for displaying plate and china, but to give rise to buffet meals on a buffet-car train. A *bazaar* was to be an English *function*—in the eighteenth century it could have been neither English nor a function. The *baton* would be wielded by a conductor as well as a soldier. Hussars would be English as well as Polish or Hungarian: *crochet* would be applied to needlework, and the housewife would use the fruit called *sultanas*[1] in cookery without cannibalistically consuming the Sultan's Lady. She would 'put out *salvage*' with no thought of the salvage of ships. *Vouchers*, as a phase of advertising, or of credit, would become specialised things, not trustworthy people. We can carry them in our *wallets*[2] which are no longer bags in two sections for distributing the weight evenly over the horse. *Wrappers* can now belong to books, and so can *jackets*, and a *jersey* is the garment rather than the wool. Roads have *kerbs* and *camber*: these words used to apply to the coping stones of wells, parts of brewers' coppers and of skylights, and to ships respectively. *Dole* and *ration* call up specific ideas for the civilian, whereas a dole was once a private charitable gift, and a ration a soldier's issue of food. A *programme* was to become political as well as cultural. And *toilet* no longer means a lady's dressing table, from which it was to depart by euphemism.

A *stoker* is no longer mainly restricted to a 'brewhouse' and a *purser* has left the naval vessel for the passenger ship: the *editor* is no longer the publisher, and a *referee* can act on a playing field as well as at a tribunal.

If words now bring to our mind people and things that did not occur to eighteenth-century minds, they may also, while standing for basically the same object, event or state, imply now a quite different attitude in the speaker. *Incident* to us tacitly implies a worrying one—'there were no incidents' is a relief to read. If a man is a *coming* actor, politician, or whatever, we believe he will go far, not that he is forward and

---

[1] *Sultana* could mean also a confection of sugar in the eighteenth century.
[2] *Pocket-book* sense from U.S.A. (nineteenth century).

pliant.[1] If he affords us *entertainment*, that need not imply 'the lower comedy' as Dr Johnson defines it. To be *conventional* in the bad sense —and to be *unconventional*—are both nineteenth-century developments: for the eighteenth, the former meant belonging to an assembly, or done in conformity to certain articles of agreement. A pamphlet need not now be upon a trifling subject, or be but meanly performed. If we *verbalise*, we put our thoughts into words—we need not be tedious in so doing. And if we answer *abstractedly*, we are doing what no eighteenth-century speakers would have described by that adverb. For them it meant 'simply' and 'free from mixture'. Dickens appears to have used it in our sense first on record.

The eighteenth-century grammarians protested against our habit of turning abstractions into concrete words. Nevertheless, we can talk of an anachronism, an atrocity, a casualty, an orphanage, the acoustics of the room being bad, where acoustics obviously does not mean the science of sound. And when we call the park or the swimming-pool or the art gallery the amenities of the town we are making a twentieth-century use of the noun. The nineteenth century made some new figures of speech. In the eighteenth *drastic* remedies were in the hands of doctors, not politicians: you could not then lead a *drab* life; you could not be *stranded* except on the beach, and you could not *floor* an opponent in argument. Nor could you *shadow*[2] anyone as a detective does, or build a *shadow factory* or be a member of a *shadow cabinet*. Eighteenth-century people *clarified* juices and decoctions or their own minds, but not positions or obscure subjects. *Snags* existed only in wood or objects of some other solid material, and though *aftermath* was used figuratively it was still part of a farming metaphor.

The eighteenth century began to shift *culture* from the sense it bears in its compounds *agriculture, horticulture*, etc. to the cultivation of the mind, thus opening up the way for the word to mean the good results of education and breeding; and also for the archaeologist's *cultures*, and those of the biologist. The word was then used as we use *cultivation*. In one part of America, the principal objects of *culture* 'should be vines, almonds, raisins . . .'[3] If we heard the phrase 'the Culture of Lucerne'[4] I think we should assume it referred to the educational contributions and social setting of the Swiss city, whereas the eighteenth

---

[1] See *O.E.D.* and eighteenty-century dictionaries s.v.
[2] A general forerunner of the special sense is recorded in *O.E.D.* from 1602— then nothing until 1876.
[3] *Gent. Mag.* xxxvii (1767), 102.　　　　[4] *Gent. Mag.* xxxvi (1766), 128.

century thought of the plant. We can see how, thanks to metaphor, the
sense has developed. 'Culture improves, and occasions elicit natural
talents . . . the soil must be cultivated, and the seasons favourable for
the fruit to have all its spirit and flavour.'[1] Gerard thinks it is only 'the
few who improve the rudiments of taste which nature has implanted,
by culture well chosen and judiciously applied'.[2]

Certain syntactical and semantic changes have occurred that enable
us to extend the ideas implicit in words in eighteenth-century use.
Shuddery then meant shivering—the epithet had not been transferred
to the shuddery ghost story. *Clinic* was an adjective, so you could not
visit the clinic. The verb *to surface* could have been used of divers, but
seems not to have been, and the invention of the submarine has made
it more needed. As a matter of fact, *O.E.D.*'s first example in the sense
of 'coming to the surface' is of fish and is dated 1898.

A character in the *Connoisseur* (xix) says he would be glad to 'dive'
with a friend into any cellar. The noun *dive* for a place of resort has
sometimes gone up in the world, figuratively speaking, since then. It
was probably lower in its U.S.A. nineteenth-century sense of an
illegal drinking den in a cellar.

Set phrases made up of words already available 200 years ago have
been made as required. It is interesting to reflect that the eighteenth
century would have had no clear notion of what we mean by *granulated
sugar*: that they would have been equally ignorant of *career girl* and
careers master; and that their dictionaries would have led them to
suppose that *nuclear fission* had something to do with cracking nuts.

Obviously it is the words ready to be used by the scientists that had
the most exciting futures.

Air travel by balloon was just beginning, and the distance we have
come in well under 200 years can be seen when we observe the juxta-
posed statements of fact and opinion in the *Monthly Review*[3] of 1784:
'M. Champmar of Paris gave notice that he should send off an aerial
diligence on Friday the 12th March. Of this last we hardly expect any
further account.' Horace Walpole foresaw[4] (frivolously it is true) air
liners and air-ports (and air-sickness), but if he could come back and
land from the one at the other, it is a fair guess that he would hardly
believe his eyes or find words to express himself. As late as 1796[5]
'aerial philosophers' were concerned with medicine, not aeronautics:

[1] *World* (120).   [2] *Essay on Taste*, p. 95.   [3] *Month. Rev.* lxx (1784), 225.
[4] Letter to the Hon. H. S. Conway, 15 Oct 1784.
[5] *Gent. Mag.* lxvi (1796), 12.

the year after, the *Gentleman's Magazine*[1] was using 'aerial space'—
air-space as we should say—not of lines of communication, broadcasting time or national skies but of the amount of space allowed to the
human cargo on a slave-ship. We are reminded that the French first
dignified the balloon's procedure by the name of 'aerial navigation'.

Capsule was used in botany, in medicine and in chemistry. The
capsule that contains nauseous doses came in the nineteenth century.
The jump from any of these to the capsule in which a cosmonaut circles
the earth is astonishing.

Satellite was still firmly fixed in Roman history, among hangers-on,
and in astronomy. It was the nineteenth century that extended it to
satellite states, and the twentieth to satellite towns and man-made
objects orbiting in space.

The invention of the motor-car gave *car* a new lease of life and
produced a progeny of compounds. The word had a lively future, but
the changed application has ruined many a line meant by its author to
be distanced and impressive. Glover in his *Athenaid* tells how 'Before
the Prytaneum stop'd the car' and worse still, says of Themistocles
that 'His car is ready'. Another minor poet declaims 'We hear the
rattling car'—and indeed we often do, so often that even his coupling
of it with 'the neighing steeds' is not enough to blot out the remem-
brance of some old jalopy.

Laboratory could appear as *Elaboratory* and be at once narrower and
more impressive. The *Annual Register*[2] reported that 'a magnificent
elaboratory' was to be set up in Dublin; and that in 1779 the Elaboratory at Woolwich blew up by accident.[3] And just how serious was the
gentleman who called milch cows 'wonderful elaboratories'?[4]

Of all the words that the eighteenth century inherited or invented,
perhaps the one that was to become most in demand and to give rise
to a large technical family was *electric(ity)*. All *Glossographia Anglicana
Nova* in 1707 can say is that electricity 'is the quality that Amber, Jet,
sealing-wax, etc., have of attracting light Bodies to them, when the
attracting Body is rubb'd or chaf'd'. Dr Johnson in 1755 says much the
same, but he knows that electrified bodies may 'emit flame' and 'be
fitted with such a quantity of the electrical vapour, as, if discharged at
once upon a human body, would endanger life'. Later the 'vapour'
has become 'this wonderful fluid'[5]—indeed our word *current* is in

[1] *Gent. Mag.* lxvii (1797), 862.   [2] *Ann. Reg.* xi (1768), 174.
[3] *Ann. Reg.* xxiv (1779), 231.   [4] Thompson, *Sentimental Tour*, p. 2.
[5] Jackson, *Four Ages*, p. 62.

tune with that idea. The authors[1] of some 'Observations on a Series of Electrical Experiments' thought *electrical* a word of 'too confined a meaning to be a proper epithet for a fluid of so universal an activity' —but the word has absorbed all the power since developed.

People received 'electrical shocks' metaphorically when they were stunned, 'driven back, and brought to the ground'.[2] The practice of giving actual shocks to cure sundry ills had a future, and *shock-treatment* itself can be a metaphor—even if it is not quite as much of a panacea as the eighteenth century believed. To be 'electrified' in this sense passed into metaphor with a different emphasis from ours: an excitable tourist,[3] a devotee of that other new craze sea-bathing, exclaims 'The billows run high, they dash, they foam—I bathe, am electrified and refreshed.' But the electronic brain was far from the thought of the *Anti-Jacobin*[4] writer who spoke of the 'bold expression of th'electric mind'. To show how the doubtful hopes of the eighteenth century have become the triumphant certainties of the twentieth, and to demonstrate that you can have the word without the thing, we need only quote a comment by the *Gentleman's Magazine*[5] in 1795: 'Perhaps the *electric batteries*, which electricians have hitherto only imagined but been afraid to put in practice, may be realized.' Naturally, our increasing control over electricity has brought new applications of old technicalities. We no longer expect to find electric points on the top of lightning conductors.[6] And old general terms like *frequency*, *vibration*, and *insulate* as well as the more specific *valve*, were to become familiar in their electrical senses.

Eighteenth-century comment reminds us that *telegraph* was originally the name of a French seventeenth-century invention: persons placed in several stations at such distances from each other that, by the help of a telescope, a man in one station may see a signal made by the next before him; he instantly repeats that signal. The invention has been adopted in France, and is so useful, thinks the *Gentleman's Magazine*[7] in 1794, that it will undoubtedly be soon introduced in this country. The telegraph, especially in civil life, has gone a long way since then and signallers are now giving way to wireless operators.

Torpedo is a word likely to puzzle the modern reader: it can take a

[1] *Month. Rev.* xv (1756), 467.
[2] *Month. Rev.* xliii (1771), 40.
[3] Thompson, *Sentimental Tour*, p. 280.
[4] *Anti-Jacobin*, ii, 421.
[5] *Gent. Mag.* lxv (1795), 141.
[6] Erasmus Darwin, *Botanic Garden*, Note XIII.
[7] *Gent. Mag.* lxiv, Pt. I (1794), 815.

great deal of context to make it clear, as we shall see. But its future as the name of a missile, whether submarine or aerial, must be mentioned here. As for *missile*, the word was applied to the quills upon the fretful porcupine, and to darts and spears—anything you could throw. The Romans began it, and the fact that we can speak of Inter-continental Missiles bears witness to the progress of science, not to any basic change in the word.

The *Gentleman's Magazine*[1] in 1782 wondered why a translator had not said of a dove that 'Forth through the rocks she *wings* her dauntless flight.' It was a difficult passage for her, and the translator had said *weaves*. The R.A.F. has improved on this with its application of the verb to the in-and-out flight of the aeroplane.

Shunt was once a general word meaning *to shove*; *tunnel* applied to a mine, and a *truck* was a carriage; *sidings* were ridges in a ploughed field. The railway has found a use for all of them. *Locomotive* and *train* both existed in eighteenth-century English, but of course quite gener-ally—'having the power of motion' and 'what is drawn', whether of people following a leader, of a lady's train, of consecutive thoughts or a line of gunpowder. *Passenger*, too, has become more technical—there are so many more ways in which one's 'passage' can be made. In the middle ages, a passenger was usually a wayfarer on foot: the tell-tale *foot-passenger* (first illustrated in *O.E.D.* from the nineteenth century) implies that now he usually is not. By the sixteenth century he was commonly going by ship. In the eighteenth century the word could still mean a passer-by or be used of any traveller, but it was growing specialised for those who went in horse-drawn vehicles. The prevailing sense of 'one who pays his fare in a public conveyance' was common in the period, and has of course been extended to air travel in the twentieth century. To be a 'passenger' metaphorically—not to pull your weight—began in nineteenth-century footballers' slang.

Fixation is at home in psychology now as well as in chemistry and a *neurotic* is now a person in need of treatment; in the eighteenth century, neurotics were tonics for the nerves. *Film* has gone to photography and the cinema from anatomy and the surface of mineral waters. Two hundred years ago *cones* had no connection with mountains or meteor-ology.

Now that tourism is a major industry in many countries, and you do not have to be a 'milord' to make a tour of Europe, it is interesting to find that the *Gentleman's Magazine*[2] was looking askance at the word

[1] *Gent. Mag.* lii (1782), 376.   [2] *Gent. Mag.* lvii, Pt. I (1787), 53.

tour in 1787, even though *Glossographia Anglicana Nova* had defined it in our sense eighty years before. The *Critical Review*[1] also disliked *touring* a country ('by which we suppose he means travelling through it?'). One senses that it was thought pretentious. Perhaps the real objection was the one Grose[2] hints at when he speaks of how the modern tradesman and his family 'take a *tower*, as they term it, in summer'.

The tour could be a working one, as it still is when we *make* a tour rather than take one. We read of a missionary[3] who made a two months' tour among the American Indians; and the word could still be used for *quality* or *tenor*—'the Tour of the Argument[4]—the chain of Ideas that forms it'. Or, 'there are three distinct *tours* in poetry; the design, the language, and the versification'.[5]

Apart from *tour de force*, the eighteenth century fixed *tour* in the holiday sense by extending it to the general public. *Tourist* (*O.E.D. c.* 1800) naturally followed; as the *Critical Review*[6] remarked in 1781, of a poetic guide book to the Lakes which was meant for *actual Tourists*, the word was 'not to be met with in Johnson's or any other English Dictionary, though the meaning of it is sufficiently obvious'. It has proved useful in itself, and as the parent of *Tourism* (not now usually depreciatory as *O.E.D.* has it), *Tourist Class, Tourist resort, Tourist Agency, Tourist Ticket*. If any eighteenth-century tourist had gone to a mountainous country, he would have found no *funicular railway* to save his labour; *funicular* still meant only 'belonging to little ropes'. Neither could he have taken some pre-packed food in a *carton*, or enjoyed Punch's *cartoons* as a reminder of home. In the eighteenth century these were variant spellings of one word that meant a preliminary design on large paper. The Raphael Cartoons, for example, keep this meaning alive. The packaging carton dates from early this century.

For good or ill, *literature, literate* and *illiterate* have widened their application noticeably in the last two centuries. *Literate* used to mean 'learned', 'skilled in letters', just as Literature meant 'Knowledge in Letters'—consider the phrase 'men of sense, literature, and patriotism'.[7] Our civilisation depends so much at all levels on the written

---

[1] *Crit. Rev.* i (1756), 464.   [2] *Olio*, p. 27.   [3] *Crit. Rev.* 26 (1768), 385.
[4] Waterland, *Doctrine of the Eucharist*, p. 232.
[5] Spence's *Anecdotes*, p. 23, quoting Pope.
[6] *Crit. Rev.* 52 (1781), re *Ode to the Genius of the Lakes in the North of England*.
[7] *Life of Beau Nash*, p. 218.

word, that we use the words more unexactingly—to be literate now simply means to be able to read and write, with no particular stress on the understanding of what you read or the quality of what you write. It would hardly have been possible in the eighteenth century to publish a book called *The Illiteracy of the Literate*. It is a witness to the widespread nature of our education and its too-frequent concomitant shallowness.

Literary, said the *Monthly Review*[1] in 1780, 'has yet acquired no appropriate significance in our language'. *Literary* Essays, thought the reviewers, told us nothing about the essays—which would not be true now, since we should know they were not on political, religious or scientific subjects, for example. To the Review *literary* was 'equally descriptive of every species of composition and characteristic of none'. Eleven years earlier[2] they had wondered whether the word could be extended to descriptions of the arts that depend on mechanical skill, which no words can convey, and which no rules can teach. Now *literature* is used of holiday brochures and begging letters—i.e. printed matter, a sense that dates from the 1890's. It was Dr Johnson in 1779 who encouraged the use of *literature* in the general way commonest at present when he speaks of Cowley's position in the ranks of literature. One suspects that the eighteenth century would have thought that early nineteenth-century invention 'light literature' a contradiction in terms, though 'light music' is spoken of in the sixteenth.

Standard English and *Standard Authors* have become technical terms: their forerunners can be seen in Gildon's[3] remarks that the Diction of an Elegy should be standard and correct. But Goldsmith's warier use may be quoted too: in his *Account of the Augustan Age in England* he says that it cannot be disowned that L'Estrange was a standard writer 'because a great many very eminent authors formed their style by his. But his standard was far from being a just one'.

It is not easy for us to see why eighteenth-century purists objected to *subject-matter*, which has proved so useful a term. Dr Armstrong[4] disliked it, but the critics had to admit—sarcastically—that it is 'so absolutely necessary both in the pulpit and at the bar, that we may as well think to close the mouths of the church, the senate, and the law, as to exclude it from the English language'. There is no need to alter *is* to *was*. It was felt to be tautologous: but it went on to acquire a sense that is not precisely that of *subject* alone or *matter* alone. After

[1] *Month. Rev.* lxii (1780), 63.   [2] *Month. Rev.* xl (1769), 2.
[3] p. 170.   [4] *Sketches by Launcelot Temple*, ix; *Crit. Rev.* 5 (1758), 383.

Dr Armstrong's death, the *Monthly Review*[1] spoke of the subject
matter of a book that obliged the printer to use a larger or smaller type
to suit the quantity of his manuscript copy. Here it means 'material
provided' rather than *treated*. The word was used by scientists and
philosophers in specialised senses, and continues a useful career in
literature and reports. *Matter* was recognised as sometimes a printers'
term.[2] 'Matter of fact', a virtual compound, was originally peculiar to
lawyers—as distinct from 'matter of law'. Its wider meaning is clear
in the contrasted phrases in 'I have got beyond all surmises, even to
the matter of fact.'[3] The adjectival extension 'in a matter-of-fact way',
'a matter-of-fact person' were eighteenth-century uses that we find
convenient.

When Dr Johnson, commenting on *The Bard*, says that 'Of the
first stanza the abrupt beginning has been celebrated, but technical
beauties can give praise only to the inventor', the critic who compiled
the *Deformities of Dr Johnson*[4] compared *technical* here with Johnson's
definitions in his Dictionary, which said 'Belonging to the arts; not
in common or popular use', illustrating it by 'technical words'. How
could this word be used of 'beauties' with propriety? A present-day
reader would assume that the beauties were those of technique rather
than idea, and surely that is what Johnson had in mind, for he mentions
the abrupt rush into the subject and the alliteration.

O.E.D. credits Coleridge with *technique* in the artistic sense, early in
the next century, but Johnson seems to have been well on the way to it.

For the eighteenth century a Bibliographer was a writer of books, as
Glossographia Anglicana Nova defines him, or, according to Dr Johnson, a transcriber. For Dyche and Pardon, he is a bookseller. The
scholar the word implies for us is conspicuously absent. He is first
recorded from 1814, along with *bibliography* in the sense of 'the science
of books'. A work containing a description of books is an extension
two decades later, and the phrase 'A bibliography' of a particular
author or subject did not arrive for another thirty years after that. This
development is a tribute to the growth of scholarship.

A group of less specialised adjectives shows eighteenth-century
words ready for nineteenth-century expansion. *Non-descript* is a technical word that has moved out into general conversation. It was a

---

[1] *Month. Rev.* lxxxi (1784), 300. The term had already had a long history.
[2] *Month. Rev.* xxv (1762), 471.
[3] *Crit. Rev.* 42 (1776), 269, from Benjamin Victor's *Original Letters.*
[4] Callender, p. 19.

naturalists' and physicians' term, used of new species of birds, beasts or diseases; its wider application appears when Tom Paine in his *Rights of Man* describes titles as a chimerical non-descript, or when in 1790 the *Annual Register*[1] uses the word for 'a villain of a species that has hitherto been non-descript'—an insulter of ladies who slashed their petticoats. The idea of scientific classification was strong.

Quaint has five definitions in Johnson's Dictionary, none of them quite our complex of old-fashioned, odd and attractive. Southey and Scott at the turn of the century are the sponsors of the modern sense.

Queer, according to *Glossographia Anglicana Nova*, is a canting word. Its meaning then was what it is now, but *queer the pitch*, *Queer Street* are nineteenth-century extensions. *Feel queer* is used by Fanny Burney's 'Daddy Crisp'.[2]

Vital meant life-giving, or 'that on which life depends'. It was the nineteenth century that invented the technical phrase *vital statistics*[3] and applied *vital* to problems. It seems appropriate enough that the Duke of Wellington should be *O.E.D.*'s first recorded authority for saying that something was 'of vital importance' (and to require reports 'in triplicate'). *Vitality* in the figurative sense of liveliness, animation, is a mid-nineteenth-century use. *Animation* itself began literally as 'the informing an Animal's body with a Soul'. Boswell in 1779 uses it of liveliness and Scott in 1818 of enlivenment.

Gray is the first on record to use *breezy* figuratively: the *Gentleman's Magazine*[4] thought it quaint and difficult. It is only literal in Johnson's Dictionary. As implying brisk, airy or fresh it has become a useful description of people.

These developments have all been useful. One which has its modern parallels is not so good. In 1797, the *Gentleman's Magazine*[5] commented on the phrase 'superior personal beauty', saying 'This is inaccurate; and this kind of inaccuracy is becoming very common. *Superior* to what? the word "*superior*", in the sense here meant, ought never to be used without a comparative reference.' The Magazine would surely repeat its dictum about this increasingly common inaccuracy if it could read the advertisements about the detergent that washes whiter and the jelly that contains more fruit.

[1] *Ann. Reg.* xxxii (1790), 207.
[2] W. H. Hutton, *Burford Papers*, 1905, quoting Letter of 1 March 1781. *O.E.D.* c. 1800.
[3] The slang sense is recent.   [4] *Gent. Mag.* li (1781), 570.
[5] ibid., lxvii (1797), 850.

Icon is Greek for 'image' and the eighteenth century so used it. We read of 'Ichons' amongst Roman antiquities, or on seals, and dictionary definitions say it is 'any cut, Picture, Image or Representation'. The special religious sense that associates Icon with the Greek Church is a nineteenth-century restriction, and the literary-critical sense in the title *The Verbal Icon* is a modern specialisation of another kind.

The eighteenth century could use *instalment* where we use *installation*, but they paid by instalments like their descendants. Figurative uses of the word are nineteenth-century.

They used *issue* in its literal sense of event, passage, outlet, or thought like Boswell that in the meaning of 'conclusion' it should remain as a law term.[1] In its nineteenth-century application to important matters involving decision, it had a great future.

In the sphere of thought and action, some words that in the eighteenth century were malodorous have become disinfected, and some that were factual then have acquired a moral colouring. *Democracy* used of a government system was not the compliment it usually is now, as understood by either West or East. We read of the 'ravages of Democracy', of 'democratic rage and anarchy', the 'sink of democracy', the 'fluctuating rage and unbridled ambition of democracies', of 'democratic licentiousness', and that democracy is 'pernicious government'.[2] These phrases are all from the 'nineties and are luridly tinged by the French Revolution. 'We may hope', said the *British Critick*[3] in 1798, 'that should the rising generation be at all tainted with democratic follies, as it grows older, it will grow wiser.' Successive generations have found it wise to encourage democracy and recent ones have been willing to die for what they believed it means now.

Imperialists, on the other hand, were then the Subjects or forces of the German Emperor as *Glossographia Anglicana Nova* says, or of any Emperor, as Dr Johnson has it. The word did not imply a policy or attitude of mind. There was no smear-word quality in *imperialist*, and *colonialism* did not exist. *Indoctrinate* had still its etymological sense— to teach or instruct, with no undertone of misused inculcation of wrong ideas as it so often has in the twentieth century.

[1] Letter to Temple, 26 July 1763.
[2] The quotations are, in order, from *Brit. Crit.* ii, 302, 400; iv, 227; *Looker-on*, p. 238; *Crit. Rev.* (1792), 82 and (1790), 297 (quoting from Robert Bisset's *Sketch of Democracy*).
[3] *Brit. Crit.* xi (1798), 416.

Chivalry, according to *Glossographia Anglicana Nova*, is merely Horsemanship or Valour. Dr Johnson's fuller analysis shows no moral quality in the word. It was Burke in 1790 who gave it the meaning of chivalrousness, with stress on the protective gentleness of the strong which the ideal knight was supposed to show.

Crusade until Jefferson's time was historical in reference to the expeditions for the conquest of the Holy Land, or some other 'holy' war. He spoke of a crusade against ignorance and since then any organised attack on any social evil can be a crusade. It is surely inappropriate to use the word of any opposition to whatever a group happens to dislike.

Eighteenth-century uses may look forward to modern slang, or be revived to serve for a modern euphemism. Many a man, especially in the U.S.A., has called his beloved 'a peach of a girl'—and indeed *peach* can be applied to anything of superlative quality. Was Sir Edward Turner[1] the first to set the example when he wrote to enquire for his friend's niece 'that orange Peach'? It looks like his pet name for her.

In 1785 the *Monthly Review*[2] remarked that modern houses have a room, perhaps several, unknown to the ancients, which is a *powdering-room* for the hair. Now it is a room for powdering the nose and for providing what the official mind thinks of as ablutionary facilities. And *ablution* first meant a scientific technical process, or (as in Keats's sonnet) referred to ritual washing. It seems to have been Smollett in the mid-eighteenth century who set it on its way to modern use.

If they gave us the word we want, to use for things they hardly dreamed of, we have sometimes found the word they wanted. In 1754 the *Gentleman's Magazine*[3] reviewed a book on 'A Method to extract sugar from common Plants such as white and red beets, or skerrits.' We feel that *beet sugar* (*O.E.D.* 1833) and *sugar beet* (*O.E.D.* 1831) must have been on the tip of the writer's tongue; it is strange that the names had to wait for three quarters of a century.

[1] Dickins and Stanton: Letters of 16 August 1754 and 21 July 1756. It was also the name of a fashionable colour—see Iris Brooke, *Dress and Undress*.
[2] *Month. Rev.* lxxiii (1785), 22.   [3] *Gent. Mag.* xxiv (1754), 9.

VIII

THE MISLEADING

Obscurity arising from an uncommon word is easily surmounted, whereas ambiguity, by misleading us ere we are aware, confounds our notion of the subject altogether.

George Campbell, *Philosophy of Rhetoric*, p. 36, footnote

FALSE FRIENDS

IF we wish to write a good style, says William Godwin,[1] 'we must have an accurate notion of the meaning of words . . . the delicate shades of meaning by which they are diversified, and the various ideas and associations they are calculated to excite, and we must have an extensive acquaintance with their history.'

All this is also true if we wish to understand what people meant by words that have shifted their ground with the passage of time, or how they reacted to them. We have already seen how the advances of the last two centuries have put ideas into our heads that lie so close to the surface that we have to think back to earlier meanings. It is natural to expect our own meanings, but the context, as we read, shows us that we look in vain. But there are words that are not merely undeveloped —they have come to a dead-end in their older sense, so that they are obsolete or so archaic that we meet them as strangers. Their modern senses are descended from some other branch of the family. To us, *dialling* suggests a telephone, not a sundial;[2] *face-painting* reminds us of cosmetics, not portraits,[3] a *queue* is the line of people waiting for a 'bus or at the theatre or ticket-office, not a form of hair-dressing;[4] a *small bag* will be a lady's handbag, not a gentleman's wig;[5] a *rat-race* is more likely to be a struggle for place and power than between real rats;[6] we should expect a *cowboy* to come from the New World rather than from an Irish farm;[7] the *goose-step* calls up a military march, not

---

[1] *Enquirer*, p. 477.
[2] *Gent. Mag.* xxxix (1769), 328.
[3] Hutcheson, *Moral Good and Evil*, p. 266.
[4] In Dyche and Pardon spelt *cue*.
[5] *Connoisseur*, lxxvii.
[6] Jackson, *Letters*, ii, 40.
[7] *Gent. Mag.* xxxvii (1767), 566: *Anti-Jacobin*, i, 300.

a fashionable dance.[1] We expect a *pulpit* to be always occupied by a
preacher and not on occasion by an auctioneer in the course of his
profession;[2] if we hear someone described as a black man (*Spectator*
(1, etc.) we expect a Negro, not merely a man of dark complexion. A
metaphorical *guinea-pig* takes its colour from experimental science,
and no longer suggests a lad going abroad on a merchantman.[3] *Water-
works*[4] suggests a public utility, not ornamental lakes, cascades and
streams in a garden. We put *whitewash*[5] on our walls, not on our faces,
and we expect glaziers only to make the windows, never to clean them.
Party gowns[6] are frocks fit for a party, not made in the colours of
political parties, and a *knocker*[7] is what some people have on their
doors, not down their backs. One's *son-in-law*[8] cannot now be one's
step-son; *Oxford Blues*[9] are sportsmen, not soldiers; and *United States*[10]
means those in America, though in the eighteenth century we read of
'Amsterdam, the capital of Holland, and indeed of all the United
States.' *Signposts*[11] are the finger-posts on the roads, not inn-signs or
advertisements.

The ideas in all these words are so different from ours that we
cannot fail to see that we are on dangerous ground. More difficult are
the words that make sense but the wrong one—the false friends rather
than the complete strangers. Their outward forms are still with us, but
they are animated by a different spirit. We expect too much of them,
or not enough, or we turn our thoughts in the wrong direction.

Slang (ours or theirs) is responsible for some disturbance. A 'very
tight middle-aged woman'[12] was certainly not tipsy; whereas a young
nobleman, who came *flustered*[13] to his box in the theatre, was.

When the *Anti-Jacobin* begins to tell us of the '*remains*[14] of our unfortunate countrymen', we expect to find the men are dead. But no—
their constitutions had weathered a series of hardships, and they were
removed from Quimper living on the strength of one herring and one

---

[1] *Town & Country Mag.* xiii (1781), 231. (Not in *O.E.D.*). A Duchess learns
the goose-step from Vestris, and stands on one leg.
[2] *Tatler* (268), 1710: 1738 in *O.E.D.*   [3] Elphinston, *Education*, 50–1.
[4] *Adventurer*, 102; Shebbeare, *Letters*, ii, 267.
[5] *Spect.* (377). The cosmetic sense is the older in the noun.
[6] Mrs Montagu, *Letters*, ii, 103.
[7] *Town & Country Mag.* xiii (1781), 192.
[8] Ruffhead, *Life of Pope*, p. 192.   [9] *Ann. Reg.* xxxiv (1792), 20.
[10] *Crit. Rev.* new arr. xi (1794), 329.
[11] Dennis, *Critical Works*, ii, 206. *Looker-on*, ii, Nos. 34, 39.
[12] *Tatler* (118).   [13] *Tatler* (3).   [14] *Anti-Jacobin*, ii, 92.

pound of bread on a march of twenty to thirty miles. The *remains* means the rest, the survivors, and had done for 300 years.

It is noteworthy that 'the execution of the sentence' is now usually shortened to 'the execution of the criminal', and we take it to mean he suffered death. The eighteenth century, during which the death-penalty was horrifyingly more frequent, still used *execution* of any sentence, capital or not. We read of the execution of Madame de la Motte, and about the executioner—but she was not 'executed' in our restricted sense[1]: she was branded on the shoulder.

At times, such wider eighteenth-century uses can be disturbing. Mr Spectator speaks of a cunning *solicitor*,[2] who would never ask a favour of a great man before dinner—the solicitor is not a lawyer, merely a man seeking a favour. The *Tatler* (131) calls a cat an innocent *domestic*, because she lives in the house. It also uses *novelist* in the sense of newspaper man; at that date there were no Novels as a recognised genre. *Furniture*[3] could include such items as a snuffbox, handkerchief, or fan. *Aborigines*[4] were not necessarily primitive tribesmen—that sense is first recorded by *O.E.D.* in 1789. A *frontispiece*[5] could be the front of a building as well as in the front of a book. When Addison visited Venice, he found them 'putting out very curious stamps of the several Edifices which are most famous for their Beauty or Magnificence'.[6] A modern tourist could report a quite different form of souvenir in various countries in exactly the same words. A reference to 'times of Vacancy'[7] could be misunderstood, were the phrase not followed by 'and Recess from Business'; the distance now between *vacancy* and *vacation* is wide. *Prosaic* now implies the bad qualities of prose—a 'quotation from our Author's Prosaic writing'[8] would hardly be complimentary now. 'Studious and curious persons' is rather ambiguous to us.[9] 'Sturdy humour' sounds approving, but what Bishop Lavington[10] meant by it was more like 'obstinate cantankerousness'.

---

[1] *Gent. Mag.* lvi (1786), 608.
[2] *Spect.* (177).
[3] *Spect.* (57).
[4] Shenstone, *Works*, ii, 230.
[5] Shaftesbury, *Characteristics*, iii, 173.
[6] *Italy*, p. 61.
[7] *Spect.* (480).
[8] Pearce, *Text of Paradise Lost*, p. 292.
[9] *Ann. Reg.* ii (1759), 149, quoting British Museum Statutes.
[10] *Enthusiasm of Methodists and Papists Compar'd*, Pt. I (1749), p. 39.

MENTAL ATTITUDES

Much more important and still more difficult are the words that reflect the gradual movement of thought—the psychological changes that alter words from expressions of approval to disapproval, from smear-word to compliment, from strength to weakness, from the real to the fictitious. Such changes may be connected with scientific knowledge, international urgency, religious belief, social decorum, and they can hardly be neatly pigeon-holed. I have chosen a representative selection of various types.

We may begin with three words that stood always or normally on firm ground in the eighteenth century but are now standing on melting ice. The difference of meaning now between the older speaker and the younger—or the purist and the carefree (or careless) is noteworthy. They are *Fruition*, *Literally* and *Fabulous*. *Fruition* is the earliest, and for most people seems to have completely altered. The eighteenth-century (or earlier) meanings are thought archaic to us even when remembered. Modern readers would wonder why the *Monthly Review*[1] in 1774 thought 'Fruition' as the title of a Nuptial Elegy was 'startling', even if the poem itself was 'by no means unmodest'. As the *Glossographia Anglicana Nova* says, the word meant enjoyment or obtaining. This is the original sense, based on *fruor*; but Cocker-Hawkins will gloss the *Review* by telling us it means 'Possession'— usually of a man's possession of a woman. Of course it was more widely used and long had been—we recall Marlowe's 'sweet fruition of an earthly crown', or Goldsmith's[2] 'fruition of restored liberties'. But the idea that *fruition* is connected directly with fruit and with maturity and harvesting did not come till late last century. It would be pedantic to insist on the earlier meaning now, but some cling to it, and it must be recognised in older English.

Literally is now so often used as a mere intensifier that we may get a well-deserved shock when we meet it in its *literal* sense. In 1796 the *Annual Register*[3] recorded two accidents. At Camden Place, Bath, a gentleman's horses rushed over the precipice, and he was *literally* dashed to pieces; even more horrifying is the incident of a lad who fell into a copper of boiling water and was *literally* flayed alive. The *Critical*

---

[1] *Month. Rev.* l (1774), 231.
[2] *Essays* (1765), xiii.
[3] *Ann. Reg.* xxxviii (1796), 16, 20. (Rivington).

Review[1] described a concordance to Shakespeare as 'literally a patch-work'. At first sight, this looks like an early example of our intensifier. There is no need to think so, for *patch-work* meant any sort of medley or muddled arrangement long before the compound was used of the patch-work quilt, the memory of which gives vividness to the metaphor we feel the word to be. But I fear there was no doubt about Boswell's slack modernity when he writes (29 March 1773) to Goldsmith that 'all the great and the gay in the British metropolis are literally hanging upon *your smiles*'.

Fabulous, thanks mainly to advertisers and the exuberant young, is becoming a word of extravagant praise. For both, what is fabulous is marvellous and desirable, despite the fact that many things told of in fable are undesirable marvels. It is true, as Dr Pearce[2] reminds Dr Bentley—and us—that 'the first and most proper sense of the word *fabula* is, something commonly talked of, whether true or false'. He claims that all the dictionaries say so, which may be true of the Latin ones, but English dictionaries of this period (and of ours unless they are very up-to-date and receptive) say 'full of lies or stories',[3] 'feigned',[4] 'invented', 'lying'.[5] The difference between this usage and the new one so widely current is made plain by the context. A modern might say the Wall of China was fabulous—i.e. wonderful, but the *Spectator* (415) says any 'Account of it would have been thought Fabulous, were not the Wall itself still extant.' Holcroft's play *The School for Arrogance*[6] represents a sister meeting a long-lost brother who does not recognise her at once. 'Ah! Nature, thy instincts are fabulous,' she says, 'for were they not, his heart would have beaten as warmly toward me, as mine has done for him.'

The University of Oxford liked to think it had flourished in the reign of Henry III with 30,000 students—but that, says Dr Wende-born,[7] 'is certainly fabulous'. It certainly would have been in the modern undergraduate's sense, if there had been any truth in the belief.

In ordinary modern English, if we make an *allegation* we must be prepared to prove it. This was often true of the eighteenth century also, but we need to bear in mind that the word was not always clouded by so sceptical a spirit. The *Glossographia Anglicana Nova* defines it as 'a citation of any Book or Author to make good any Point or Assertion'—it is the equivalent of 'supporting quotation'.

[1] *Crit. Rev.* 65 (1788), 107.   [2] *Text of Paradise Lost*, p. 117.
[3] *Gloss. Ang. Nov.* s.v.   [4] Bailey, Johnson, s.v.
[5] Dyche and Pardon, s.v.   [6] p. 25.   [7] *View*, ii, 156.

Dyche and Pardon say it is 'a making of any assertion good by due proof', and that to allege is to affirm, bring as proof, quote, or bring in precedents. So a reviewer for the *Gentleman's Magazine*[1] speaks of proving the meaning of a word 'by an allegation of numerous authorities'.

We take a happier view of *amusement* than our ancestors did in the earlier part of the century, when to *amuse* was often much the same as to *bemuse*. *Glossographia Anglicana Nova* and Bailey agree that it is to stop someone with a trifling story, to feed him with vain expectations. *Amusement* is 'an idle or trifling employment to pass away the time, a *pastime*, a Toy, Divertisement; also the making of vain Promises to gain time'. There is some implication of throwing dust in the eyes. Clearly our meaning was there too, but sometimes in contexts where we should not choose the word because the idea of trifling, however pleasant, seems out of place. The *Spectator* will illustrate all three uses. Adam, during Eve's absence, says Addison, remains in 'Impatience and Amusement'[2]—i.e. perplexity. Similes in Odes and Epic poems are introduced partly 'to amuse and relax the Mind of the Reader'[3] (where both verbs agree with our usage); Milton's 'Account of the Hymns which our first Parents' heard the Angels sing 'is altogether Divine and inexpressibly amusing to the Imagination'.[4] Here *pleasing* sounds more suitable—even Dr Johnson's 'entertaining with tranquillity' is hardly enough to justify 'amusing' in so exalted a context. The word takes a good deal of getting in focus. We should not be *amused* with vague propositions of reformation.[5] In 'priests, having retired in gloomy and lonely habitations, find it in their interest to deceive, amuse and terrify the vulgar',[6] the company the word keeps shows us that such 'amusement' is undesirable. We should hardly say seriously that we had been amused by anything as solid as a biographical dictionary.[7] A thunderstorm that damaged a large area in London, and caused a number of deaths, would hardly be described as accompanied by lightning that *amused* the spectators very much.[8]

Lackington[9] thinks we should not amuse ourselves with hope or fear and Hanway[10] that we should not amuse ourselves with vain conjectures. Hogarth[11] admits that his title *Analysis of beauty* has amused

---

[1] *Gent. Mag.* xxvii (1758), 57.   [2] *Spect.* (351).   [3] *Spect.* (303).   [4] *Spect.* (321).
[5] *Gent. Mag.* xxii (1752), 352.   [6] James Beattie, *Dissertations*, p. 520.
[7] Letter to *Gent. Mag.* lv (1785), 359.
[8] James Beattie, *London Diary*, 13 Aug. 1773.
[9] *Memoirs*, p. 105.   [10] *Journal*, i, 242.   [11] Pref., A 2.

and raised the expectations of the curious, and that his 'line of beauty' amused them as much as any hieroglyph. Lawson[1] thinks poets always seek for amusing and roundabout ways of expression. *Interest, delude, dazzle, puzzle* would be our words. French propaganda is called *Amusements*[2]—*Artifices* to us: it was not *amusing*[3] in our sense at a time of expected imminent invasion to hear that the French had collected flat-bottom boats at Havre de Grace, while the real force was somewhere else. We should not describe Thomson's *Seasons* as captivating and amusing,[4] or call conjectures about the magic shield in *The Squire's Tale* amusing to the imagination,[5] or, with Dr Johnson,[6] characterise *Coriolanus* as one of Shakespeare's most amusing performances. The Looker-on[7] is not being frivolous when he hopes that in his Essay on Immortality he will be able to mix more than ordinary amusement.

Hanway[8] considers caring for the poor a pious amusement for ladies —an absorbing interest? Ferguson[9] implies that sense when he says men 'are best amused with exercises that engage them most, that awaken their affections, and occupy their talents. For this reason, the more serious and urgent occupations are to be preferred to the more light and apparently pleasant.' A modern widower would not *amuse*[10] his grief by composing poetry; and we should not consider it 'a most amusing speculation' to trace the unfolding of Benjamin Franklin's genius.[11]

Our sense of 'entertainment' did run parallel, and is clear beyond all doubt in H. J. Pye's *Amusement: a Poetical Essay* in 1790 which sings of all the popular sports and pastimes in a comprehensive not to say higgledy-piggledly way—hunting, dancing, fencing, chess, tennis, bowls, billiards, shooting, the theatre, concerts, races, visits to Bath or the sea-side, cards, fairs and boxing.

CHANGED TONE

If *amusing* encroaches on *interesting*, that word and its relatives have a stronger sense of involvement, moral or physical, than they sometimes have now. Our interests are so frequently merely our amuse-

[1] *Oratory*, p. 290. He uses it as we do, too.
[2] *Review*, v, 279:   [3] Henry Grenville in Dickins and Stanton (1759), p. 410.
[4] Warton on *Pope*, i, 42.   [5] Warton on *Faerie Queene*, i, 153.
[6] *General Observations*.   [7] *Essay* 31.
[8] *Journal*, ii, 118.   [9] *Institutes*, p. 154.
[10] Graves, *Columella*, ii, 182.   [11] *Crit. Rev.* new arr. viii (1793), 361.

ments, and interesting people, places and things merely entertaining
ones, that we need to watch eighteenth-century phrasing with some
alertness. Remembering 'an interested party', 'in one's own interest'
we can feel the slur intended in 'bad and interested physicians'[1] and
size up the lady who was 'selfish and interested, under all the agreeable
Qualities in the World'.[2] One gets the impression that Goldsmith's
English people who live abroad 'from interest or choice'[3] were doing
so because it was to their interest rather than because they were interested in foreign countries. Ferguson[4] tells us that mankind are
slavish, interested, insidious, deceitful, lazy. It is as though no self-
interest can be honourable. This is the frame of mind negatived by
disinterested: we shall be throwing away a useful tool if we persist in
levelling *disinterested* and *uninterested* now that we have come to believe
that interest can be good.

The *Gentleman's Magazine* in 1790[5] reports that the French have
received a very interesting account of insurrections among the Blacks
at Port au Prince, Domingo, Petit Grace and Martinico. As these were
mainly her colonies, France was bound to be affected and involved—it
was not just an 'interesting' piece of news as we read it now. The same
is true of numbers of public situations. In 1788[6] the Magazine considers that the Russo-Turkish war of those days has become interesting, because 'it threatens to involve all Europe in its consequences'.
Two years earlier it had been noticed that the disputes in Holland were
becoming interesting[7] to all Europe. Here the student of international
relations is looking uneasily at the possible consequences of local up-
heavals. At home, Junius[8] comments that the constitution is a common
cause in which we are all interested—it concerns us all. So an injury
offered to an individual is interesting to society.[9] In the unlikely event
of a modern government decreeing a fast, we should hardly term it 'an
awful and interesting occasion'; but in 1756[10] every citizen was—or
was meant to be—at once impressed and involved. Samuel Richardson[11]
couples the same two words in an account of a public execution—a
spectacle 'so awful and so interesting, to all who consider themselves
of the same species with the unhappy sufferers'. This is one of the rare

---

[1] Lyttelton, *Dialogues of the Dead*, xxiv.   [2] *Guardian* (5).
[3] *Present State of Polite Learning*, xiii.
[4] *Civil Society*, p. 171.   [5] *Gent. Mag.* lx (1790), 170.
[6] *Gent. Mag.* lviii (1788), 71.   [7] *European Mag.* x (1786), 324.
[8] *Letters*, ii, 3.   [9] *Letters*, i, 136.
[10] *New Universal Mag.* (March), p. 101.   [11] *Familiar Letters*, clx.

sentences where even for us *awful* resumes its power; and where *interesting* ought to suggest 'There, but for the grace of God, go I.' But both words are even better illustrated, because of the deeper involvement imagined, in certain reflections on the execution of Lords Kilmarnock and Balmerino, published in the *Westminster Journal*[1] in 1746: 'To meet certain and immediate death . . . is certainly the most awful and interesting situation that human nature can possibly be in.'

Such a situation might well give rise to the most terrible *apprehension*. But the eighteenth century used this word where we should use *comprehension* in the sense of grasp, understanding. Our feeling of fear is not present in the remark that punctuation is a useful artifice for leading 'the Reader's Apprehension into the Track of the Writer's Meaning',[2] or in a reference to our apprehension[3] that the air is hot, which is not fear of a storm but simply our perception of the physical fact. Some folk are too self-assured ever to be apprehensive. *Assurance*, says Trusler in his book on synonyms (1783) 'is the faculty of possessing a man's self—the just mean between bashfulness and impudence'. *Assured* has kept its ground; but *assurance* seems to have moved nearer to impudence, apart from its commercial, legal and theological uses.

APPROVAL AND DISAPPROVAL

Candour and *Candid* are now usually taken in the sense Dyche and Pardon give for the noun—they imply 'plain downright dealing' often with an overtone that a little less plainness would be more acceptable. But eighteenth-century Dictionaries give the adjective the warmer senses of gentle, favourable, benevolent, courteous, kind. When we receive the home-thrusts of our candid friends, however well-intentioned, we may doubt whether these are the adjectives we should choose, either for them or their remarks. We stress the sincerity at the expense of the good-will—and sometimes we doubt the good-will. Sheridan's Mrs Candour is a hint that the later eighteenth century was beginning to do so too. Etymologically, *candour* implies literally brightness, and so to the figurative innocence, and there are still traces of these basic senses when *Glossographia Anglicana Nova* says candid means 'White, also Innocent', and when Blacklock writes of 'vice indulg'd' that may *stain* Candour. Dr King's epitaph on Beau Nash recalls that the 'King' of Bath

[1] Quoted *Gent. Mag.* xvi (1746).   [2] Burrow, *Essay on Punctuation*, p. 12.
[3] Priestley, *Universal Grammar*, p. 107.

cuncta insignia, etiam regium diadema rejiciens, Caput contentus fuit *ornare GALERO ALBO, Manifesto animi sui candoris signo.*

This was translated as 'the ornamental ensign of a white hat, a symbol of the candour of his mind'.[1]

But the usual eighteenth-century sense is that of kindness. Candour goes with benevolence and humility, with liberality of sentiment, with compassion and indulgence, as well as with impartiality. It is a favourite word with Charles Churchill, who contrasts it with Rancour, and declares that

> CANDOUR, with the charity of Paul
> Still thinks the best, when e'er she thinks at all,
> With the sweet milk of human kindness bless'd.[2]

Unless we keep this emphasis in mind, we shall feel many eighteenth-century remarks inconsistent and take them in a sense incompatible with their real one.

People who declare 'they will not in candour disclose what they know',[3] would now exemplify their candour by disclosure. Shenstone[4] would not now think that 'the merit of a single part will strike a most candid judge so strongly as to make him overlook multitudes of faults'. Faults are what we should expect him to look for. A correspondent of the *Monthly Review*[5] in 1765 thinks people in general 'are much mistaken in the ideas they affix' to *Candour.* 'For they are apt to imagine, that every commendation or at least abstinence from blame of a work is an instance of the Critic's candour.' He would hardly make the same accusation now. Ferguson[6] defines Candour as 'the just allowance given to the pretensions or merits of other men in opposition to prejudice, or to the suggestions of interest'. Dr Johnson's[7] words in his *Preface to Shakespeare* (1768) seem out of focus to us, when he says that little regard is 'due to that bigotry which sets candour higher than truth', or when he remarks of the lesser critics that 'the little which they have been able to perform might have taught them more candour to the endeavours of others'.

But we feel at home when Francis Grose,[8] in his *Essay on Advertisements*, admits 'Candour has obliged me to insert some articles which

---

[1] *Life of Beau Nash*, p. 189.   [2] *Epistle to Hogarth*, l. 55.
[3] Knox, *Essays*, i, 60.   [4] Quoted *London Mag.* (1764), 452.
[5] *Month. Rev.* xxxii (1765), 485.   [6] *Institutes*, p. 245.
[7] In Murphy's edition, p. 30; *Johnson on Shakespeare*, ed. Raleigh, 1940, p. 51.
[8] *Olio*, p. 256.

do not tend to the honour of the parties concerned, or that of the country wherein they are suffered; such as those relative to the sale of seats in Parliament and guardians offering to dispose of their wards.' And in the 'nineties, one of the *Anti-Jacobin*[1] writers is praying

Save me from the *candid Friend*

just as we might—and giving a new adjective to the noun in the phrase *canting candour*. Though they could still use the noun in its old kindly sense,[2] it strikes us as the odd man out in their appeal that the country should 'hear no more at such a time, of amiability and gentleness—of candour, liberality and moderation—of conciliatory, mild, and generous feelings'.

Our candid friends keep watch over our complacency. This word could carry a more respectable idea than it usually does now. *Complacency* was delight in other people or in external things, an inherited sense we need to remember in *Paradise Lost*. Now, *complacency* implies being pleased—indeed, too pleased—with oneself. The *Concise Oxford Dictionary* gives its first meaning as 'tranquil pleasure', which is Dr Johnson's definition of amusement, we remember, but it is the second definition—'self-satisfaction' which is the common one now.[3]

The *Tatler* (95) speaks of one man's complacency to another's inclinations; the *Spectator* (588) wonders what *Complacency* the divine Mind could have in Man. 'Fitzosborne' can talk of 'a most disinterested Complacency'[4] when someone benefits him, which implies pleasure in the friend as much as in himself. Vicesimus Knox[5] thinks we cannot look at 'the playful Lamb' without complacency, and that paintings of animals and scenery inspire a complacency but do not warm with sentiment or animate to virtue. On the other hand, it is only too easy to read the modern tone into Sarah Fielding's description of Octavia 'approaching with a Complacence that approved her conscious Virtue'.[6] To be conscious of one's virtue (or of any other quality or possession) and to show it, is precisely what gives rise to our reading of the word, though it is far from Miss Fielding's conception of her heroine's character.

We do not look on condescension as an amiable quality; for Dr Johnson the word means 'voluntary humiliation: descent from

[1] *Anti-Jacobin*, ii, 630.   [2] ibid., p. 572.
[3] See Fowler's *Modern English Usage*, and Partridge's *Usage and Abusage* on this, and the French twin *Complaisance*.
[4] Melmoth, *Letters*, p. 105.   [5] *Essays*, i, 34.   [6] *Octavia*, p. 147.

superiority'. *Condescendingly* means 'by way of kind concession'. So Reid[1] puts it among the 'moral virtues which in a peculiar manner constitute a lovely character: Innocence, gentleness, condescension, humanity, natural affection, public spirit, and the whole train of the soft and gentle virtues'. He is not snobbish when he says good breeding 'consists of all the external signs of due respect to our superiors, condescension to our inferiors, politeness to all'. It is strange to the modern mind to hear of an author who resigns 'his judgment with entire Condescension to his Superiors'.[2] The nature of condescension turns on the spirit and manner of those who practise it: it seems all too clear that most people have been patronising—and that too is a word that could be good in the eighteenth century, despite Dr Johnson's celebrated reference to the patron in the *Vanity of Human Wishes*. There is nothing in his Dictionary s.v. *patronise* to suggest any uncomfortable relationship. If we patronise our friends, the worse for us—but we may patronise a shop or hotel in all innocence.

Imbecility now suggests readiness for a mental home. In the eighteenth century it was primarily weakness of body, but was used also of judgment. That it was not essentially connected with the brain is clear from a remark about a man whom misfortune had reduced to a state of 'almost complete mental imbecillity'.[3] If 'praise of goodness of heart is usually accompanied with an oblique insinuation of intellectual imbecility',[4] there is no hint of a *mental* breakdown. Knox[5] speaks generally of the 'common imbecilities attendant on the most improved state of human nature', and Ruffhead comments on the imbecility of Pope's frame and of his extravagant attachment to Lord Bolingbroke[6] —but Ruffhead was far from implying that Pope was mad, except as in modern slang one might be 'mad on' a friend. It would be easy to read too strong a sense into the word.

Imbecility is close to its Latin sense. So is *impertinent*, which throughout the period implies not so much rudeness as irrelevance and the out of place. The votive offerings Addison saw in Italy bore *impertinent* inscriptions;[7] the *impertinencies* of a wretch in pain[8] could be the wanderings of delirium or his expressions of feelings in which his

---

[1] *Intellectual Powers of Man*, ii, 514.
[2] Shaftesbury, *Characteristics*, iii, 71.
[3] *Ann. Reg.* xxxvii (1795), 13 (Rivington).
[4] Knox, *Essays*, ii, 86. The spelling wavers between one *l* and two.
[5] ibid., p. 126.   [6] *Life of Pope*, ii, 531.
[7] *Italy*, p. 47.   [8] *Spect.* (374).

visitor cannot share. The *Universal Spectator*[1] has a definition of *impertinence* followed by an amusing catalogue of *impertinents*—it is 'a certain Giddiness of the Mind, occasioned by a redundant Liveliness of the Imagination, accompanied usually with a Stupefaction of Judgment'. Silvia engrosses all the conversation with her own life-story, Novellus talks only of foreign news; Clarissa sings Italian airs and some from *The Beggar's Opera*; Aunt Priscilla *will* talk of house-keeping, Father of astrology. And then there are the 'Manual imperti-nents who scratch plates and cut tables as if they did not see Folks, or, what is worse, despised them.' They are all self-centred, not willing to take part in social converse and determined to talk only on matters of interest to themselves; it is a form of rudeness, but thoughtless rather than deliberately impudent. 'Nothing to the Purpose, idle Discourse,' says Cocker-Hawkins. But we can see how the transition could be made when we read[2] 'of the impertinence of the sophist who read a lecture to Hannibal on the art of war'. Certainly it was 'nothing to the purpose', and if Hannibal thought it impudence, who could blame him?

More obviously literal is one of the eighteenth century's uses of *levity* (now felt as rare) which was used of physical lightness—the opposite of *gravity* before Newton transformed it. Adam Smith[3] men-tions the 'superior levity' of fire, which fits in with *Glossographia Anglicana Nova*'s definition of 'the want of weight in any Body when compared with another that is heavier'. Erasmus Darwin[4] makes Mont-golfier ascend 'on levity of wing'—which suggests a plane rather than a balloon. With the familiar figurative uses there was one that was not derogatory as ours normally is—the *Annual Register* in the preface to its first volume promises to intermingle with its solid historical facts 'matters of a lighter nature, but pleasing even by their levity'.

No doubt levity could and can descend to lubricity. *Lubricity* then as now could be literal or figurative, and could then be used with no suggestion of disapproval. The gentleman who displayed 'lubricity' of manner and alienation of thought,[5] was only absent-minded—he could not get a grip on his thoughts. There is no implication of moral obliquity in a reference to 'the lubricity of all those principles which are not grounded in the real circumstances of man, and in the constitution of nature'.[6] Mortality in 'a state of lubricity and deception'[7] refers to the uncertain incidence of death; the lubricity of a language arises from

[1] Quoted *Gent. Mag.* i (1731), 205.   [2] Knox, *Essays*, ii, 104.
[3] *Works*, v, 198.   [4] *The Botanic Garden*, iv, 146.
[5] *Looker-on*, i, 312.   [6] *Looker-on*, ii, 24.   [7] ibid., iii, 4.

an 'exuberancy of vocal sounds',[1] because vowels are the most subject to change. A 'lubricous' dimpled smile is one that 'prints itself in every corner of the countenance'[2] and the observer clearly enjoys it. The prevailing modern sense of moral slipperiness was often there, but cannot be always assumed.

Nor is *dissipation* always an adverse comment on improper indulgence of a physical sort—indeed William Cowper is recorded as the first to apply it in that way. Dr Johnson accuses himself of living a dissipated and useless life[3]—without concentration and purpose, he means. It can be contrasted to *collected*. Ferguson[4] defines it as 'a weakness of the mind disabling it from chusing or prosecuting the occupations that would engage it most effectually and with most advantage'. Boswell[5] records that even in church he was too dissipated to fix his attention—i.e. he could not control his wandering thoughts. If we suspect that these were concerned with dissipation in our stronger sense, it is due to our knowledge of Boswell and the later uses of the English tongue.

EXTENSION AND RESTRICTION

We moderns apply *national* to all sorts of things—widely to sentiment and character, art and literature, narrowly to the Coal Board or the Health Service; the particularising of the word is a measure of our changed political and social patterns. *Nationality* goes with being a 'national' of a given nation. We are therefore held up for a moment when we find the word obviously meaning nationalism, good or bad. Hutcheson[6] equates national love with love of one's country; Dr Johnson defines *national* as 'bigotted to one's country'—and a Scottish[7] observer remarks that 'What is patriotism with the English is nationality with the Scots'—from the English viewpoint, of course.

Dr Bentley[8] disapproved of Milton's 'signs of remorse and passion' because *passion* had too wide a signification to be proper—it comprehends disdain and rage 'quite contrary to Remorse'. The young man[9] who was rendered miserable by his overbearing father, told his story

---

[1] *Lælius and Hortensia*, p. 421.   [2] *Looker-on*, i, 146.
[3] Written on Easter Eve 1761. Cp. Repton, *Variety*, xviii, which equates *dissipation* with *amusement* and *relaxation*.
[4] *Institutes*, p. 256.   [5] *London Journal*, p. 254.
[6] *Moral Good and Evil*, p. 163.   [7] *Gent. Mag.* lvi (1786), 845.
[8] Re *Paradise Lost*, i, 605.
[9] *New Letters to the Tatler and Spectator*, p. 148.

in tears, yet in the height of his passion would say his father 'designed him well'. He was not in a fit of anger. By the 'nineties, however, Mrs Piozzi[1] thinks *passionate* the synonym of *angry* most in use—which is hardly still true. We could use *indignant*, and *wrathful* is not rare outside theological circles. We might easily misunderstand the reference of *passionate* and the atmosphere of *wrathful*.

Change is the spice of life; it amounts to much the same if you say 'Vicissitude is essential to every state of durable enjoyment.'[2] Pleasure and Pain may well come turn and turn about; it is hardly to be wondered at that pain leaves the deeper impress and that therefore *vicissitude* mainly suggests the uncomfortable variations of life. We should hardly say that 'the leaves of the tree undergo a pleasing vicissitude'.[3] Another sort of pessimism is betrayed by the fact that in the eighteenth century a *diatribe* was still not necessarily a vicious attack; it could, also, be merely the place where a disputation was held, according to Bailey's Dictionary.

We are used to hurrying crowds, and all we mean is large numbers of people bent on getting somewhere quickly. The eighteenth century meant a great deal more by both words. *Hurry* implied tumult, agitation, confusion. A great storm gives us the 'Apprehension of Danger, which puts the Passions in a Hurry';[4] according to Trusler to 'be in a hurry, is proof that the business we embark on confuses us, and is too great for us, whereas to be in haste . . . is a mark of diligence'. During Parliamentary elections, all the kingdom might be 'in a hurry'[5]—an upheaval. Defoe[6] describes a riot at Edinburgh as 'a Hurry'—one that was 'continued in a Terrible Manner'. Parliamentary business he thinks of as a Hurry, and also the subject of French trade.[7]

The muscular sense of *crowd* is kept today much more in the verb than the noun—it is a verbal witness to the improvement of our manners. The *World* (66) describes a fashionable Assembly in terms we should be more likely to adapt to a paragraph about a rush at the Sales—Woman is 'a creature formed for crowding and being crowded; a crowded assembly breaks her hoop, tears her ruffles, puts her in a horrid fluster, makes her a fright'—nevertheless, to game in a crowd was the thing.

---

[1] *Brit. Syn.*, i, 88.   [2] Knox, *Essays*, i, 168.   [3] ibid., ii, 39.
[4] Baillie, *Essay on the Sublime*, p. 40.
[5] Hertford-Pomfret Correspondence, iii, 279.
[6] Letters to Harley, 24 Oct. 1706.
[7] Letters to Harley, 18 July 1713; 19 Oct. 1713.

A gentleman going to the theatre has the same experience: 'At the door I waited near half an hour with the utmost impatience; and the moment it was open, rushed in, driven forward by the crowd that gathered round one.'[1]

So Dennis[2] had understood the word earlier. To him, Pope's *close-embodied crowd* was tautology—'As if every crowd were not *close* . . . A crowd of anything implies Confusion.'

The Duchess of Northumberland[3] puts it, by implication, in a nutshell, for she records in her Diary that at a royal Ball there were 'a vast many people, yet there was no crowd'. She sounds pleasantly surprised at such orderly behaviour: we could easily feel she was contradicting herself.

Now and then the eighteenth century gave a more concrete application to a word we see in the abstract; and it may work the other way.

The *Anti-Jacobin*[4] records an Angelo-Isabella story in real life, with no happy ending: the woman, who sacrificed herself to save her husband from death, was judicially murdered in particularly humiliating circumstances. The *Anti-Jacobin* describes the act of the treacherous official as 'a trait so atrocious as to surpass all ever read of in history —such a trait alone would serve to dishonour a whole nation'. Here *trait* is action rather than quality.

Casualty on the other hand, was much more the abstraction—misfortune, hurt or damage rather than *those* dead or injured by the chance of war or calamity. It is noteworthy that both *casualty* and *accident* have moved to the area of unpleasant chance, and *incident* seems to be following them. Dr Armstrong[5] speaks of being 'by custom steel'd

To every casualty of varied life'—

though in the beginning of the century Jeremy Collier[6] could still write of changes of custom, honour and language as casualties. The modern reader who tends to connect the word with people, will be surprised at the items listed under *Casualties* in the magazines. The first volume of the *Gentleman's Magazine* includes fatal accidents, murders, suicides, fires, an accidental poisoning. *Casual(ly)* had not acquired any implication of nonchalance, and formed the equivalent of *accidental*. Dyche and Pardon define *chance-medley* as 'the killing of a person casually',

[1] *Adventurer* (24).   [2] *Critical Works*, ii, 124.
[3] *Diaries of a Duchess*, ed. Greig. 9 Sept. 1761.
[4] *Anti-Jacobin*, i, 329.
[5] *Art of Preserving Health*, iii, 29.   [6] *Essays*, p. 11.

which would certainly imply the worst kind of murder now. A discussion of whether the Government of the World is Casual, Fatal, or Providential[1] would imply different philosophies in two out of three of the adjectives now. The sense of happy-go-lucky existed, but not that of 'off-hand' which is a twentieth-century extension.

If we fall into a reverie, its substance will depend on our mental furniture. It is characteristic of the rational eighteenth century that it so often thought of reveries as wild, chaotic and impossible. Fielding's[2] *Champion* speaks of falling 'into a Sort of Reverie . . . the pure Result of the Imagination, heated with' reading Lucian—and Lucian is enough of himself to show its nature. The *British Critick*[3] thought two shillings exorbitant for fifty small pages of quotations and twenty of the author's own reveries. The Looker-on[4] declares himself no friend to the Platonic system of ravings and reveries; allegories would be unpardonable romantic reveries but for their mystical meaning. Duff[5] argues that judgment must be essential to genius—otherwise we cannot distinguish between the flights of genius and the reveries of a lunatic. The author[6] of some *Physiological Reveries* modestly apologised for troubling the public with thoughts so crude as to merit the term of reveries. There is a certain ambiguity about the word: Charles Johnstone's book *The Reverie*[7] begins with an account of how he 'sunk into that suspension of sense which is called A Reverie; when the soul only wakes, and, breaking through its corporeal incumbrances, ranges at will over the boundless expanse of creation, and joins in converse with congenial spirits'. Indeed the book has the uncertainty and range of a daydream. The introduction leads us to expect lofty flights of imagination—but the subtitle is *A Flight to the Paradise of Fools*.

The eighteenth century is full of attempts to pin down that elusive entity genius. This is no place to try to sum up the philosophical and literary essays,[8] but it may be useful to remind the student that the word could be used to mean nothing more than mental capacity, even a bent towards some study or occupation.

While the higher sense of genius was being analysed by the philosopher and critic, the man in the street was applying it to everything. In the mid-century, the *Connoisseur*[9] was laughing at the 'modern acceptation of the word, by which it signifies a very silly young fellow,

[1] ibid., p. 22.   [2] i, 200.   [3] *Brit. Crit.* x, 321.
[4] *Looker-on*, i, 85.   [5] *Essay on Original Genius*, p. 24.
[6] *Crit. Rev.* xx (1765), 301.   [7] 1763.
[8] See Bibliography.   [9] xc, 15 Oct. 1755.

who from his extravagance has obtained the name of a Genius...'
and the magazine continues

> Genius, blest term of meaning wide!
> (For sure no term so misapply'd)
> How many bear the sacred name,
> That never felt a real flame!
> Proud of the specious appellation,
> Thus fools have christ'ned inclination.

And by 1799[1] a gentleman who signs himself *No Genius*, is wishing for peace with France so that he can retire to the Continent among 'a few plain dull fellows' like himself, with no 'risk of being knocked down by a Genius at every turning'. There are geniuses at shoe-making and furnishing, any dauber or rhymer is a genius, his daughter is a genius at mincemeat, his son at skating. Cannot some scheme be proposed 'for the reduction of geniuses, that business may not stand still?'

COMPLIMENTS?

It would be easy to read too much into Lyttelton's[2] remark that 'to meet danger with courage, is manly; but to be insensible of it, is brutal stupidity'. *Brutal* was often the adjective of *brute* (beast); to us it implies savagery in the human. There is indeed a long catalogue of adjectives whose eighteenth-century overtones have been changed. The *Critical Review*[3] in 1766 said what we should say when it censured Blackstone for being 'addicted to the study of the Law', which struck the reviewers as very improper, because *addicted* does very generally, and should always infer a vicious pursuit'. But Blackstone had various supporters. Priestley[4] is surely not blaming the sea-ports of Asia Minor for being addicted to commerce; Junius[5] speaks of being addicted to useful reading; Wendeborn[6] of people addicted to cleanliness. A historian wrote of people addicted to woollen-manufacture or castle-building—the *Critical Review*[7] thought it too vulgar for history; and disliked Baretti's[8] 'addicted to arts and sciences'. Clearly we cannot be sure it implies disapproval.

[1] Quoted from *St James' Chronicle* by *Gent. Mag.* lxix (1799), 199–200.
[2] *Dialogues of the Dead*, VII.
[3] *Crit. Rev.* xxi (1766), 12.
[4] *Universal Grammar*, p. 172.
[5] *Letters*, ii, 129.
[6] *View*, i, 264.
[7] *Crit. Rev.* 45 (1778), 43.
[8] *Crit. Rev.* 3 (1757), 40.

If we described anyone as 'alert' we should be paying him a compliment; but Dr Johnson says the word implies some degree of censure and contempt, and commonly means brisk, pert, petulant, smart. *Smart* now leads a double life, and *brisk* is good—but Bunyan's Mr Brisk reminds us that it was not always a word of unqualified praise. On the other hand, *artful* to us does imply censure: the Artful Dodger has left too many descendants. The eighteenth century offers us a perplexing set of variations on the meanings of *artful, artist,* and *artificial. Artful* can be approving, and mean that the rules of a particular art (or craft) have been followed. A building could be artfully executed, a grove artfully laid out. Pope[1] refers to Abelard's fate with 'artful decency'; Chaucer's[2] plan of the *Canterbury Tales* is artful and entertaining; if *The Bard* had ended with 'To triumph and to die are mine', the reader 'would have been left in a pleasing and artful suspense.'[3] *St Cecilia's Day* is an artful poem.[4] On the other hand, the *Guardian* (68, 65) recognises 'the Dissolute, Gay and Artful of the Fair Sex', and those who are artful and insincere in business, and Hutcheson[5] speaks of the *covetous, mean-spirited,* but *artful* citizen who will serve his country no further than it is for his private interest. The good and the bad senses turn on whether the artful are full of Art or of arts. As Uvedale Price[6] says, there are words 'that have a good and a bad sense; such as *simplicity* and *simple, art* and *artful;* which as often express our contempt as our admiration'.

An artist could be a practitioner of any art, not necessarily of any of the Fine Arts—'an ingenious Workman' as *Glossographia Anglicana Nova* has it. It was an 'ingenious artist', in the words of the *Critical Review,*[7] who wrote a dissertation on the Construction of Locks. Dyer[8] writes of the artists from populous Leeds, and Cowper[9] of the cobbler, 'leather-carving artist', and a gentleman in the *Mirror*[10] wears buttons 'made by one of the most eminent artists in Birmingham'. The *Spectator* (56) includes under Works of Art such things as Knives, Boats and Looking-glasses (*Artifact* did not come till 1835). Work of Art in the strict modern sense dates from 1883; though the phrase occurs in the index of vol. vi of the *Spectator* in 1739 it refers to gardens which may be artistically or artificially laid out, but were not works of

---

[1] Warton on *Pope*, i, 324.   [2] ibid., ii, 4.
[3] ibid., ii, 43.   [4] Ruffhead's *Life of Pope*, p. 59.
[5] *Passions and Affections*, p. 296.   [6] *Essay*, i, 386.
[7] *Crit. Rev.* 65 (1788), 77.   [8] *Fleece*, ii, 60.
[9] *Verses written at Bath*, 9.   [10] *Mirror* (5).

art in the sense current in Museums and Galleries or at Sotheby's any more than the utilitarian articles just mentioned.

Bland had acquired no tinge of irony, so the *Looker-on*[1] could speak of the 'bland and unerring powers of instinct that cause the hen to gather her brood under her wing'. *Charming* turns up in what seem to us strange contexts. Horace Walpole[2] tells us that after forty years of miserable sufferings, Lord Dacre's death was charming; and a lady[3] describes the view of a public execution as charming—which leaves us in doubt whether we need to adjust ourselves to the word or the lady's outlook. 'Pleasing in the highest degree', says Dr Johnson. *Pretty* may strike us as weakly out of place. We should not say that King's College Chapel, Cambridge, was elaborately pretty as Mrs Piozzi does.[4] It was not that she was deficient in either words or appreciation—she goes on to say it gives delight to every beholder. Nor should we say a statue of Handel looked pretty enough[5] or that in any form Mr Thynne's murder was prettily represented.[6] Bailey tells us the word can mean handsome.

Sedate now has a touch of smugness about it, a spice of unnatural calm. For the eighteenth century it was simply quiet, undisturbed, composed. We may compare *sedative*. The difference can be felt in context more easily than analysed. Sublimity—a storm at sea, thunder —will inspire sedateness, which suggests awestruck quiet.[7] It is an amiable quality like sagacity and sweetness:[8] sedateness of reason makes up a triad with purity of discernment and elegance of mind.[9] King Lear's 'Pray do not mock me . . .' is a speech in which 'humility, calmness and sedateness' are 'opposed to former rage and indignation'.[10] Sedate tempers are contrasted with passionate ones. Poussin's landscapes are characterised by 'sedate, solemn dignity'.[11] Poetic numbers have a 'sedate majesty'.[12] Caesar weighed the war sedately.[13] One does not now as a rule have 'any sedate Malice against any Person'[14]—we should prefer *settled, deliberate*. Lady Pomfret[15] must have been one of the first to appreciate Alpine scenery, even if her appreciation was

[1] i, 65.
[2] Quoted Dickins and Stanton, p. 438.
[3] Mrs Montagu, *Letters*, i, 254.
[4] *Brit. Syn.*, i, 39.
[5] Richardson, *Familiar Letters*, cliv.
[6] ibid., clvi.
[7] Gerard, *Essay on Taste*, p. 16.
[8] ibid., p. 46.
[9] ibid., p. 233.
[10] *Adventurer* (122).
[11] Uvedale Price, *Essay*, ii, 241. *On Architecture and Building.*
[12] W. Mitford, *Essay upon the Harmony of Language*, p. 79.
[13] Brooke, *Universal Beauty*, iv, 261.
[14] Hutcheson, *Moral Good and Evil*, p. 153.
[15] Hertford-Pomfret Correspondence, ii, 254.

224   THE MISLEADING

encouraged by appropriate amenities of civilisation. The approaches
to the Brenner Pass were so easy, the roads so good, dangerous places
so carefully walled or railed, that she could 'with great pleasure and
sedateness contemplate the variety which this fine country affords'.
    Considerate now implies concern for others, especially those over
whom one has some power. It can be colder in the eighteenth century,
implying thought rather than altruistic thoughtfulness—reflection,
prudence, the result of taking into one's consideration—though it
could also have our meaning, for Dyche and Pardon say it can mean
compassionate. Dr Johnson does not go beyond moderate, not rigor-
ous. So we meet with a considerate and unprejudiced reader, and a
learned and considerate writer. Age is considerate, and judgment is
cool, attentive and considerate. 'A considerate person cannot pass a
coxcomb . . . without being sensibly hurt at the reflection that such a
calamity is incident to human nature.'[1]
    Coy, according to Dr Johnson, is modest, decent, reserved, not
accessible, and the *Concise Oxford Dictionary* agrees. It seems to be
moving towards the appearance of modesty rather than the reality, in
so far as it applies to people. To be coy is compatible with a 'Come-
hither look': the *Oxford Illustrated Dictionary* (1962) admits the
declension. Another meaning much stronger than the dictionaries
acknowledge, seems to be given the word by Jerningham,[2] when he
describes efforts to make Huguenots recant on their deathbeds to
prevent the confiscation of their property—

>   from th'alarmed reluctant mind to wrest
>   The coy assentment to the hateful test.

This is surely 'having reservations', not just 'reserved'.
    Decent was changing its tone; 'Grave, not gaudy, not ostentatious',
says Dr Johnson, along with 'convenient' and 'not immodest'. So
Parnell[3] speaks of the decent eyes of the shining seraphim. Collins'
Simplicity is 'a decent maid'—the atmosphere is very different from
'she's a decent girl' or a 'decent sort'. Knox in his essay on Decency
thinks that Pope uses the word as the opposite to *sprightly*. But the
later eighteenth century, like the twentieth, was puzzled as to just what
Pope meant when he said Archbishop Secker was decent. One critic[4]
thought it a 'negative, niggardly' commendation, but supposed that the
meaning he gave it was 'perhaps very different from that which is

[1] *World*, p. 88.
[3] *Poetical Works*, p. 204.
[2] *Enthusiasm*, p. 12.
[4] *Crit. Rev.* 50 (1780), 95.

carried in its common acceptation'. The *British Critick*[1] thinks that Pope intended to transfer into our language the classical sense of 'decens' which is sometimes used to denote personal beauty and sometimes moral good. Pope probably 'attempted injudiciously to give dignity to a word which was too much debased by its familiar acceptation to admit of such an exaltation'. *O.E.D.* doubts whether Pope had any such exaltation in mind—he meant that Secker fulfilled the duties of his station. The *Critick* noticed that the poet was apt to use unacceptable epithets: he thought Allen would take 'low-born' as a compliment, and altered it to 'humble' when he did not—a word whose ambiguity can have hardly made it much better.

Genteel has likewise gone down. It once conveyed the ideas of politeness, gracefulness, elegance of dress and manner, but declined through indiscriminate use and affectation. It was not a vulgarism, and had no ironic turn. Defoe couples it with its doublet *gentle*. Lord Lovat, before his execution in 1747 for his part in the "Forty-five', sent for his wig betimes, that the barber might have time to comb it out genteely[2] (*sic*). Genteel life is contrasted with low life, a genteel wit with scurrilous buffoonery. Hogarth[3] thinks we should all wish to be genteel and graceful in our carriage. Dyche and Pardon define *polite* as 'accomplished with all manner of genteel arts and useful learning'. Vergil, according to Spence, wrote 'genteel pastorals' and Horace's wit was of the genteelest sort.[4] Mr Crosbie the balloonist had a genteel figure: he needed it, to set off his aerial costume which 'consisted of a robe of oiled silk, lined with white fur, his waistcoat and breeches in one, of white satin quilted, and Morocco boots and a Montero cap of leopard-skin'.[5] But the word was slipping when it was applied to those who look like gentlemen but are not—when the butler and footmen are genteel men-servants, dressed and powdered out like gentlemen.[6] Materials that are at once cheap and genteel[7] open the way for doubt. When the body of a street robber was rescued and revived after a hanging, he was pardoned and a genteel collection[8] made for him. Did it enable him to set up as a gentleman, or was it worthy of the gentlemen who subscribed? The same question arises when we read of a genteel annuity left to a steward.

[1] *Brit. Crit.* viii (1796), 252.
[2] *Gent. Mag.* xvii (1747), 160.
[3] *Analysis of Beauty*, p. 138.
[4] *Polymetis*, pp. 17, 21.
[5] *Ann. Reg.* xxvii (1784–5), 224.
[6] *Columella*, ii, 19.
[7] *Spect.* (283).
[8] *Ann. Reg.* x (1767), 51.

WEAKENING

Horrid still carried its full weight of horror in a way it does not now. Horrid children are not now really horrifying, though they may be nuisances. In the eighteenth century we find the word used of a woman who poisoned her husband and five children,[1] and of such acts as the execution of Lady Lisle[2] and Louis XVI. It applies to the Inquisition, war, blasphemy, pestilence, suicide, the massacre of defenceless prisoners. It is used of the eyes of a Fury, of Druidical rites, of the spectacle of a murderer's dissected body, of the Gordon Riots. It goes with barbarity, catastrophe, tragedy, violence. We should prefer *horrible*, *horrific* or *horrifying* in all such contexts. It is also used of the literary description of horrors—that of a wretch broken on the wheel,[3] or the flaying of Marsyas.[4]

When it is used of scenery, there can be little doubt that the speaker was feeling shocked at barren or overpowering nature: it filled him with fear and revulsion. His reaction is not always ours. Iceland is rendered horrid by its black and stinking waterfalls;[5] the mountains and valleys round Trondheim are horrid barren places;[6] Glaciers in the Alps make a horrid noise,[7] and Vesuvius in eruption is a glorious and horrid scene.[8] Now and then we meet the word in its full Latin sense of bristling, as in *Eloisa to Abelard*—'Ye grots and caverns shagg'd with horrid thorn'; 'the hairy skins of goats all horrid'[9] combines distaste and shagginess, but is comparatively weak.

Erasmus Darwin[10] offers a careful analysis of *horrid* when he says it combines the ideas of distress and disgust, and is allied to hate, whereas *tragic* is made up of distress and pity, and is allied to love.

Many a situation described as *horrid* could also have been described as *deplorable*. The modern tone of the word was there, but there was also a kindlier attitude. When we find the situation deplorable, we are readier to make a protest than to weep over it according to the etymology. But it was pity that the *Literary Magazine*[11] was expressing

[1] *Gent. Mag.* xliv (1774), 89.
[2] Alice Lisle was beheaded in Winchester Market Square, after the Bloody Assize, for sheltering two fugitives from Sedgemoor.
[3] *Crit. Rev.* 42 (1776), 195.   [4] Spence, *Polymetis*, p. 96.
[5] *Gent. Mag.* xxviii (1758), 22–3, re Horrebow's *Account of Iceland*.
[6] *European Mag*, x (1786), 376.   [7] *Crit. Rev.* 41 (1776), 373.
[8] *Ann. Reg.* x (1767), 202.   [9] Glover in Chalmers' *English Poets*, xvii, 107.
[10] *Loves of the Plants*, p. 91.   [11] *Literary Mag.* v (1790), 149.

when it described as *deplorable* the state of 1,000 men starving for lack of work. So the *Annual Register*[1] speaks of the deplorable feelings of an unhappy father who shot his son in mistake for a burglar. There was a deplorable hurricane in Barbados:[2] we cannot protest against the devastations of nature. If we thought the ruin left by a fire deplorable, we should be hinting that it ought to have been prevented. And we may be quite sure that the *Anti-Jacobin*[3] was not being moved to tears either, when it referred to that deplorable young man the journalist who wrote for the *Morning Chronicle* without any proper knowledge of geography.

FROM FACTUAL TO EVALUATIVE

Some adjectives which could then be factual, non-committal or wholly approving are disapproving now. 'Hot thoughts', said the *Gentleman's Magazine*[4] in 1758, 'are in poetic language, always understood to be pure, vigorous, soaring and splendid; such being the properties of fire; for this reason they are said to be *ardent, glowing, sparkling, radiant* and *aspiring*.' All true—except as to *hot* itself. Again, 'persons who are eminent for these ardent glowing thoughts are frequently, in common speech, said to be *hot-headed*'. It is not the word we should choose now.

Dennis[5] talks without disparagement of prosaic diction—i.e. the diction proper to prose: Knox[6] writes of 'simplicity of style in Prosaic Composition', and Jackson[7] defines the word—'What is generally understood by prosaic, is sentences having the common form of structure, whereas poetry consists of inversions and a dignity of expression, which suit not with prose.' We have made it mean 'having the uninspired nature of flat prose where we have a right to expect poetic fire', and so we apply the word not to prose itself but to poetry and mental outlook.

Revolting to us—unless we are linguistically aware enough to pun— means inspiring revulsion. People are not necessarily literally revolting when they revolt or are in revolt. You could not now say you had 'revolting thoughts'[8] without danger of misunderstanding. In the eighteenth century it means rebellious.

[1] *Ann. Reg.* xvii (1774), 142.   [2] *Ann. Reg.* xxviii (1786), 211.
[3] *Anti-Jacobin*, ii, 531.   [4] *Gent. Mag.* xxviii (1758), 283.
[5] *Critical Works*, i, 215.   [6] *Essays*, ii, 72.
[7] *Four Ages*, p. 284.   [8] *New Letters to the Tatler and Spectator*, p. 91.

Shocking, which George III[1] uses literally of the electricity that gives a shock, is used in a good sense when the *Monthly Review*[2] in 1776 considers one of Hannah More's poems a 'shocking performance'. It is clear that they were deeply impressed by it, and were using *shocking* to mean that its pathos had shocked their sensibilities.

FROM PRAISE TO DOUBT

Dr Johnson tells us that *sensuous* means tender, pathetic, full of passion, and is not in use. So Adam Smith[3] calls the pleasure of an opera more *sensual* than that of a common comedy or tragedy. It appeals to our senses through its music, presumably. Now a sensual opera might have trouble with the censor.

The common eighteenth-century sense of *smug* is clean, neat, spruce, well-dressed, with no overtone of self-satisfaction. Lyttelton,[4] speaking of the smug looks of soldiers, is referring to their smart appearance. A razor-strop will help to make 'your Person more smug', says the *Spectator* (428). Now it is our minds, not our persons, that can be smug, and it is no suitable state to be in: the first clear examples of it come in the mid-nineteenth century, though there may well be earlier ones, as *O.E.D.* points out—the good sense slides imperceptibly into the bad.

To be *voluble*, says Cocker-Hawkins, is to be quick, ready in speech, elegant. To us it is not elegant, and much too ready. Mrs Piozzi[5] talks of 'sweet volubility' in talk, and by her parallel use of *fluency* literally of a stream, and of the verb *to flow*, reminds us of the basic 'rolling on' sense of the word. Not so obvious is James Beattie's[6] remark that 'flags and streamers, flying in the wind, gratify the eye, by the varying shades of colour, and by their easy volubility'.

It is doubtful whether any one now would couple *serene* and *vacant*, and whether any great man would take the pair as an indivisible compliment. When Glover's[7] Aristides 'descends At once to affability and ease' he can do so because he is *vacant*—i.e. free from engagements. And *vacancy* is now so much at home in the Posts Vacant columns that it sounds to us out of place when in a visionary Hall of Fame a *Vacancy* is *reserved* for a hero.[8]

---

[1] Letter to Bute of 23 Dec. 1759.
[2] liv (1776), 89. The word could be used as we use it; see *O.E.D.*
[3] *Works*, v, 295.   [4] *Persian Letters*, xxiv.
[5] *Brit. Syn.*, i, 242.   [6] *Dissertations*, p. 127.
[7] Chalmers' *English Poets*, xvii, 89.   [8] ibid., xvii, 92.

The context of all these words shows them to be words of praise, while to us they are words of blame or mere statements of fact. There are others that were complimentary then and now, but whereas they used to be generous, they are now grudging. *Respectable* then really could imply 'worthy of all respect', whether for one's character, one's projects, one's deeds or one's power. If we read it in our sense, which is practically the equivalent of so-so, not immoral, or at the best good with no particular need to be enthusiastic about it, it may sound anything from inadequate to rude, or even blasphemous. The 'most respectable of all known perfections',[1] predicated of God, sounds at least more inadequate than human language need be even in such a case. In our sense, it seems out of tune when applied to Benjamin Franklin,[2] the Bishop of London, the Archbishop of York and prelates generally,[3] to the Professors of Botany at Oxford, Cambridge and Edinburgh, and that great master of the English tongue, Dr Samuel Johnson.[4]

It is true that 'General Washington is a character which will always, with every impartial mind, ... be very respectable'[5]—but one would now say much more, and so with Pope's respectable mentions of Dryden, for whom he felt admiration,[6] the 'respectable Corporation of the City of London'[7], and the respectable personages at the Board of British Admiralty.[8] The Bible and Shakespeare are respectable authorities.[9] Chester is a respectable city[10] and Milan a respectable University.[11] We deny none of these statements, but nowadays none of the persons concerned—individual or corporate—would feel flattered or even justly dealt with. In the international sphere, nations now talk of making themselves respected. The eighteenth century spoke of respectable nations and argued, like us, as to what justifies the epithet. Wendeborn[12] considers that 'an empire is not rendered powerful, rich and respectable by wars and conquests'. Ferguson[13] thinks the most respectable nations have always had a sea-board. In 1765[14] a statement from Sweden was translated 'The armaments of our neighbours have made it necessary

---

[1] *Month. Rev.* xx (1759), 8.   [2] *Gent. Mag.* lvi (1786), 951.
[3] *Gent. Mag.* lxvi (1796), 904. Preface to Byrom's *Universal English Shorthand*, 1767.
[4] *Crit. Rev.* 55 (1783), 21.   [5] *Crit. Rev.* 49 (1780), 472.
[6] Ruffhead, *Life of Pope*, p. 23.
[7] Lord Lieutenant of Ireland, quoted in *Anti-Jacobin*, i, 358.
[8] *Crit. Rev.* 28 (1769), 160.   [9] *Crit. Rev.* new arr. iv (1792), 565.
[10] *Brit. Syn.*, i, 323.   [11] *Crit. Rev.* 52 (1781), 396.
[12] *View*, i, 137.   [13] *Civil Society*, p. 200.   [14] *New Universal Mag.* x, 235.

for both this kingdom and Denmark to put their borders and fleets
into a more respectable condition': indeed the Danes[1] were reported
to have said that their navy had been put into such a respectable condition that the greatest powers in Europe were watchful upon its
destination.

Worthy is in a like state. Both adjectives are the least we can say,
and we hardly feel positively enough about them to call them agreeable,
as Mrs Piozzi does.[2] She thinks *worthy* is a good word for 'our old
English country gentleman' whose useful, unspectacular life is 'particularly favourable to that steady and honourable conduct, that truly
estimable and worthy disposition, which never glowing up into enthusiastic fervour of liberality, is yet incapable of degenerating into
meanness, or suffering a base action to infest their family'.

NEW WORDS OF PRAISE

A few adjectives have gone up in the world, in that they stand for
qualities we admire, or which enjoy our respect even if we should not
think they could ever be applied to ourselves. *Ideal, intriguing, mystic*
and *enthusiastic* bear witness to this fact in their different ways.

Dr Johnson defines *ideal* as mental, intellectual, and disapproves of
'the *idea* of an argument or proposition';[3] the primary meaning of
modern colloquial speech is not there—'answering to one's highest
conception', and no one in the eighteenth century talked commonly as
we do of his 'ideals' or made 'idealistic' plans. *Glossographia Anglicana
Nova* and Dyche and Pardon say *ideal* means imaginary, so that an
ideal commonwealth was one that existed only in the imagination. But
what we imagine is naturally wish-fulfilment, and we wish things to
be better than they are. And so the ideal Utopia in their sense becomes
the ideal Utopia in ours. The contrast between actual and imaginary
is brought out well when Lord Kames[4] regrets 'the want of proper
words to describe *ideal* presence and to distinguish it from real presence'. He is thinking of the pictures we see with the mind's eye—our
'waking dream'. To use the historic present 'aids the conception of
ideal presence'.

When the Monthly Reviewers[5] in 1772 discussed a travel book
about 'the Terra Australis' they thought it 'quite as ideal as Robinson
Crusoe' which suggests they thought it fictitious. *Robinson Crusoe* is

---

[1] ibid., p. 14.   [2] *Brit. Syn.*, ii, 394.   [3] *Life*, iii, 196.
[4] *Elements of Criticism*, p. 90.   [5] *Month. Rev.* xlvii (1772), 501.

an account of an 'unknown or rather, an Ideal' country.[1] The closeness of the adjective to its popular noun comes out in a scrap of conversation in Lewis's *The Monk*.[2] 'The idea of ghosts is ridiculous . . . and if you continue to be swayed by ideal terrors'—'Ideal?—Why, we heard it ourselves, Signor.' Warton[3] speaks of the ideal inhabitants of hell, and Aristotle, we are told, opened his Art of Poetry with an ideal monster.[4] Christ, according to the French papers—as reported by the *Anti-Jacobin*[5]—is as ideal as Bacchus; the value of money is ideal;[6] and Ver-Vert the parrot may have dreamed of 'Ideal cracknels or ideal creams.'[7]

The philosophers sometimes objected to the increasing popular use of the word *idea*; Reid[8] notes its double use, and that in popular language it means conception, apprehension, notion, even opinion. This, he considers, is more French than English, though good authors —even Locke—use it. Why must they introduce an ambiguous term when we have several words which are either originally English, or have been long naturalised? He has to admit that '*notion* is a word in common language whose meaning agrees exactly with the popular meaning of the word *idea*, but not with the philosophical. On the other hand, Dugald Stewart[9] says he uses *idea* uniformly in the popular sense because it is so difficult to avoid ambiguity. *Glossographia Anglicana Nova* defines Idea thus—'properly the Image or Representation of any sensible Object, transmitted into the Brain thro' the Organ of Sight—but in a more general Sense it is taken for the immediate Object of Understanding, whatever it may be'.

If we stay to think, we should accept *intriguing* as the present participle of *to intrigue* in the basic sense of *plot*; but the meaning 'arousing interest and curiosity' which the *Concise Oxford Dictionary* in 1929 called a journalistic gallicism seems to be gaining enough ground to necessitate wariness. The *Critical Review*[10] was not expressing pleasurable interest but stating a political fact when it described the times of Cardinal de Retz as 'one of the most intriguing periods' in the history of France. Lady Craven[11] was not pleased with her intriguing guide who tried to delay her journey.

[1] Reeve, *Progress of Romance*, i, 124.   [2] p. 329.
[3] *Observations on Fairy Queen*, p. 61.   [4] *Lælius and Hortensia*, p. 12.
[5] *Anti-Jacobin*, ii, 618.   [6] Shebbeare, *Letters*, ii, 185.
[7] trans. quoted in *Crit. Rev.* new arr. viii (1793), 390.
[8] *Intellectual Powers*, i, 38–9.
[9] *Elements of the Philosophy of the Human Mind*, pp. 160–1, note on Reid.
[10] *Crit. Rev.* 40 (1775), 166.   [11] *Journey*, p. 296.

'The Age of Prose and Reason' had little use for *mystic* and its congeners. Count von Zinzendorf's religious zeal did not seem sensible: the *Annual Register*[1] quotes approvingly the sentiments of a French writer who considered the Count had 'shown all Europe, that in the most enlightened age, perseverance, supported by enthusiasm and devotion, could recall that zeal, that *Mysticity*, those extraordinary follies, which one would think proper only for the dark and barbarous ages'. Dr Johnson shows that *mystic* had been used by Hooker to mean 'sacredly obscure' and by Taylor as 'emblematical' but it seems clear enough that for some it was equivalent to 'what I don't follow'. Richard Jago,[2] writing of weavers at Coventry, describes how 'their active feet

> In mystic movement, press the subtle stops'

of the loom's complicated frame. Did it look like some strange ritual? We think better of Mystics and Mysticism now, and if we coupled them with Enthusiasts and Enthusiasm, we should be praising them for their zeal. Of all the changed words, *Enthusiasm*, *Enthusiast* and *Enthusiastic* have made the most astonishing move from detestation to warm approval—in every realm, that is, except Poetry, where the family has been in general good repute from the start.

A correspondent of the *Radio Times* in 1961 commented on Sir Brian Horrocks' 'superb enthusiasm' for Nelson, and recalled Sir Barry Jackson's dictum that 'In drama, as in everything else in this world, enthusiasm is the touchstone.' Eighteenth-century readers would perhaps have agreed as to the drama, but would have been shocked at the generalisation. In reverse, we are puzzled by their use of *enthusiasm* and its relatives as obvious smear-words. We meet with 'enthusiasm, and delusion',[3] 'the Blindness of enthusiasm',[4] 'bigotry and enthusiasm',[5] 'enthusiastic and sanguinary reformers',[6] 'Knavery, artifice, absurdity and enthusiasm'.[7]

There are too the tell-tale *buts* that qualify the testimonials—'the late respectable but enthusiastic Mr Cruden'[8]—'He enjoys a good deal of yᵉ grace of God, but with a touch of Enthusiasm.'[9] And there is the

[1] *Ann. Reg.* iii (1760), 108.   [2] Chalmers' *English Poets*, xvii, 296.
[3] *A Caution against Enthusiasm*, by the Bishop of London (1739; ed. 1772).
[4] *Gent. Mag.* lxix (1799), 1064.   [5] *Month. Rev.* (1749), 132.
[6] *Crit. Rev.* 53 (1782), 160.   [7] Soame Jenyns, *Works*, iii, 289.
[8] *Gent. Mag.* liii (1783), 941.
[9] Letter of 1772 (displayed in Epworth Old Rectory) from John Wesley. *Letters*, v, 347.

doubt implied in Godwin's reference to 'zeal, perhaps a little extravagant and enthusiastic'.[1] A still clearer call for adjustment is implied in the remark 'I have praised virtue wherever I found it, guarding at the same time against the enthusiasm it inspires.'[2] Mgr Ronald Knox's[3] conclusion that the eighteenth century used *enthusiasm* with 'singular lack of accuracy' is understandable: but preachers, philosophers, politicians, poets, literary critics and people in general may have a general agreement on the meaning of a word, even of one so 'dark and ambiguous',[4] and nevertheless disagree on its referends, especially when moral questions are involved, and different ends in view.

In general, the word is an expression of disapproval in religion and morals all through the period, but approving in literary reference: in politics it is beginning to work itself clear by the last decade; used of things at large, it begins as a derogatory term, wavers between condemnation and approval, and ends up as we know it today. Boswell frequently uses it of his own feelings with self-satisfaction. *Enthusiasm* is by etymology a religious word, as the eighteenth-century dictionaries and critics were well aware. Defoe[5] gives us the etymological sense and the current connotation: 'I am none of those that... Dream of Inspirations, and fancy themselves on the other side of Time; that call strong Imagination Revelation, and every Wind of the Brain an impulse of the Spirit: and this I meant when I said formerly that *I am no Enthusiastick*, knowing at the same time, that the true and original meaning of the Word Enthusiasm, was Divine Inspiration.'

The bad odour of the word-group arises from the assumption that the divine inspiration is not, as a matter of fact, there, that those who claim it are self-deceived. Indeed, there are plenty of incidents that demonstrate this all too well.

Enthusiasm, says Bailey in 1721, is 'a prophetick or poetical rage or fury, which transports the mind, raises and enflames the imagination, and makes it think and express things extraordinary and surprizing'. Dyche and Pardon quote this, adding with their usual ungrammatical exuberance, 'but the word is generally applied to those persons, who pretend to have divine revelation, to support some monstrous, ridiculous or absurd notions in religious matters, and thereby takes away both reason and revelation, and substitutes in the room thereof the groundless fancies and obstinate result of self-willedness, by using

[1] Godwin, *Enquirer*, p. 38.   [2] *Gent. Mag.* xxii (1752), 467.
[3] *Enthusiasm*, p. 449.
[4] Wesley, *Nature of Enthusiasm*, p. 34.   [5] *Review*, viii, 94.

extravagant gestures and words pretending to things not only improbable but also impossible'. So, an enthusiast commonly means a person 'poisoned with the notion of being divinely inspired when he is not, and upon that account commits a great number of irregularities in words and actions'.

Accordingly, the word was used of one Jacob Romart who murdered a Thomas Wentworth believing he had a divine commission for doing so: he was 'a gloomy visionary enthusiast'.[1] Caleb Elliott, 'starved to death' in Devon in 1789, was 'a visionary enthusiast' too.[2] Charlotte Corday was described as enthusiastic by the author of *A Residence in France*.[3] A murder of equally national note was committed by a young friar who prayed all night, was shriven, bought a dagger and killed Henry III of France—which shows 'what enthusiasm is capable of effecting'.[4] Suicides in Denmark who wished to save themselves from worldly contamination,[5] those who practised suttee,[6] Margery Kempe,[7] Madame Guyon,[8] Swedenborg,[9] William Law,[10] the Puritans[11] and the Methodists[12] were all enthusiasts in the bad sense according to one critic or another. The classic period-piece on the matter is Bishop Lavington's the *Enthusiasm of Methodists and Papists Compar'd* (1749)—learned, comprehensive, by any standard, and funny or infuriating according to how you look at it. His attitude to St Francis of Assisi is like that of Langhorne[13] in his *Letters on Religious Retirement* when he refers to 'the extravagant Francis' preaching to swallows and fishes. For Lavington,[14] St Francis and St Ignatius were 'a couple of crackbrain'd Enthusiasts'. The religious norm is summed up by those who uphold 'calm and rational piety'[15] and are thankful that the Church of England is 'equally removed from fanaticism and infidelity—pious without enthusiasm, and liberal without laxity'.[16] Opinions differed then as now: it is proper to recall George III's[17] remark to Dr James Beattie that people said Lord Dartmouth was an enthusiast—'but surely he says on the subject of religion but what every christian may

[1] *Ann. Reg.* i (1758), 99.   [2] *Gent. Mag.* lix (1789), 1211.
[3] Quoted, *Brit. Crit.* ix (1797), 282.   [4] *Art of Poetry*, p. 362.
[5] *London Mag.* (1768), 55.   [6] *Gent. Mag.* xxi (1751), 54.
[7] *Month. Rev.* viii (1753), 125.   [8] Lyttelton, *Dialogues of the Dead*, iii.
[9] So called by Warburton, *Doctrine of Grace*, viii, 272.
[10] *Gent. Mag.* lix (1789), 32.   [11] *World* (42).
[12] *passim*. But see esp. Lavington's book, published 1749–51.   [13] *Letters*, v, 16.
[14] *Enthusiasm*, Pt. III (1751), 22.   [15] Mrs Montagu, *Letters*, ii, 79.
[16] *Crit. Rev.* new arr. xxiv (1798), 208, quoting Bisset's *Sketch of Democracy*.
[17] *London Diary*, 24 Aug. 1773.

and ought to say'. We ourselves are more likely to agree with the writer who was 'enthusiastic' about the genius and learning of Erasmus than with the Monthly Reviewer who found the quotations from his work 'mere rant'.[1] How easily enthusiasm was detected can be seen in Sir John Hawkins'[2] comments on Dr Johnson's religion: it 'had a tincture of enthusiasm, arising, as it is conjectured, from the fervour of his imagination, and the perusal of St Augustine ... and Kempis and the ascetics, which prompted him to the employment of composing meditations and doctrinal exercises'.

Lack of reason and self-control, and a refusal to be bound by the conventions, could be demonstrated in other ways. 'The French Revolution has proved', said the *Anti-Jacobin*,[3] 'that Enthusiasm does not belong only to Religion'—it could be directed against religion. Also, 'there is a holy mistaken zeal in politics as well as religion'[4] and in the state as in the church 'no evil is more to be feared than a rancorous and enthusiastical zeal'.[5] It leads to riot and murder. The *Critical Review*[6] sums up the religio-political dangers of Enthusiasm by declaring that 'Enthusiasm, which has in former ages provided the most fatal effects, when victims unnumbered have been sacrificed to the sanguinary idol, is still productive of evils; not indeed to be compared to the massacre of Paris, or the evil commotions by which England was torn during the reign of Charles I, but which call loudly for reformation, as the peace of individuals, often of whole families, has but too frequently felt the baleful influence of this mental disease.'

There were social and scholarly enthusiasms that were foolish if no worse to some eighteenth-century critics. Not all welcomed Rousseau's enthusiasm for the simple life:[7] it could be held that any idea of abolishing the slave trade was enthusiastic:[8] there is no doubt of the disapproving tone in a reference to those political enthusiasts who 'labour to expel subordination from civil society'.[9] Edward Young's[10] enthusiasm for St Thomas Aquinas is clearly regarded as rather unreasonable. So is that of the 'linguist'[11] for whom Hebrew was the mother of all tongues. Nothing but enthusiasm could allow one to persist in believing that Charles I was a model of straight dealing.[12]

---

[1] *Month. Rev.* lxx (1784), 369.   [2] *Life of Johnson*, p. 70.
[3] *Anti-Jacobin*, ii, 562.   [4] *Letters of Junius*, i, 271.
[5] Lyttelton, *Dialogues of the Dead*, I.   [6] *Crit. Rev.* 10 (1760), 207.
[7] *Crit. Rev.* 68 (1789), 114.   [8] Letter to *Gent. Mag.* lix (1789), 334.
[9] *Crit. Rev.* new arr. iv (1792), 358.   [10] Knox, *Essays*, i, 282.
[11] *Month. Rev.* lxviii (1783), 232.   [12] *Crit. Rev.* 23 (1767), 251.

On the other hand, absorption in a cause, interest, or hobby does lead to enthusiasm in the modern sense, and this is how the word grows into a compliment—if the cause or speciality is a good one.

'Fitzosborne'[1] is an early critic who in 1739 notes the divergent paths enthusiasm can take. After we have expelled her from her religious dominions, he entreats us to leave her in the undisturbed enjoyment of her civil profession. 'I look upon Enthusiasm', he says, 'in all other points but that of religion, to be a very necessary turn of mind; as indeed it is a vein which Nature seems to have marked with more or less strength in the tempers of most men.' You cannot pursue business, pleasures, or the fine arts unless you do so *con amore*: 'and inamoratores of every kind are all enthusiasts'.

The critics appreciate Gray's enthusiasm for Nature,[2] and every Englishman's enthusiasm for Shakespeare.[3] Enthusiasm is a friend of civil liberty.[4] The Bastille fell to the enthusiasm[5] of heroism; the Swiss[6] resisted the French with an enthusiasm that made up for their lack of military skill; Howard[7] could not have investigated prisons without enthusiasm. In time we meet the enthusiast for Chinese agriculture,[8] or the art of public-speaking,[9] or mountains,[10] for such artists as Poussin or Claude,[11] for the ancient ruins[12] or architecture,[13] for fame, ease of friendship or scenery.[14] But there may still be a shade of disapproval—as when the word is used of a chemist[15] who still believes in the Philosopher's Stone, when it is said that only enthusiasm could lead a man to relish fox-hunting,[16] or when Chatterton enthusiasts are said to be undiscerning or classical enthusiasts unreasonable.[17] As late as 1796 Uvedale Price[18] was saying that 'Hogarth had a most enthusiastic admiration of what he called the line of beauty, and enthusiasm always leads to the verge of ridicule, and seldom keeps totally within it'. Likewise, his reference to Michael Angelo is double-edged—'his enthusiasm produced the grandest and most striking attitudes but also

---

[1] Melmoth, *Letters*, pp. 1–2.
[2] *Month. Rev.* lii (1775), 577.
[3] Uvedale Price, *Essay*, i, 118.
[4] Hume, *Essays*, p. 149.
[5] *Literary Mag.* vi (1791), 267.
[6] *Anti-Jacobin*, ii, 62.
[7] *Gent. Mag.* lx (1790), 288.
[8] *Crit. Rev.* 28 (1769), 107.
[9] *Crit. Rev.* 36 (1773), 454.
[10] Gray, *Correspondence*, p. 1086.
[11] Uvedale Price, *Essay*, i, 12.
[12] *Gent. Mag.* lxvii (1797), 1033.
[13] Alison, *Taste*, p. 368.
[14] *Month. Rev.* lxxx (1789), 60. *Crit. Rev.* 69 (1790), 273.
[15] *Diary of Sylas Neville*, 29 March 1772. [16] *Month. Rev.* lxv (1781), 216.
[17] *Gent. Mag.* lix (1789), 538. *Crit. Rev.* ix new arr. (1793), 12.
[18] *Essay*, ii, 269, 265.

led him to twist the human figure into such singular and capricious forms as borders on caricatura'.

In reference to literature, this word-group seems to have been nearly always free of derogation. Dennis,[1] writing on Milton or Nathaniel Lee, is all for enthusiasm at the beginning of the century, and towards the end we read[2] that 'Enthusiasm is the very soul of poetry, and there is such an indissoluble connection between them that the same word in the learned languages was indifferently applied to a poet and a prophet.'

In poetry, Invention and Enthusiasm constitute genius:[3] 'thought, enthusiasm and picture ... are the body, soul and robe of poetry'.[4] *The Bard* displays lyric enthusiasm,[5] Burns generous enthusiasm.[6] Dido's rage shows noble enthusiasm.[7] Enthusiasm of sentiment leads to happiness of language,[8] and the enthusiastic love of liberty produces energy of poetic composition.[9] Odes and epics[10] depend on enthusiasm —indeed, without it,

> The Soldier, patriot and the bard is faint.[11]

Yet even here an occasional doubt is felt. It was said[12] *à propos* Collins that the 'enthusiasm of poetry, like that of religion, has frequently a powerful influence on the conduct of life, and either throws it into the retreat of uniform obscurity ... or marks it with the irregularities that lead to misery and disquiet'. It is as if Collins' poetry were being blamed for his mental break-down, in accordance with the common conception of enthusiasm as a nervous disorder.

In general, the twentieth-century reader should expect enthusiasm in the eighteenth century to be essential to poetry, a disease in religion, and a doubtful element in politics, where it depends entirely on what you have enthusiasm for.

As late as 1794[13] an enquirer remarks 'A definition of the word *Enthusiasm* will ... be ... acceptable as I cannot find anything satisfactory thereon.' What he would have found satisfactory of course we

---

[1] *Critical Works*, ii, 169, 122.   [2] James Usher, *Clio*, p. 99.
[3] Goldsmith, *Essays*, xv.   [4] Young, *On Lyric Poetry*, p. 61.
[5] *Crit. Rev.* 40 (1775), 469.   [6] *Crit. Rev.* 63 (1787), 388.
[7] Dennis, *Critical Works*, ii, 351.   [8] Godwin, *Enquirer*, p. 460.
[9] *Crit. Rev.* new arr. xvii (1796), 209.
[10] *Guardian* (12) 1713. *Gent. Mag.* vii (1737), 292.
[11] Glover in Chalmers' *English Poets* xvii, 183.
[12] *Crit. Rev.* 19 (1765), 199, quoting Langhorne.
[13] *Gent. Mag.* lxiv (1794), 220.

do not know, but if he had found nothing, it was not for want of trying on the part of a variety of people. John Byrom in 1757 and Edward Jerningham in 1789 had written poems on Enthusiasm, true and false, religious and secular. Shaftesbury had discussed its varieties. John Wesley, so often called an enthusiast though he flatly rejected the term,[1] had preached a sermon to define its use for both genuine and deluded religious experience, and had incorporated a note on its everyday uses. Various people had worked out schematic tables[2] to show precisely how religious enthusiasm differed from superstition on the one hand and reason on the other; and Duff, in his *Essay on Original Genius*,[3] had chosen the word to illustrate how meanings can degenerate. It is the more noteworthy, that now we incline to look on Enthusiasm as the example of the term that has changed from smear-word to compliment. But the back-formation 'to enthuse' may serve to remind us that enthusiasm still has dangers.

LOSS OF ETYMOLOGICAL SENSE

The primary meaning of *Enormous* (despite *enormity*) and *tremendous* (despite *tremor*) is now simply 'big' for most people. That should not blind us to their more etymological sense 200 years ago. 'Irregular, vast, monstrous,' said Richardson,[4] when he glossed Milton's 'Enormous Brood', which shows our common meaning was there, but not so exclusively. Indeed the word is usually compounded of all three ideas. Dyche and Pardon give the basic sense as 'out of rule, order or square'; and the secondary one 'heinous or very bad'. 'What can be more enormous than for men, not to say Christians and friends, to thirst for the blood of each other?'[5] This is defiance of moral order. It is a defiance of literary decorum that produces mixed metaphors— the *Spectator* (595) calls it 'that enormous Stile'. It was an enormous criminal who poisoned his parents, two sisters and the maid by arsenic.[6] We could substitute *great* here, but not in the other two instances. So with 'enormous solecism'—one that resoundingly breaks the norm of usage (or what grammarians considered should be usage). Trusler[7] says it implies greatness in size even to deformity and dreadfulness. An

---

[1] He says an enthusiast is as like him as he is like a centaur. (Comment on Thomas Church's *Remarks on Mr Wesley's Last Journal*, 1744.)
[2] e.g., the *Old Whig*, quoted in *Gent. Mag.* viii (1738), 89.
[3] pp. 169–70.   [4] *Explanatory notes*, p. 33.   [5] *Gent. Mag.* lix (1789), 521.
[6] *Ann. Reg.* xvii (1774), 115.   [7] *Synonyms*, s.v.

enormous appetite may still be *abnormal* and we *can* use the word approvingly—we could experience an enormous satisfaction or relief if we felt strongly enough. The *Concise Oxford Dictionary* gives no other sense than 'huge, very large'.

Tremendous sometimes keeps more of its suggestion of the terrible, but in colloquial use it too means only big, or even merely considerable. The eighteenth-century writers are far more conscious that basically the word meant that before which we tremble, that which is to be feared. Dr Johnson says it means dreadful, horrible, astonishingly terrible. So God is 'that great and tremendous Being'[1] 'in tremendous pomp array'd'.[2] This is as strong as the 'Rex tremendae maiestatis' of the *Dies Irae*.

Jupiter thunders with a tremendous tone.[3] There are 'tremendous powr's ... Whose voice is thunder and whose nod is fate.'[4] Medusa's head stares tremendous—over the chimney (and the satirical description gains in force if we keep the full meaning in mind),[5] Discord is tremendous;[6] Vacuity, Darkness, Solitude and Silence are images of tremendous dignity at the mouth of Vergil's Hell.[7] War is tremendous and death may be.[8] A Spartan 'phalanx turns A face tremendous on recoiling swarms Of squadron'd Persians'[9] and an English naval broadside is tremendous.[10] Those who lived through the French Revolution lived in an eventful and tremendous period and survived a tremendous crisis.[11] Darkness, Solitude and Silence oppress the mind by a tremendous sensation.[12] Arthur Murphy felt that a funeral with full ceremonies is tremendous.[13] George Garrick found Dr Johnson 'tremendous'—he was struck, or rather stunned, by his manner.[14] Applied to natural scenery, the word has a sense of overpowering majesty. Mt Etna in eruption is tremendous.[15] The natural arch at 'Pystyll Rhaid'r', seventy-eight feet above a torrent, was crossed by a heroine (described admiringly as a 'virago'). If she did not find it tremendous, the journalists did.[16] I doubt whether Bristolians would

---

[1] Burke, *Sublime and Beautiful*, p. 117.   [2] Blacklock, *Psalm I*, p. 45.
[3] *Babler*, xciii.   [4] Blacklock, *Elegy on* ... *Pope*, pp. 177–8.   [5] *World* (15).
[6] Blacklock, *To Happiness*, p. 35.   [7] Burke, op. cit., p. 125.
[8] Glover on Sir Isaac Newton, Chalmers' *English Poets*, xvii, p. 15. *Crit. Rev.* 49 (1780), 194.
[9] Glover, in Chalmers' *English Poets*, xvii, 179.   [10] *Anti-Jacobin*, i, 108.
[11] ibid., i, 3; ii, 570.   [12] Usher, *Clio*, p. 114.
[13] Letter to Mrs Thrale, quoted H. L. Dunbar, p. 291.
[14] Boswell, *Life*, iii, 139.   [15] *Crit. Rev.* 41 (1776), 80.
[16] *Literary Mag.* vi (1791), 157.

apply the word to St Vincent's Rock above the Avon Gorge, but a
Survey of the Bath Road[1] describes it as 'stupendous' and overhanging
the Avon 'in tremendous cliffs of prodigious height'. The travellers
of the period were more easily impressed than we are. Perhaps the word
is weakening where thunder and lightning are called tremendous,
though obviously both can do fearful damage: and the rush towards the
doors of a chapel when the congregation believed the roof was about
to fall in undoubtedly was both the result of fear and productive of it.[2]
A fire at Copenhagen[3] that threatened to engulf the whole neighbourhood must have been fearful as well as big. The Mohocks and members
of the Hell-fire Club certainly left a literally tremendous memory.[4]
But how much must we read into the reference to the old custom of
keeping children at *tremendous* distance from their parents?[5] It sounds
as if parents once set themselves out to be awe-inspiring but not,
apparently, in 1787. And when an orator speaks of his tremendous
convictions, we begin to lose the awe-inspiring overtones, especially
when the speech is a take-off.[6]

DEGENERACY

Tremendous and *enormous* have developed naturally out of part of
their eighteenth-century meanings. The same can hardly be said of that
mishandled group *awful, blasted, blooming, blinking* and *bloody*. These
are all spoiled for literary or dignified use, unless we keep a very firm
hand on ourselves and resolutely refuse to recognise their slangy or
'low' associations—there can be no doubt at all that 'low' (if with
varying degrees of depth) is what the eighteenth century would call
them, if it could meet them now. A sufficiently powerful context will
disinfect them, but most people are not prepared to take any risks. So
it is as well to remember that *Blasted* is the only one that seriously fell
in the eighteenth century, though there are signs that *awful* and *bloody*
were about to do so. No doubt literature lagged behind colloquial
speech.

Blast, the noun, according to Dr Johnson is a gust of wind, or the
stroke from a malignant planet; the verb means to strike with some
sudden plague, to injure, invalidate, confound, strike with terror. It is

---

[1] Quoted *Crit. Rev.* new arr. x (1794), 422.
[2] *Ann. Reg.* xl (1798), 60 (Rivington).   [3] *Anti-Jacobin*, ii, 176.
[4] *Connoisseur*, l (1755). See the *Oxford Companion to English Literature*.
[5] *European Mag.* xi (1787), 320.   [6] *Anti-Jacobin*, i, 98.

frequent in poetic use, a conventional symbol of killing weather, and offered an obvious metaphor. We have no real trouble with noun or verb. It is easy to transfer our minds from high explosive to storms though we may easily overlook the astrological references. The tone is the same. Pope's 'cheeks now fading at the blast of death',[1] and Thomson's 'baleful blast',[2] are good poetic figures. But the past participle is a different matter. 'Wide o'er the blasted fields the tempest sweeps' is safe by its context: so is Lady Winchilsea's[3]

> Nor would th' ensuing blasted spring
> One purple violet revive.

But the 'blasted lordlings of the day'[4] is not so easy: here it means vicious. The *Looker-on*[5] has a letter allegedly from Ben Crump to Dr Olivebranch about his master's London nephew who was 'as glib with his *damns* and *blasts* and as natural' as those who knew no better: indeed the scullion had asked Ben whether he mightn't 'sware upon his honour if gemmen takes to b—sting of eyes'. We can see why the *British Critick*[6] was concerned about an author who, in expressing his great indignation against the United Irishmen, had called the organisation 'that blasted institution'. He would not have done so 'had he been studious of literary praise'. Presumably all he meant was 'discredited' or 'defeated'.

Blast finds its proper contrast in *bloom*. So Thomson[7] says that fantastic woes 'blast the bloom of life', and *blooming* is a good and serious metaphor applied to young folk in the bloom of youth, or to flourishing and pleasant conditions. Thomson[8] writes of 'the blooming blessings of the former day' and of 'every blooming pleasure'.[9] Less obvious, and all the better for that, is Whitehead's[10] phrase in his poem on Nobility about 'blooming coronets on parchment trees'; and Brooke's[11] interesting lines in his *Fables* tell us how

> Lybia's golden orchard grew
> Blooming temptation to the view.

[1] *Elegy to ... an Unfortunate Lady*, l. 32.   [2] *Spring*, l. 116.
[3] Pope's *Iliad*, xiii, 1001; Lady Winchilsea, *Death of Sir Thomas Twisden*, p. 10.
[4] Knox, *Essays*, ii, 314.   [5] iii, 171.
[6] *Brit. Crit.* xiv (1799), 208.
[7] *Spring*, l. 1003. A good instance of Thomson's troubles with the word is described on p. 27 of Douglas Grant's study of the poet. But they were not ours.
[8] ibid., l. 246.   [9] *Summer*, l. 79.
[10] Chalmers' *English Poets*, xvii, 209.   [11] ibid., p. 406.

In the sense of *luxuriant*, it appears in the most serious sort of context, as in Carey's[1] question

> What then forbids that we should jointly raise
> Our blooming fancies or employ our lays
> To sing and celebrate our Maker's praise?

But given the blast-bloom opposition it was all too easy to use *blooming* as irony, euphemism, or shunt-word. And it must be admitted that eighteenth-century versifiers were much too fond of *blooming*. A 'blooming boy', the 'blooming banks of Tay' and a lady described as 'blooming Bertha' are too many for one short ballad.[2] The word is too conventionally and indiscriminately thrown about. Even where the context makes the metaphor strong and clear, the modern must be firm, as with Hutcheson's[3] remark that 'a Poppy bending its Stalk, or a Flower withering when cut by the Plow, resembles the Death of a Blooming Hero'. The phrase was used with a very different ring by the genuine heroes who lie under the Flanders poppies in our time.

When Pope[4] depicts Paris snatching an hour with Helen who 'clasped the blooming hero in her arms', the character of Paris is apt to insinuate the thought that the slang sense would not be quite inappropriate. In light verse, the effect is ruinous, as in the lines Garrick[5] left on the table of the Duchess of Devonshire at noon, when she was still not up:

> What makes thy looks so fair and bright,
>   Divine Aurora, say?
> —'Because, from slumbers short and light,
>   I rise to wake the day!'
>
> O hide for shame thy blushing face,
>   'Tis all poetic fiction!
> To tales like these see Devon's Grace,
>   A blooming contradiction.

Blinking was still merely the present participle of the verb *to blink*. But it becomes a transferred epithet in a comment made by the *Monthly Review*[6] on a new version of Homer. The translator wrote

> O thou with wine o'er charg'd who bear'st to view
> A dog's bold eye—

---

[1] *Poems*, p. 57.   [2] Hannah More, *Sir Eldred of the Bower*.
[3] *Beauty and Virtue*, p. 42.   [4] *Iliad*, iii, 558.
[5] Quoted *Gent. Mag.* xlix (1779), 262.   [6] *Month. Rev.* xii (1755), 358.

'Possibly', says the *Review*, 'the very new expression of *bearing to view* a dog's eye (which gives us some idea of an anatomist's displaying one to his pupils, in comparison with, or for want of, a human eye) may atone for this blinking omission.' The eighteenth century could read of Shakespeare's 'blinking idiot' without our distractions.

Whether the modern intensifying *bloody* is the ordinary adjective of *blood* has been needlessly doubted.[1] The widespread notion that it is a corruption of *by our Lady* ought to be dead by now (though it is not), and there seems no real reason to suppose it to be other than it seems, though the exact connotation of blood seems doubtful. Early in the eighteenth century it meant excellent—like a man or beast showing good blood. The *Monthly Review*[2] makes no adverse comment on the practice of theatrical managers employing a man because he can sing 'a bloody good song', and equally the *Critical Review*[3] sees nothing out of the way in dismissing *The Bloodhounds, a Political Tale* as 'A Bloody bad performance indeed.' Both were staid and dignified critical journals ever on the watch for linguistic or moral impropriety. But thirty years later, the *Critical Review*[4] did not think 'bloody cruelty' sounded very classical, though the epithet is as obviously suitable as it is in Soame Jenyn's[5] reference to the fact that the soldier's

> Scarlet, glowing from afar
> Shows that his bloody occupation's war

In 1796, a criminal was reported[6] to have said after his crime 'Damn him, I've cut his bloody eyes out'—where the general tone of the words suggest the degenerate use, though clearly the word also carried its literal meaning.

Awful and *awfully* belong here, though their history is more complex. There is a weakening of the connection with awe, which is an impoverishment of the language in that we hardly know what to use instead, substituting *awesome* or the spelling 'awe-full'. At times there is a shift from fear to joy—we can be 'awfully pleased' or say 'it's an awful relief'. The words are intensifiers, not meaning anything more precise than *much* or *very*. But they are at home in polite society and

---

[1] See Eric Partridge, *Origins*, and E. Weekley, *Etymological English Dictionary*. Cp. John Orr, *Old French and Modern English Idiom*, pp. 42–3. He disagrees with *O.E.D.* but does not offer enough evidence for *literary* uses of the word.

[2] *Month. Rev.* xiii (1755), 2.   [3] *Crit. Rev.* 16 (1763), 478.

[4] *Crit. Rev.* new arr. x (1794), 70; *à propos* of *Annual Register*.

[5] *The Art of Dancing. Works*, ii, 6.

[6] *Ann. Reg.* xxxviii (1796), 65 (Rivington).

cannot be used to shock either purist or 'puritan'. But given the right
context—which means attachment to the right noun—the full meaning is still there or easily restored. *Awful* is one of the many words
that lead a double life, and will therefore serve to introduce some of
those that do so in the eighteenth century, though for itself it mostly
belongs with the preceding group of degenerates. The transfer, according to *O.E.D.*'s written sources, is a nineteenth-century one, paralleled
by *dreadful* and *terrible*, and similar extensions in other languages. So in
eighteenth-century literature we should always expect the full meaning
of 'Apt to strike terror into' or 'to be revered or reverenced', as Bailey
has it, or more succinctly with Dyche and Pardon, 'majestick, dreadful,
powerful, fearful'. But in eighteenth-century colloquial use, the shift
had begun if Mrs Piozzi is not belying her sex. She thinks[1] *awful* ought
to be used with caution and a due sense of its importance, but she has
'heard even well-bred ladies now and then attribute that term too
lightly in their common conversation, connecting it with substances
beneath its dignity'. Usually, however, *awful* occurs where we should
feel safer with *impressive* or *awe-inspiring*. That does not mean we
should always be impressed where our ancestors were. Should we really
be affected by the dropping cave at Staines 'with the most awful
dread'?[2] Do we feel in these democratic days that any illustrious Person
is awful in his station?[3] Should we think a royal birthday banquet 'at
once awful and impressive'?[4] Do we feel that awful homage which is
due to such remains of antiquity as Stonehenge?[5] When we read that
the balloonist Mr Crosbie mounted awfully majestic[6] it sounds almost
comic in these days of cosmonauts. But there is no mistaking the
potency of the word when Dr Johnson, asked to compose some new
collects, replies 'Do not talk thus of what is so awful',[7] or when
Young[8] thinks of the awful confines of eternity; or when even a light
Magazine[9] speaks of the 'awful dispensations' of God or the 'awful
benediction' of the church. A poet uses 'awful imagery', to present
the genius of Rome;[10] the beginning of Pope's 'Essay on Man' is
awful.[11] Some found Gothic architecture awful, and some thought likewise of the forms of Gothic—i.e. medieval—superstition. To compare

[1] *Brit. Syn.*, i, 31.   [2] *Gent. Mag.* xl (1770), 536.
[3] Shaftesbury, *Advice to an Author*, p. 225.
[4] *Ann. Reg.* xxx (1788), reporting function of 12 Aug.
[5] Hanway, *Journal*, i, 162.   [6] *Ann. Reg.* xxvii (1785), 224.
[7] Boswell, *Life*, iv, 294.   [8] *Conjectures on Original Composition*, p. 45.
[9] *Babler*, xciii.   [10] Ruffhead, *Life of Pope*, p. 97.
[11] J. Warton, *Essay on Pope*, ii, 124.

Aeneas in his armour, springing to action, to Mt Apennine shaking the
frozen forests on its sides raises an awful idea of the hero's 'force and
dignity'.[1] Reid[2] tells us that there are awful virtues—magnanimity,
fortitude, self-command, superiority to pain and labour, and to pleasure. Dr Pearce[3] holds that awe has nothing to do with fear: it is
'respect or reverence paid to one whom we love and Love excludes
Fear'; but fear is frequently present in the eighteenth-century uses of
awful.

On the other hand, we have re-instated *vast* and may therefore
read too much into that vogue word. We may wonder why the
Monthly Review[4] thought it vulgar to write of viewing a 'glorious chief
with vast delight'—it sounds merely hyperbolic to us. But we should
not call anything 'vastly little'.

GOOD SENSE, BAD SENSE

Dr Johnson considers that we always use *admirable* in a good sense,
but that its noun and verb are not always so applied, though they
usually are. Earlier, *to admire* meant to wonder at, whether the cause
were agreeable or not. You could admire at the proceedings of villains
and tyrants, like Catiline or Tiberius, until you found that the one was
actuated by jealousy, the other by ambition.[5] This was an inheritance
from earlier times.

Pompous in Dr Johnson's view could still be used with no suggestion
of pomposity. When Dennis[6] writes of the 'greatness and elevation'
of 'the pompous Preparative with which *Milton* ushers in his Account'
of Creation, the word is clearly complimentary, but we may have our
doubts when Wendeborn[7] considers a congregation of Quakers 'more
solemn than the most pompous celebration of divine service'. Pope[8]
cannot have intended any derogation when he called the turrets of
Windsor Castle or the columns of his Temple of Fame or of the house
of Paris, *pompous*.

We should call no virtue comely and *plausible*: generosity was then
so called. When the *Gentleman's Magazine*[9] thought an author's intent
plausible, and some of his observations just, the one statement is as
complimentary as the other, but the double sense is recognized by

[1] Gildon, *Art of Poetry*, p. 285.   [2] *Intellectual Powers of Man*, ii, 514.
[3] *Text of Paradise Lost*, p. 348.   [4] *Month. Rev.* liii (1775), 114.
[5] *Spect.* (408).   [6] *Critical Works*, i, 274.   [7] *View*, ii, 282.
[8] *Windsor Forest*, l. 352.   [9] *Gent. Mag.* xlvi (1776), 301.

Glossographia Anglicana Nova nearly seventy years earlier—'acceptable, received with applause and favour; also seemingly fair and honest'.

In the earlier part of the eighteenth century *painful* could still mean painstaking as well as causing pain: the *Spectator* (172) mentions 'painful' artificers.

When the *Critical Review*[1] informs us that in the *Shadows of Shakespeare* the author makes the characters of the plays appear in 'shady' forms, it reminds us that the word could mean both *shady* and *shadowy* —it did not acquire its disreputable meaning till the nineteenth century.

As late as 1769 the *Monthly Review*[2] was objecting to *obnoxious* for *offensive* or *culpable*. Its older meaning had been 'liable to'. So the *Gentleman's Magazine*[3] in 1754 had said Latin *obnoxius* in plain English means 'in danger of'. *Glossographia Anglicana Nova* had defined the English word as 'guilty' or 'faulty', 'liable to punishment'. Early in the century, the *Spectator* (589) had described Aeneas's ships as 'obnoxious' to the power of winds and waves, and as late as 1795 the *Critical Review*[4] was declaring that nothing was further from its thoughts than any exercise of criticism that can be 'obnoxious to the slightest imputation of partiality or malice'. But despite the *Monthly Review*, both senses were running parallel—indeed, in 1783, it quoted[5] a reference to itself as 'that obnoxious Journal'! The *Gentleman's Magazine* quoted a reference to 'obnoxious words' fifty years before that.[6]

We should have to be in a particularly pastoral and escapist mood to call whey a 'luscious draught',[7] though we should agree about luscious plums[8] and the luscious temptation of a fine juicy ham,[9] or luscious oysters. We use the word so much as a term of praise for food that we find it out of place in literary criticism. If we do use it, we probably agree that sweetness of style 'ought to be distinguished from lusciousness',[10] which quickly cloys and palls the appetite. What surprises us— and could easily mislead us—is the use of the word to mean licentious, either morally or politically. The food and drink metaphor is clear when Shebbeare[11] accuses English freedom of drinking draughts of luscious licentiousness. Oddly enough, for us, Dyche and Pardon,

[1] *Crit. Rev.* 47 (1779), 233.   [2] *Month. Rev.* xl (1769), 83.
[3] *Gent. Mag.* xxiv (1754), 592.   [4] *Crit. Rev.* new arr. xv (1795), 32.
[5] *Month. Rev.* lxix (1783), 301.   [6] *Gent. Mag.* iii (1733), 296.
[7] R. Dodsley, *Agriculture*, 1753, iii, 408.   [8] ibid., i, 463.
[9] *Connoisseur*, lxviii.   [10] Knox, *Essays*, ii, 102.   [11] *Letters*, ii, 125.

s.v. *Racy* say that wine is agreeable when it has 'lost its sweet offensive, luscious quality'. Caroline lyrics are summed up disapprovingly by the *Connoisseur* (CXVIII) as 'luscious love-songs'. Mr Spectator (51) observes how some people always go to the opening performance of a play, 'lest it should prove too luscious to admit their going with any countenance' on the second day. Ovid and Catullus would have us believe that 'luscious Verses' are consistent with personal chastity— the eighteenth-century critic[1] is not so sure, and the *Anti-Jacobin*[2] contrasts the luscious novels of one versatile Revolutionary with his severe decrees. There is more in this than just a suggestion of cloying bad taste.

The critics of the time disliked the use of erotic language in religious discourse: John Wesley[3] spoke for many when he doubted whether any real holiness can be gathered 'from that amorous way of praying ... or that luscious way of preaching. ...' Needless to say, sentimental novels could be luscious: how they could be *sentimental* is a story in itself.[4]

Sentimental began of course as the adjective of *sentiment*, whose earliest sense was simply Opinion, Judgment, as it still is when we say 'these are my sentiments on that matter'. As late as 1762 the *Critical Review*[5] could write about verbal and sentimental criticism—criticism of expression and content. But in the 'sixties and 'seventies sentiment may tacitly imply the finer feelings—a delicate sensibility—and then a sickly sentimentality. In this sense, *sentiment* was, as the *Looker-on*[6] said 'a word of modern origin'. These essays give *O.E.D.* its first example of *sentimentalist* with the apt definition that it is used of people 'who love to repine upon sorrows without relieving them'. Somewhat later,[7] a contributor, the Rev. James Beresford, is laughing at a 'Sensibility Advertisement', the author of which pledges that in a twelvemonth he will 'turn out of his academy such a tribe of snivellers, whimperers, sobbers and blubberers, at funerals, charity sermons, hanging bouts, and tragedies, as shall raise a very sentimental uproar through his majesty's three kingdoms'.

Clearly *sentimental* had fallen from the good sense which the *Critical Review* could still give it—in the same year as it used it in its older

---

[1] John Jones, re Diaper's *Halieuticks*, quoted in Broughton's edn., p. lix.
[2] *Anti-Jacobin*, ii, 632.
[3] J. Wesley to Fletcher, March 1768, quoted in R. Knox, *Enthusiasm*, p. 500.
[4] See Erämetsä, *A Study of the word 'sentimental'*.
[5] *Crit. Rev.* 13 (1762), 489.   [6] ii, 299.   [7] op. cit., No. 64, p. 311.

dispassionate meaning—when it considered[1] the last sentence of Uncle Toby's will 'a concert of genius, glowing with the warmth of a heart truly sentimental'. It may well be argued that Sterne gave the word its brief glory and set it on its road to decline as well. Dr Wendeborn[2] tells us that when he first came to England,

what is called *sentimental* was the hobby-horse of many moral writers and of such persons as pretended to have finer feelings, and tenderer moral nerves than others, though they contradicted it frequently by their actions. The public, however, grew tired of this . . . and many persons of both sexes may now be seen, smiling with a kind of contempt, though often without reason, and very little to their honour, at everything which appears to come under the denomination of sentimental.

The *Critical Review*[3] supports the general public—'This same Lady Sentimentality, of whom we are apt to hear so much in modern publications, we are sorry to say is but too apt to quarrel with her elder brother Common-sense.'

The philosophers tried to keep the word exact, but were not agreed as to what it should mean. Beattie,[4] in his essay on *Poetry and Ridicule*, says that laughter caused by tickling or gladness is different from the laughter that arises on reading *A Tale of a Tub*. 'The former may be called *Animal* laughter, the latter (if it may be lawful to adopt a new word which has become very common of late) I should term Sentimental.' George Campbell[5] notes that the word is rather modern, but 'nevertheless convenient, as it fills a vacant room, and doth not, like most of our new-fangled words, justle out older and worthier occupants, to the no small detriment of the language. It occupies so to speak, the middle place between the pathetic [of the feelings] and that which is addressed to the imagination, and partakes of both, adding to the warmth of the former the grace and attractions of the latter.'

The *Monthly Review*[6] summed up the clash of old and new when it used a volume of 'occasional attempts at Sentimental Poetry' as the text for extended comment.

The word *sentimental* is, like *continental*, a barbarism that has but lately disgraced our language, and it is not always easy to conceive what is meant by it. We have before seen a *Sentimental* Novel, and a *Sentimental* Journey, and now we have Attempts at *Sentimental* Poetry. Our own old English word

---

[1] *Crit. Rev.* 13 (1762), 69. [2] *View*, ii. 84. [3] *Crit. Rev.* 29 (1770), 110.
[4] Quoted, *Month. Rev.* lvii (1777), 109. [5] *Phil. of Rhet.*, p. 80.
[6] *Month. Rev.* xli (1769), Art. 12 in Monthly Catalogue.

sentiment means only thought, notion, opinion: the French word *sentiment* seems to mean *intellectual sensation*, a sense of conduct and opinion, distinct from the sense of qualities that affect us by the taste, sight, smell, touch, and hearing: it has a place in the cant of our travelled gentry, many of whom show by their use of it, that they neither know the meaning of it in English nor French: to the fashionable use of the word *sentiment*, however, we owe the use of the word *sentimental*, which, from polite conversation, has, at length, found its way to the press.

Just what did the *Monthly Review*[1] itself mean when it spoke disapprovingly of these times of 'sentimental liberality' in which 'mistaken Zealots' try to 'revive the dying cause of Mystery and Superstition'? That their opinions were too lax, or sentimental in the bad modern sense? The exaltation of feelings, easily strengthened into passions, at the expense of thought and morality, taints the word. Knox[2] puts it well when he writes

The sentimental manner ... has given an amiable name to vice, and has obliquely excused the extravagance of the passions, by representing them as the effect of lovely sensibility. The least refined affections of humanity have lost their indelicate nature, in the ideas of many, when dignified by the epithet of sentimental; and transgressions forbidden by the laws of God and man, have been absurdly palliated, as proceeding from an excess of those finer feelings, which vanity has arrogated to itself as elegant and amiable distinctions. A softened appellation has given a degree of gracefulness to moral depravity.

One sympathises with the *Critical Review's*[3] comment that the 'epithet *Sentimental* is used now so frequently that we are at a loss to guess what idea some writers have of it'.

AMBIGUITY

The related *sensible* had then as now distinct meanings—'what is perceptible by the senses' and 'showing common-sense'. The *Looker-on* (24) contrasts *sensible* and *tangible* with *ideal* and *intellectual*, and this sense is now frequent in philosophical or scientific language. In colloquial speech we prefer *sensitive*, the word we should use of tender skin instead of the eighteenth-century's *sensible*, of any 'sensible and living organ'[4] and of an overwrought nervous system.[5] Occasionally

[1] *Month. Rev.* xxxix (1768), 313.   [2] *Essays*, i, 70.   [3] *Crit. Rev.* 33 (1772), 325.
[4] Adam Smith, *Works*, v, 354.   [5] James Beattie, *Dissertations*, p. 199.

we must translate 'perceptible to the senses' in phrases that at first sight sound startling. Addison[1] tells us that from Venice to Ancona, the tide comes in very sensibly; it is interesting that *insensibly* offers no stumbling-block of ambiguity when we read that all the soil on that side of Ravenna has been left there insensibly by the sea's discharging itself for so many Ages.[2]

When the *Tatler* (58) says of a man that he has 'too sensible a Spirit to see the most lovely of all Objects without being moved with Passion', *sensible* sets us off on a false scent: *sensitive* is our word, but this sense came in the nineteenth century.

William Godwin[3] believes that sensible pleasures are to be avoided, when they tend to impair the corporeal faculties—the connection between sensible and corporeal suggests that here *sensible* means felt by the senses; the same is implied by his contrast when he says it is a mistake to suppose that sensible pleasures and intellectual ones are incompatible.

It is something of a shock to find Dr Johnson stigmatising our two common meanings as 'low'. To use sensible to mean convinced, persuaded—('I am sensible of the fact that . . .') is low; and in 'low conversation it has sometimes the sense of reasonable; judicious; wise'. Yet it is clear from the company it keeps that this latter is the meaning the word had for many people about whose standing there could be no question. Lady Hertford[4] describes Lord Cathcart as 'an extremely good officer and a sensible man'—it seems unlikely that she meant sensitive. Dennis[5] says that all the sensible world are agreed that public diversions ought not to be barbarous, sensual, base or effeminate (*sensible* here might mean *sensitive*), and that generous and sensible audiences scorn to use their interest for a foolish play; and that Pope cannot hope to impose on the sensible and impartial world. The *Annual Register*[6] describing Swift's decay speaks of his last sensible word, and reports[7] how a fanatic at New York killed his baby to ensure the happiness of its soul but 'talked very sensibly except on the particular subject of his uneasiness'. Sylas Neville[8] thought sensible people cannot believe in absurdities, and once met 'a sensible gent.' who hoped for the independence of the American colonies. Surely all these were gifted with common sense rather than sensitivity. But was the 'elegantly

[1] *Italy*, p. 74.   [2] ibid., p. 76.
[3] *Enquirer*, p. 242.   [4] Hertford-Pomfret Correspondence, iii, 7.
[5] *Critical Works*, ii, 300: 276.   [6] *Ann. Reg.* ii (1759), 328.
[7] *Ann. Reg.* viii (1765), 113.   [8] *Diary*, pp. 63, 36.

sensible'[1] Lord Lyttelton sensible as we take it, or sensitive? The 'humane and sensible[2] author of a letter on the state of the poor in Ireland might have been both; this is true too of a 'sensible and exact' commentator.

It is possible to find two senses within a few pages or even a few lines of each other. The *Annual Register* reports a 'very sensible shock' of an earthquake on p. 148 of its fourth volume, and, on p. 153 that the royal academy of sciences at Paris have given a 'very sensible and polite' answer to a paper. Miss Arundel in *Columella*[3] hoped her lover would never act contrary to the filial duty which, he was sensible, every young person owed his parents; and the oldest member of the party commented that she was 'a very sensible' young woman.

HESITATION

Resentment then as now usually meant a feeling of anger, not, as its etymology would imply, any feeling in reply to one's treatment, good or bad. Dr Johnson says that to resent is to take well or ill, but that to take ill is the most usual sense. It had been, from the word's introduction in the seventeenth century. George Campbell[4] seems to be trying to keep the basic meaning when he describes gratitude as 'the resentment of a favour' and anger as 'the resentment of injury'. This was a special eighteenth-century use. Hutcheson[5] uses the verb more non-committally than we do when he points out that if 'we had no moral sense Villany, Treachery, Cruelty, would be as meekly resented as a Blast or Mildew or an overflowing stream'. For Lord Kames,[6] resentment comes under the heading of anger, and is in every stage painful. In the *Spectator* papers the word was used in both senses: 'nothing renders a Person more unworthy of a Benefit than his being without all Resentment of it', says No. 588, whereas in No. 604 there were people 'who resented the satyr which they imagined I had directed against them'.

Vulgar is another word hesitating between matter-of-fact description and disapproval. *Glossographia Anglicana Nova* says it means common, trivial: Cocker-Hawkins, rude, vile, common; Bailey, common, ordinary, general, ungenteel. These definitions are tricky, for in this period or in the present-day United States *ordinary* can mean bad;

[1] Knox, *Essays*, ii, 379. [2] *Crit. Rev.* 51 (1781), 389.
[3] i, 163. [4] *Phil. of Rhet.*, p. 129.
[5] *Moral Good and Evil*, p. 112. [6] *Elements*, i, 110.

common and *mean* are equally double-edged. The modern advertiser's *exclusive* is a counterblast. But sometimes eighteenth-century usage implies trivial at the worst and ordinary at the best. Lyttelton's *Dialogues of the Dead*[1] makes Plato praise Fénelon for giving dignity to the most vulgar and obvious truths. Junius[2] declares that if unquestionable truths make no impression, 'it is because they are too vulgar and notorious'—and there is no bad tinge in *notorious*. Dr Johnson's[3] characterizing of *Lycidas* as 'easy, vulgar, and therefore disgusting' should be seen in the light of the less colourful sense of vulgar and the weaker—'displeasing'—sense of *disgusting*.

Apparent sometimes seems to have turned a complete somersault. *Glossographia Anglicana Nova* speaks for the older sense (still found in 'It is apparent that...')—Visible, Certain, Evident. Bailey agrees. Johnson adds *seeming*. After all, Appearances may be deceptive. We have to be guided by context. When the *Adventurer* (4) says that in both Epic and Romance 'truth is apparently violated' the facts demand *obviously*, and so too when Shaftesbury[4] says credentials should be open, visible and apparent. Dennis's[5] meaning is clear when he speaks of a moral which is 'so apparently the Foundation of the Dramatic Action, and must appear to every Spectator and Reader to be the genuine Result of it'. When Jack Ketch the hangman is made to say he is apparently the first Minister to Law and Justice, there is no question of his seeming only.[6] Nor can we be in any doubt about the meaning in Junius' Fifteenth Letter—'Cutting off ears and noses might still be inflicted by a resolute judge: but I will be candid [i.e. kind] enough to suppose that penalties so apparently shocking to humanity would not be hazarded in these times.' 'Apparent reluctance' to us usually means assumed reluctance: but it was real and obvious when the lady[7] refused to stay at home and her husband would not urge her to stay—for to stay with apparent [i.e. obvious] reluctance would not have gratified his wish.

When a twentieth-century woman was found 'apparently dead' in her bath, artificial respiration was tried for some time before a doctor confirmed she was dead. The early eighteenth century would hardly have used *apparently* if any one had felt she was perhaps alive, and the word would have been ambiguous at any time. George Campbell[8]

[1] *Dialogues of the Dead*, III.
[2] *Letters*, p. ix.
[3] 'Life of Milton.'
[4] *Characteristics*, iii, 338.
[5] *Critical Works*, ii, 103.
[6] *Champion*, ii, 154.
[7] *Adventurer*, 36.
[8] *Phil. of Rhet.*, p. 194.

accepted the usual modern sense and was concerned about the ambiguity. It is, he says, 'often equivocal and can hardly ever be accounted
proper. Both etymology and the most frequent use lead us so directly
to the signification of *seeming* as opposed to *real*, or *visible* as opposed
to *concealed*, that at first we are always in hazard of mistaking it.' For
the same reason, he disliked *to make appear* (though a very common
phrase) for *to prove, to evince, to show*. 'By the aid of sophistry, a man
may *make* a thing *appear* to be what it is not.'

The real and the assumed clash in *Pretender*. Dr Johnson defines *to
pretend* as to put in a claim truly or falsely. 'It is seldom used without a
shade of censure'—which amounts to an admission that false claims
are what we think of when we use the word. Historically, Pretenders
are those who lay claims to throne—and to those who actually occupy
them, such claims must be false. The *Gentleman's Magazine*[1] says that
Pretender is the term used in Parliamentary language, but notes that
Mr Boswell did not think it a gentlemanly expression. Obviously no
Jacobite could.

Stricture now usually implies adverse criticism. The sense is the
result of confusion between two Latin homophones, one meaning a
light touch and one firm binding—connected with *stringent*. The slight
touch is the modest sense intended by authors who published strictures
on military discipline,[2] on the gout,[3] on the confessional,[4] on agriculture,[5] on painting.[6] Dr Johnson[7] uses the word neutrally, in contrast
to *censure* and *praise* when he adds 'short strictures, containing a general
censure of faults or praise of excellence' to his edition of Shakespeare.
The *Critical Review*[8] speaks of 'lively strictures' which indicate a
writer of genius, and the *Monthly Review*[9] notices a pamphlet which
claimed to contain 'genteel strictures' but was, in the *Review*'s opinion,
a 'most virulent and indecent attack'. The writers on military discipline
and on the confessional thought both in need of improvement. It is
easy to see how the word attained its bad meaning. It must be added
that the meaning of 'slight trace' was helped by the current idea that
Vergil's *stricturae* meant sparks from the anvil rather than iron bars.

[1] *Gent. Mag.* lviii, 2 (1788), 677.
[2] Reviewed in *Month. Rev.* liii (1775), 84.
[3] Quack Advertisement, *Month. Rev.* liv (1770), 420.
[4] Reviewed in *Month. Rev.* 41 (1775), 461.
[5] Reviewed in *Month. Rev.* lix (1778), 350.
[6] *Gent. Mag.* l (1780), 26.   [7] *Preface to Shakespeare.*
[8] *Crit. Rev.* 41 (1776), 155.   [9] *Month. Rev.* lvii (1777), 337.

WORDS IN CHANGED CONTEXTS

A number of verbs have differences of tone. We are more likely to say *exposed to cold* than to *sunshine*, but the *Monthly Review*[1] was uncomfortable with 'to expose public misconduct and base practices'—the very things that the verb would have us to expect. Shenstone thought this sense equally contrary to good nature and the laws of etymology. *Exposition* goes with *expound* rather than *expose*, especially as what in French is an *exposition* in English is an *exhibition*. It is equally noteworthy that if we make an exhibition of ourselves, the implication is that we ought to know better, even if exhibitions of art or science are wholly desirable. Certainly no trader would now write to a newspaper after the fashion of a letter to the *Tatler* (92) 'to beg the Favour of being advantageously exposed' as a Purveyor of Snuff or of any other commodity.

In kinder mood we may extenuate offences, and so did the eighteenth century. But we should hardly 'extenuate our obligations', or speak of 'extenuating the value of antiquarian research'.[2] We certainly should not extenuate a favourable report,[3] though we might doubt or contradict it. Here *to extenuate* is to belittle or depreciate.

We may realise our hopes or our assets and realise that this or that is true. The eighteenth century used the verb in the former sense more than we do; often *to realise* is literally to make real, not only to feel it imaginatively true. 'Oh that you could realize the golden bough' means 'find it in reality'—but it 'does not grow in this country'.[4] In a vivid description of Etna 'as much as words can realize objects, they are realized'.[5] Of course words can only make scenery real to the mind's eye—but Kent 'realized his landscapes'[6] in all the estates he laid out. A poet of strong imagination and stronger vanity, might naturally enough 'realize the world's mere compliment'—believe it was really true—and think himself inspired.[7] When Charles Wesley[8] prays that God will 'realize' the Eucharistic symbols, he is obviously asking for efficacy, not understanding.

We have killed the liveliness that *vegetate* once conveyed. *To*

[1] *Month. Rev.* i (1749), August, reviewing a History of Scotland.
[2] Mandeville, *Enquiry*, p. 106; Knox, *Essays*, i, 315.
[3] Knox, *Essays*, ii, 112.   [4] Clara Reeve, *Progress of Romance*, ii, 55.
[5] Jackson, *Letters*, p. 116.   [6] Mason, *English Garden*, i, 513.
[7] Young, *Original Composition*, p. 23.
[8] Hymn: 'Come, Holy Ghost, Thine influence shed.'

vegetate is to be like a vegetable, without motion or thought. In this period it could still imply growth. 'There are a few who vegetate freely and take the bias of the unfettered human genius.'[1] And in 'youth that borders on infancy the passions are in a state of vegetation, they only appear in full bloom in maturity'.[2] They are developing, even if immature, and associated with the young, not with the onset of age. But it was the eighteenth century that developed the lazy meaning.

If we might read less into these verbs than our ancestors, we are likely to read both more and less into *elope*. To us it is not to be used specially of a married woman running off to a lover and bilking her creditors[3]—it is more likely to be a young couple running off without parental consent. But in the eighteenth century it was possible for no love-affair to be involved. Lackington[4] has a tale of a lady who 'eloped' because she was too spiritually-minded for her husband: no other man came into it. The verb and noun were used of any going away by stealth, as Bailey defines their meaning. So we meet a girl weeping for the elopement of her monkey,[5] a magpie eloping from its cage in an Aesop fable,[6] the overgrown schoolboys who go off on a short elopement to London[7] and the young man who went on the stage and was cut off with a shilling by his father in the first rage after his discovery of the elopement.[8]

The verb *to shift* can present a double problem. When Hutcheson[9] tells us that Sparta chiefly desired to abound in a 'hardy, shifting youth' he means self-reliant young men able to shift for themselves. We tend to associate *shifting* with *shifty*. And Mr Bickerstaff[10] would be socially out of key now if he were still to order people unsuitably dressed to 'go Home immediately and shift themselves'. Likewise, to *let down* sounds colloquial now but as *O.E.D.* shows was dignified up to the nineteenth century. It would sound incongruous now in such a sentence as 'the humanity of Eneas seems to be let down by his seizing so many youths to be sacrificed to the *manes* of his friend Pallas'.[11]

A *treat* suggests a children's outing or party or some adult indulgence. We are surprised to meet it used also of a discussion on philosophy and art, as at the table of Polymetis[12] whose friends seldom went

[1] Usher, *Clio*, p. 40.   [2] ibid., p. 80.   [3] Cocker-Hawkins, s.v.
[4] *Memoirs*, pp. 142–3.   [5] Hanway, *Journal*, i, 109.
[6] *Ann. Reg.* iii, 271, re *Fables of Æsop*, by Mr Dodsley.
[7] Gildon, *Art of Poetry*, p. 259.   [8] Knox, *Essays*, ii, 118.
[9] *Moral Good and Evil*, p. 203.   [10] *Tatler* (30).
[11] Gildon, *Art of Poetry*, p. 315.   [12] Spence, *Polymetis*, p. 1.

away 'without being pleased, and perhaps improved by this treat'.
The lesser sense was there too: a burlesque poem addressed to George
Whitefield scoffs

> Methodists still[1] love to eat
> And always fondly praise a treat.

So Pope uses the word in *The Rape of the Lock* (i, 96; iii, 169).

Recruits suggests primarily new servicemen: in the eighteenth century an assembly could be in 'good Humour, having received some
Recruits of French claret'[2]—a treat, no doubt. We still recruit our
strength.

If *recruit* has narrowed, so has *refuse*. Dr Johnson says the noun
means 'that which remains disregarded when the rest is taken'. That is
true of the refuse we put in the dustbin, but we should not now talk
of the refuse of our correspondence.[3] The word was weaker then. So
was *gust(o)*. Often it is taste—the vigour of modern *gusto* need not be
there. Gildon's[4] Mrs Lamonde thinks Italian opera in English could
not have been borne by 'Ears of any tolerable gusto': he[5] wants to
gratify 'the *goust* of the ladies'. Spirit of Lavender 'delights the gust'.[6]
Even one of the least gusto cannot be indifferent to Raphael and
Rubens.[7] Pope's 'Destroy all creatures for thy sport or gust'[8] is hardly
more than pleasure, or whim.

Undoubtedly any chalice is a *moveable*,[9] but the word seems inadequate to us to describe the 'emerald' chalice of Genoa—'il sacro
catino' held by some to be the cup of the Last Supper itself.

No householder in his most poetical flights would now call his house
a *Dome*. To the eighteenth century this need be no more than a building, not one with a cupola, not even a home according to the Latin
sense. Dyer[10] uses it of a factory, and of the abodes of mountain goats.
Smart and Thomson use it of birds' nests.[11] We can paint our 'Domes'
with distemper and the pet dog can catch distemper. But we do not
suffer from distemper ourselves, and so might well get the wrong
impression from 'Sir, I am extremely well-born: pedigree is my distemper'[12]—it could so easily be Pompey the Little speaking or 'his
Highness' dog at Kew' rather than a man. Lunatics at Bedlam would

---

[1] *still* means *always*. *The Methodists . . .* addressed to . . . Whitefield, 1739.
[2] *Spec.* (440).   [3] *Adventurer* (89).   [4] *Art of Poetry*, pp. 102–4.
[5] ibid., p. 101.   [6] *Tatler* (224).   [7] Gildon, *Art of Poetry*, p. 27.
[8] *Essay on Man*, l. 117.   [9] *Ann. Reg.* vi (1763), Characters 168.
[10] *Fleece*, iii, 261.
[11] e.g. Hymn XIII (Smart on the bluecap), *Spring*, l. 647.   [12] *World* (195).

not be distempered now: gout is not an 'acute Distemper': neither is
influenza.[1]

SPECIALISATION

So far we have considered differences of tone imposed upon a fundamental identity of reference, or specialisations justified by etymology.
There are many words where the application and the referend have
changed enough to dig deeper pits for us. If, for example, we heard a
man advised to 'live on such diet as is not provocative of *acrimony*',[2]
we should think of his temper, not his digestion.

We do not always distinguish our *Vocations* and our *Avocations*.
Etymologically, our Avocation is, as Dyche and Pardon say, 'the
calling one off or taking some one from his business that he is about,
an interruption, lett or hindrance', and so the eighteenth century uses
it at times. We read of an author who was early initiated into the
company of the Muses, 'and tho' he might have small avocations, yet
he soon returned again with greater eagerness to his beloved studies'.[3]
But the doubt as to whether your vocation or your avocation were the
more important began in the eighteenth century, and the sense of
'ordinary occupation' develops accordingly.

If we receive emoluments for our work, we expect them to be tangible, if not in hard cash. The eighteenth century used the word to
mean, as *Glossographia Anglicana Nova* says, Advantage, Profit, in
the abstract. Newspapers were stuck up at Temple Bar 'to the great
emolument of the hackney-coachmen';[4] the dispatch of business 'when
it turns to the Publick Emolument' is a great satisfaction;[5] and a
gentleman might have projects conducive 'to the Emolument of the
Publick' including a reformation of Street Cries.[6] If we said that
Elocution would be a suitable part of a Street Crier's training, the
eighteenth century might have misunderstood, for some people then
spoke of Elocution as consisting of finding '*proper*, *polite*, and *ornamental* Expressions to signify our Thoughts'. Its parts are 'Composition, Elegance and Dignity'[7]—it is eloquence rather than elocution.
But there were also those who equated Elocution with Pronunciation.

[1] *Tatler* (27). *Ann. Reg.* v (1762), 82.
[2] *Gent. Mag.* xxiii, 1753, 527. See Donald Davie, *The Language of Science and
the Language of Literature*, 1700–1740.
[3] Upton, *Critical Observations on Shakespeare*, p. 15.
[4] *Connoisseur*, lxxxvi.   [5] *Tatler* (103).
[6] *Spectator* (251).   [7] Holmes, *Art of Rhetoric*, i, 25.

The 'fulminations' of a footman[1] would make us suppose he had lost his temper: it refers only to his thunderous knocking on a door in announcing a visitor.

If a traitor joins the invaders of his country, we should not speak of his *junction*.[2] We understand the *prevalence* of principles or fashions but not the *prevalence* of an army.[3] Nor do we use *preference* for 'the quality that makes us prefer'—the superiority—as the *Critical Review*[4] does when it mentions a book which offered some observations in the preference of the English Language in several instances as compared with Greek and Latin. To us a recess is an alcove or a holiday, so 'Accesses and Recesses of passion',[5] or the 'joint appearance and recess of the engaging arts'[6] give us pause. We prefer *Recession* or *Receding*.

We are so used to applying *denomination* to religious sects that it surprises us to find 'the good of all denominations'[7] used with no ecclesiastical reference whatever.

When we use *vicinity* we mean neighbourhood, not nearness by measurement, so 'the great vicinity to Jupiter'[8] of one of its satellites sounds awkward.

In all these, the key is to be found in the *literal* meanings of the Latin originals without our modern transfers and emphases.

Different concrete objects may share the same name in various periods, even when the things and the names exist simultaneously. The name may be commoner in one period applied to this, in another to that, and so the modern will be shocked, amused, or misled as the case may be. *Bottom* existed then as now in the same senses, but the distribution varies. A trader now would be in danger of raising a laugh if he said his trade was still further improveable because he hoped to enlarge his bottom.[9] 'The basis of his undertaking' would be better now. Mr Spectator's 'Creatures with no other Bottom but Self-love'[10] would now be 'foundation'. The clash between *bottom*, the lowest point below the surface (*O.E.D.*, 2) and the most remote part of a recess or bay or the like (*O.E.D.*, 6) has for us a comic ambiguity in the report that the Marquess of Montcalm was informed 'that the English had assembled at the bottom of Lake Sacrament an army of 20,000 militia

---

[1] Knox, *Essays*, i, 328.
[2] *Gent. Mag.* xlix (1779), 14.
[3] Gildon, *Art of Poetry*, p. 98.
[4] *Crit. Rev.* 56 (1783), 78.
[5] Gildon, *Art of Poetry*, p. 96.
[6] Usher, *Clio*, p. 37.
[7] Ruffhead, *Life of Pope*, p. 360.
[8] *Month. Rev.* xlii (1770), 53.
[9] Richardson, *Familiar Letters*, xviii.
[10] *Spect.* (588).

and 6,000 regular forces'.[1] Apart from the technical and figurative uses, we think of *inlets* mainly as watery, but in the eighteenth century you could make inlets by thinning clumps of trees,[2] regard the sense of feeling as an inlet of beauty,[3] and describe a blind poet as having his chief inlets for poetical ideas totally barred up.[4]

From the middle ages, *engine* had implied any sort of ingenious contrivance or contraption, and in particular whichever one was most impressive or most in demand at the time. It has meant an engine of war or of torture, a fire engine, a locomotive, the internal combustion engine of the car, the jet engine of the plane. According to Dyche and Pardon the eighteenth century thought first of fire-engines. *Glossographia Anglicana Nova* says it is 'any Mechanick Instrument composed of Wheels, Screws, etc. in order to raise, cast or sustain Weight' —there is no idea of motion. But the word could still be used much more widely, as we use *instrument* today. Defoe[5] speaks of writing with 'Mouth, Foot or any other Engine', Hutcheson[6] of the various Engines that 'might have attain'd the same ends' as a human muscle. George Campbell[7] calls the voice the only engine by which a man can operate on the passions of his hearers. A person can be an engine of oppression. Comets, meteors, lightnings and thunders are the engines of God's vengeance.[8] Roman religion was 'scarce anything more than an engine of state';[9] religion and the sense of shame are the 'two great engines of government'.[10] At the other end of the scale, the scissors in the *Rape of the Lock* are the 'fatal engine' and—to go to a much lighter poet—William Woty[11] uses the word of corkscrew, tobacco-stopper and looking-glass. There is an element of mock heroic here.

Machine too is much more widely applied, and to things of which we should never use it. A warship is a wooden machine[12] and so is the State Barge of Venice.[13] A fan is 'that little modish Machine',[14] the Treaty of Pilaitz is 'this extensive and complicated machine'.[15] The earth is 'the firm machine'.[16] Feathers are 'a curious Sort of Machines adapted to many admirable Uses'.[17]

---

[1] *Gent. Mag.* xxviii (1758), 496.　　[2] Uvedale Price, *Essay*, ii, 80.
[3] Hogarth, *Analysis of Beauty*, p. 13.　　[4] Spence on Blacklock, p. vii.
[5] *Review*, ii, 59.　　[6] *Beauty and Virtue*, p. 23.　　[7] *Phil. of Rhet.*, p. iii.
[8] J. Smith, *Last Judgment*, quoted *Crit. Rev.* 55 (1783), 33.
[9] Spence, *Polymetis*, p. 20.　　[10] Shebbeare, *Letters*, i, 203.
[11] *Poetical Works*, i, 40, 46, 62.　　[12] Knox, *Essays*, i, 237.
[13] Hertford-Pomfret Correspondence, iii, 214.　　[14] *Spect.* (102).
[15] *Anti-Jacobin*, ii, 41.　　[16] Blacklock, *Hymn to the Supreme Being*, l. 24.
[17] Hutcheson, *Beauty and Virtue*, p. 26.

To us *mechanism* implies machinery—how it works—or the soulless nature of machinery in contrast with the caprice and variety of men. A 'mechanical inquiry' would suggest a perfunctory one, but that is not implied in *A mechanical inquiry into the nature, causes and seat and cure of the diabetes*. There are *Observations on the Mechanism of the horse's foot* and *Thoughts on the Mechanism of Societies*, both being studies of what makes them work.[1]

Mechanic, with our greater respect for machinery and greater need of the expert, has gone up in status as well as being specialised. In this period it could be used of a newspaper man or a tailor.[2] On the other hand, a derogatory connection with the machine and a protest against such a reading of it, are both clear in the remark that 'By the word *mechanic* is generally meant a person who makes but little use of his rational faculty, but it must be remembered that *mechanical contrivance* is one of the highest departments of reason, depending as it does on mathematics.'[3]

If we have both narrowed and exalted *mechanic* we have also specialised a variety of other general words. A gentleman[4] who published his work in *parcels*—periodical instalments—sounds odd now, for we assume that a parcel is a package. We talk of the 'papers', not the 'prints'[5] which to us are illustrations—as they could also have been then—or textiles (which they could not). We do not define a University as a Nursery[6] where youth is instructed in the Languages, Arts and Sciences. If it is odd to find a word suggestive of children or plants used of an adult institution, it is equally strange to us to find *Stipend*—which we connect with the professions—used of weekly pocket-money for schoolboys.[7]

Nor should we use *Natural History* as the heading for notes on the following multifarious topics, all of which come under it in the Third Volume of the *Annual Register*—a remarkable nervous case, accounts of a sleep-walker and a boy with convulsive fits, of a negress whose skin changed colour, of a lad whose tendons and muscles turned into bone, of a Polish dwarf, of the Irish Giant Cornelius McGrath, an explanation of why the Atlantic runs into the Mediterranean, an account

[1] *Gent. Mag.* xv (1745), 448; *Gent. Mag.* lxv (1795), 505; *Month. Rev.* lxxvi (1787), 301.

[2] *World* (197); Knox, *Essays*, i, 9.

[3] Jackson, *Letters on Slavery*, quoted *Literary Mag., and British Rev.* ii (1788), 284.

[4] *Month. Rev.* xiii (1755), 267.   [5] Bailey's *Dictionary*, s.v.

[6] Knox, *Essays*, i, 29.   [7] Knox, *Essays*, ii, 245.

of the North Sea commonly called the Ice Sea, of the ostrich, of the heat of the weather in Georgia, a waterspout at Cockermouth, Scotch lime-stone quarries, etc. Here come 'histories of enthusiasm, wanderings, and madness' for they are 'always very deserving of attention'.

A study of trees, shrubs and flowers would be part of Natural History as we understand it, but we should not expect them all to be covered by the one word *greens*. That is so tied up with the idea of brassicas that any other sense in a context where the vegetable would be possible is apt to produce a more or less comic incongruity. According to a lady in the *Spectator* (282) the parish clerk, who had been a gardener, 'so overdeckt the Church' at Christmas 'with Greens' that he spoilt her view. Evergreens we should expect, but the gardener inevitably turns our minds to cabbages and their like. The skit on the absurdities of topiary work in the *Guardian* (173) mentions a cook who 'beautified his Country Seat with a Coronation Dinner in greens'—shrubs—and a Catalogue of Greens to be disposed of by an eminent Town-Gardener. Addison's[1] picture of the land 'with sudden greens and herbage crown'd' concerns trees or shrubs. And the lady who decorated her fireplaces with 'greens' during the summer would now say *greenery*. Although a *green* now probably suggests a golfing green it could also suggest a village green, as it clearly did to Dr Bentley[2] when he read in *Paradise Lost*

> a tuft of shade, that on a green
> Stood whispering.

'*On a green*', he declares, 'is poor stuff indeed. He seems to have fancied himself in some country village.'

If we placed a collection of birds in our garden we should not call it a *menagerie*,[3] which for us is a collection of beasts, though there is no etymological reason why it should be. Dr Johnson does not include the word, though he gives '*menage*, a collection of animals'. Both are based on *mansio*, a household. We should enjoy the *warbling* of the birds, but that is no word to apply now to 'cats and scritch-owls'.[4]

'A Discourse on the Torpedo' was delivered at the Anniversary Meeting of the Royal Society in 1774. It could still be done in the 1960's, but it is unlikely that it would be on the same topic. So a head-line which read 'Torpedos found on the Coast of England'[5] would

---

[1] *Spect.* (441). *Greenery* is first recorded in *Kubla Khan* (1797).
[2] re *Paradise Lost* (IV), 325. [3] *London Mag.* xxxvii (1768), 71.
[4] *Crit. Rev.* 39 (1775), 44. [5] *Month. Rev.* lii (1775), 332.

have a very different reference now from that of the same words nearly 200 years ago. Even when we read on and find that the torpedo is 'the electric ray' we might see no reason to rid our minds of warlike devices. But when we find that it 'frequents the shores of this island' we begin to think of fish, and realise the word is not out of place when we are told how

> Torpedoes, Sharks, Rays, Porpus, Dolphin pour
> Their twinkling squadrons round the glittering shore—.[1]

Nevertheless, 'A live torpedo placed upon the table in a napkin',[2] sounds like a dangerous experiment (if it could be done).

We should not naturally think a torpedo causes lethargy—to our minds it causes explosions—but it was a common metaphor where we prefer 'bromide'. Dr Johnson[3] observed 'that some authors produce the same effect as the torpedo, they benumb the faculties and reward with torpid insensibility the rash hero that ventures to touch them'. We are told in the *Life of Beau Nash*[4] that he 'was not born a writer; for whatever humour he might have in conversation, he used to call a pen his torpedo. Whenever he grasped it, it numbed all his faculties.'

Toy has grown so associated with children's playthings that we need to notice that its earlier uses were much wider. A toy, says Dr Johnson, is 'a pretty commodity'. It could be used of needles, knitting-needles, tape, thread, scissors, bodkins, fans, play-books, gloves, silks and ribbons.[5] You could buy a pair of superb candlesticks for 100 guineas at Mr Grimstead's, the great toyshop near St Paul's.[6] The *Guardian* has a paper (106) about a Dreamer who could see into ladies' hearts. 'The first Images I discoverer'd in it were Furs, Silks, Ribbons, Laces, and many other Gew-gaws, which lay so thick together that the whole Heart was nothing else but a Toy-shop.' Indeed 'the moving Toy-shop of their Heart'. The word had other figurative uses— Birmingham is 'the grand toy-shop of Europe', the place where 'all ingenuity and mechanism have united to dazzle and astonish the world',[7] and in the eyes of the rational and cynical Bernard Mandeville,[8] the Church of Rome is 'that Holy Toy-Shop' which puts off 'contemptible Baubles . . . in the face of the Sun for richest Merchandize'.

---

[1] Darwin, *Loves of the Plants*, ii, 252.
[2] *Ann. Reg.* xv (1772), 135.
[3] *Crit. Rev.* 63 (1787), 339.
[4] p. 34.   [5] Steele, *Tender Husband*, p. 23; *Tatler* (151).
[6] *Babler*, lxxviii.
[7] *Crit. Rev.* 68 (1789), 41.   [8] *Enquiry*, p. 50.

MISTAKEN IDENTITY

In eighteenth-century literature we meet a number of people whose occupation, standing or nationality are not what their names suggest to us. An *amateur* was still usually the lover of an art or subject—indeed Gildon[1] speaks of 'any Gentleman and *Lover*, as they call it', who may have a taste for painting 'without being able to draw a stroak'. The 'amateurs of the horrid'[2] would be entertained by the *Phantom of the Castle*. The modern notion of an amateur as some one who follows a pursuit or sport out of interest, perhaps inexpertly, certainly without financial gain, is a later development; it was just coming in late in the century, when, according to the *European Magazine* of 1786,[3] the scientific writings of Dr Percival showed that he wrote 'as an *amateur* rather than as a master'. We expect a Professor to be an academic, or at least the teacher of some art, though we have narrowed it to exponents of a particular standing in one profession only. Vicesimus Knox[4] reminds us of the older sense when he says that almost all professions have some characteristic manners, which the professors adopt.

Why should a *locum tenens* suggest a medical man? Etymologically it could be any understudy or substitute. So we read that Sir Robert Ladbroke, locum tenens, presided at a civic banquet for the King of Denmark, 'the right hon. the Lord-Mayor being indisposed'.[5] We expect a *florist* to sell flowers as well as to cultivate them and be an expert on them: the first of these senses is missing in the eighteenth century, though it seems the one uppermost in our minds. We prefer *horticulturalist* and *botanist* for the other two. The 'eminent florists in Holland'[6] raised hyacinths; and the Greek poet who made all his flowers 'blow at the same time without regard to their seasons', must have been no good florist.[7]

There is a large slice of social and industrial history wrapped up in the fact that in the eighteenth century a manufacturer was the man who worked with his hands, not a member of the Board of Directors; the employee, not the capitalist, as indeed the etymology of the word must have at first indicated.

[1] *Art of Poetry*, p. 225.
[2] *Crit. Rev.* new arr. xxiii (1798), 473.
[3] *European Mag.* x (1786), 421.
[4] *Essays*, i, 91.
[5] *Ann. Reg.* xi (1768), 167.
[6] *Month. Rev.* ix (1753), 314.
[7] *Gent. Mag.* li (1781), 333.

We may occupy ourselves with any sort of business, and be occupiers of houses—the eighteenth century could have called us housekeepers —but we are not 'occupiers of the glass trade'[1] or any other.

A bookmaker made books, but with no idea of a book for recording bets. That sense is only just 100 years old. The *Monthly Review* of 1760,[2] discussing a biblical commentary, remarked that 'by its publication in sixpenny numbers, and thus taking in the mob of Readers, we are told it has likewise answered *another intention*, which most Book-makers have principally in view'. (*Take in* meaning deceive was in use by the 'forties, but is unlikely here: we should say 'reach', 'be available to'). *Chapman* for us is a surname or a word appropriate to a historical novel, while we use *chaps* colloquially in friendly reference or greeting. In this period it may mean a buyer as well as a seller, which we should not expect. It is interesting to find Dr Johnson commenting on *Love's Labour's Lost*, II. i. 15, 'Not uttered by base sale of chapmen's tongues.' 'Chapman here seems to signify the *seller*, not as now commonly the buyer.' Actually Shakespeare has it in the sense of 'buyer' in *Troilus and Cressida*, IV. i. 75.

The history of the word *American* (and *Canadian*) is a commentary on political development. An American could be what we particularise as an American Indian—the same applies to the Canadian—or a White citizen of the New World, either the continent, or the West Indies— and a Loyalist living in Canada. *American* in reference to the original inhabitants is common. Mrs Piozzi,[3] in the last decade of the century, speaks of 'wild Americans, who hunt the wood and fish the rivers'. Warton,[4] discussing Pope's projected *American Eclogues*, notices rather tartly that the Turks, Persians and Americans of our poets are in reality distinguished from Englishmen only by their turbans and feathers. Ferguson[5] argues that in a primitive stage of culture, there can be nothing to 'distinguish a German or a Briton . . . from an American, who, like him, with his bow and his dart is left to traverse the forest'. The Americans who believe in animism in the *Spectator* (56) are marked as Indians by their beliefs as much as the Americans[6] in Brazil by their 'plume of feathers'. That there could be ambiguity is shown by the note of an author who writes in 1752[7] on 'a fair American—by an American I do not mean an Indian, but one descended of British parents born in America'. Of course now an American need not be of

[1] *Gent. Mag.* xvi (1746), 161.   [2] *Month. Rev.* xxiii (1760), 415.
[3] *Brit. Syn.*, i, 254.   [4] *Essay on Pope*, i, 285.   [5] *Civil Society*, p. 133.
[6] *Ann. Reg.* iv (1761), 106.   [7] *Gent. Mag.* xxii (1752), 281.

British descent. The gay West Indian who is described as 'this American in a Summer-Island Suit' in the *Spectator* (80) is obviously a White. American Intelligence in the *Gentleman's Magazine* of 1793[1] includes news from Quebec—the adjective did not immediately suggest the U.S.A. as we tend to let it do now. One item of news was that H.R.H. Prince Edward was just returned to Quebec after reviewing the Royal Americans. Perhaps the best comment on the growing confident nationalism of the U.S.A. was made by implication in a plan for establishing public schools put forward by a Professor of Chemistry[2] in Pennsylvania and reported in 1786. He advocated training in the classics as 'the best foundation for a correct and extensive knowledge of the language of our Country. Too much pains cannot be taken to teach our youth to read and write our American language with elegance and propriety.'

ADJECTIVES IN CHANGED CONTEXTS

There are numerous adjectives which differ in their application. Things may go awry nowadays: one could put on one's hat awry, but we should not report that the foundations of a building were awry like those of the 'Spaw House' at Scarborough in 1738.[3] We talk lightly of things and people that are the bane of our lives, or more seriously of baneful influences, and we know such plant-names as *henbane* and *leopard's bane*. We do not think of any of them as actual killers, though that is the Germanic meaning of the word. We must recall this if we are not to be puzzled by the remark that laurel 'is in its nature hurtful, and a distillation from it not only poisonous but actually *baneful*'.[4] We should be *chary* of meddling with such a liquid: but what do we make of Defoe's phrase 'this chary piece' Liberty and Property?[5] *Chary* meaning 'requiring care or careful handling' according to *O.E.D.*, is rare; it occurs in Mulcaster in 1581: and *chary* meaning precious has no illustration between Philemon Holland and Sir Walter Scott. But Bailey says it means choice as well as sparing and careful, and there seems no evidence that 'choice' could still mean 'choosy' as in the seventeenth century. The context suggests that the jewel needs constant care if it is not to be lost: and of course that implies it is precious.

[1] *Gent. Mag.* lxiii (1793), 1143.
[2] *Gent. Mag.* lvi (1786), Pt. II, 777.
[3] *Gent. Mag.* viii (1738), January.
[4] *Brit. Syn.*, ii, 68.   [5] *Little Review*, p. 71.

Chastening and *chastized* make us think of punishments: we should never refer to a 'pleasing chastising tint' amid the verdure of foliage[1] or speak of 'a warm but chastized imagination'.[1] *Chaste* would be better now.

We contrast *conscious* with *unconscious*; in everyday use it means physically in command of one's faculties. If we are conscious of this or that, it means we are aware of it in our mind. Both are nineteenth-century developments. In the eighteenth century it can mean 'in the know' as in

> A hint which like the mason's sign
> The conscious can alone define.[2]

This was its earliest sense. *Glossographia Anglicana Nova* says it means 'inwardly guilty', but now one can be conscious of rectitude or innocence. Reid[3] argues that it is improper to say 'I am conscious of the table which is before me; I perceive it, I see it, but do not say I am conscious of it.' We do say it, nevertheless.

We so often apply *deciduous* technically to trees—only one of its botanical and zoological applications—that Erasmus Darwin's 'deciduous day' and 'deciduous shades'[4] jolt us, until we notice that the word literally means 'falling away', and so 'declining'.

If we heard *desultory*, we should expect it to be concerned with thought or discourse, or a walk. We should hardly expect to hear of 'an uneven desultory noise' or of 'desultory or ill-compounded words'. Unmethodical is one sense. There is enlightenment on the word in the *Idler's* story (xix) of Jack Whirler who begins his dinner at home, goes off to a neighbour's, sits down, and then after the soup 'makes a short excuse to the company and continues through another street his desultory dinner'. He is literally jumping from one place to another; but we use the word mainly of abstractions. We might consider Jack's behaviour as undignified. In the eighteenth century *dignified* meant 'advanced to a dignity, especially an ecclesiastical one'—it goes with dignitary, not dignity. The meaning 'stately' dates from the nineteenth century.

'Dogged determination', 'dogged hard work': the adjective implies persistence, fidelity, tenacity, and we approve of them in dog or man.

[1] Gilpin—*Observations relative to the Picturesque*, quoted *Month. Rev.* lxxvii (1788), 316.

[2] Brooke in Chalmers' *English Poets*, xvii, 409.

[3] *Intellectual Powers of Man*, i, 31.

[4] *Botanic Garden*, i, 173: 322.

This sense, says *O.E.D.*, is first found in Dr Johnson in 1779. Its earlier meaning was sullen, surly, crabbed—other canine qualities. Dr John Rutty[1] kept a Spiritual Diary in which he noted with regret his 'doggedness' or the sad fact 'dogged: ate too much'—or that he was 'mechanically and sinfully dogged'.

We should not say that 'undoubtedly the stones of Stonehenge are natural and not fictitious':[2] *fictitious* goes with fiction as an art—or with the inventions of the artful. The contrast here is between natural and artificial or man-made.

It is easy to see that 'im-per-vious' once meant 'where there is no way through', but we use it figuratively rather than of real roads. It could be literal in the eighteenth century. The *Monthly Review*[3] saw that air transport implied 'the gigantic idea of crossing chains of mountains hitherto impervious'; the *Critical Review*[4] spoke of glaciers enclosed 'within the bosom of almost impervious mountains', and a figurative use in which the word is very much alive appears when Felton[5] writes 'Your Lordship need not wonder, that fine Countries have strait Avenues [i.e. narrow approaches] when the Regions of Happiness, like those of Knowledge, are impervious and shut to lazy Travellers.' The non-scientist might agree that water is 'absolutely incomprehensible', but when Adam Smith[6] used the word, he meant that by nature water cannot be compressed, not that it cannot be understood.

Inanimate seems never to be used now as the opposite of *animated* but Sylas Neville[7] once heard a bishop preach an inanimate sermon.

Lucid to us suggests argument, style, or the lucid intervals of the mentally ill. It may still mean 'bright' for the poet, and in the eighteenth century was a favourite epithet for the spheres, floods, snow, meteors, eyes, mother-of-pearl; but it could also be used in plain prose. In the periodicals we read of comets with lucid tails; and of a storm during which some people affirmed that they saw several flashes of lightning, that the sky seemed to separate and that 'terrible lucid streams emitted from the openings'.[8]

Mawkish we use of style and taste, but they used to be able to say that a drunkard goes senseless to bed and rises mawkish in the morning[9] suffering from satiety, not 'causing' it.

[1] Quoted, *Crit. Rev.* 43 (1777), 204–6.   [2] *Gent. Mag.* lxi (1791), 53.
[3] *Month. Rev.* lxix (1783), 560.   [4] *Crit. Rev.* 41 (1776), 369.
[5] *On Reading the Classics*, 12.   [6] *Works*, v, 340.   [7] *Diary*, p. 175.
[8] *New Universal Mag.* Feb. 1756, p. 78.   [9] *Connoisseur*, lxxxii.

Our modern indiscriminate use of *nice* could easily lead us to wrong interpretations of older writing. If the Dog is 'an animal of the nicest smell'[1] we might say it depends on the dog; of course it means 'keenest'. Our difficulty is that often the modern meaning makes sense —but not the right sense, or enough sense. It isn't an expression of general approval—indeed we fail to use it *nicely* in the earlier sense of that adverb. A 'nice and delicate reader',[2] 'a nice correspondence in the sound' of rhymes[3] all imply exactness—the reader is exacting, the rhymes exact.

'Young readers are seldom very nice as to manner, provided the matter does but afford them amusement'[4]—probably a true remark, which could now be much more uncomplimentary than it is. A chisel could be nice;[5] chess, according to Dr Johnson,[6] is a nice and abstruse game; the tongue is a nice organ;[7] people who weave 'gradated' colours into every flower and leaf are 'the nicest needleworkers'.[8] The *Annual Register*[9] reports a forged note which 'was so nicely executed' that the cashier could hardly tell the true from the false. Shebbeare[10] talks of a cry of hounds so nicely taught that they would quit the prey in full chase. Then there is the expert on wines who would not pretend to a tolerable palate if he couldn't distinguish 'the Wines of France from those of Portugal; and if he is perfectly nice, he will tell you, with his Eyes shut what Province, what Mountain supplied the Liquor'.[11]

The sense of 'ticklish' appears in Boswell's[12] dictum that 'elections are very nice things', and in the *Gentleman's Magazine's*[13] remark about the 'nice trial' of a man who killed a person that assisted at an arrest, under the sanction of a special warrant. Dr Johnson says that *nice* often implies a culpable delicacy—or fastidiousness; this is what is meant by the poor man whose wife, of a very nice and delicate disposition, carried out so many nice operations that every room was filled with soap and brickdust.[14] The Chintz Bedroom was too nice for a dirty country squire. He admits he is far from being a nice man [i.e. a fussy one] yet he prefers his own dirt to other people's! Dr Johnson defines a minx as a nice trifling girl—clearly not a nice girl in our sense. But when he comments on *Antony and Cleopatra*, III. xii. 180, he

[1] *Month. Rev.* ii (1749), 112.
[2] *Month. Rev.* iii (1750), 363.
[3] *Month. Rev.* x (1754), 218.
[4] *Month. Rev.* xxv (1762), 229.
[5] Darwin, *Botanic Garden*, ii, 100.
[6] Dictionary, s.v. *Chess*.
[7] Burke's *Sublime and Beautiful*, p. 295.
[8] Hogarth, *Analysis*, p. 97.
[9] *Ann. Reg.* xxx (1788), 195.
[10] *Letters*, ii, 99.
[11] *Englishman*, 7.
[12] *London Journal*, p. 172.
[13] *Gent. Mag.* xxix (1759), 423.
[14] *Babler*, lxxiii.

considers that nice means not delicate and courtly as Warburton
thought, but rather 'just fit for my purpose'. 'So we vulgarly say of
anything that is done better than was expected, it is nice.' Here we are
ready for 'the best share of every nicer dish' or 'a nice shoulder of
lamb'. Nowadays, does *nice* mean any more than 'I like it'? There is
more than that in Uvedale Price's[1] remark that any one 'who can make
a nice asparagus bed, has one of the most essential qualifications of an
improver, and may soon learn the whole mystery of slopes and hanging
levels'. It is a perfectly arranged bed, not merely one that looks pretty
or produces tasty asparagus.

In the eighteenth century Swift's aphorism that a nice man is a man
of nasty ideas was not the paradox it seems now, since *nice* means
squeamish. Pope's *Essay on Criticism* affords the right comment when
he bids us

> shun their fault, who, scandalously nice
> Will needs mistake an author into vice.

Authors who excel 'in giving minute pictures of manners, and of the
nice features of character'[2] could include many features far from nice
in our sense. And when Junius[3] remarks 'You have nice feelings, my
Lord, if we may judge from your resentment', he is not crediting the
Duke of Bedford with anything we should call nice feelings today, but
only with being easily annoyed.

It is clear that *nice* must be judged by its context.

We talk of both *oral* vaccines, and *oral* delivery: but when we read
of an 'oral injunction' we naturally expect it to be by word of mouth.
Actually it means an injunction relating to the mouth—'to keep it
religiously clean'.[4]

It is disconcerting that *plastic* has ceased to be mainly the property
of poets and philosophers, and come into the hands of manufacturers
and advertisers, and indeed of all of us for our domestic concerns. 'The
poet's plastic soul',[5] 'Earth's fair orb shap'd by the plastic flood',[6]
metal brightening into fame under plastic hands,[7] are preserved by their
context. But it requires strength of mind to react properly to Mason's[8]
exhortation to

> take thy plastic spade,
> It is thy pencil.

[1] *Essay*, i, 125.
[2] *Lounger* (49).
[3] *Letters*, i, 181.
[4] *Month. Rev.* xxiv (1761), 145.
[5] Stockdale *Inquiry*, p. 78.
[6] Jago in Chalmers' *English Poets*, xvii, 288.
[7] ibid., p. 302.
[8] *English Garden*, i, 275.

And 'the art which goes under the technical name of Plastick'—i.e. 'founding metal, papier maché, wood, earthenware', seems to include everything but what Plastic means to us.[1]

Spirituous now primarily suggests 'liquor', a sense developed in the eighteenth century: but it was not the only sense, and it gives us something of a jolt when Young[2] writes that the 'Ode, as it is the eldest kind of poetry, so it is more spirituous and more remote from prose than any other'.

'I am become so stout,' says a gentleman in 1745,[3] 'I can travel in any manner. Three days ago I walk'd five miles to dinner.' Becoming stout to our minds is no qualification for a five-mile walk: but the adjective merely means strong with no reference to size. If a rake is a 'poor *unweildy* wretch'[4] the adjective refers to his moral lack of self-control, not to any bodily awkwardness.

Strident, says Ash's Dictionary, is stridulous, making a small noise. Strident tones now make a loud one. The basic sense is creaking, which, used of grasshoppers, gives rise to Ash's definition. Before the nineteenth century it was a dictionary word, but it is not in Johnson. Thackeray gives *O.E.D.*'s first example of it used of a voice, which is what it is commonly associated with today.

Outmoded schoolboy slang may stand between us and a word used seriously, when an almanac in 1718 prognosticates some *topping* Priest in danger of death,[5] or the *Guardian* (174) describes a '*topping* Ben Johnson in Lawrel'.

If here we read too little, we may read too much into *transient* which for us has a serious aura, something of the colour of 'Sic transit gloria mundi'. Nothing of this is implied by the *Critical Review*'s[6] statement that an author takes a transient view of the present state of the nation, or only once transiently refers to a matter—it is 'in passing', literally.

We have decided that *various* shall imply plurality as well as variety —or in preference to it, and so we expect it to construct with a plural noun, as indeed it could do in the eighteenth century. But it could mean changeable, fluctuating, inconstant—not necessarily in any derogatory sense. 'Various people' to us does not necessarily mean other than several: the idea of varying was stronger 200 years ago. So, 'Mr Cowper is extremely various'[7]—versatile in manner and subjects: birds

[1] Wendeborn, *View*, ii, 221.   [2] *Lyric Poetry*, p. 57.
[3] Dickins and Stanton, p. 114.   [4] *Tatler* (27).
[5] *Merlinus Liberatus*, November.
[6] *Crit. Rev.* 48 (1779), 222.   [7] *Gent. Mag.* lvi (1786), 5.

swell their various throat—the multicoloured feathers—or sing their various lay. The 'various child of man'[1] implies human variety: nature's various face stresses her multifariousness. A various reading is what we call a variant reading. There is some food for thought in Elphinston's lines

> As various culture tempers various clay,
> So various tempers various rule obey.[2]

Frederick the Great was admired as a man and a philosopher 'unallayed by the king and unsullied by the warrior':[3] *unallayed* suggests to us fears or doubts, and so sets our minds off on the wrong track. In eighteenth-century usage *unallayed* was still undifferentiated from the *unalloyed* we use for the pleasant and desirable.

MISLEADING VERBS

It is perhaps characteristic of eighteenth-century dogmatism over against modern enquiry that to *ascertain* then meant 'to assert for certain', and specifically to fix price, measure or weight, whereas to us the stress is on the *process* of finding out certainty. Soame Jenyns[4] talks of ascertaining Judges' salaries where we should say fixing them: and we should doubt whether we could ascertain the reputation of dead authors beyond re-appraisal.[5]

Our acquaintance with *discarded* clothes today may lead us to read a too vague tone into statements that a Captain was discarded after a serious crime[6] or that Jupiter discarded the deities out of heaven.[7] It is to discharge from service, not merely to lay aside. We might dispense with people's services and so completely misunderstand the remark that it is only on the principle of the English delight in compounds that the expression 'listless limbs' can be *dispensed with*.[8] The critic believes, wrongly, that *list* must be a verb, and that *listless* is as odd as *thinkless* would be. He means, therefore, that we 'put up with' such expressions, whereas he would clearly prefer 'to dispense with them' in our sense of doing without them. To disengage oneself from monastic vows was 'a liberty Sir Thomas More thought no man could conscientiously

---

[1] Brooke in Chalmers' *English Poets*, xvii, 406.
[2] *Education*, iii, 57–8.   [3] *Ann. Reg.* i (1758), 237.
[4] *Works*, ii, 202.   [5] Clara Reeve, *Progress of Romance*, ii, 4.
[6] *Gent. Mag.* xv (1745), 51.
[7] *Spect.* (389).   [8] *Month. Rev.* xx (1759), 8.

dispense with', says Shebbeare,[1] another sentence that to the twentieth-century reader suggests the opposite of what it means. But we should here remember that one may obtain a dispensation.

Discover now, like *ascertain*, implies finding out something new—continents, planets, scientific or historical fact. So it did in the eighteenth century, but beside this sense was the older one of *uncover, reveal, display*. So dress, furniture and equipage will discover a good or bad taste;[2] a picture could discover naked skin;[3] another prediction in *Merlinus Liberatus* declares that 'the Parties will not discover their true Interests or be open and clear one with another'. God 'keeps his Creatures in Suspense, neither discovering nor hiding himself'.[4] Pope did not discover 'any great degree of genius for painting', but he did discover poetic enthusiasm.[5]

Those who 'discover, that they hope, by cruelty, to wring the payment from their friends' are not finding out the depth of their villainy but making it manifest;[6] similarly 'the resentment will burn on in secret of which shame hinders the discovery'.[7] If you praise an author you have never read, don't be too minute on any particulars you may have heard of him, for fear of discovering that you have *only* heard of them.[8] Sometimes the senses of finding out and revealing appear at close quarters. Gildon[9] says he cannot discover how a good translation makes a good poet—and then adds that a poet must 'discover a supream Judgment and Genius'.

'Children discover the rudiments of taste'—surely 'give signs of it'. But Gerard[10] goes on to notice that they are very quick in discovering oddity and highly entertained with the discovery of it. Does that mean that they enjoy making fun of it, or that they are pleased they have noticed it? Either sense (or both together) would do in the anecdote[11] of the child who was believed to have a golden tooth: a silver-smith 'discovered' it to be an ordinary tooth to which some gold leaves had been applied. He did this by unexpectedly surprising the child's mouth—incidentally a good example of *surprise* meaning 'take by surprise'. The *unexpectedly* is surely needless.

[1] *Letters*, i, 59.   [2] Gerard, *Essay on Taste*, p. 93.
[3] *Universal Spectator*, quoted *Gent. Mag.* iv (1734), 245.
[4] *Spect.* (635).
[5] Gerard, *Genius*, p. 433. Warton, *Essay on Pope*, i, 24.
[6] *Idler* (22).   [7] *Idler* (23).   [8] *World* (107).
[9] *Art of Poetry*, Introd. p. xv.
[10] Gerard, *Essay on Taste*, p. 93.
[11] *Gent. Mag.* iii (1733), 84, from *Grub St Journal*.

No wonder a gentleman of the law in 1757 took exception to the formula of the oath required of recruits for the Militia:

'I, A.B., do swear that I shall and will, at all times, prevent and discover, with intent to prevent . . . all treasons . . . which I shall know or credibly hear of.'

'It is scarce conceivable', he writes to the *Monthly Review*,[1] 'how so much nonsense could be crowded in such a narrow compass. Not to mention the shocking impropriety of making a man swear that he *shall* do any act, We would ask the Author, with what safety of conscience any one can *swear* that he shall and will *discover* treasons, etc.? The word *discover* is too equivocal an expression to be used in this place: it often means to *find out*; and no man alive can swear that he shall and will *find out* treasons etc.'

But ought not a legal formula to be explained, and taken according to the meaning intended? The law still uses *discover* in the sense of reveal: in September 1961 a man was sentenced at Bedford Quarter Sessions[2] for failing to report the fact that his brother had committed a crime—i.e. for 'concealing, keeping secret and neglecting to discover it'—in other words, for misprision of felony.

'Tea exploded' says the index to the *Gentleman's Magazine*, volume vii.[3] It would make a striking headline: we could imagine the paragraph to go with it—a booby-trap, a concealed home-made bomb. The entry merely directs attention to an attack on the bad properties of tea, a drink which moralists like Jonas Hanway delighted to debunk. *To explode*, says *Glossographia Anglicana Nova*, remembering its etymology, is to hiss or cry down. For Dyche and Pardon it is to find fault with, expose, render contemptible. So we read of exploding plum porridge,[4] or the explosion of the Dutch manner of gardening,[5] of words that have been exploded[6] and solecisms that ought to be.[7] The high explosive sense which seems to us the obvious one comes for the verb only in the 'nineties. *Explosion* in this sense appears in the 'forties, and the adjective *explosive* not till nearly the end of the century.

Supply is so often used now to mean *provide*, without any thought of replacement, that we could miss the point of the criticism on one of our forerunners in this use who wrote

> The bright subject, tow'ring high
> Shall meaner requisites supply

[1] *Month. Rev.* xvii (1757), 568.   [2] Case of R. *v.* Tudor Davies.
[3] (1737).   [4] *World* (103).   [5] Knox, *Essays*, ii, 301.
[6] *Month. Rev.* iv (1751), 520.   [7] *Crit. Rev.* 57 (1784), 479.

on which the *Gentleman's Magazine*[1] remarks that requisites are said to be supplied, instead of the want of them. So eighteenth-century writers supply defects, and define the word as 'to make up what was wanting'. So we read[2] of a step-mother whose step-daughter didn't know how to behave, and wasn't fit to be seen; the lady chose rather to conceal the girl's defects by excluding her from company, than to supply them by putting her to a boarding schoool. Dodsley,[3] in his lines on Agriculture, thinks that 'Toil's unceasing hand' may 'supply the dunghill's sordid and extraneous aid'. He has given the argument against manuring, so *supply* here means 'do instead of', not 'furnish'.

To *want* began with the meaning 'to lack'; but as we like to have what we haven't got when it is pleasant, the sense easily slides into 'desire'. In this period it can clearly mean to 'lack' here and to 'desire' there, and it is sometimes ambiguous. As the century wears on, English speakers came to feel the older sense was Scottish.[4] 'To lack' is obviously the meaning when we read 'You will not contend that mankind want a taste for that which they all desire',[5] or when John Wesley[6] castigates those 'Men of fair speech and Behaviour, who want nothing of Godliness but the Power, nothing of Religion but the Spirit.' Either sense would be valid in the reflection that gaming 'will ever be the pleasure of the rich, while men . . . fancy more happiness in being possessed of what they want, than they experience pleasure in the fruition of what they have'.[7]

We should be unlikely to see anything ambiguous in the lines from an Elegy to the Memory of a worthy Family in Westmorland—

> A hand to give and pity to relieve,
> Was all they wanted, and they wish'd no more—

à propos of which the *Critical Review*[8] asks 'Are we to understand by this that they neither pitied nor wished to relieve the wretched?'

'To take place' now is to occur: 'to take pride of place' or 'first place' may help us to notice that earlier the unadorned phrase meant 'to take precedence' or 'to take effect'. We could easily be caught out by the remark that 'Spires were never used till the Saracen mode took place',[9] or that 'the learn'd, the able, and disinterested Historian' took

---

[1] *Gent. Mag.* xxxvii (1767), 561.

[2] *Adventurer* (7).   [3] *Agriculture*, ii, 83–4.

[4] e.g. *Crit. Rev.* 53 (1782), 243, re *Observations on the Scottish Dialect*, by John Sinclair.

[5] Usher, *Clio*, p. 6.   [6] *Sermons*, p. 93.   [7] *Life of Beau Nash*, p. 22.

[8] *Crit. Rev.* 62 (1786), 422.   [9] Warton, *Fairy Queen*, ii, 195.

place,[1] or when a critic admits 'so many concur in this last Reading that I am very much in doubt whether it ought not to take place'.[2]

The Duke of Richmond's tame wolf broke his chain, nature took place and he marched off to the country.[3] The phrase is more literal in an account of an exchange of shots between an officer of justice and a criminal—'Both their Balls took Place, and both immediately expired'[4]—a sentence that depends more on common sense than on the efficient use of our pronouns.

CHANGED ADVERBIAL USAGE

There is a small group of adverbs that could mislead the unwary reader. *Immediately* and *occasionally* have developed their temporal elements more strongly now. We should hardly define 'to broil' as Dyche and Pardon do—'to roast meat upon the coals immediately, or mediately upon a gridiron laid upon the coals'—a statement which lights up both adverbs. *Occasional* meant 'suitable to the occasion' and its adverb follows it, but as the occasion may be a rare occurrence, the idea of 'infrequently', 'now and then', gains ground. Occasional tables are for particular occasions, naturally not everyday events. We should never call a kitchen table occasional, though it certainly serves for 'necessary business', which is Dyche and Pardon's definition of *occasion*. The adverb could be modernised into 'as the occasion arises' when Warton[5] says 'incidental imitations of romance' in the *Fairie Queene* will be pointed out occasionally. So with Dyche and Pardon's definition of *salvatory* as 'a surgeon's little box in which are put various sorts of salve, ointment, etc., to be used occasionally'. When Waterland[6] says St Paul's doctrine of the Eucharist is of great moment, 'tho but occasionally delivered', he means 'for a specific reason at a particular time'. Both ideas, of cause and time, may well be combined when the *European Magazine*[7] of 1787 deplores the lack of an index in a new edition of the *Tatler*—it makes it difficult for 'the numerous class of readers who take up such books for the mere purpose of consulting them occasionally'.

Doubtless now suggests if not a doubt, at least a lack of conviction, just as, so the cynic claims, 'to be frank' implies concealment, and

---

[1] Shaftesbury, *Characteristics*, i, 224.
[2] *Spect.* (470).   [3] *Ann. Reg.* xiii (1770), 104.
[4] *Tatler* (172).   [5] op. cit., i, 55.   [6] *Review*, p. 267.   [7] xi, 334.

'Honestly, . . .' a lie. But Elphinston[1] had no doubts about the Roman historian's greatness when he wrote

> Sage copious *Livy* proves the roman theme,
> Of Rome's recorders doubtless the supream,

nor had Duff[2] any doubt when he said Newton 'was doubtless in Philosophy an original Genius of the first rank'. So does our state of mind influence our words, whether it be one of bluff, deceit or uncertainty.

Practically seems to be loosening its link with *practice*. We often use it to mean 'more or less', 'nearly'—starting from the approximation in 'It'll do in practice', which implies that it falls short of ideal theory. The construction of arched bridges, according to Uvedale Price,[3] is 'a practice in building, with which every common stone-mason is practically acquainted'.

Of course has changed its tone. The eighteenth-century meaning was likely to be 'in due course', 'in the natural order', 'as a logical consequence' and often 'according to convention'. The modern overtones may variously imply 'Whatever do you ask that for?'; 'How could you doubt it?'; 'I grant that'; 'What else do you expect?'—and frequently in society columns 'I must assume out of politeness that you know who I'm talking about, but I don't really suppose you do, so let's make sure'—the tone of 'Miss X is of course a cousin of Lord Y.'

'He had no illness, but the wheels of the machine being worn out, it stopt of course.' So wrote Lackington[4] of John Wesley's death. Richardson[5] thinks of a less peaceful course of events when he says of a sick man, 'His surgeon took him first, a fever next, then his doctor, and then, as it were of course, death.' 'An animal whose body is at rest, and who does not reflect, must be disposed to sleep, of course.'[6] The ancients considered speech as the substance and writing as the shadow which followed it of course.[7] If you make a rattle jingle, music comes of course.[8] In ancient Rome every citizen whose fortune amounted to 400,000 sesterces was inrolled of course as a knight.[9] William the Conqueror's absolute dominion devolved of course upon his

[1] *Education*, iii, 217–18.   [2] *On Genius*, p. 119.
[3] *Essay*, ii, 329. On *Architecture and Building*.
[4] *Memoirs*, p. 186.   [5] *Familiar Letters*, lxxvi.
[6] Quoted by Dugald Steward, *Elements*, p. 311, from Jefferson's *Notes on Virginia*.
[7] *Month. Rev.* lxiii (1780), 244.   [8] Churchill, *Gotham*, ii, 10.
[9] Reynolds' Reading Notes, quoted Hilles, p. 203.

successors.[1] Parliament, at the end of its term, expires of course.[2] It would be easy to mistake the tone of the coach driver who says 'I shall stop of course at the White Horse'—it is the scheduled stop.[3]

All these suggest a natural, social, or legal order of consequences. There is nothing offhand in Cowper's lines[4]

> Man's obligations infinite, of course
> His life should prove that he perceives their force.

'What happens naturally and what cannot be avoided' are both implied in Vicesimus Knox's[5] account of the man who came on a hovel where the wife had died in childbirth, leaving a husband and seven children: if 'he had not seen the case, it would have passed on as a common affair and a thing of course'.

The idea of the conventional is frequent. Sermons and charges at the ordination of the dissenting clergy are things of course; and generally consist of nothing but trite observations—i.e. they are always happening and there isn't much new to say, at least in the opinion of the *Critical Review*.[6]

There are constant complaints about 'words of course'—the formulae the occasion requires. So 'the modes of address and politeness though the terms are expressive of the profoundest respect and homage, yet through constant use and frequency of repetition, soon degenerate into mere verbal forms and *words of course*'.[7] Common expletives, like 'upon my word', 'upon my honour', 'whatever sense they might formerly bear, are at present understood as words of course without meaning'.[8] A visitor frightens an invalid by telling him he doesn't look well. 'It is no excuse', says the *Gentleman's Magazine*,[9] 'to say "I meant no harm, and they were words of course." These words *of course*, as they are called, do more execution sometimes than a bad shot from the mouth of a cannon.'

The most interesting comment on 'words of course' comes from Lord Chief Justice Mansfield.[10] During court proceedings arising from the publication of the *Letters of Junius*, 'in his charge to the jury, he said they had nothing to do with the *intention*, nor with the other words in the information, such as *malicious*, *seditious*, etc. which he affirmed

[1] Hurd, *Dialogues*, ii, 103–4.   [2] *Letters of Junius*, pp. iii–iv.
[3] Graves, *Columella*, ii, 235.   [4] *Truth*, i, 197–8.
[5] *Essays*, ii, 274.   [6] *Crit. Rev.* 41 (1776), 76.
[7] *Month. Rev.* xlv (1771), 234. Cp. *Spect.* (103).   [8] *Connoisseur*, cviii.
[9] *Gent. Mag.* lxi (1791), 137.   [10] *Ann. Reg.* xiii (1770), 117.

were words of course: just as it is said in an indictment for *murder*, *that the person* did, etc., at the instigation of *the devil.* . . .'

Legal language is notoriously archaic: but surely this use of strong adjectives which are to be taken to mean nothing must have brought it into disrepute.

EPILOGUE

'STYLE and manner', said the *British Critick*[1] in 1793, 'are, from the fabrication of our language, and its present cultivated state, so readily attainable, that it is perhaps rather a disgrace to want, than a merit to possess them; but the diffusion of this attainment beyond the Atlantic, and to commercial men, reflects a lustre on the present age, and greatly tends to confirm our hope that the English language will survive the ravages of time, and be looked up to by future nations with the same reverence that we now pay to the classical dialects of antiquity.' It is a credo of optimism. The critic was reviewing a history of the West Indies, by a gentleman of those parts. He could hardly have foreseen the growth of American literature and the use of English for official and cultural purposes in many African states: and Austral English was barely born. The hope that English might take the place of the Classics must become a reality in our present system of education if the best thought of Western Civilisation is to be preserved and handed on in this age of diminishing Latin and vanishing Greek. What was once patriotic piety is now plain necessity, and in our situation we must cultivate the mother-tongue if no other, preserving what is good in it, transforming what is bad in it, and developing it wherever growth is needed.

The *British Critick*'s words themselves show that changes come— here *fabrication* has no hint of deceit, and when the writer says 'it is rather a disgrace to want them' we could easily suppose him to mean that it would be somewhat disgraceful to wish for a good style and manner, or that the phrase 'style and manner' stands for a mannerism we should be better without.

And this process of shift in meaning and use is the outstanding lesson we learn from any prolonged look at words and their ways.

We cannot always see why the change should have taken place. 'A large man', says Trusler,[2] 'is as great an impropriety as a big field: and we need only mention a *big* or *large* pleasure to show the absurdity'. We agree about the pleasure (though a welcome can be big) but not

---

[1] *Brit. Crit.* ii, 1.

[2] *Synonyms.* For fuller discussion see *Encyclopedia Britannica*, 1773. s.v. *Dictionaries*.

about the field. But the large man is now big in physique, while the big man may be small as to frame but big in importance, though he may not. We are indeed more willing to accept variety of idiom. Eighteenth-century purists[1] disapprove of 'Act *one*, scene *three*' instead of 'Act the *first*, Scene the *third*'—we prefer the shorter form, but should not think the longer incorrect.

Dr Johnson tells us in his Dictionary that the plural form *wages* is the only form used in his time: we have invented living wage, wage-rate, wage-slave. The language does not stand still. Nor are we bound by the categorical dicta of our ancestors. 'We cannot say "I have come"', says the *Gentleman's Magazine*[2] in 1775—we can if we want to, making a subtle distinction between 'I am come' (Here I am) and 'I have come' which suggests some additional or explanatory clause to follow. As a matter of fact 'have come' is on record from at least the early sixteenth century.

'*People*', says the purist,[3] 'cannot be connected with a determinate number: as for instance, four, five, or six people: but . . . *persons* may.' To us, 'six people' sounds natural and friendly—'six persons' sounds like a legal document or a public notice. To Trusler, *tired* is stronger than *weary*, and to Adam Smith[4] *intolerable* is stronger than *insufferable*. We seem to have attached *weary* more to the spirit than the body and *insufferable* to people rather than to things: do degrees of intensity enter into these pairs now?

Laughing at strange words has been a pastime at least since the fifteenth century: it is at once chastening and instructive to note that what is ridiculous to one age is accepted in another. The critic[5] who found Dr Johnson's style full of 'deformities' tells us that he has consulted men of eminent learning who disown all acquaintance with such words as *aberrant, abrasion, abstention, adulation, amalgamate, angularity, anthology, Archaeology, articulateness, Austral.* He laughs too at *turpitude, nefarious, repercussion, resuscitation, homogeneous, celebrity, hilarity, concatenation, mercantile, implacable.* None of these would cause any worry to an educated man now—and education is much more widely spread than in Mr Callender's time. The *Critical Review*[6] said no more than the truth when it remarked that 'our

---

[1] *Month. Rev.* xxiii (1760), 9.
[2] *Gent. Mag.* xlv, Critical Remarks on Lowth's English Grammar.
[3] Trusler, op. cit.   [4] *Lectures on Rhetoric*, ii.
[5] Callender, *Deformities of Dr Johnson*, p. 182.
[6] *Crit. Rev.* xxi, 30, re Johnson's edition of Shakespeare.

language has not only migrated from place to place, but from rank to rank of subjects. Terms that in Shakespeare's time were familiar to a peer, are now common with a cobler'—thanks of course to Shakespeare, the Press and the Radio.

It is clear that the people of a given age can be trusted to know, if only in broad outline, about what comes within their own experience. But they cannot necessarily be trusted where historical evidence is required. If they say that an expression is low, or fashionable, we can trust them if they are persons of judgment. If they say it is rare, we can trust them if they are people of education who move in the world at large. But, we cannot assume they are right if they say it is new, unheard of before; it may be new only to them. Universal affirmatives and negatives are easy but dangerous—there was no *Oxford English Dictionary* in the eighteenth century to offer guidance to date and usage. We have no such excuse,[1] and can profit from our ancestors' slips. People who, for instance, believe that *Commando, Concentration Camps* and *camouflage* date from the Second World War could correct themselves if they used the right authorities. So could those purists who insist that *none* must *always* be constructed with a singular verb, and that *between* must never be used of more than two. There is no getting away from George Campbell's conclusion that we cannot learn 'ideal grammar'—every language, he points out, offends the grammar of every other at some point. In formulating our own ideal of correctness, we are entitled to appeal to 'the tribunal of use, as to the supreme authority, and consequently, in every grammatical controversy, this is the last resort'. Grammarians' laws and decisions are second to it, and 'this order of subordination ought never, on any account to be reversed'.[2] Of course, the questions inevitably follow—Whose use? Why theirs? How do we know what it is? Campbell's answer is that the use must be *reputable, national,* and *present,* and though again none of these terms is definable with mathematical precision, they do give us a general guide. We must agree, too, with Mrs Piozzi[3] that there are 'niceties of language that books never teach, and conversation alone can establish'.

Looking back, it may give us a salutary jolt to see forerunners of our worse selves in various eighteenth-century pillories. It seems unlikely that nowadays 'a person of no mean appearance' who has mislaid

[1] I can only hope I am not here condemning myself.
[2] *Phil. of Rhet.,* ii, 139–41.
[3] *Brit. Syn.,* ii, 29.

his hat at a ball, supposing he took one, would call out 'Pray, Gentle-men, has not nobody seen never a hat nowhere?'[1] So crass a violation of modern grammar doesn't touch us—but what about our expletives, our hesitancies, our pet phrases? Mr Spectator[2] tells us of a man who invited half a dozen friends, each with a pet phrase, to listen to each other and observe how silly the constant repetitions sounded—'as, *d'ye hear me, d'ye see, that is, and so Sir*'.

Inexpert speakers still do it—'Well, you know, I mean to say, it's like this, sort of.' Officials might still write 'till such time as' though I doubt whether any of us would waste time introducing a remark with 'if so be in case as how'[3]—which is said to have been 'not uncommon with people above the middle class as well in rank as in understanding'.

There are, too, plenty of moderns, jingoistic, ignorant, inarticulate, like the armchair critic[4] who knew how he would use our troops abroad: 'I'd land them; and then I'd ambuscade all the Spaniards' back settle-ment; and take from them all their (... you know what I mean well enough, all their—all them damn'd hard names mentioned in the newspapers).'

The eighteenth century did not level out varieties of speech, regional or social, and neither have we done so. We know more about them, thanks to travel, broadcasting and both the exigencies and the opportunities of the world we live in. We should hardly now regret that a modern Burns should write in a provincial dialect difficult to read. But there is something to be said for Thomas Sheridan's[5] idea that if all the subjects of the crown spoke with the same accent we should be in a fair way to heal many of our social divisions. Our solu-tion seems rather to be in accepting far more varieties of English as culturally and socially good. And we are growing out of irrational objections to Scots and American.

Looking back, it is exciting to see how easily the language rises to the occasion. We are never finally at a loss for words even if sometimes their coming is long delayed. Once the eighteenth century had in-vented *aeronaut* the twentieth would have no difficulty in providing itself with *cosmonaut*. On a more earthy level, the eighteenth century saw that a new expert had arrived whom it called a civil engineer:[6] after that, it was easy, as science developed, to produce and name the electrical engineers and the mechanical and aeronautical ones.

[1] *Gent. Mag.* xxxiv (1764), 559.   [2] *Spect.* (371).
[3] *Gent. Mag.* as above.   [4] *Gent. Mag.* xxxv (1765), 404.
[5] *Lectures on Elocution*, p. 249.   [6] See *O.E.D.* s.v. *Engineer*.

We have seen that the language reflects our beliefs and values too. There is an account,[1] surely shocking in every way to us, of a small girl who ran amok and killed two younger children. She was executed in the public square in the presence of the local school-children collected there to see this *exemplary* punishment. True, it happened (in 1768) in Munich and not in England—but the English report uses the tell-tale adjective. It is some measure of the gulf between their thinking and ours. But have we no expressions of our own that condemn us out of our own mouths? What will the future think of 'preventive war' or 'clean' bombs?

Comments on the meaninglessness of political terms and the degradation of *patriotism* may sound strange to our politically less corrupt and more internationally-minded age—and we have *jingoism* to help to distinguish false patriotism from true. But we cannot forget our own use of smear-words and indeed that it is we who feel the need for that term.

History, which sets events and ideas in perspective, tends to correct period aberrations, leaving the older language behind. So with *Protestant*. The eighteenth century was well aware of its historical origins in sixteenth-century Germany, but in 1787, the *Gentleman's Magazine*[2] was remarking that the name 'seems now to be confined to those who protest against the Christian religion itself . . . and call those doctrines erroneous which have been held by the Church . . . in all ages'. However many varying beliefs are held within Protestant Christendom, that is no longer true in so sweeping a form. Point of view words, doctrinal words (whether religious or political) are amongst the hardest to tie down. They are the chameleons of the vocabulary. For 'words, by representing ideas, become the picture of our thoughts, and communicate them with the greatest fidelity. But they are not only the signs of sensible ideas [i.e. mental pictures of things perceptible to the senses], they exhibit the very image, and distinguishing likeness of the mind that uses them.'[3]

Dr Johnson wishes that the elements of our language 'might obtain the firmness and immutability of the primogenial and constituent particles of matter, that they might retain their substance while they alter their appearance, and be varied and compounded, yet not destroyed'. But he recognises that though 'art may sometimes prolong' the duration of words, 'it will rarely give them perpetuity, and their changes

[1] *Gent. Mag.* xxxviii (1768), 345.
[2] *Gent. Mag.* lvii (1787), 870.   [3] James Usher, *Clio*, p. 83.

will be almost always informing us that language is the work of man, of a being from whom permanence and stability cannot be derived'.[1]

And yet, change there must be, unless we are to be stultified, regimented, brain-washed and turned into robots. The Protean shape is a shape of life: English changes as occasion calls, elusive but, we ought to hope, undying. It is only dead languages that never change.

[1] *Plan of an English Dictionary*, in Murphy's edition, pp. 17, 18.

APPENDIX

A NOTE ON EIGHTEENTH-CENTURY PERIODICALS

In the eighteenth century, periodicals of every kind proliferated. They appeared daily, weekly, monthly, annually, at other regular intervals, or intermittently, and they might be political, scientific, literary, broadly informative or purely entertaining. Some ran for a long time with several changes of title. Some lasted for a month or two; some, like the *Monthly Review* and the *Critical Review*, survived into the next century: the *Gentleman's Magazine* lasted into this century; the *Annual Register* reached its bicentenary in 1958 and is still triumphantly with us; so are the *Transactions of the Royal Society*, first published in 1665.

Some periodicals were the projects of famous men—for example, Defoe's *Review*, Addison and Steele's *Spectator*, Fielding's *Champion*, Goldsmith's short-lived *Bee*, Johnson's *Rambler* and *Idler*. Some commanded the services of famous men—for example Smollett in the *Critical Review*, Chesterfield in the *World*, Burke in the *Annual Register*.

It was in 1731 that Edward Cave ('Sylvanus Urban') founded the *Gentleman's Magazine*, which set the pattern for many miscellanies. At first it merely collected extracts from other periodicals, but soon, on Samuel Johnson's advice, it began to present news (including obituaries, promotions, market prices and weather reports), and to provide a poetry section, reviews of books, antiquarian articles and mathematical problems. Johnson and Goldsmith both wrote for it.

The London Magazine was a venture in business rivalry with Cave, brought out by a group of publishers in 1732 and lasting for over fifty years. Hawkesworth's bi-weekly *Adventurer*, to which Johnson also contributed, ran for two years; the *World* was a challenge to it supported by Chesterfield and Soame Jenyns. Johnson replied with his *Idler* in 1758.

The *Town and Country Magazine* 1769–96 had a taste for scandal (with engravings of the parties involved) and fiction. In 1749 Ralph Griffiths saw the need for a more strictly literary periodical and issued the *Monthly Review*. His staff of reviewers were experts in their special fields, and their articles were lavishly illustrated with extracts from the books they dealt with. In politics they were mainly Whig, in religious affiliation non-conformist, so it was natural that in 1756 the *Critical Review* should be founded in the interests of the Tory party and the Church of England, though its founder was the Edinburgh printer Archibald Hamilton.

The *Annual Register* presents some problems of reference. Its various sections—the history of events abroad, with the chronicle of those at home—are discontinuously paginated from the literary and antiquarian material. Unless otherwise stated, my page-references imply the 'Chronicles' part of the book. Further, in 1790, James Dodsley, brother of the founder Robert Dodsley, died, and F. and C. Rivington bought the copyright of the volumes to date. S. Otridge and others bought the stock, and both parties issued continuations. The Rivington edition lasted from 1791 to 1827: the other line is the one with us now, and is the one I refer to unless Rivingtons' is specified.

The *Critical Review* ran continuously to 1791 and was then issued with new numbering; it is referred to as the New Arrangement, with the numbers beginning again. I have given the original series in Arabic, the new in Roman.

The *British Critic* began in 1793 under W. Beloe and R. Nares. In 1826 it was united with the *Quarterly Theological Review*, and the publication continued under their joint titles till 1843.

BIBLIOGRAPHY

The Bibliography consists of four sections: (I) a list of dictionaries and other reference books; (II) a list of the periodicals quoted in the text; (III) a list of general primary sources; (IV) a list of modern books and articles that throw light on language, biography and history.

Where editions other than the first have been used, the date of the original publication is given first, and that of the later edition or reprint in brackets. Works published anonymously are entered in their alphabetical place and cross-referenced to their authors where these are known or suggested. Pseudonymous works are ascribed to their known or probable authors with their names in inverted commas. Periodicals wholly or mainly the work of a single author are entered under his name as well as in the periodical list. Where only the date of the work is given, it is the sole indication I could find of the author's floruit. Essays are referred to by number, except for the longer productions of Vicesimus Knox which are quoted by volume and page.

I. BOOKS OF REFERENCE

i. *Eighteenth-century Dictionaries*

Ash, John (1704?–79). *New Complete Dictionary*, 1775.

Bailey, Nathan (d. 1742). *An Universal Etymological English Dictionary*, 1721 (1730). Last edition 1802.

Cocker, Edward (1631–76) and Hawkins, John (d. 1692). The English Dictionary ascribed to them first appeared in 1704 and is considered a booksellers' compilation. I used the revised third edition of 1724. Cocker was primarily a mathematician, and is recalled in the phrase 'according to Cocker' to imply precision.

Dyche, Thomas (d. between 1731 and 1735) and Pardon, William (of whom no information seems available). *A New General English Dictionary*, 1735 (4th edn., 1744). First published 1735, with eighteen editions and several reprints to 1794.

Glossographia Anglicana Nova, 1707. Often considered a version of Thomas Blount's *Glossographia*, 1656, but see Starnes and Noyes.

Johnson, Samuel (1709–84). *A Dictionary of the English Language*, 1755 (1784). The fourth edition, of 1784, was the last published in his lifetime. See Sledd and Kolb.

Kenrick, William (1723–79). *A New Dictionary of the English Language*, 1773.

Sheridan, Thomas. *A Complete Dictionary of the English Language*, 1789.

Trusler, John (1735–1820). *Synonyms*, 1783.
The Encyclopaedia Britannica for 1773, s.v. Dictionaries.

ii. *Modern*

A New English Dictionary on Historical Principles, based on the materials of
    the Philological Society, 1884–1928. Reprinted, with a supplement, 1933,
    under the title of
The Oxford English Dictionary. To this my obligations are constant and
    paramount.
The Oxford Dictionary of English Etymology, ed. C. T. Onions, 1966.
The Stanford Dictionary of Anglicised Words and Phrases, ed. C. A. M.
    Fennell, 1892; reprinted, 1965.
Partridge, Eric H. *Origins, a short etymological dictionary of Modern English*,
    1958.
—. *Usage and Abusage*, 1947.
Weekley, E. *Etymological English Dictionary*, 1921.
English Dialect Dictionary, ed. Joseph Wright, 1898–1905.

iii. *Chronological and Biographical Material*

Alston, R. C. *A Bibliography of the English Language . . . to the year 1800*
    1965 continuing.
The Cambridge Bibliography of English Literature, 1940.
The Dictionary of Anonymous and Pseudonymous Writings, ed. S. Halkett,
    J. Laing and others, 1882–1926.
The Oxford Companion to English Literature, ed. Sir Paul Harvey, 1932.
The Dictionary of National Biography, 1885–1900, with several later sup-
    plements.
The Catalogues of the British Museum and the Bodleian Libraries.

II. EIGHTEENTH-CENTURY PERIODICALS QUOTED

The Adventurer, 1732–4, ed. John Hawkesworth (1715?–73) (1797).
The Annual Register, 1758–. Edmund Burke contributed to it for thirty
    years.
The Anti-Jacobin, 1797–8, ed. William Gifford (1756–1826) (1798).
The Babler, 1763, ed. Hugh Kelly (1739–77). Collected Essays from *Owen's
    Weekly Chronicle*, 1763–7 (1786).
The British Critic, 1793–1826.
The Champion, 1739–40, by Henry Fielding (1707–54) and James Ralph
    (1705?–62).
Common Sense, 1737–43(?). Chesterfield, Lyttelton, Molloy (d. 1767).
The Connoisseur, 1754–6, ed. George Colman the Elder (1732–94) and
    Bonnell Thornton (1724–68).

The Craftsman, 1706–7, ed. Nicholas Amhurst, with Lord Bolingbroke, William Pulteney and Thomas Cooke.

The Critical Review, 1756–1817. Notable editors Tobias Smollett (1721–71) and Percival Stockdale (1736–1811). New arrangement with new numeration from 1791.

The Daily Courant, 1702.

The European Magazine, 1782–1826.

Fog's Weekly Journal. It began as *The Weekly Journal*, 1716–25, continued as *Mist's Weekly Journal* to 1728, and as *Fog's Weekly Journal* till 1737. Ed. Nathaniel Mist, with Defoe and Charles Molloy.

The Free Briton, 1729.

The Free Thinker, 1718–23, ed. Ambrose Philips (1675?–1749).

The Gentleman's Magazine, 1731–1922, ed. Edward Cave (1691–1754).

Gray's Inn Journal, 1753–4, ed. Arthur Murphy (1727–1803).

The Guardian, 1713, ed. Sir Richard Steele (1672–1729) (1726).

The Literary Magazine, and British Review, 1788–94.

The Looker-on, 1772–4, ed. William Roberts (1767–1849), James Beresford (1764–1840), Alexander Chalmers (1759–1834). Additional essays in collected editions of 1794, '95, '96.

The Lounger, 1785–7, ed. H. Mackenzie and others (2nd edn. 1787).

The Mirror, 1779, ed. H. Mackenzie (1791).

The Monthly Review, 1749–1845, ed. Ralph Griffiths (1720–1805).

The New Universal Magazine, or Gentleman and Lady's Polite Instructor, 1755–65.

The Old Whig, 1735–9, ed. Samuel Chandler and others.

The Present State of the Republic of Letters, 1728–33.

The Royal Society, London, *Philosophical Transactions*, 1665–. First edited by H. Oldenburg, later by a committee.

St James' Chronicle, 1761–1866.

The Spectator, 1711–12; 1714. Addison and Steele (1739).

The Tatler, 1709–11. Steele and Addison.

The Town and Country Magazine, 1769–96.

The Universal Magazine of Knowledge and Pleasure, 1747–1803, editors include P. Stockdale.

The Universal Museum and Complete Magazine of Knowledge and Pleasure, 1764–70, ed. Arthur Young (1741–1820).

The Universal Spectator, 1728–48, ed. H. Baker and W. Guthrie.

Variety, 1788. Variously ascribed to Humphry Repton (1752–1818) and Anna Seward (1747–1809) qq.v.

The Westminster Journal, or, New Weekly Miscellany, 1741–59. A continuation of the *New Westminster Miscellany* of 1741. Ran under variously modified titles till 1825.

The Whig Examiner, 1710. Addison.

III. GENERAL PRIMARY SOURCES

Addison, Joseph (1672–1719). 'An Essay on Virgil's Georgics' in *The Miscellaneous Works of Joseph Addison*, ed. A. C. Guthkelch, 1914, ii.

—. *Remarks on Several Parts of Italy*, 1701; 1705 (1761).

—. *The Spectator* (with Steele), 1711–12 (1739).

—. *The Whig Examiner*, 1710 (1753). See also *The Spectator* (periodical).

Alison, Archibald (1757–1839). *Essays on the Nature and Principles of Taste*, 1790.

'Angeloni Battista'. See Shebbeare.

Anstey, Christopher (1724–1815). *The New Bath Guide*, 1766 (3rd edn. of same year).

Armstrong, John (1709–79). *Art of Preserving Health*, 1744 (1774).

—. *On Taste*, 1753.

—. *Sketches by Launcelot Temple*, 1758 (1786).

The Art of Poetry on a New Plan, printed for J. Newbery, 1702. By Newberry, with revisions by Goldsmith?

Atterbury, Lewis (1656–1731). *A Vindication of Archbishop Tillotson's Sermons*, 1709

Baillie, John. *An Essay on the Sublime*, 1747.

Baker, Robert. *Remarks on the English Language*, 1770 (2nd edn. 1779). Title of 1st edn. is *Reflections on the English Language*.

Beattie, James (1735–1813). *Dissertations Moral and Critical*, 1783.

—. *London Diary*, ed. R. S. Walker, 1947.

Beattie, James Hay (1768–90). *Dialogues of the Dead*, appended to *The Minstrel* by James Beattie Sr, 1799. Vol. ii includes J. H. Beattie's *Miscellanies* of 1794.

'Beaumont, Sir Harry'. See Spence.

Beckford, William (1760–1844). *Modern Novel Writing: or The Elegant Enthusiast*, 1796.

Bedford, John, Fourth Duke of. *Correspondence*, ed. Lord John Russell, 1842–6.

Belsham, William (1752–1827). *Essays*, 1789.

Bentley, Richard (1662–1742), ed. *Paradise Lost*, 1732.

Berkeley, George (1685–1753). *Common-place Book*, ed. A. C. Fraser, 1901.

Blacklock, Thomas (1721–91). *Poems*, ed. Spence, 1754 (1756). 'To which is prefix'd An Account of the Life, Character and Writings, of the Author.'

Blair, Hugh (1718–1800). *Lectures on Rhetoric and Belles Lettres*, 1783.

Bond, Richmond P., ed. *New Letters to the Tatler and Spectator*, 1959.

Boswell, James (1740–95). *Boswell on the Grand Tour*, i, ed. F. Brady, 1953; ii, ed. F. Brady and F. A. Pottle, 1955.

—. *Boswell in Holland*, ed. F. A. Pottle, 1952.

—. *Boswell's London Journal*, ed. F. A. Pottle, 1930.

—. *Boswell in Search of a Wife*, ed. F. Brady and F. A. Pottle, 1957.

Boswell, James (1740–95). *Letters of James Boswell*, ed. C. B. Tinker, 2 vols., 1924.

—. *Letters to the Rev. W. J. Temple*, ed. Thomas Seccombe, 1908.

—. *Life of Johnson*, ed. G. B. Hill and L. F. Powell, 1935.

Brooke, Henry (1703?–83). *Universal Beauty*, in Chalmers' *English Poets*, xvii.

Browne, Isaac H. *Poems upon Various Subjects*, 1768, in Chalmers' *English Poets*, xvii.

Buchanan, James. *A Regular English Syntax*, 1769.

Burke, Edmund (1729–97). *A Philosophical Enquiry into the Origin of our Ideas of the Sublime and Beautiful*, 1756 (5th edn. 1767 'more full and satisfactory than the first').

Burrow, Sir James (1701–82). *An Essay on Punctuation*, 1772. Enlarged version of *De Ratione et Usu Interpungendi*.

Byron, John (1692–1763). *Miscellaneous Poems*, 1773 (1814).

—. *Private Journal and Literary Remains*, ed. R. Parkinson, Chetham Society, xliv, 1857.

Bysshe, Edward (fl. 1712). *The Art of English Poetry*, 1702.

Callender, James Thomson (d. 1803). *The Deformities of Dr. Johnson*, 1782.

Campbell, Archibald (1726?–80). *Lexiphanes, A Dialogue*, 1767 (2nd edn. same year).

Campbell, George (1719–96). *The Philosophy of Rhetoric*, 1776.

Carey, Henry (1687?–1743). *Poems*, ed. F. T. Wood, 1930.

A Caution against Enthusiasm. See Gibson.

A Caution to Gentlemen who use Sheridan's Dictionary, 1789 (3rd edn., 1790).

Chalmers, Alexander (1759–1834). *The Works of the English Poets*. Vol. xvii contains Brooke, Browne, Glover, Jago, Scott and W. Whitehead. See also *The Looker-on*.

Cheyne, George (1671–1747). *The English Malady, or a Treatise of Nervous Disorders of all kinds*, 1733. Cited in O.E.D. as *On Nervous Disorders*.

Church, Thomas (1707–56). *Remarks on Mr. Wesley's Last Journal*, 1745.

Churchill, Charles (1731–64). *Poetical Works*, ed. Douglas Grant, 1956.

Cole, Charles Nalson (1723–1804). *Sketches of the Life of Soame Jenyns*. See Jenyns.

Collier, Jeremy (1650–1726). *Essays upon Several Moral Subjects* (*of Duelling, concerning Cloaths*), 1703 (6th edn., 1722).

Collins, Anthony (1676–1729). *A Discourse concerning Ridicule and Irony in Writing*, 1729.

—. *A Philosophical Inquiry concerning Human Society*, 1717.

'Copywell J.' See Woty, W.

Cowper, William (1731–1800). *Poetical Works*, ed. H. S. Milford, 1911.

Craven, Elizabeth Lady (1750–1828). *A Journey through the Crimea to Constantinople in the year MDCCLXXXVI*, 1789.

Darwin, Erasmus (1731–1802). *The Loves of the Plants*, 1789; republished with additions as *The Botanic Garden*, pt. II, 1790.

Defoe, Daniel (1660?–1731). *Letters*, ed. G. H. Heeley, 1955.
—. *The Review*, 1704. (Facsimile edition ed. A. W. Secord, 1938.)
The Deformities of Dr. Johnson. See Callender.
Dennis, John (1657–1734). *Critical Works*, ed. E. N. Hooker, 2 vols., 1939 and 1943.
Diaper, William (1685–1717). *Complete Works*, 1712–14, ed. Dorothy Broughton, 1951.
—. *Halieuticks*, completed by John Jones and published 1722.
Diaries of a Duchess (Elizabeth Percy, later Smithson 1716–76), ed. James Grieg, 1926.
Dickins, L. and Stanton, M. *An Eighteenth-century Correspondence*, 1910. (Letters to Sanderson Miller Esq. of Radway.)
Dodsley, Robert (1703–64). *Agriculture*, 1753.
Dryden, John (1631–1700). *Dedication of the Æneis*, 1697.
—. *Marriage à la Mode*, 1673.
Duff, William (1732–1815). *Essay on Original Genius*, 1767.
Dyer, John (1700?–58). *Ruins of Rome*, 1740 (in *Minor Poets of the Eighteenth Century*, ed. H. I'. Fausset, 1930.)
Edwards, Thomas (1699–1757). *Canons of Criticism*, 1748 (1765).
Elphinston, James (1721–1809). *Education*, a Poem, 1763.
Enfield, William (1741–97). *Sermons on Practical Subjects* (with a Memoir by J. Aitkin), 1798.
An Essay upon the Harmony of Languages intended principally to illustrate that of the English Language. See Mitford.
Felton, Henry (1679–1740). *A Dissertation on Reading the Classics and Forming a Just Style*, 1709. (5th edn. 1753, with some alterations and notes.)
Ferguson, Adam (1723–1816). *An Essay on the History of Civil Society*, 1767 (4th edn. revised and corrected, 1773).
—. *Institutes of Moral Philosophy*, 1769.
Fielding, Sarah (1710–68). *Lives of Cleopatra and Octavia*, 1757 (1925).
'Fitzosborne, Sir Thomas'. See Melmoth.
Letters from George III to Bute, 1756–66, ed. R. Sedgwick, 1939.
'Paul Gemsege'. See Pegge.
Gerard, Alexander (1728–95). *An Essay on Taste*, 1759 ('To which is now added Part the Fourth, of the Standard of Taste: with Observations concerning the Imitative Nature of Poetry', 3rd edn. 1780).
—. *An Essay on Genius*, 1774.
Gibbon, Edward (1737–94). *The Decline and Fall of the Roman Empire*, 1776–88 (World's Classics edn. 1903 sqq.).
Gibson, Edmund (1669–1748). *A Caution against Enthusiasm*, 1739 (1772).
Gildon, Charles (1665–1724). *The Complete Art of Poetry*, 1718.
Gilpin, William (1724–1824). *Observations on the River Wye*, 1782 (4th edn. 1800).

Glover, Richard. *Athenaid* in Chalmers' *English Poets*, xvii.
Godwin, William (1756–1836). *The Enquirer*, 1797.
Goldsmith, Oliver (1730?–74). *An Account of the Augustan Age in England* (in *The Bee*).
—. *Present State of Polite Learning*, 1759.
—. *Essays originally published in the year*, 1756.
—. *The Bee*, 1759.
—. *Life of Beau Nash*, 1762.
(The above items in *Works*, ed. Cunningham, 1854.)
—. See also *Art of Poetry*.
Gordon, Ian A., ed. *Shenstone's Miscellany*, 1765 (1952).
Graves, Richard, of Claverton (1715–1814). *Columella*, 1779.
Gray, Thomas (1716–71). *Complete Poems*, ed. H. W. Starr and J. R. Hendrickson, 1966. Contains *Luna Habitabilis* with an English version.
—. *Correspondence*, ed. P. Toynbee and L. Whitby, 1935.
Grose, Francis (1731?–91). *The Olio*, 1796. 2nd edn. corrected and enlarged includes The Grumbler's Essays.
Hanway, Jonas (1712–86). His essays appear in two volumes described as the second edition enlarged and corrected, 1757. It is really the first edition; apparently Hanway meant to have the MS bound and regarded that as the first edition. The publication bears a comprehensive but somewhat inconsequent title:
A Journal of eight days journey from Portsmouth to Kingston-upon-Thames; through Southampton, Wiltshire, etc., with Miscellaneous thoughts, moral and religious, in sixty-four letters: Addressed to the Ladies of the Partie. To which is added an Essay on Tea—with several Political Reflections: and Thoughts on Public Love: in Thirty-two Letters to Ladies.
Harris, James (1709–80). *Philosophical Arrangements*, 1775.
Harrison, James. *British Classicks*, 1785–7.
Harwood, Edward (1729–94). *A Liberal Translation of the New Testament*, 1768.
Hawkesworth, John (1715?–73). See *The Adventurer* (periodical essays).
Hawkins, Sir John (1719–89). *The Life of Samuel Johnson*, 1787 (ed. B. H. Davis, 1962).
Hertford-Pomfret Correspondence, ed. 1805. i.e. *Correspondence between Frances Seymour, Countess of Hertford and Henrietta Louisa, Countess of Pomfret, between the years 1738 and 1741.*
Hogarth, William (1697–1764). *The Analysis of Beauty*, 1753.
Holcroft, Thomas (1745–1809). *The School for Arrogance*, 1791.
Holmes, J. *The Art of Rhetoric*, 1738 (1739).
The Humble Petition of Z. See *Gent. Mag.* lii (1783).
Hume, David (1711–76). *Essays, Moral and Political*, 1742.

Hume, David (1711–76). *Enquiries concerning the Human Understanding*, 1748, ed. from posthumous edn. of 1777 by L. A. Selby-Bigge, 1888.

Hurd, Richard (1720–1808). *Lectures on Chivalry and Romance*, 1762 (1772).

—. *Moral and Political Dialogues*, 1759–63 (1771).

Hutcheson, Francis (1694–1747). *An Essay on the Nature and Content of the Passions and Affections*, 1728 (1730).

—. *An Inquiry into the Original of our Ideas of Beauty and Virtue*, 1725 (1729). Includes *An Inquiry concerning Moral Good and Evil*.

Hutton, W. H. *Burford Papers*, 1905. Includes letters of 'Daddy' Crisp.

Jackson, William, 'of Exeter' (1730–1803). *Thirty Letters on Various Subjects*, 2nd edn. corrected and improved, 1784.

—. *The Four Ages; together with Essays on Various Subjects*, 1798.

Jago, Richard (1715–81). *Poems* in Chalmers' *English Poets*, xvii.

Jenyns, Soame (1704–87). *Works*, ed. C. N. Cole, 1790, 1793.

Jerningham, Edward (1727–1812). *Enthusiasm*, a Poem, 1789.

Johnson, Samuel (1709–84). *Diaries, Prayers and Annals*, ed. E. L. McAdam, 1958.

—. *A Dictionary of the English Language*, 1755 (1784).

—. *General Observations on Shakespeare's Plays* in Murphy, xii.

—. *The Idler*, 1758–60 (1783).

—. *The Lives of the Poets*, 1779–81 (ed. G. B. Hill, 1905).

—. *Notes on Shakespeare* (Augustan Reprints, 19, 56, 57, 58).

—. *The Patriot*, 1774 in Murphy, viii.

—. *Plan for a Dictionary*, 1747 in Murphy, xii.

—. *The Rambler*, 1750–2 (1785).

Johnstone, Charles (1719?–1800). *The Reverie: or, A Flight to the Paradise of Fools*, 1762 (1763).

'Junius'. *Letters*, 1772. Edition printed for T. Bensley, 1797; no editor's name.

Kames, Henry Home, Lord (1696–1782). *Elements of Criticism*, 1762. 7th edn. with the author's last corrections and additions, 1788.

Kenrick, William (1725?–79). *A New Dictionary of the English Language*, 1773.

—. *The Kapelion*, or Poetical Ordinary, 1750–1. 'By Archimagirus Metaphoricus.'

Knox, Vicesimus (1752–1821). *Essays Moral and Literary*, 1779 (1782).

Lackington, James (1746–1815). *Memoirs*, 1791 (13th edn. 1810).

Laelius and Hortensia, 1782. See Stedman.

Langhorne, John (1735–79). *Letters on Religious Retirement and Melancholy*, 1762.

Lavington, George (1684–1762). *The Enthusiasm of the Methodists and Papists compar'd*, three pts. 1749–51 (1754).

Lawson, John (1712–59). *Lectures concerning Oratory*, 1758 (2nd edn. 1759).

Leland, Thomas (1722–85). *Dissertation on the Principles of Human Eloquence*, 1764.

Lewis, Matthew Gregory ('Monk') (1775–1818). *The Monk*, 1795 (1832). *Life of Beau Nash*, 1762. See Goldsmith.

Lloyd, Evan (1734–76). *The Conversation: A Poem*, 1767.

George, 1st Lord Lyttelton (1709-73). *Dialogues of the Dead*, 1760–5.

—. *Persian Letters*, 1735.

Mackenzie, Henry (1745–1831). Editor of *The Mirror*, q.v.

Mallett, David (1703?–65). *Verbal Criticism*, a Poem, 1733.

Mandeville, Bernard de (1670–1733). *An Enquiry into the origin of Honour, and the Usefulness of Christianity in War*, 1732.

Mason, John (1706–63). *An Essay on Elocution, or Pronunciation*, 1748 (4th edn. 1757).

Mason, William (1725–97). *The English Garden*, 1772–82.

Melmoth, William (1710–99). *Letters of Sir Thomas Fitzosborne*, 1742 (1795).

Merlinus Liberatus, An Almanack for 1718. Ascribed to John Partridge on the title page. He died in 1715. 'Merlinus Liberatus, by John Partridge' appeared as late as 1890.

Mickle, William Julius (1734–38). *Syr Martyn* in Chalmers' *English Poets*, xvii.

Miller, James (1706–44). *The Man of Taste*, 1734.

Milns, William. *The Well-bred Scholar*, 1794.

Milton Restor'd and Bentley Depos'd, 1732.

Mitford, John (1744–1827). *An Essay upon the Harmony of Languages intended principally to illustrate that of the English Language*, 1774.

Monboddo, James Burnett, Lord (1714–99). *Of the Origin and Progress of Language*, 1773–6.

Moore, John. *View of Society and Manners in Italy*, 1781.

More, Hannah (1745–1833). *Sir Eldred of the Bower*, 1775.

Murphy, Arthur (1727–1815), ed. *The Works of Samuel Johnson LL.D*, 12 vols., 'with an essay on his life and genius', 1816.

—. *Gray's Inn Journal*, 1753.

Neville, Sylas (1707–88), *Diary*, ed. Basil Cozens-Hardy, 1950.

Paine, Thomas (1737–1809). *Rights of Man*, 1791–2.

Parnell, Thomas (1679–1778). *Poems* (in *Minor Poets of the Eighteenth-century*, ed. H. I'. Fausset, 1930).

Pearce, Zachary (1690–1774). *A Review of the Text of the Twelve Books of Milton's Paradise Lost in Which the Chief of Dr. Bentley's Emendations are considered*, 1733.

Pegge, Samuel alias Paul Gemsege (1733–1800). *Anecdotes of the English Language*, 1803, ed. John Nichols.

Philips, Ambrose (1675?–1747). See *The Free-Thinker* (periodical).

Philips, John (1676–1709). *Cyder, a Poem*, 1709.

Piozzi, Hester Lynch (*née* Thrale) (1741–1821). *British Synonymy*, 1794.

—. *The Intimate Letters of Hester Piozzi and Penelope Pennington*, 1788–1822, ed. O. G. Knapp, 1914.

Pope, Alexander (1688–1744). *Poetical Works* (Everyman's Library).

—. Translation of *Iliad*, 1715–20, in World's Classics edn. 1902; of *Odyssey*, 1725, World's Classics edn. 1903.

Price, Richard (1723–91). *Additional Observations on Civil Liberty*, 1777.

Price, Sir Uvedale (1747–1829). *An Essay on the Picturesque*, 1794–8, 2 vols.

Priestley, Joseph (1733–1804). *A Course of Lectures on Oratory and Criticism*, 1777, composed when Tutor . . . in the Academy at Warrington and . . . first delivered in 1762.

—. *A Course of Lectures on the Theory of Language and Universal Grammar*, 1762.

—. *Observations on Education*, 1778.

Pye, Henry James (1743–1813). *Amusement*, 1790.

Ralph, James (1705?–62). *The Champion*. With Fielding.

Reeve, Clara (1729–1807). *The Progress of Romance through Times, Countries and Manners*, 1785.

Reid, Thomas (1710–96). *A Brief Account of Aristotle's Logic*, 1773.

—. *Essays on the Intellectual Powers of Man*, 1785 (1812).

—. *Essays on the Powers of the Human Mind*, 1764.

Repton, Humphry (1767–1818). *Sketches of Hints on Landscape Gardening*, 1793.

—. *Variety* (?). See also Anna Seward.

Reynolds, Sir Joshua (1723–92). *A Journey to Flanders and Holland*, 1797 (in *Works*, ed. Malone, ii, 1809).

—. *Portraits*, ed. F. W. Hilles, 1952.

Richardson, Jonathan Sr (1665–1745) and Richardson, Jonathan Jr (1684–1771). *Explanatory Notes and Remarks on Milton's Paradise Lost*, 1734. Referred to in footnotes as the Richardsons' commentary.

Richardson, Samuel (1689–1761). *Familiar Letters*, ed. B. W. Downs, 1928.

Romaine, William (1714–95). *Letters from the late Rev. William Romaine*, 1793.

Ruffhead, Owen (1723–69). *The Life of Alexander Pope, Esq.*, 1769.

Salisbury, William. *Two Grammatical Essays*, 1768.

Scott, John (1720–83). *Poems* in Chalmers' *English Poets*, xvii.

Seward, Anna (1747–1809). *Variety* (?).

Shaftesbury, Anthony Ashley Cooper, 3rd Earl of (1671–1713). *Advice to an Author*, 1710.

—. *Characteristics of Men, Manners, Opinions, Times*, Treatise I, *A letter concerning Enthusiasm*, 1711 (1714).

—. *The Moralists*, 1711 (1714).

Shebbeare, John (1709–88). *Letters to the English Nation*, 1756.

Shenstone, William (1714–63). *Works*, ed. R. and J. Dodsley, 1764. See also Gordon.

Sheridan, Thomas (1719–88). *A Course of Lectures on Elocution*, 1762 (2nd edn. 1764).

—. *A Complete Dictionary of the English Language*, 1789.

Smart, Christopher (1722–71). *Collected Poems*, ed. Norman Callan, 1949.

Smith, Adam (1723–92). *Works*, ed. Dugald Stewart, 1811. Vol. v contains essays on History of Astronomy, Formation of Languages, Imitative Arts, Ancient Physics, Logic and Metaphysics.

—. *Lectures on Rhetoric and Belles Lettres*, ed. J. H. Lothian, 1963.

Spence, Joseph (1699–1768). *Anecdotes*, ed. S. W. Singer, 1820.

—. *Essay on Pope's Odyssey*, 1726. 1st edn. in two parts, but the first part is not so designated. No division in later editions.

—. *Polymetis*, 1747.

—. ('Sir Harry Beaumont'.) *Crito*, 1752.

—. ('Sir Harry Beaumont'.) *Moralities*, 1753.

See also Blacklock.

Stedman, J. *Laelius and Hortensia*, 1782. The work was published anonymously.

Steele, Sir Richard (1672–1729). *The Funeral or Grief à la Mode*, a Comedy, 1721 (1735).

—. *The Guardian*, 1713 (1726).

—. *The Tatler*, 1709–11.

—. *The Tender Husband*, 1705 (1735).

See also *The Spectator* (periodical).

Stevens, William Bagshaw. *Journal*, ed. G. Galbraith, 1965.

Stewart, Dugald (1753–1828). *Elements of the Philosophy of the Human Mind*, 1792.

Stockdale, Percival (1736–1811). *An Inquiry into the Nature and Genuine Laws of Poetry*, 1778. See also the *Critical Review*, the *Universal Magazine*.

Swift, Jonathan (1667–1745). *Polite Conversation*, 1738.

Symonds, John (1729–1807). *Observations upon revising the Epistles*, 1794.

—. *Observations upon revising the Gospels*, 1789.

'Temple, Launcelot'. See Armstrong.

Theobald, Lewis (1688–1744). *Shakespeare Restored*, 1726.

Thomas, E., *An Account of the Trial of the Letter Y*, 1753.

Thompson, George, of Esk-Bank Academy, Longtown. *A Sentimental Tour*, 1798.

Trinder, William Martin (1747–1818). *An Essay on the English Grammar*, 1781.

Upton, John (1707–60). *Critical Observations upon Shakespeare*, 1747.
—. *Spenser's Faerie Queene*: a new edition with a glossary and notes explanatory and critical, 1758.
Usher, James (1720–72). *Clio: or, A Discourse on Taste addressed to a young Lady by I.V.*, 1767 (4th edn. with large additions, 1778).
Vertue, George (1684–1756). *Anecdotes of Painting*, 1762–3.
Warburton, William (1698–1779). *A Critical and Philosophical Commentary on Mr. Pope's Essay on Man*, 1742.
—. *The Divine Legation of Moses Demonstrated*, 1737–42.
—. *Doctrine of Grace*, 1762.
   (The above items in *Works*, ed. Richard Hurd, 1811.)
Ward, John (1679?–1758). *System of Oratory*, 1759.
Warton, Joseph (1722–1800). *An essay on the genius and writings of Pope*, 1756 (3rd edn. corrected, 1772).
Warton, Thomas (1728–90). *Observations on the Fairy Queen of Spenser*, 1754 (2nd edn. corrected and enlarged, 1762). Spelt 'Faerie Queene' in 1st edn.
—. *The Oxford Sausage*, 1763.
Waterland, Daniel (1683–1740). *A Review of the Doctrine of the Eucharist*, 1737.
Wendeborn, Gebhardt Friedrich August. *View of England*, 1791. Originally published in German, 1785–8, and translated by the Author.
Wesley, John (1703–91). *Letters*, ed. John Telford, 1931.
—. *Sermons upon Several Occasions*, 1760.
—. Sermon XXXII on the 'Nature of Enthusiasm' (in *Standard Sermons*, ed. E. H. Sugden, xi, 1921).
West, Gilbert (1703–56). *Education: In Imitation of Spenser's Fairy Queen*, 1751.
Whitehead, William (1713–85). *Poems* in Chalmers' *English Poets*, xvii.
Winchilsea, Anne Finch, Countess of (1666–1720). *Poems* (in *Minor Poets of the Eighteenth Century*, ed. H. I'. Fausset, 1930).
Withers, Philip (d. 1790). *Aristarchus, or The Principles of Composition*, 1791.
Woty, William (1731–91). *Poems on Several Occasions*, 1780.
—. *Poetical Amusements*, 1789.
—. *Poetical Works of Mr. William Woty*, 1770.
—. *Shrubs on Parnassus*, by 'J. Copywell'.
Wraxall, Sir Nathaniel A. (1751–1831). *A Tour through some of the Northern Parts of Europe*, 1775 (3rd edn. corrected 1776).
Young, Edward (1683–1765). *Conjectures on Original Composition*, 1759 (ed. E. J. Morley, 1918).
—. *On Lyric Poetry*, 1728 (ed. Morley, 1918).

IV. SELECT MODERN CRITICISM
AND BACKGROUND MATERIAL

i. *Historical, Biographical and Critical*

Allen, B. Sprague. *Modes in English Taste*, 1927.

Atkins, J. W. H. *English Literary Criticism 17th and 18th Centuries*, 1931.

Bate, W. J. *The Achievement of Samuel Johnson*, 1955.

Bettany, Lewis. *Edward Jerningham and his friends*, 1919.

Bond, Richmond P. *Studies in the Early English Periodical*, 1957.

Brett, R. L. *The Third Earl of Shaftesbury*, 1951.

Brooke, Iris. *Dress and Undress; the Restoration and Eighteenth Century*, 1958.

Carlson, C. L. *The First Magazine: A History of the Gentleman's Magazine*, 1938.

Clark, Kenneth. *The Gothic Revival*, 1950.

Clifford, J. L. and Landa, L. A. *Pope and his Contemporaries: essays presented to George Sherburn*, 1949.

Collins, A. S. *Authorship in the Days of Johnson*, 1927.

Connely, Willard. *The True Chesterfield*, 1937.

Copeland, T. W. *Edmund Burke, Six Essays*, 1950.

Coxon, Roger. *Chesterfield and his Critics*, 1925.

Craig, M. E. *The Scottish Periodical Press 1750-89*, 1931.

Cruikshank, A. H. 'Thomas Parnell' in *Essays and Studies by Members of the English Association*, 1921.

Deane, C. V. *Aspects of Eighteenth-Century Nature Poetry*, 1935.

Dobrée, Bonamy. *English Literature in the Early Eighteenth Century*, 1959.

Dobson, Austin. *At Prior Park, and other Papers*, 1912.

Dunbar, H. L. *The Dramatic Career of Arthur Murphy*, 1946.

Dyson, H. V. D. and Butt, J. *Augustans and Romantics*, 1950.

Elton, Oliver. 'Reason and Enthusiasm in the Eighteenth Century' in *Essays and Studies by Members of the English Association*, 1924.

Evans, A. W. *Warburton and the Warburtonians*, 1932.

Fitzgerald, Percy. *Life of Lawrence Sterne*. 1906.

Foster, James R. *History of the Pre-romantic Novel in England*, 1949.

Furlong, I. J. *Imagination*, 1961.

Graham, Walter. *The Beginnings of English Literary Periodicals*, 1926.

Grant, Douglas. *James Thomson, Poet of 'The Seasons'*, 1957.

Hill, G. B. *Johnsonian Miscellanies*, 1897.

—. ed. *The Age of Johnson*, 1949.

Hilles, F. W. *The Literary Career of Sir Joshua Reynolds*, 1936.

Hipple, Walter J. *The Beautiful, the Sublime and the Picturesque*, 1937.

Hopkins, K. *The Poets Laureate*, 1954.

Humphreys, A. R. *The Augustan World*, 1954.

—. *William Shenstone, An Eighteenth Century Portrait*, 1937.

Hutchins, John H. *Jonas Hanway*, 1947.
Ketton-Cremer, R. W. *Thomas Gray*, 1955.
Kliger, Samuel. 'The Goths in England', *Modern Philology*, xliii (1945).
Knight, Douglas. *Pope and the Heroic Tradition*, 1951.
Knox, Ronald. *Enthusiasm*, 1950.
Lounsbury, Thomas R. *The First Editors of Shakespeare*, 1906.
Lovejoy, A. O. *Reflections on Human Nature*, 1961.
Lyles, Albert M. *Methodism Mocked*, 1960.
Monk, Samuel H. *The Sublime*, 1935.
Morley, Edith. *Eighteenth-century Ideals*. Royal Society of Literature, xvi (1937).
Nangle, Benjamin. *The Monthly Review, First Series 1749–89*: Indexes of Contributors and Articles, 1934.
Partridge, Eric. *A Critical Medley*, 1926.
Paston, George. *Sidelights on the Georgian Period*, 1907.
Payne, W. L. *Mr Review*, 1947.
Piggott, Stewart. *William Stukeley, An Eighteenth Century Antiquary*, 1950.
Powell, L. F. 'William Huggins and Tobias Smollett', *Modern Philology*, xxxix (1936).
Reith, Charles. *The Police Idea*, 1938.
Renwick, W. L. *English Literature, 1789–1815*, 1963.
Sledd, J. H. and Kolb, G. J. *Dr. Johnson's Dictionary: Essays on the Biography of a Book*, 1955.
Starnes, De Witt and Noyes, Gertrude E. *The English Dictionary from Cawdrey to Johnson 1604–1755*, 1946.
Steffen, Truman G. *The Social Argument against Enthusiasm*, 1941 (Texas Studies in English).
Sutherland, James. *Defoe*, 2nd edn. 1950.
Tillotson, Geoffrey. *Augustan Studies*, 1961.
—. *On the Poetry of Pope*, 1938.
Tucker, S. I. and Gifford, H. 'Johnson's Poetic Imagination', *Review of English Studies*, New Series, vi (1955).
Tuveson, Ernest Lee. *The Imagination as a Means of Grace*, 1966.
Utley, F. L. *The Forward Movement of the Fourteenth Century*, 1961.
Warren, Austin. *Alexander Pope. Critic and Humanist*, 1929.
Wellek, René. *A History of Modern Criticism*, i, 1955.
Werkmeister, Lucyle. *The London Daily Press, 1772–92*, 1963.
Wright, Austin. *Joseph Spence. A Critical Biography*, 1950.

ii. *Linguistic*

de Beer, E. S. 'Gothic: Origin and Diffusion of the Term', *Journal of the Warburg and Courtauld Institute*, xi (1948).

Davie, Donald. *The Language of Science and the Language of Literature 1700–1740*, 1963.
—. *Purity of Diction in English Verse*, 1952.
Erämetsä, Erik. *A Study of the word 'sentimental' and of other linguistic characteristics of eighteenth-century sentimentalism in England*, 1951 (Annales Academicæ Scientiarium Fennicæ).
Fowler, H. W. *A Dictionary of Modern English Usage*, 1926.
Fries, Charles C. 'The Periphrastic Future with *Shall* and *Will*', *P.M.L.A.* 1925.
Havens, R. D. 'The Poetic Diction of the English Classicists' in *Kittredge Anniversary Papers*, 1913.
Hulbert, J. R. 'On the Origin of the Grammarians' Rules for the use of *Shall* and *Will*', *P.M.L.A.* 1947.
Hussey, C. E. C. *The Picturesque*, 1927.
Ito, Hiroyuki, 'The Language of *The Spectator*' in *Anglica*, i (1962).
Lawton, George. *John Wesley's English*, 1962.
Leonard, Sterling A. *The Doctrine of Correctness in English Usage, 1700–1800*, 1929.
Lewis, C. S. *Studies in Words*, 1960.
McKnight, George H. and Emsley, B. *Modern English in the Making*, 1928.
Orr, John. *Old French and Modern English Idiom*, 1962.
Partridge, Eric. *Eighteenth-Century Romantic Poetry*, 1924.
—. *Slang today and yesterday*, 1933.
—. *Usage and Abusage*, 1947.
Smith, Logan Pearsall. 'Four Romantic Words' in *Words and Idioms*, 1925.
Society for Pure English. Tract 15: *On the Picturesque*.
—. Tract 48: *On Linguistic Self-Criticism*.
—. Tract 49: *On the Compound Epithet in English Poetry*.
Souter, Alexandre. *A Glossary of Later Latin*, 1957.
Strang, Barbara H. *Modern English Structure*, 1962.
Sutherland, James. *An Introduction to Eighteenth-Century Poetry*, 1948.
Tucker, S. I. 'Dr. Johnson and Lady Macbeth', *Notes and Queries*, New Series, iii (1956).
Vallins, G. H. *The Best English*, 1960.
Whelan, H. K. *Enthusiasm in English Poetry of the Eighteenth Century*, 1935.
Wiley, Margaret L. *Genius: a Problem in Definition*, 1950.
Wimsatt, W. K. *Philosophic Words*, 1948.
—. *The Prose Style of Samuel Johnson*, 1941.

INDEX OF WORDS AND TOPICS

Words in square brackets are post-eighteenth-century.
Entries in italics refer to topics.

'a Mr. X', 4, 52
aback, 68
abash, 169
abattement, 105
Abbreviation, 3, 5, 89–
90
aberrant, 280
ablution, 203
aborigines, 206
abrasion, 280
absentee, 190
abstention, 280
abstractedly, 193
abundance, 169
abut, 68
access, 258
accident 5, 137–8, 219
accord (vb), 35
acme, 115
acquire, 65
acrimony, 257
actual, 35
acumen, 38, 44, 45
acute, 90
acuteness, 44
addicted, 221
Address, modes of, 158–
162
adduce, 47
admirable, 245
admire, 245
ado, 169
adulation, 280
adumbration, 186
ad valorem, 39
advertisement, 189
advertising (pr. part.),
68
Advertising language,
83–5

advise, 75
aerial, 5, 194
aeronaut(ics), 107, 282
aerost(ation), 107, 108
aerostatation, 108
Affectation, 49–54, 87,
169–70
affix, 62
affray, 169
affront, 169
aftermath, 193
aggrieve, 57
agnation, 45
agreeable, 71
agriculturalist, 34
air-sickness, 194
airs, 171
alarm, 181
alarmist, 96
alarum, 6, 181
Alcoran, 2
alert, 222
algid, 44
allegation, 208–9
aloof, 169
amalgam (-ate), 181,
280
amateur, 110, 263
amatorial, 45
Ambiguity, 23–5, 249–
254, 271–4
amelioration, 35
American, 264–5
Americanisms, 46
amuse (-ment), 209–10
anfractuousness, 43
angina pectoris, 20
angularity, 280
animation, 201
annexion, 34

annihilation, 62
anon, 67
ant (vb), 3
anthology, 280
anthropology, 27
anticipative, 43
anvil, on the, 37
Apology, 91–5
apparent, 252
apparently, 6, 65, 252
appendage, 35
appendix, 189
appetency, 45, 46
apply to, 48
apprehension, 212
approbation, 34
approval, 34
à propos, 106, 109
Arcadian language, 53,
54
arch (adj.), 71
archaeology, 280
Archaism, 67–9, 167–9
arch-enemy, 169
architrave, 72
ardent, 227
ardour, 178
ardour-drunk, 165
arrangements, 55
array, 169
arrest, 65
artful, 222
articulateness, 280
[artifact], 222
artificial, 222
artist, 222
artistly, 45
as Monday, 74
ascension, 187
ascent, 187

ascertain, 271
askance, 169
asphyxia, 20
aspiring, 227
assistant-planter, 8, 56
assurance, 212
astonishment, 6, 29, 30
astounded, 68
asylum, 189–90
atom, 62, 77
attainder, 129
auctioneer, 80
Austral, 280
authoress, 34
authorise, 97
avalanche, 12
avenue, 267
average, 191
averse, 51
avocation, 257
await, 181
awful, 212, 240, 243–5
awry, 265
ay (e), 158
azure, 190, 191

bag (wig), 130, 204
bagatelle, 109
bale (-ful), 67, 169
baneful, 265
bang-beggar, 6
baptise, 67
basalt (-es, -ine), 13
baseness, 36
bashaw, 2
bassa, 2
basset, 130
bastion, 72
baton, 192
battle, 118
bazaar, 192
beach, 169
beard, 2
bearskins, 178
beat hollow, 80
beaten, 131
beau, 31
beautiful, 6

beauty, 29
[beet-sugar], 203
behest, 6, 67, 169
belabour, 61
Belles Lettres, 110
benevolent, 5
bent (propensity), 169
besprent, 68
best company, 51
bestowment, 46
betide, 169
between, 117, 281
beverage, 67
bevy, 169
bewitch, 31
Biblical language, 62–7
bibliographer, 200
bibliography, 200
big, 279
bigotry, 143
bilious, 35
billet (vb), 171
billet-doux, 109
bishop, 67
bishop (drink), 130
bite(r), 25
bivouac, 105
black man, 205
blackguard, 61
[black-marketeer], 80
blanch, 131
bland, 223
blank verse, 115
blanket, 59
blast (-ed), 240–1
blessed, 66
blinking, 240, 242–3
blockhead, 173, 174
blocking-guard, 105
blood-guiltiness, 67
bloods, 26, 55
bloodthirsty, 67
bloody, 240, 243
blooming, 167, 240–2
Blue Laws, 7
blunderize, 97
blunt (n.), 121
board (table), 60

bob (wig), 130
boddice, 178
bold stroke, 105
bold to do, 74
bookmaker, 264
Bombast, 48
bon mot, 109
bookist, 97
book of hope, 60
bore (n.), 38, 80
bosom-friend, 6, 20
[bottle-green], 124
bottom, 55, 258–9
boue de Paris, 123
bounty-blessing, 167
bracer, 141
brake, 169
brand (sword), 169
brazenface, 61
breathless, 166–7
breezy, 201
bribe, 55
bridle (vb), 165
brisk, 222
bristle up, 172
Bristol milk, 81
broad sunshine, 87
brochure, 96
brood (vb), 163
brown-brow'd, 166
brutal, 221
brute, 221
bubble-and-squeak, 2
bucks, 26
budge, 61
budget, 174–5
buffet, 192
bulk, 129
bumper, 19
bung your eye, 55
Burlesque, 58–9
burn (stream), 19
bury one's head, 87

cabal, 81
caddy, 19
cage, 171
caitiff, 69

cajole, 61
callous, 131
camber, 192
camisado, 38
[camouflage], 281
Canadian, 264
cancer, 20
Candia, 6
candid, 212, 214
candour, 6, 212–14
cannon, 168
canon(ise), 94
Cant, 75, 80–1
Canterbury Tale, 148
caprice, 109
capricious, 165
capsule, 195
capture (a ship), 4, 52
car, 168, 195
caravan, 135
carcasse, 105
[careers master], 194
caricature, 18
carol, 169, 171
carousal, 157
carouse, 16, 65
carpet, on the, 37
carrier-pigeon, 81
carte blanche, 112
cartel, 132
carton, 198
cartoon, 198
case-hardened, 172
cash, 75
casino, 16
cast (n.), 130
cast about for, 4
casual (-ly), 219–20
casualty, 219
catcall, 181
catch (cold), 4
catched, 4
caudee, 19
cavalcade, 72
cavalier (in fortifica-
   tion), 105
cavalry, 65
cede, 115

celebrity, 42, 280
cement (vb), 92
cent per cent, 75
cephalick, 76
chaff, 63
chair, 167
chairman, 60, 120
chamade, 105
chance-medley, 219
chapel, 142
chapman, 264
character, 18
charade, 17
chariot, 169
charity, 66
charming, 71, 223
chary, 265
chaste(ning), 266
chastising, 266
chause-trappe, 105
checkmate (slang), 80
cheery, 61
chenille, 112
chevaux de Frise, 105
chicken loo, 130
Children's language, 75
chimney doctor, 49
china shop, ox in, 177
chink (money), 75
chip of the old block,
   174
chitchat, 61
chitterling (frill), 130
chivalry, 203
chives, 185
chop off, 65
christen the apples, 176
church, 67, 142
churlish, 131
cicerone, 14
ci-devant, 110
cit, 46
citess, 46
citizeness, 46
clarify, 193
clavis, 132
clay-coloured, 124
[clean bomb], 283

cleped, 67
clergy (-man), 142
climax, 155
clime, 169
clinic, 194
clip the King's English,
   80
cloister, 31
close (vb), 73
clue, 179–80
clump, 21
clust'ring, 169
clutches, 65
clutter, 61
coarse, 131
coarse-throng'd, 167
code, 190
collecting, 83
colour (vb), 61
[colour-bar], 160
[colour-blindness], 103
coming (adj.), 192
commanding, 62
[commando], 281
Commercialese, 75
committal, 34
common, 117, 118, 252
common parlance, 76
commotion, 133
compassionable, 71
compassionate, 71
complacency, 214
complaisance, 28, 214
compleat, 71
Compliments?, 221
comrade, 65
concatenation, 280
[Concentration Camp],
   281
Concord, 3, 40
concussion, 133
condemnable, 35
condense, 134
condescension, 214–15
cone, 197
confoundedly, 61
Confusions, 5, 24–5,
   117–20

congenial, 91
congress, 74
conjobble, 61
connexity, 34
connoisseur, 109, 110
conscience, in all, 61
conscious, 266
conscription, 190
considerate, 224
constitute, 65
consummation, 118
contact, 187
contagion, 187
contemptible, 24, 25
contemptuous(ly), 24,
    25
continent, 186
continental, 248
contingent, 44
convention, 74
convention tent, 66
conventional, 193
convoke, 62
convolvulus, 134
cordial, 55, 170
cordon, 112
corianders (money), 75
cornice, 72
corporation (slang), 80
correctness, 30
corregiesque, 98
corymb (-us), 102
[cosmonaut], 282
counsellor, 50
counter-scarp, 72
counter-stroke, 169
coup de main, 105
coup d'œil, 18, 38
coup de théâtre, 108
courage, 38
courier, 62
of course, 276-8
courtier, 82
cowboy, 204
coxcomb, 139
coy, 224
crack a joke, 4, 176
cramp, 87

credulist, 115
cremation, 43
crescendo, 115
Crete, 6, 169
crimp (n.) (game), 130
criticism, 111
critique, 111
crochet, 192
[crop-mark], 103
cross-eyed, 101
crowd, 218-19
crow's foot, 105
crucial experiment, 114
cruise, 192
crusade, 203
cry (n.), 88
culminate, 72
culture, 193-4
cultured, 162
cummerbund, 16
curious, 206
curly, 167
curry favour, 6
cursedly, 61
cut out for, 95, 173
'cute, 90

daffa-down-dilly, 135
daffodil, 135
daisied, 162
[Daltonism], 103
damnable, 61
danger, out of, 76
dank, 169
dealings, 143
death-dew-dropping,
    166
debark, 37
debonair, 169
debonnaireté, 38
débris, 112
decadence, 45
decamp, 172
decent, 224
deciduous, 266
decorum, 121
decrepid, 165
dedicator, 31

deficit, 112
Degeneracy, 240-9
degenerate, 156
degradation, 21
degree, to a, 52
deject, 134
delight, 122
dell, 68
demand, 35
demean, 118
demeanour, 118
democracy, 202
democratic, 202
demon, 66
demonise, 97
demurrage, 74
denary, 65
denomination, 258
dénouement, 112
dense, 191
depend, 134
deplorable, 226-7
derange, 37
descend, 35
desiderate, 52
destination, 133
destiny, 133
desultory, 266
deterred, 42
devastate, 35
develop, 36
devil, 66
devil, talk of the, 176
devious, 178
dial (vb), 204
Dialect, 19
diatribe, 218
die hard, 176
dignified, 70, 266
dignity, 70
dint, 87, 169
dip, 67
disarrange, 37
disassociate, 37
discard, 271
disclaimer, 35
discover, 6, 272-3
discovery, 88

disembark, 37
disgusting, 252
dishabillé, 109
[disincentive], 37
disinterested, 211
dismal ditty, 171
disorderliness, 35
dispense with, 271–2
dissenter, 42
dissipation, 217
dissocial, 121
distemper, 256–7
Distinctions, 28, 29–30, 88, 115–16, 120–2, 123, 125, 133
distinctiveness, 35
ditto, 39, 75
divan, 15
dive (n. and vb), 194
divers, 68
divine, 143
divinity, angel of, 66
do better for, 176
doctor (n.), 49, (vb), 61
dodge, 61
doff, 78, 169
dogged, 266–7
doings, 61
dole, 192
Dolly Pinup, 5
dome, 256
domestic (n.), 206
domiciliate, 45
don (vb), 169
donative, 65
donkey, 19
don't-know-howish-ness, 100
door-wise, 167
Doric pillars, 72
dormitory, 192
double entendre, 187
doubtless, 275
douceur, 109
doughtie, 169
down in black and white, 80
dozen, 61

drab, 193
dragon (cane), 129; (serpent), 136
dragoon, 31
drastic, 193
dreare, 169
dreary, 169
droll, 156–7
drummist, 97
dubious, 156
ductile, 134
dumbfound, 57
duplicity, 187
dusting-places, 100

each, 169
eagerness, 36
easie, 76
Eau de millefleurs, 55
ebb, lowest, 175
eccentric, 182
éclair, 136
éclaircissement, 109
eclipse (vb), 92
ecliptic, 72
editor, 192
effluvium, 187
egotism, 37, 112
Eidophusicon, 102
Eidouranion, 102
ejectment, 66
elaboratory, 195
eld, 68
electorate, 190
electric (-al, -ian, -ity), 5, 195–6
electric battery, 96, 196
electrify, 196
elegant, 55, 155
elocution, 257
elope, 255
emanate, 35
embers, 92
emblematize, 34
embonpoint, 108, 109
embrace (vb), 165
emigrant, 2
eminent, 50

emolument, 257
emperor's eye, 123
emporium, 192
empressement, 36
enchant, 31
encroachment, 106
encumber, 92
enfilade, 105
enflure, 109
engagement, 118
engine, 259
engineer, 282
English conversation, 177
English gardening, 124
English pineapples, 100
enjoy bad health, 4, 72
enlargedness, 46
enlighten, 172
ennui, 38, 112
enormity, 238
enormous, 6, 238, 240
ensemble, 111
entertainmatic, 102
entertainment, 193
enthusiasm (-ast, -astic), 5, 230, 232–8
Equator, 72
eradicate, 179
erewhile, 60, 67
erst, 67, 68, 69
eschew, 68
esquire, 160
etiquette, 109
Euphemism, 8, 54–6
evanescency, 45
evaporate, 73
evening-sneaks, 81
eventuality, 44
ever-shady, 98
everybody, 51
exacerbation, 43
excavate, 43
excellency, 101
excise, 5, 83
exclusive, 252
excogitation, 43
execution, 206

exemplary, 5, 283
exertment, 46
exility, 45
existence, 52
expire (-y), 54
explanation, 74
explode, 273
expose, 254
extenuate, 254
extra, 89
extravagant, 134
extremity, 35
extricate, 62
exuberant, 41

fabrication, 279
fabulous, 148, 207, 208
face-painting, 204
facile, 172
facsimile, 39
faculties, 35
fadeless, 167
fag-end, 172
faggot, 130
fairy, 67
family of Languages, 113
[fan: enthusiast], 68
fanatic (-al), 68, 144, 169
fancy, 6
fantasque, 129
fantasy, 67
fare, 169
fascination, 182–3
faunist, 163
favour, 66, 75
fay, 169
fell (skin), 68
fell (adj.), 169
felo de se, 174
female, 57
fervent (-id, -our), 178
fictious, 34
fictitious, 267
fiddle-faddle, 61
fight (n.), 118

Figurative language, 164, 172–6, 178–86, 193, 201
figure (vb), 138
filemot, 123
film, 197
[finalise], 97
fine (adj.), 79
fine fellow, 25, 26
fine linen, 65
finesse, 109
fire, 76
fire-ball, 105
fixation, 197
flagrant, 162
flambeau, 57
flanking-fire, 105
flash in the pan, 6, 172–3
flee, 117
fleering, 28
flegm, 76
flimsy, 190–1
flirtation, 61
flood of tears, 64
floor (vb), 193
Florence (wine), 129
florist, 263
floury, 162–3
fluency, 228
fluent, 134
[flueologist], 50
fluidity, 113
flummery, 26
flustered, 205
fly (vb), 117
foible, 109
foiblesse, 35
followers, 157
footsteps, 132
fop, 139
[forcing-house], 179 (cp. 18th-cent. forcing-frame)
foreboding, 107
forlorn, 169
forlorn hope, 183
formalities, 131, 132

formidable, 36
formlessness, 114
fort (i.e. forte), 38
fowl, 24
fracas, 109
fragrant, 162
fraischeur, 35
Franklin, à la, 98
Franklinian, 98
Franklinism, 98
fray (n.), 67
free to do, 74
free-thinker, 116
frequency, 196
freshness, 35
fribble, 26
fricassée, 109
friend, 159
Friendly Society, 190
fright, die of, 174
frightful, 61
frolic, 139
frontispiece, 206
fruition, 207
fulmination, 258
function, 192
fundamentally, 55
funicular, 198
funk, 61
furniture, 206
fuss, 61
future, for the, 52
future, in, 52

gain-insidious, 166
gainsay, 60
gale, 85
galley-slave, work like, 173
Gallicism, 35, 36–8, 105–13
gambler, 61
gamgarou, 103
gan, 68
garbage, 171
garble, 183
garnish, 186–7
gauntlet glove, 190

gear, 67
generalise, 94
generate, 69, 156
generator, 70
generosity (-ous), 156
genius, 12, 29, 91, 220–221
genius-kindly, 166
genteel, 225
gentleman, 50–1
Georgian account, 99
Georgium Sidus, 99
Georgy, 99
get, 65
get nothing by it, 76
Giants' Causeway, 13, 14
gibbeting, 21
Gibbonian, 98
give a dog a bad name, 174
glacier, 12
glade, 169
glaring, 171
glass, head of, 177
glazier, 205
glee, 6, 60, 169
gleeful, 68
glen, 13, 169
glib (-ness), 60, 95
glowing, 227
glue (vb), 61
glum, 61
good company, 80
good mind to, have a, 176
good nature, 145
goose-step, 204
gore (vb), 169
got, 5
Gothic, 5, 149–55
governance, 69
governess, 158
grace, 66
gradated, 268
grade, 37
grain, against the, 174
granulated, 194

gravel (vb), 61
gravity, 216
gray peas, 130
Great Man, 76
greaves, 59
green(s), 261
greenery, 261
grewing, 48
grievousness, 67
grimalkined, 100
groping, 61
gross, 129
grotto, 169
ground, 168
group, 92, 93
gruesome, 48
guerdon, 169
guillotine, 2
guinea-pig, 205
guise, 169
gulph, 169
gun, 168
gust(o), 256

habit (-ude), 43
hackneyed, 65, 179
had rather, 3
half-seas-over, 80
hand of ginger, 21
hands off, 61
hanged, 118
hank, 175–6
hanker, 61
happy, 66
hard, 87
harpist, 97
hattist, 97
havoc, 169
heap, 129, 183
'Hear, hear,' 176
heart of oak, 174
hearty, 87
hecatomb, 93
henbane, 265
hero, 24
Hibernian, 43
hideous, 6, 169
High church, 143

Highflyer, 82
high roads, 66
higher (of punctuation), 131
hight, 67
hilarity, 280
hold out, 175
Holophusicon, 102
homogeneous, 280
honest fellow, 55
honied, 162
honour, upon my, 76
honourable, 161
hook or crook, by, 61
hookah, 15
horrid, 226
horrify, 101, 226
horse, enough to kill, 174
horseman, 65
[hospitalise], 97
hot, 227
hotbed, 179
hot-headed, 227
hot water, 177
hum (-bug), 25, 80
human, 88
humane, 88
humanise, 5, 94
humour, 206
hung, 118
Hungarian twins, 177
hurry, 218
hurtle, 68, 169
husbandman, 34
Hussar, 192
hyp, 113
hyper, 90
hypothesis, 41

Ic(h)on, 202
idea(l), 230–1
Idiom, 78, 87, 158
illiterate, 198
ill-persuading, 98
imagination, 6
imbecil(l)ity, 215
immediately, 275

immerse, 67
immolate, 64
immolation, 43
imp, 68
impeachment, 129
impend, 134
imperialist, 202
imperium, 45
impertinence (-ent),
    151, 215–16
impervious, 267
implacable, 280
implicated, 134
implicit, 41
improve (ment), 124
inanimate, 267
inanity, 43
inarticulately, 62
incarnate, 78
in case, 68
incident, 192, 219
incipient, 43
incog(nito), 65, 89
incomprehensible, 267
incumberment, 34
incur, 169
index, 32
indictment, 76
indifferently, 68
indiscerp(t)ible (-ity),
    43
individuating, 44
indoctrinate, 202
infiltration, 112
inflation, 189
influence, 5
influenza, 20
ingeniety, 119–20
ingenious (-ness), 108,
    119
ingenuity, 119
ingenuosity, 120
ingenuous, 108, 119
ingenuousness, 120
ingurgitate, 52
inhume, 78
inimical, 2
inlet, 259

in place of, 48
Ins and Outs, 82
insanity, 157
inscience, 133
inspect, 65
instalment, 202
instead of, 48
insubordination, 96
insufferable, 280
insulate, 37, 196
insulation, 62
insurrection, 43
int, 3
interest (-ed, -ing),
    210–12
interference, 44
interposition, 44
interpretation, 74
inthrall, 68
intolerable, 280
intriguing, 230, 231
intumescent, 43
invention, 88
involve, 134
ireful, 67
irritation, 187
isolate, 37
issue, 202
-ist, 97
Italian characters, 170
Italianisms, 14, 38, 39
item, 39
-ize, 97

jacket, 192
Jacobite, 82
jambee, 129
jealousy (plant), 135
je ne sçai quoi, 109, 111
jeopardy, 68
jersey, 192
jeu d'esprit, 109
jigger-dubbers, 81
[jingoism], 283
jocund, 169
Johnsonian, 98
jointed columns, 13
jökul, 12

jot, 58
jot down, 47
jujube, 190
jump (vb), 167
junction, 258
juncture, 134
junk (rubbish), 171
junket (vb), 65; (n.),
    129

kangaroo, 103
ken, 69
kerb, 192
kiddy-napper, 81
king, 141
kiosk, 16
Kitty Fisher (bonnet),
    130
knocker, 205
knowing, 139
Koran, 2

laboratory, 195
laboured (adj.), 172
labyrinth, 179, 180
lack, 68
lad, 61, 65, 169
lad of mettle, 55
lady, 50
laid on the shelf, 176
lair, 169, 186
lament (n.), 169
landscape-gardening,
    96, 124
languorous, 68
larboard, 168
large, 279
lash (vb), 65, 163
lassitude, 71, 112
latent, 134
Latinisms, 39–46, 134
latitude, 133
launch (a campaign),
    165
launch into eternity,
    175
lawyer, 49
lay (n.), 169

lay (vb), 5, 117
lay a-dying, 63
Lay me down softly, 55
lead, in the, 61
leave in the lurch, 4, 61
legerity, 35
legitimate, 62
leisure, 2
lengthy, 46
let down, 255
levée, 109
Levels of language,
    57–61, 85–8, 176,
    254–6, 282
levity, 216
Lexiphantic, 98
liberal, 144
lie (vb) (tell untruths), 5
life-line, 21
light literature, 199
light music, 199
Lillebulero (vb), 100
limp, 19
line, 26–7
line of demarcation, 93
lingo, 61
link (torch), 57
liquor, in, 80
listlessness, 112
literally, 207–8
literary, 199
literate, 198
literature, 198–9
lithe, 169
litigious, 2
living (n.), 60
Loan Words, 2, 11–19,
    20, 35–6, 38–9,
    105–12
locate, 45, 46
locomotive, 197
locum-tenens, 263
log(g)erhead, 174
longitude, 133
lorgnette, 17
lounge (18th-cent. n.),
    139; (20th-cent. n.),
    32

love, 66
love-exalting, 81
lovesome, 68
low, 85–6
Low church, 143
Low words, 61, 65, 87,
    90, 95, 106, 168, 250
lozenge, 190
l.s.d., 39
lubricity, 216
lubricous, 217
lucid, 267
luggage, 32
luminousness, 102
lumping, 61
Lunardi (bonnet), 130
lunch, 32
luscious, 56, 246–7
luxuriate, 146
luxurious, 146
luxury, 146–7
Lyceum, 102
lymphatic, 44

macaroni, 26
machine, 259
madam, 159
magazine, 187
maiden, 2
mainland, 186
mainmast, 72
majestatic, 34
major (wig), 130
make up one's mind, 4,
    176
mamma, 158
manage, 107
manœuvre, 105, 109
mansion house, 188
manufacturer, 263
maraud, 112
Marlborough's Battles,
    130
marmalade, 157
martinet, 18
matron, 86
matter, 200
matter of fact, 200

mauvaise honte, 109
mawkish, 267
mavis, 68
maze, 179, 180
meads, 170
mean (adj.), 118, 252
meanness, 70
meat-offering, 65
mechanic(k), 32, 260
mechanism, 260
mediator, 74
meed, 169
meet (adj.), 68
meeting-house, 142
mellifluous, 81
memorandal, 51
memory, 116
ménage, 261
mendacious, 78
mentally, 80
mercantile, 280
mess (n.), 19
mess (vb), 65
Metaphor, 92–3, 163–5,
    178
methinks, 3
Methodism (-ist), 96,
    144
microcosm, 78
mirror-writing, 34
misanthrope, 35
miscellaneous, 43
mischievousness, 67
Misnomers, 69–72
Miss, 158–9
missile, 197
mistress, 158
mistressly, 100
mizzen, 72
mob [-law, -violence],
    89, 90
Modernisation, problems
    of, 62–7
modulation, 55
money, 21
mortuary, 190
mote, 63
[Motorcade], 72

mould, 169
mount (in fortification), 105
moveable (n.), 256
Mr, 160–1
Mr Nobody, 177
Mrs, 159
Mrs How d'ye call, 177
multifarious, 43
mumper, 129
murk, 67
murkie, 169
murmur, 71
muslin, 65
muster (vb), 65
mutual, 117, 118
mystery, 5, 230, 232
mystic (-ity), 232

nab, 61
nabob, 15
naif, 108
naïve (-ity), 108
nathless, 69, 78
national (-ity), 217
natural, 76
natural history, 260
natural philosophy, 133
Nautical Language, 84–5
N.B., 39
need (vb: 3rd pers. sing.), 2
needful, the, 75
nefarious, 280
negligent (wig), 130
nemesis, 115
nemine contradicente, 39
Neologism, 34, 96–9, 101, 113–14, 282
Neptune, 99
nervish, 120
nervy, 120
net (vb,) 52
neurotic, 197
nice, 267–9
niggardliness, 68

[nihilism], 43
nihility, 43
noble stroke, 59
nobody, 51
Nonce-words, 100
nonchalant, 112
non-descript, 200–1
non-plus, 61
normal, 191
notion, 231
notorious, 252
novel (adj.), 52
novelist, 206
[nuclear fission], 194
nudity, 43
number (vb), 65
nursery, 260

object (vb), 41
obnoxious, 246
obtund, 43
obtuse, 43
occasionally, 275
occident, 35
occupier, 264
occupy (trade), 63
odour, 187
oft(en), 89
oilman, 32
oil on troubled waters, 173
olden, 68
ombre, 130
omnium, 39
onction, 109
one, 79
opera, 147
operation, 105
operose, 44
opinionâtre, 36
oral, 269
orb, 23
ordinary, 251
orgasm, 45, 46
orgy, 17, 169
orient, 23, 35
original, 91
orthography, 72

ostracism, 129
outdo (-ings), 188
out-of-the-wayest, 100
outré, 18–19
overdrove, 21
overshoes (adv.), 59
Oxford Blues, 205

pacha, 2
painterly, 45
palisade, 72
palpable, 169
Panorama, 102
Pantheon, 102
paper currency, 46
par, above, below, 75
parachute (bonnet), 130
Paradisiacal, 91
paralyse, 37
paramour, 62, 68
parcels, 260
Parfait Amour, 55
parley, 105
Parliamentary language, 74
parlour, 32
part, 36
partial, 41
particular, 118, 119
party gowns, 205
pasha, 2
passage (game), 130
passenger, 197
passion, 217–18
passionate, 218
Passover, 66
patch-work, 208
pathetic, 245
patriot (-ism), 82, 83, 283
patron, 31
patronise, 31, 215
peach, 203
peculation, 190
peculiar, 119
pedant (-ry), 12, 28–9
Pedantry, 29, 42, 280
peerage (vb), 100

peevish, 139–40
penchant, 36
pendent, 134
pen-knife, 170
people, 280
per, 39, 75
peradventure, 67
perplex, 134
persiflage, 96, 112
person, 280
pest, 58
pesthouse, 58
pestiferated, 101
pet, 190
pharmocopolist, 50
philology, 27–8
philosophism (-ist), 107
physical, 93
physician, 50
pick out, 65
pickle (metaphorical), 55
picturesque, 6, 125–126
Pinchbeck's metal, 170
pinion, 169
piquante, 125
placard, 2
plaguy, 61
plastic, 269
platina, 133
[platinum], 133
platitude, 109, 111
Platonician, 34
platoon, 136
plausible, 245–6
plebeian, 43
plenteousness, 67
plit, 114
plod, 134–5
ply, 134
poetess, 34
Poetic Diction, 98, 102–5, 166–9
Point of View Words, 144–7, 282
polar, 177
police, 121

policy (adj.), 122
polite, 110, 225
Political language, 82, 115
pompous, 151, 245
ponder, 169
porridge, 19
port (= larboard), 168
portent, 78
portentous, 169
posse, 61
posture of affairs, 57
potential, 93
powdered, 59
powdering-room, 203
powderize, 97
practically, 276
preaching-house, 142
precinct, 92
precipitate, 36
preference, 258
prejudice, 47
preliminaries, 74
preluding, 51
premature, 70
premier, 109
premises, 61
prenticide, 100
preparedness, 46
prepossession, 47
presage, 107
pre-sensation, 107
present (n.), 55
pre-sentiment, 107
presently, 47
preside, 26
pretend (-er), 253
pretty, 223
prevalence, 258
prevent, 68
[preventive war], 183
prickt, 130
pride, 116
print, 260
priorly, 117
privateer, 80
privy council, 62
produce (vb), 69

Professional language, 74, 76–7, 84–5, 88
professor, 14, 263
profundity, 133
programme, 192
progress, 185
project (-or), 141
promontory, 169
Pronunciation, 2, 3
propagate, 70
propelled, 35
Proper Names, 52, 53, 60, 98–9
propose, 115
prosaic, 206, 227
prospect, 84
prosperousness, 35
Protestant, 5, 283
prowling, 169
proximate, 117
prude (vb), 100
psychology, 27
Public house, 171
publican ('tax-collector'), 66
puddling, 113, 114
pugilist (-ic, -ical, -ically), 49
pulpit, 205
pulverise, 97
punyism, 100
puppybility, 100
purlieu, 169
purloin, 62
purport, 106
purpose (vb), 118
purser, 192
purveyor, 50
put in a good way, 176
puzzleation, 100

quadruped, 43
quaint, 201
Quaker (bonnet), 130
quantum, 93
quarry (prey), 169
quatrain, 115
queer, 201

queue, 204
quiet (-ude), 43
quietism, 188
quite away, 61

Raca, 65
[Racketeer], 80
racy, 247
radiant, 227
ragoût, 109
raisonné, 18
ramble (vb), 65
ramification, 43
Ramilie (wig), 130
Ranelagh, 102
rantipoll, 61
ratiocination, 43
ration, 192
rat-race, 204
ready rhino, 75
realise, 140, 254
rear, 24
recess (-ion), 258
recherché, 108
recipe, 170
reciprocation, 43
recollection, 116
reconnoitre, 112
recruit, 256
red flag, 5, 142
red-letter day, 93
redoubtable, 35
referee, 192
reference, 74
referral, 34
reform(ation), 52
refrigerated, 43
refugee, 190
refund, 134
refuse (n.), 256
regatta, 17
regency, 62
relations, 189
relax (-ed), 140–1
relief, 122
religion-lifted, 167
remains, 205–6
remplissage, 109

[renaissance], 154
repercussion, 280
repertory, 192
replace, 37
reptile, 134
resentment, 215
respectable, 229–30
resuscitation, 280
return chaise, 130
reverie, 220
revolting, 227
ricochet, 105
right now, 67
rigidity, 44
rigour, 44
ripe to do, 74
risible, 41
rivality, 34
riven, 169
Robinson Crusoe (vb),
    100
rogue, 55
rôle, 36
Rolly Polly, 130
romance, 45, 148–9
[Romanesque Architec-
    ture], 6, 103
romantic, 148
rosy, 31
rouge, 109
roulette, 130
Rousseauistic, 98
route, 109
rubric, 135
ruddy, 169
rue (vb), 169
ruination, 68
run (n.), 55
ruthless, 67

sack, be given the, 176
saint-encyphered, 166
sally out, 65
saloon, 192
salvage, 192
salvatory, 275
sanction, 34
satellite, 195

saunter, 134
scant, 68
sceptic, 115
science, 133
sciolto viso, 38
scissors, 86
score (reckoning), 169
Scotticisms, 2, 3, 47–8
scout (vb), 52
scrape acquaintance, 61
scream out, 65
scrub(by), 170
sea-calf, 6
seal (animal), 6, 169
sedate (-ness), 223
seeing life, 55
seeing that, 67
seemly, 169
see-saw (Whist), 165
seethe, 170
Self and Co., 75
self-same, 67
semblance, 67
seminary, 50
senatorial, 43
seneschal, 67
sensible (-ility), 249–
    251
sensitive, 250
sensual, 228
sensuous, 68, 228
sentiment (-al, -ality),
    29, 76, 247–9
septentrion, 35
serenitude, 68
serpent-maze, 98
set-down (n.), 130
set off, 65
set one's heart upon, 87
shabbily, 61
shadow, 193
shady, 246
shake-down, 48
[shake-up], 133
Shall and will, 47, 63
sham, 61
shapelessness, 114
shark, 61

sharps, go to, 130
shear, 134
shed (roof), 136
sheen, 78
shepherdess (bonnet), 130
shift (-ing), 255
shocking, 228
[shock-treatment], 196
shore-tumbrils, 81
short day, 74
shrill (vb), 169
shrink, 163
shuddery, 194
shunt, 197
siding, 197
signpost, 205
silhouette, 111
silvan, 169
sine qua non, 39
Sir, 159, 160
ski (-ing), 13
Skipover, 66
skirtings, 163
Slang, 7, 205, 234
slap (vb), 65
slave, 8, 56
[slenderise], 97
slim, 61
slip away, 65
slit, 21
slump, 189
slur over, 92
smack (ship), 192
smart, 222
smash, 19
smug, 228
snag, 193
snap-judgment, 76
snip-snap, 61
snow-ball, 12
snow-fall, 12
so, 79
sodden, 170
sods, 6, 169
solemnify, 34
solicitor, 206
solidity, 113

somehow, 79
son-in-law, 205
sophisticate (-ion), 183
sorry, very, 158
sortie, 112
[sort of (adv.)], 282
sot, 65
sovereign, 132
spar (vb), 171
sparkling, 227
special stick of wood, 174
species, 62
speculatist, 115
Spelling, 7, 94, 150, 215
sphere, 182
sphere-inspiring, 167
spick and span, 61
Spirit of Adonis, 55
spirituous, 270
splinter, 63
splutter (n.), 61
sporting, 52, 55
spouse, 57
spread (n.), 143
spume, 169
squabble, 61
squall (n.), 65
squeakation, 100
squeeze, 65
squelch, 61
stamina, 185
stamp, 206
stand one's ground, 87
standard, 199
Standards of English, 1, 5, 281
starboard, 72
stark, 172
startled, 65
staunch, 87
stigma, 6
still (adv.), 256
stingy, 61
stipend, 260
[stockist], 97
stoker, 192
storm, 85

stout, 270
strain (n.), 67
strait, 267
stranded, 193
strapping, 19
strata, 186
[stream of consciousness], 94
stricture, 253
strident, 270
strike (industrial), 96
Strip me naked, 55
strong language, 24
stronghold, 178
sturdy, 206
style, 76
subject-matter, 199–200
sublime, 6
subnormal, 191
succedaneum, 44
success, 70
succinct, 41
succumb, 47
such, 79
[sugar beet], 203
[suicide squad], 183
suit of ribbons, 129
sultana, 192
sunburnt, 157
[sunshade], 186
super, 90
supercilious, 178
superior, 201
supernal, 34, 169
supply, 6, 273–4
sure (to be), 60, 61
surface, (vb), 194
surprise, 6, 29, 30
swan-song, 163
swap, 61
sway (n.), 6, 169
swear, 74
sweat, 54, 85
sweet mouth (-tooth), 60
swell (n.), 115
swerve, 169
swindling, 6

swinging, 60
Sylphish, 91
symbolize, 34
symphonia, 135
synopsis, 134
Syntax, 3–4, 40, 117, 280
280

tabernacle, 66
take cold, 4
take in (cheat), 61, 264
take in (include), 264
take place, 274–5
take the field, 93
tame (flat), 61
tapis, sur le, 37
task, 132
taste, 6, 12, 29, 122
tattoo (ornament), 16
tax, 132
tax-gatherer, 66
[tea-break], 148
tea-things, 96
technical, 200
Technical terms, 12–14, 72–4, 88, 101–106, 113–15, 124, 189, 196–8
[technique], 200
telegraph, 196
temper, 155–6
temperance, 138
temperate, 92
tenor, 67, 169
tepid, 169
terrible, 36
tête à tête, 109–10
texture, 169
the (Siddons), 52
thrall, 169
thread, 180
thrill (vb), 185–6
thwacking, 60
thwart (vb), 172
tidy, 19

tiff, 61
tight, 205
time-corroded, 166
timeously, 47
time-unlettered, 166
tinted ideas, 35
tired, 28
Titles, 159–61
toddling, 19
toilet, 192
ton, the, 99
Tone, 210–12, 276
tonic, 141
tontine, 7
topical, 133
topping, 61, 270
torch, 57
torpedo, 196, 261–2
torrid, 169
torso, 19
tortuous, 169
Tory, 82
tour [tourism], tourist, 109, 198
toute ensemble, 111, 112
toy (-shop), 262
trade (n.), 65
traffic (n.), 65
tragacanth, 73
tragopon, 73
train, 58, 197
traipse, 61
trait, 218
tranquillity, 35
tranquilly, 35
transcend, 188
transcendental, 43
transferral, 34
[Transferred epithet],[1] 114
transient, 270
transpierce, 71
transpire, 37
trash, 171

treat (n.), 255–6
tree-felling, 105
tremendous, 238–40
tribulation, 67
trilithon, 115
trimestre, 113, 114
trite, 131
trivial, 178
trombonist, 97
troublous, 68
truck, 197
truculent, 191
truism, 34
trumpetist, 97
trunk, 19
tube, 168
Tullian, 98
tunnel, 197
Turf, the, 96
Turkey Merchant, 50
Turkey stone, 170
turn (n.), 76
turnspike, 105
turpitude, 280
Tyburn hat, 130

ult., 89, 90
ultimatum, 39
Ultramarine, 130, 131
umbrage, 186
umbrella, 186
unallayed, 271
analloyed, 271
unconventional, 193
uncouth, 169
unction (-ous), 109, 172
undertaker, 23
underwrite, 75
unearth, 67
uneducated, 95
unfortunate, 55
ungenerous, 156
[ungood], 37
uninterested, 211

[1] It occurs in Alexander Bain's *English Composition and Rhetoric*, 1866, p. 24. Not in *O.E.D.* as a technical phrase.

uninterestingness, 35
unique, 51
United States (of the Netherlands), 205
unity, 76
unkempt, 68, 169
unpolish, 95
unrest, 169
unwell, 158
unwieldy, 270
[Uranius, Uranus], 99
urbane, 28
urbanity, 28

vacancy, 206, 228
vacant, 228
vacation, 206
valve, 196
vampire, 15
vaporosity, 113
vapours, 113
Variants, 176-7
various, 270-1
vast, 245
vaunt, 169
Vauxhall, 102
vegetables, 171
vegetate (-ion), 254-255
vehicle, 169
Venetian red, 170
verbalize, 193
verbiage, 109
verbosity, 109
vestige, 133
veterans, 190
via, 39
viands, 67
vibration, 196
vicinage, 84
vicinity, 258
vicissitude, 218

victorious, 2
villa, 96
virago, 240
virtuoso, 14
vis à vis, 109
visionary, 147
visit (-ation), 120
vital (-ity), 201
[vital statistics], 201
vixen, 157
vocation, 257
Vogue Words, 25-7, 78-80
volatile, 134
volley, 136
voluble (-ility), 228
volupté, 36
voucher, 192
vulgar, 251-2

wabble, 61
waft, 134
[wage-rate (-slave)], 280
wages, 280
wallet, 192
want (vb), 68, 274
Wanted words, 6, 103, 203
wanting-to-be-diverted, 100
war (vb), 68
warbling, 261
wars of principle, 56
watering-places, 100
water-works, 204
ways, 66
wealth-puffed, 167
weary, 280
weave, 197
ween, 78
Welsh-rabbit, 105

weltering, 169
wench, 65
Werter (bonnet), 130
whenas, 67
Whig, 5, 82
whilom (e), 67, 68
white bears, 178
white gold, 133
white lie, 96
white sauce, 157
whiten, 163
whitewash, (n.) 205; (vb), 131
who and which, 4, 68
width, 61
win, 70, 71
wing (vb), 197
-wise, 167
wiseacre, 68
wit, do you to, 63
womanette, 100
Women's language, 61, 78-80
wonder, 6, 30
wonderment, 61
wooden piece of business, 174
world, for all the, 61
worthy, 230
wrapper, 192
wrathful, 218

yea, 158
yeoman, 22
yes, 158
youths, 171
Yule, 19

zenith, 72
Zerdusht, 2
zig-zag, 180
Zoroaster, 2

INDEX OF PERSONS

Occasionally eighteenth-century conventions differ from ours in the form of foreign names. These are noted.

Abelard, Peter, 222

Addison, Joseph, 34, 72, 91, 104, 152, 165, 206, 209, 215, 250, 261

Aikin, John, vi

Alison, Archibald, 121, 123, 125, 154

Allen, Ralph, 225

Anstey, Christopher, 50

Aquinas, St Thomas, 31, 235

Ariosto, Ludovico, 148

Armstrong, John, 3, 123, 191, 199, 219

Ash, John, 81, 188, 270

Augustine, St, of Hippo, 205

Austen, Jane, 89

Badcock, Samuel, 168

Baden-Durlach, Karl Friedrich, Margrave of, 46–7

Bailey, Nathan, 27, 35, 50, 94, 114, 137, 151, 184, 186, 188, 209, 218, 223, 233, 244, 251, 255, 263

Baker, R., 24, 107, 117, 118, 119

Banks, Sir Joseph, 103

Barber, Francis, 160

Baretti, Giuseppe Marc Antonio, 14, 221

Barruel, Augustin, 106

Beattie, James, 3, 4, 52, 68, 72, 80, 86–7, 228, 234, 248

Beattie, James Hay, 34, 49, 52, 175, 234

Beckford, William, 54

Bentley, Richard (Master of Trinity College, Cambridge), 6, 23, 59, 60, 88, 148, 162–3, 167–8, 208, 217

Beresford, James, 247

Bernard, St, of Clairvaux, 148

Bicknell, Alexander, 34

Blacklock, Thomas, 212

Blackstone, Sir William, 22, 221

Blair, Robert, 4, 71, 85, 119

Blayney, Benjamin, 62–3

Bode, Johann Elert, 99

Bolingbroke, Henry St John, 1st viscount, 36, 185, 215

Boswell, James, 44, 47, 85, 140, 177, 201, 208, 217, 233, 253, 268

Brindley, James, 114

Brooke, Henry, 241

Brown, Lancelot ('Capability'), 124, 180

Browne, Isaac Hawkins (the elder), 78

Buchanan, James, 158

Bunyan, John, 185, 222

Burke, Edmund, v, 24, 34, 35, 44, 45, 46, 48, 93, 110, 122, 140, 155

Burney, Fanny (Madame D'Arblay), 35, 201

Burns, Robert, 19, 282

Burrow, Sir James, 131

Byrom, John, 173, 238

Bysshe, Edward, 3, 106

Caesar, C. Julius, 223

Callender, James Thomson, 43, 280

Campbell, Archibald (naval officer), 40, 98, 281

Campbell, George, 2, 3, 27, 34, 41, 67, 88, 89–90, 92–3, 94, 190, 248, 251, 252–3, 259, 281

Carey, Henry, 141, 242

Carlyle, Thomas, 114

Caxton, William, 47

Chambers, Sir William, 137

Charles I of Great Britain and Ireland, 235

Chatterton, Thomas, 236

Chaucer, Geoffrey, 50, 62, 73, 97, 148, 168, 169, 177, 222

Chesterfield, Philip Dormer Stanhope, 4th earl of, 38, 100, 121, 158

Cheyne, George, 120

Churchill, Charles, 213
Churchill, Sir Winston, 74
Cicero, M. Tullius, 43, 143
Claude Lorraine (Claude Gellée), 125, 236
Coleridge, Samuel Taylor, 6, 29, 93, 114, 124, 167, 200
Collier, Jeremy, 130, 133, 170, 219
Collins, William, 224, 237
Cook, Charles, 43
Cook, James, 16
Corday, Charlotte, 234
Cowley, Abraham, 199
Cowper, William, 41–2, 58, 101, 182, 183, 217, 222, 277
Craven, Elizabeth, Lady (later Margravine of Anspach), 16, 17, 51, 101, 138, 231
Crisp, Samuel, 201
Croft, Sir Herbert, 104
Crosbie (the aeronaut), 225, 244
Cruden, Alexander, 232
Cumberland, Richard, 60
Cumberland, William Augustus, duke of, 5

Dalton, John, 103
D'Arblay, Madame, see Burney
Dartmouth, William Legge, 2nd earl of, 235
Darwin, Erasmus, 73, 99, 180, 191, 216, 226, 266
Defoe, Daniel, 19, 28, 93, 146, 150, 159, 183, 218, 225, 233, 259, 264
Dennis, John, 58, 71, 96, 108, 150, 219, 227, 237, 245, 250, 252
De Quincey, Thomas, 46
Diaper, William, 134
Dickens, Charles, 157, 193
D'Israeli, Isaac, 45
Dodd, William, 55
Dodsley, Robert, 274
Dryden, John, 3, 24, 31, 36, 57, 62, 98, 160, 168, 229
Duff, William, 91, 93, 238, 276
Dyche, Thomas and Pardon, William, 26, 27, 31, 94, 137, 142, 149, 151, 157, 171, 172, 181, 200, 209, 212,
219, 224, 225, 230, 233, 238, 244, 246, 257, 259, 273, 275
Dyer, William, 185, 222, 256

E.K., 13
Elphinston, James, 271, 276
Enfield, William, vi, 34
Evelyn, John, 183

Felton, Henry, 267
Fénelon, François de Salignac de la Mothe-, 252
Ferguson, Adam, 140, 147, 210, 211, 213, 217, 229
Fielding, Henry, 76, 130, 146, 161, 174, 219
Fielding, Sarah, 214
Francis, St, of Assisi, 184, 234
Franklin, Benjamin, 98, 173, 229
Frederick I of Prussia (Friedrich Wilhelm), 44
Frederick the Great, of Prussia, 271

Galle, Johann Gottfried, 99
Garrick, David, 3, 59, 175, 242
Garrick, George, 289
Geddes, Alexander, 48
George III of Great Britain and Ireland, 228, 234
Gerard, Alexander, 113, 114, 152, 178, 194, 272
Gibbon, Edward, 35, 71, 98
Gildon, Charles, 45, 79, 199, 256, 263, 272
Gilpin, William, 152
Glover, Richard, 134, 172, 179, 191, 195, 228, 272
Godwin, William, 87, 105, 180, 185, 204, 233, 250
Goldsmith, Oliver, v, 86, 115, 145, 199, 207, 208, 211
Gower, John, 122
Grainger, James, 35, 72
Graves, Richard (of Claverton near Bath), 24, 53, 126
Gray, Thomas, 7, 70, 162, 201, 236
Green, William, 63
Gregory the Great, Pope, 41

Griffiths, Ralph, 95

Grose, Francis, 53, 71, 72, 83, 119, 198, 213

Grosvenor, Richard, 1st earl, 5

Gustavus Adolphus, of Sweden, 38

Guyon, Madame, 234

Handel, George Frederic, 223

Hanway, Jonas, 146, 148, 191, 209, 210, 273

Harris, James, 28

Harte, Walter, 44

Harwood, Edward, 62, 64, 65, 85, 144

Hawkesworth, John, 285

Hawkins, Sir John, 55, 74, 235

Heberden, William, 20

Henry VIII, 159

Herbert, Sir Alan P., 5, 75

Herbert, George, 177

Herschel, Sir William, 99

Hertford, Henrietta, Countess of, 136, 250

Hervey, James, 167

Hirons, John, 64

Hogarth, William, 18, 22, 31, 95, 111, 138, 209, 225, 236

Holland, Philemon, 265

Homer, 24

Hooker, Richard, 232

Horrebow, Nils, 12

Howard, John, 236

Hoyle, Edmund, 165–6

Hume, David, 2, 108, 116, 122, 164

Hunter, John, 95

Hurd, Richard, 92–3, 155

Hutcheson, Francis, 122, 217, 222, 242, 251, 255, 259

Ignatius Loyola, St, 234

Jackson, Sir Barry, 232

Jackson, William, 60, 73, 99, 115, 124, 125, 227

Jago, Richard, 125, 232

Jefferson, Thomas, 203

Jenyns, Soame, 174, 180, 243, 271

Jerningham, Edward, 224, 238

Jespersen, Otto, 40

Johnson, Samuel, v, 13, 14, 19, 20, 22, 25, 26, 27, 31, 32, 33, 34, 35, 36, 37, 40, 42, 43, 44, 45, 46, 48, 50, 55, 59, 60, 61, 67, 68, 73, 74, 76, 78, 80, 82–83, 85–6, 89, 93–4, 98, 109, 114, 115, 118–19, 120, 121, 129, 132, 134, 137, 142, 146, 160, 162, 165, 169, 171, 177, 179, 183, 185, 186, 189, 193, 195, 198, 199, 200, 201, 202, 203, 209, 210, 213, 214, 215, 217, 222, 223, 224, 228, 229, 230, 232, 235, 239, 240, 244, 245, 250, 251, 252, 253, 256, 261, 262, 264, 267, 268, 280, 283

Johnstone, Charles, 82, 220

Junius, 157, 185, 211, 221, 252, 269

Kames, Henry Home, Lord, 21, 70, 114, 121, 230, 251

Keats, John, 203

Kelly, Hugh, 5, 50

Kempe, Margery, 231

Kempis, Thomas à, 235

Kenrick, William, 61, 68, 191

Kent, William, 92, 254

King, William, 212

Knox, Ronald, 62, 233

Knox, Vicesimus, 27, 92, 119, 123, 135, 138, 139, 153, 173, 179, 214, 215, 224, 227, 277

Lackington, James, 27, 209, 255, 276

Langhorne, John, 146, 163, 234

Laver, Sir Ashton, 102

Lavington, George, 148, 206, 234

Law, William, 234

Lawson, John, 95, 154, 210

Le Brun, Charles, 178

Lee, Nathaniel, 237

Lennox, Charlotte, 158

L'Estrange, Sir Roger, 199

Lewis, Matthew Gregory, 155, 231

Lindsay, Theophilus, 69

Lisle, Lady Alice, 22

Lloyd, Evan, 166

Louis XVI of France, 226

Loutherbourg, Philip James de, 102

Lucian, 219

Luxborough, Henrietta Knight, Lady, 26

Lyttelton, George, 1st baron, 14, 40, 140, 150, 221, 228, 251, 252

Malory, Sir Thomas, 4

Mandeville, Bernard de, 262

Mansfield, Sir James (Lord Chief Justice of the Common Pleas), 3, 277

Marlowe, Christopher, 207

Marshall, William, 114

Martyn, Thomas, 101

Mason, John, 89

Mason, William, 125, 134, 153, 191, 269

Michael Angelo, usual eighteenth-century name for Michelangelo Buonarotti), 236

Michaelis, Johann David, 101

Mickle, William Julius, 67

Miller, Sanderson, 18

Milton, John, 17, 59, 60, 61, 69, 72, 88, 148, 162, 167, 169, 187, 209, 217, 237, 238, 245

Mitchel, Charles, 21

Molière (i.e. Jean Baptiste Poquelin), 156

Montagu, Elizabeth, 56, 110, 113, 151, 181

Montagu, Lady Mary Wortley, 106

Montesquieu, Charles Louis de Secondat de, 45, 153

Montgolfier, Joseph Michel and Jacques Etienne, 216

Moore, John (physician and writer of travel books), 17

More, Hannah, 228, 242

More, Sir Thomas, 271

Motte, Madame de la, 206

Murphy, Arthur, 239

Nash, Richard, 25, 100, 130, 212, 262

Neville, Sylas, 135, 250, 267

Newton, Sir Isaac, 216, 276

Northumberland, Elizabeth, 1st duchess of, 219

Omiah, of Tahiti, 149

Orwell, George (pseudonym of Eric Blair), 37

Paine, Thomas, 100, 201

Parkinson, Sydney, 103

Parnell, Thomas, 224

Partridge, Eric H., 135

Patkul, Johan Reinhold, 150

Peacock, Thomas Love, 133

Pearce, Zachary, 23, 59, 60, 208, 245

Pegge, Samuel, alias Paul Gemsege, 21, 67, 70, 71, 97, 102, 120, 146

Pennant, Thomas, 13

Philips, Ambrose, 116, 134

Piozzi, Hester Lynch (née Salusbury, then Thrale), 35, 37, 75, 79, 90, 115, 119, 120, 123, 139, 140, 156, 157, 178, 179, 184, 191, 218, 223, 228, 230, 244, 264, 281

Pliny (Gaius Plinius Secundus), 178

Polwhele, Richard, 163

Pomfret, Frances, countess of, 94, 136, 223

Pontoppidan, Erick (Erich), 13

Pope, Alexander, 25, 35–6, 41, 42, 58, 71, 77, 86, 91, 96, 97, 109, 125, 140, 148, 154, 161, 185, 191, 215, 219, 222, 224–5, 229, 241, 242, 245, 250, 256, 269

Poussin, Nicholas, 223, 236

Pownall, Thomas, 45

Price, Richard, 174

Price, Sir Uvedale, 21, 111, 114, 125, 141, 144, 152, 187, 222, 236, 269, 276

Priestley, John Boynton, 81

Priestley, Joseph, 30, 63, 77, 96, 104, 113, 115, 144, 164, 185, 221

Pritchard, Hannah, 108

Pye, Henry James, 210

Quin, James, 181

Radcliffe, Ann, 155

Raphael (Raffaello Sanzio), 198, 256

Reeve, Clara, 50, 148, 154, 185

Reid, Thomas, 12, 78, 129, 215, 231, 245, 266

Repton, Humphry, 7, 124, 217
Reynolds, Sir Joshua, 94, 125, 140, 189
Rich, John, 102
Richardson, Jonathan, Sr and Jr, 6, 17, 23, 59, 187, 238
Richardson, Samuel, 137, 211, 276
Roberts, William, 48, 177
Romaine, William, 46
Rosa, Salvator, 125
Rousseau, Jean-Jacques, 147, 235
Rubens, Sir Peter Paul, 94, 256
Ruffhead, Owen, 43, 44, 86, 109, 141, 148, 189, 215
Rutty, John, 267

Sayers, Dorothy L., 135
Scarlett, Nathaniel, 66–7
Scott, John, of Amwell, 125
Scott, Sir Walter, 201, 265
Secker, Thomas, 224–5
Shaftesbury, Anthony Ashley Cooper, 3rd earl of, 143, 144, 145, 238, 252
Shakespeare, William, 6, 30, 35, 54, 59, 60, 62, 67, 70, 88, 100, 160, 186, 208, 210, 229, 236, 243, 264, 281
Shaw, George Bernard, 3
Shebbeare, John, 14, 135, 184, 246, 268, 272, 277
Shenstone, William, 26, 108, 154, 215
Sheridan, Richard Brinsley, 212
Sheridan, Thomas (elocutionist), 2, 282
Sinclair, Sir John, 47
Sloane, Sir Hans, 14
Smart, Christopher, 256
Smith, Adam, 29, 46, 92, 95, 180, 216, 228, 267, 280
Smollett, Tobias George, v, 62, 180
Spence, Joseph, alias Sir Harry Beaumont, 14, 41, 58, 67, 97–8, 109, 111, 123, 178, 225
Spenser, Edmund, 13, 59, 88, 148, 154, 168, 169
Steele, Sir Richard, 25, 52, 148, 177
Sterne, Laurence, 248
Stevens, William Bagshaw, 166–7
Stewart, Dugald, 94, 102, 110, 231

Stockdale, Percival, 188, 269
Stukeley, William, 103, 115
Swedenborg (Swedberg), Emanuel, 234
Swift, Deane, 18
Swift, Jonathan, 20, 34, 89, 92, 250, 269
Symonds, John, 1, 66

Tasso, Torquato, 154
Taylor, Jeremy, 232
Taylor, Thomas, 68
Tennyson, Alfred, 1st baron, 4
Thompson, George, 195, 196
Thomson, James, 140, 186, 210, 241, 256
Thrale, Hester Lynch, 13, see Piozzi
Thynne, Thomas, of Longleat, 223
Trusler, John, 118, 212, 218, 238, 279, 280
Tull, Jethro, 98
Turner, Sir Edward, 203
Tyndale, William, 66, 142

Upton, John, 6, 13, 59, 87, 148, 169
Usher, James, 149

Vauban, Sébastien le Prestre de, 105
Voltaire (name assumed by François Marie Arouet), 107

Wakefield, Gilbert, 66
Walker, Adam, 102
Walpole, Horace, 38, 52, 170, 194, 223
Walpole, Sir Robert, 76, 175
Warburton, William, 59, 146, 165, 269
Warton, Joseph, 67, 264
Warton, Thomas (the younger), 88, 275
Washington, George, 37, 229
Waterland, Daniel, 139, 275
Watts, Isaac, 107
Weldon, James, 22
Wellington, Arthur Wellesley, 1st duke of, 46, 201
Wendeborn, Gebhardt Friedrich August, vi, 15, 82, 92, 142–3, 150, 159, 177, 221, 229, 245, 248
Wesley, Charles, 70, 254

Wesley, John, 238, 247, 274, 276

Whitefield, George, 143, 256

Whitehead, William, 23, 73, 143, 241, 256

Whitney, William Dwight, 114

Wiclif, John, 35

Wilkins, John, 137

Williams, William, 64–5

Willis, John, 66

Winchilsea, Anne Finch, countess of, 241

Withers, Philip, 4, 5, 39, 117–18

Woffington, Margaret ('Peg'), 52

Wordsworth, William, 116, 167

Worsley, John, 63

Woty, William, alias J. Copywell, 50, 84, 153, 259

Wren, Sir Christopher, 153

Wynne, Richard, 40

Young, Edward, 89, 115, 154, 235, 244, 270

Zinzendorf, Nikolaus Ludwig, Graf von, 232